DISTANCE EDUCATION

Principles, Potentialities and Perspectives

DISTANCE EDUCATION

Principles, Potentialities and Perspectives

DR. ARUNA GOEL

Chairperson, Department of Correspondence Studies, and
Honorary Director, Centre for Women Studies and Development
Former Professor of Sanskrit, Panjab University, Chandigarh,
Member, University Grants Commission,
Member, Indian Institute of Advanced Study, Shimla, and
Member, Sahitya Academy, Government of India, New Delhi
(Sanskrit Board)

and

DR. S.L. GOEL

Editor, The Indian Journal of Public Administration, New Delhi
Former Member of UGC, Management Board AICTE, DEC
Director, State Bank of India, Northern Region
Vice-President of IIPA and Emeritus Professor of Public
Administration, UGC
Professor of Public Administration (Retd.)
Panjab University, Chandigarh

DEEP & DEEP PUBLICATIONS PVT. LTD.

F-159, Rajouri Garden, New Delhi-110027

DISTANCE EDUCATION
Principles, Potentialities and Perspectives

ISBN 978-81-8450-141-4

Typeset by S.S. COMPOSERS,
3190, Mohindra Park, Shakur Basti, Delhi-110034.

Printed in India at MAYUR ENTERPRISES,
WZ Plot No. 3, Gujjar Market, Tihar Village, New Delhi-110018.

Published by DEEP & DEEP PUBLICATIONS PVT. LTD.,
F-159, Rajouri Garden, New Delhi-110027.
Phones: 25435369, 25440916
E-mail: ddpbooks@yahoo.co.in • ddpubs@gmail.com
Showroom:
2/13, Ansari Road, Daryaganj, New Delhi-110002 • Telefax: 23245122

Contents

Preface

Open learning system has revolutionised the present mode of education. The growing population of a country demands a system of education which can bring learning to the door-step, so that the percentage of the population living in the remote areas, working in the offices and involved in business and agriculture may be benefited. The women can also take advantage of this system even when they are leading a domestic life. In short, that percentage of the population which cannot be benefited by the conventional education system can be benefited by the open learning system. The open learning system of education is new and helps people in achieving higher education without any formality of attending regular classes like that in the conventional educational institutions. The university which imparts distance learning is known as Open University which can simply be considered as "University without walls or border." On the other hand, conventional universities are referred to as 'universities within the walls' which arrange regular classroom teaching and face to face interaction between the students and the teachers. The formal conventional type of education has created a number of barriers which debar those people from taking education who cannot afford to come to the colleges and the university for higher education because of various reasons and constraints. In such circumstances the open learning system by imparting distance learning came to their rescue. The increasing popularity of open universities functioning abroad and in India is supportive of the fact that this system has helped people in their knowledge and skill towards achieving purposeful goal of life.

The emergence of distance education as a part of traditional formal education is largely a post-World Ward II event in contrast to formal education that dates from 10th century AD. It began as a 'second chance' for those who were left out or for the dropouts of formal education during World War II and thereafter.

In addition to war, knowledge explosion and the need of professional workforce gave impetus to distance education. In Australia, UK, Canada, USA and other developed and developing countries, distance education expanded in a big way. Large number of States in USA have adopted this system

The inadequacy of traditional system of education system to cope with the ever increasing frontiers of knowledge and aspirants led to the emergence of distance education all over the world with the setting up of first correspondence courses institute in Delhi University in 1962, led to great expansion.

Access to education through the Open Distance Learning system is expanding rapidly. The Indira Gandhi National Open University (IGNOU) now has a cumulative enrolment of about 15 lakhs. The University introduced 16 new programmes during 2006-07. The Distance Education Council (DEC), an authority of IGNOU's is coordinating the activities of 13 state Open Universities and 119 Institutes of Correspondence Courses in conventional universities. DEC has been accorded statutory status. National Institute of Open Schooling (NIOS) has registered more than 20 lakh learners since inception.

K. Aludiapllai observes that Distance Education today is slowly acquiring the characteristics of industry. Industry is not only cost conscious but also quality conscious. Any dilution in quality will eventually lead to the easing out of scenario. All out efforts should be made to ensure customer satisfaction. The education offered by open universities has to be designed for the masses, cost effective, customer oriented, and on top it all, responsive to the changing needs of the times.

As of now, the hope for the future in the realm of education in terms of access, cost effectiveness and societal needs lies in the growth and effective functioning of open universities. They may well serve as a panacea for many of the ills affecting education. Never before has such an opportunity been thrown open. It has to be seized and fully utilized for the good of all.

Dr. M. Anandakrishnan, Vice-Chairman, Tamil Nadu State Council for Higher Education delivered the Convocation address at the First Convocation of Periyar University, Salem on March 19, 2001. He said, "The internationalization of the higher education system is rapidly gaining ground in India. Our own standards are being compared with world-class institutions. Benchmarking the performance of our institutions against some of the renowned institutions is becoming a necessity. We need to pay serious attention to the accreditation process of our institutions."

Human mind is the major resource for creation of wealth far more than the land and mineral resources. The wealthiest persons of recent origin have used their minds, rather than materials, to create their assets. The universities engaged in training of the minds should advise their students that the syllabi and the degree do not constitute the finality of the knowledge system in any discipline. Some of it will become obsolete with time. The students should be encouraged to continuously engage in further learning not only in their domain but also in associated fields for success in their occupations. They should be able to keep pace with the changing demands of the knowledge system both the content and the context. All this is possible, through well designed Distance Education System.

The Parliamentary Standing Committee on HRD in its 172nd Report has recommended that for a vast country like India where accessibility to higher education is quite low, Open Universities have the vast potential for taking Higher Education to more and more people irrespective of different barriers. This system caters also for in-service persons for whom it is second chance as well as for regular learners. It, therefore needs to be provided greater thrust by integrating utility courses with personal development with socio-economic problems. The courses offered could be mainly job-oriented as far as possible. High priority should be given for opening more study organization particularly covering rural and remote areas with concentration of SCs/STs and other backward communities students.

11th Five Year Plan approach paper suggests that the Open University system is an important instrument for expanding higher education since it overcomes the infrastructure constraint. Until a larger network of accessible and well supported colleges is developed, the open schooling programme should be strengthened and expanded. In case of subjects that do not require laboratory work, it will be helpful for students to access pre-recorded selections of lectures, tutorials, and standardized test available at internet kiosks. Testing and examination centres where students can take standardized examinations in parts can reduce the pressure. For this autonomous institutions charged with the responsibility of testing and examination will have to be developed. The 11th plan should pay attention to creation of electronically available content and testing mechanism so that the pressure on infrastructure can be eased. The present condition of dichotomy between distance and traditional education is farce.

Another reality is that there are many unanswered questions that pose real challenges to judge the effectiveness of distance learning. If one losses sight of the distinctive characteristics of distance education, wrong assumptions and faulty priorities may result in distance education losing its relevance and suffering from problems related to Interior quality. The existing form of open distant education that was relevant in the 20th century when it all started to cater to the left outs and drops outs of the mainstream will need radical change for remaining relevant in the 21st century. Now it is an adult and continuing education for life long learners who already have substantial formal campus education. Is there a sound research base to base the radical changes on?

The reality is that there are many inconclusive and not so clear aspects in distance education that need to be sorted out. It looks as though the changes introduced in distance and open learning hinges on novelty rather than the rationale. The World Bank publication entitled, "Tertiary Education in the Twenty-first Century: Challenges and Opportunities" (Salmi, 2000) and the review done in 1999 by the Institute for Higher Education Policy (IHEP) in USA on "what the research in distance education tells us and does not tell us" highlights many of those critical aspects that need rather urgent attention.

One should quickly find the answers to some of the following questions through research or pilot studies, 'not depending only on the wisdom of the elder' academics to uphold the relevance of distance education:

* How to promote sufficient Interaction in distance Education courses, in order to build up critical thinking and social learning? What is an appropriate mix of face to face and distance teaching?
* How can students acquire the values needed to live as responsible citizens through open and distance learning?
* Which is a better way to organize programms and courses for a learning society of all age groups—Separate strategies or in an integrated way?
* How to choose technologies suitable to the affordability of the "learning society" without compromising on the curricular and pedagogical objectives.
* How to avoid over-reliance on technological gimmicks and loss of hands-on training opportunities?
* How to preserve linguistic and cultural identity as communication in a major world language becomes more and more imperative.
* How to finance the new educational technologies and related infrastructures in a sustainable way?
* How to reconcile to growing digital divide among the haves and have-nots?
* What should be the policy of the national governments to subsidize the adult learners who cannot afford to meet their further educational needs?
* What does research say about the different learning styles of students and how they relate to the use of particular technologies?
* How effective are the digital libraries for the distance education learners?
* Does research explain why the dropout rate is high among distance learners?
* Finding an answer to these questions that have been conveniently neglected so far is not an easy task. One's not sure how far the fund starved distance education units of the traditional universities will be able to take up these issues as they get into the distributed education mode to serve concurrently both teen-age and adult learners.[1]

National Knowledge Commission has also stressed the same. To quote: The lack of convergence between programmes run by open universities and correspondence courses offered by the distance education

1. A. Ganam and Antony Stella, Myths and Realities of Distance Education, *University News*, March 24-30, 2004, p. 8.

wings of conventional educational institutions is a cause of great concern.

Rather than function as parallel systems at odds with each other, open universities must forge organizational alignment with conventional universities geared towards common goals and strategies. They must engage each other in the collaborative creation of pedagogical resources via OER and its delivery along shared modes. Programmes and courses offered by each should be subject to the same stringent norms of quality assurance. This implies that the distance education departments operating within conventional universities must he encouraged to put correspondence courses through the NETS for purposes of assessment. At the same time, universities must also ensure that their distance education programmes do not stand-alone, but should benefit from regular interaction with university departments in concerned disciplines. The aim of such convergence is to eventually enable learners to move freely from one system to the other.

B. Murahari in his article, "Teaching Today for Tomorrow" in *University News*, April 14-20, 2008 observes:

People require a change in the teaching-learning process from the traditional one-size-fits all to differentiated teaching. Education in the digital world of today can actually make that meaningful shift by ensuring that if students do not learn the way they are taught, they can be taught the way they learn. This pedagogical shift, when integrated into educational software and appropriate technology, can make learning exciting and enjoyable while securing successful learning outcomes in shorter time frames. While colleges and universities globally lend to use asynchronous or delayed technologies with an instructor as the basis of e-learning, and thereby include tools like online discussion forums, electronic books, online exams and grading, online mentoring, web-linked shared tools, student profiling and course material, synchronous presentation tools which include application sharing, web browsing, audio and video streaming, chat rooms, surveying and polling are all gaining ground as emerging and enhanced pedagogy. As the 11th Plan approach paper states 'The 11th Plan provides an opportunity to restructure policies to achieve a new vision of growth that will be much more broad based and inclusive, bringing about a faster reduction in poverty and helping bridge the divides that are currently the focus of so much attention'. While it recognizes that 'Information and Communication Technology (ICT) has a great potential for enhancing learning levels and improving quality of education', managing this professionally, with help of the private sector engaged in education, may make the difference between rhetoric and the achievement of desired results.

Brenda Gourley in his article, "Open Education: The Virtual Reality of the Present Era" in *University News*, April 14-20, 2008 observes:

'Indeed the world we now inhabit is vastly different from the world in which the Open Universities in the UK and India were conceived. I believe (and I am not alone) that we are witnessing a seismic shift in

Higher Education. The demands of a knowledge society require citizens to be better educated in this globalised world—and citizens themselves recognise the imperatives and are hungry for education. We are witnessing in our time a massive expansion of university students worldwide—and this is most encouraging. We can only applaud as people who only a few decades ago would have had no chance to demonstrate their intellectual capacity are now demonstrating, over and over again, their ability to engage and succeed—if only given the chance. Coupled with this change we have the most dazzling technological advances—the Internet and mobile phones to name two important ones amongst many—which have made educational opportunities accessible to some of the remotest areas of the world'.

The consequences for the HE system are colossal—for traditional providers of course, who cannot even begin to cope with the demand, but also for distance education providers who will come into their own if they are able to deliver quality learning experiences. No higher education provider can afford to ignore these seismic shifts, and we are all engaged in adjusting to this new world.

The future of distance education is bleak as the quality of distance education is deteriorating. The National Knowledge Commission (NKC) believes that a radical reform of the system of Open and Distance Education (ODE) is imperative to achieve the objectives of expansion, inclusion and excellence in higher education. The significance is obvious. For one more than one-fifth of the students enrolled in higher education are in the ODE stream. For another, ODE has an enormous potential to spread higher education opportunities beyond the brick and mortar world. But there are reasons for concern. First the quality of higher education provided in large segments of ODE, particularly in correspondence courses in universities, leaves much to be desired. Second, it is not sufficiently recognized that ODE provides educational opportunities not only to those who discontinue formal education on account of economic or social compulsions, but also to young school Ieavers who are simply unable to secure admission in the formal stream at universities. It is time to address these problems. There is a clear need to improve the quality of ODE and to make it more appropriate to the needs of society. It is just as important to expand opportunities in higher education through the use of technology in ODE. It would not be possible to attain a gross enrolment ratio of 15% by 2015 without a massive expansion in ODE. In this endeavour, we must not forget that ODE is seen as inferior to conventional classroom Iearning. This perception, and the reality, both need change. We must realize that ODE is not simply a mode of educational delivery, but an integrated discipline engaged in the creation of knowledge.

The targets fixed by XIth Five Year Plan is are 30 per cent of overall enrollment in higher education in the country which means an addition of nearly 7 million students. In addition, the thrust during XIth Plan would be to develop professional, vocational and career-oriented programmes.

Reliable external assessment is valued by employers, students and other stakeholders in the given context of a market driven economy. In view of this, a rating system to assess the standard of all institutions imparting ODE must be evolved and made publicly available. The Standing Committee would stipulate grading norms and independent rating agencies would be licensed by IRAHE to carry out this function. In addition, it is recommended that every ODE institution has an internal quality assurance cell to ensure that statutory quality compliances are regularly met.

Establishment of the new organizations proposed above, namely, the National Education Testing Service, the Credit Bank, the National Educational Foundation for developing common open resources, the Technical Advisory Group and the Advisory Group on Pedagogical Content Management would initially require financial support from the government. Additional finances for networking ODE institutions and creating access centres, developing training programmes for educators and administrators and providing scholarships and services for needy students would also be required.

Thus, distance education has expanded without quality being kept intact. Quality of distance education is deteriorating. We may have to take concrete steps to ensure quality before further expansion otherwise we may lose the merit of distance education.

At present, there are 13 states open universities. Eleventh Plan has proposed to add 8 more universities and 100 CCIS will be supported for their quality upgradation.

The present book, "Distance Education: Principles, Potentialities and Perspectives" has been divided into 17 chapters. Chapter 1 deals with meaning, scope, nature, significance and challenges of Educational Administration followed by Chapter 2 covering meaning, extent rationale, issues, problems and suggestions relating to distance education. Chapter 3 emphasizes need of Good Governance essential to maintain standards in Distance Education system, Chapters 4 and 5 deal with instructional material through lecture scripts and New Technology. New Technology has become ornamental as there is a lot of propaganda about it with little use in practice. Chapter 6 deals with Personal Contact Programme. Chapters 7 and 8 deal with Response Sheets and Students Support Services. Chapter 9 deals with Quality control in Distance Education which has become very difficult without benchmarks. Chapter 10 deals with Financial Administration in a Distance Education. Chapter 11 examines Organization and Management of Distance Education System. Chapter 12 concentrates on Qualities of teachers in Distance Education. Chapter 13 examines working of Distance Education Council. Chapter 14 examines future of Distance Education which appears to be bleak. Chapter 15 deals with Infrastructural Facilities in Distance Education System. Chapter 16 deals with Dichotomy between Distance Education and Formal Education System—A Farce. Chapter 17 discusses conclusion.

All the chapters have been illustrated with charts, facts, suggestions, case studies, etc. Analysis and suggestions have been made wherever needed.

It is hoped that this book on "Distance Education: Principles, Potentialities and Perspectives" would make a modest contribution to the knowledge and existing literature on this expanding field. Besides, this would help the academicians, national education officials, educational administrators, education research workers and the policy-makers and planners in the proper understanding of distance education delivery system. We will consider our labour well rewarded if the findings of the study are translated to provide decent distance education to the millions of people deprived of higher education. Comments and suggestions from the readers would always be welcome.

Chandigarh

ARUNA GOEL
S.L. GOEL

Acronyms and Initials

ASC	Academic Staff College
AVRC	Audio-Visual Research Centre
AICTE	All India Council for Technical Education
AIU	All India Universities Association
BC	Backward Classes
CABE	Central Advisory Board of Education
CCI	Correspondence Course Institute
CEDOK	Centre for Entrepreneurship Development of Karnataka
COL	Commonwealth of Learning
CU	Conventional University
DEC	Distance Education Council
DE	Distance Education
DCS	Department/Directorate of Correspondence Studies
DCCs	Directorate of Correspondence Courses
DEI	Distance Education Institute
EDEN	European Distance Education Network
EMRC	Educational Media Research Centre.
EADTU	European Association of Distance Teaching Universities
EDI	Entrepreneurship Development of India
GOI	Government of India
HRD	Human Resource Development
IGNOU	Indira Gandhi National Open University
ICDE	International Council for Distance Education
KOU	Kota Open University
MHRD	Ministry of Human Resource Development
MIS	Management Information System
MBO	Management By Objectives
NPE	National Policy on Education
NCERT	National Council of Education Research and Training
NCHE	National Council of Higher Education
NCTE	National Council of Teachers' Education
NOS	National Open School
OU	Open University
OLPE	Open Learning Programme in Entrepreneurship
OPENET	Open University Network
PUC	Panjab University, Chandigarh

PCP	Personal Contact Programme
POA	Programme of Action
RSA	Response Sheet Assignment
RC	Regional Centre
SC	Scheduled Castes
STRIDE	Staff Training and Research in Distance Education
SOU	State Open University
TV	Television
UGC	University Grants Commission
UNESCO	United Nations Educational, Scientific and Cultural Organization
UNICEF	United Nations Children Educational Fund
VC	Vice-Chancellor

Meaning, Scope, Nature, Significance and Challenges of Education Administration

"Education is the basic tool for the development of consciousness and reconstitution of Society"

—Mahatma Gandhi

(A) IMPORTANCE OF EDUCATION

Education is one of the most important factors in achieving the developmental goals of the country. It is the key to the national development. It is an investment in the human resources. If the fruits of education have to reach the common man, it must be adequately and properly administered.

The importance of education can be interpreted from the reply to the question asked from Aristotle. The question asked was, "How much better educated men were than those who were uneducated." The reply was, "As much as the living are than the dead."

Dr. A.P.J. Abdul Kalam has beautifully explained the need of education to young minds—

Our young minds have to be ignited,
This ignition is more powerful,
Compared to any resource on the earth,
Under the earth, above the earth

He further adds:

Where there is righteousness in mind
There is beauty in Character

Where there is beauty in character
There is order in family;
Where there is an order in the family
There is harmony in society;
Where there is harmony in society
There is unity in nation;
Where there is unity in nation
There is peace in the world

M. Karpaga Vinayagam, Hon'ble Chief Justice, Jharkhand High Court, Jharkhand, delivered the Convocation Address on 22nd Convocation of Bharathiar University, Coimbatore on 22 January, 2007. He said, "The meaningful education should stimulate all aspects of human intellectual potentials. You should not simply emphasize on needs of responsibility and the authority of knowledge, science, technology and management, but you should also uphold the values supported by the time honoured and potentially valuable disciplines of the humanity. It is true that there is explosion of knowledge, but we should not forget there is an erosion of values. There is no replacement for essence of values. It is essential that the students acquire knowledge and understanding of the facts with a sense of respect to the values. You must be morally good, otherwise you with your specialized knowledge will resemble as a well trained dog than a harmoniously developed man." Excerpts.

Kothari Commission observed: "The destiny of India is now being shaped in her classrooms. This, we believe, is no more rhetoric. In a world based on science and technology, it is education that determines the level of prosperity, welfare and security of the people. On the quality and number of persons coming out of our schools and colleges will depend our success in the great enterprise of national reconstruction, the principal objective of which is to raise the standard of living of our people. The universities must serve as the conscience of the nation; encourage individuality, variety and dissent, within a climate of tolerance; assist schools in their attempt to qualitative self-improvement; improve standards by symbiotic development of teaching and research; and create a few centres of world class competence."

In the present age of science and technology, it has been increasingly realized that one needs to be educated not only to become a better man and a better social being, but he should also be a better creative and productive being. Education has come to be recognized as the main instrument of socio-economic change. That is why it has been rightly said that the destiny of a nation is shaped by quantity and quality of students coming out of schools and colleges. Education has been accepted as an instrument of development and for strengthening the values of democracy.

The First Five Year Plan stated, "Education is of basic importance in the planned development of a country. The educational system has also an intimate bearing on the attainment of the general objective of the plan in as much as it largely determines the quality of the manpower and the social climate of the Community." In a democratic set-up the role of education becomes crucial since it can function effectively only if there is an intelligent participation of the masses in the affairs of the country.

The Second Plan stated, "The system of education has a determining influence on the rate at which economic progress is achieved and the benefits which can be derived from it. Economic development naturally makes growing demands on human resources and in a democratic set-up it calls for values and attitudes in the building of which the quality of education is an important element."[1]

The Third Plan underlines the significance of education in national development and aptly describes education as "the focal point of planned development."[2] The document stated, "Education is the most important single factor in achieving rapid economic development and technological progress and increasing a social order founded on the values of freedom, social justice and equal opportunity. Programmes of education, lie at the base of the effort to forge the bonds of Common citizenship, to harness the energies of the people and to develop the natural and human resources of every part of the country."[2] In a word education is regarded as the key to national development and the fundamental pre-requisite of social and economic justice which are the twin pillars of the Welfare State and the socialistic pattern of society. In the Fourth Five Year Plan (Draft), the importance of education was underlined in the following terms:

(1) Education as an investment in human resources plays an important role among the factors which contributes to Economic growth.

(2). It secures returns in the form of skilled manpower-geared to the needs of development and also creates the right attitudes and climate for development.

(3) It exposes the farmers and workers to new ideas, stirs their ambition and bends them to change.

(4) It seeks to create an environment of discipline, harmony, understanding and team work which is conducive *to* the implementation of production plans.

(5) Education is essential both for accelerating economic development and for improving the quality of the society which we are seeking to create. It is essential that planning should establish a firm and purposive link between education and development.

In the Sixth Five Year Plan (1980-85) education was accorded a high priority as a means of human resource development. Programmes of human resource development have a four-fold perspective: (i) to prepare individuals for assuming their role as responsible citizens; (ii) *to* develop in them scientific outlook, awareness of their rights and responsibilities as well as a consciousness of the process of development, (iii) to sensitise them to ethical, social and cultural values which go to make an enlightened nation; and (iv) to impart to them knowledge, skills and attitudes which would enable them to contribute to the productive programmes in the national development.

Seventh Five Year Plan has rightly pinpointed the linkage between Education and development. To quote the Plan, "Human resources development has necessarily to be assigned a key role in any development strategy, particularly in a country with a large population. Trained and educated on sound lines, a large population can itself become an asset in accelerating economic growth and in ensuring social change in desired directions. Education develops basic skills and abilities and fosters a value system conducive to, and in support of national development goals, both long-term and immediate. In a world where knowledge is increasing at an exponential rate, the task of education in the diffusion of new knowledge and at the same time in the preservation and promotion of what is basic to India's culture and ethos, is both complex and challenging."

"In a world based on Science and Technology, it is education that determines the level of prosperity, welfare and security of the people."[3]

The major emphasis in higher education during the Eighth Plan was on: (i) integrated approach to higher education, (ii) excellence and equity, (iii) relevance of higher education, (iv) promotion of value education, and (v) strengthening of management system in university institutions.

Ninth Five Year Plan states that education is the most crucial investment in human development. Education strongly influences improvement in health, hygiene, demographic profile, productivity and practically all that is connected with the quality of life. The policies and approach to investment in the education sector and its development in the next decade assume critical significance from this standpoint. The Ninth Plan treats education as the most crucial investment in human development. The Prime Minister's Special Action Plan (SAP) has identified the expansion and improvement of social infrastructure in education as a critical area.

The excellence of our university products and professionals is well acknowledged both at home and abroad. The competitive advantage of the country can be maintained and improved only if the university and higher education sectors perform well. Their contribution to improving our capability to interact effectively with the fast expanding global and techno-economic systems has been significant and their potential needs to be harnessed to the full.

Tenth Five Year Plan states that the importance of education, especially higher education, has grown in the 21st century, since knowledge-based industries are now occupying the center stage in development. Though the modern higher education system in India is almost 135 years old, its growth has been much faster after India became independent.

It is increasingly recognized that in the context of major economic and technological changes, the system of higher education should equip students with adequate skills to enable their full participation in the emerging social, economic and cultural environment. Universities are thus witnessing a sea change in their outlook and perspective. Also, information and communication technologies are leading to fundamental changes in the structure, management and mode of delivery of the entire educational system.

The 11th Five Year Plan approach paper states that the importance of education, especially higher education, has grown in the 21st century, since knowledge-based industries are now occupying the centre stage in development. Through the modern higher education system in India is almost 135 years old, its growth has been much faster after India became independent.

The New Education Policy also accords high priority to Education in the process of development. To quote the policy; education has an acculturating role. It refines sensitivities and perceptions that contribute to national cohesion, a scientific temper and independence of mind and spirit —thus furthering the goals of socialism, secularism and democracy enshrined in our Constitution. Education develops manpower for different levels of the economy. It is also the substrate on which research and development flourish, being the ultimate guarantee of national self-reliance. In sum, Education is a unique investment in the present and the future. This cardinal principle is the key to the National Policy on Education.[4]

Prof. Dayanand Dangaonkar, Secretary General, Association of Indian Universities, New Delhi said, "Education is universally recognized to be an investment in human resources. In the present information age, new knowledge and technology are crucial for improving productivity of human and material resources. As we all know the green revolution in agriculture resulted in high productivity with the use of technology with vigor and effort, a similar revolution in education that embraces information and communication technologies, that fosters freedom and innovation and induces a market-oriented competitive environment, is vital for the progress and prosperity of the country. This requires not only the commitment, seriousness and devotion of students and faculty but also efforts for widening the base of human capital formation through education, training, research and development activities."[5]

Globalization and Education

S.K. Panneerselvam in his article, "Impact of Globalization on Human Development and Education in the 21st Century", in the *University News*, May 24-30, 2004 observes that Globalization indicates "Interconnectivity" of technologies. These technologies have rapidly made the world a 'global village'. They have shrunk geographical frontiers. Nations, organizations, individuals, business and commercial corporations are integrated by globalization. Even the scientific community is becoming a world community. The scientific community shares concepts, exchanges ideas, collaborations on projects and uses international standards and benchmarks. The Global era has immense implications for education, with at least the following five important thrusts:

- Demands on students and teachers to develop global consciousness and global concerns;
- Necessity to arrive at the "frontiers of knowledge" as rapidly as possible by closing existing gaps and thereafter to keep up pace;
- Emphasis on the development of communications skills, with increasing mastery over information technology; and
- Development of a global civilization and the necessity to share values that can sustain humanity in the global era.

Private Higher Education

The wide spectrum of institutions internationally makes it very difficult to generalize about private higher education. Institutions range from prestigious universities such as Harward in the United States, Waseda in Japan, and Yonesi in South Korea, to "garage universities" in El Salvador and other countries. The private sector will certainly continue to expand and thrive in the contemporary higher education marketplace. It is clear that the private higher education sector makes many important contributions—the most notable among them providing study opportunities for many students who would otherwise not be able to find a place at a public institution. Many have argued that the private sector has created a degree of competition in the moribund public system, has focused on students, and had other benefits. However, the growth of private higher education poses many challenges to higher education systems worldwide.

While private higher education has been part of the academic system since the origin of Western universities in the 13th century, it has become a central feature of academic in the 21st century. How to perceive the private sector and integrate it into the broader academic system in a country—and worldwide—is a key challenge. The newer private institutions are quite different—structure, orientation, financial background, and in other ways—from the traditional private universities. Without question, understanding, integrating, and creating an appropriate policy framework for private higher education are central issue of the current period to ensure quality, transparency and service institution and not profit motive.

(B) OVERVIEW OF EDUCATIONAL DEVELOPMENTS

Let us review the developments in different areas of education which impinge directly and indirectly on planning and administration of Education. The developments are not merely numerical but also of qualitative in nature. The enumeration of these developments would help in understanding the dynamics of educational administration in a better way.

(a) Growth of Institutions

As on 2004-05, there were 767520 Primary Junior basic schools, 274731 Middle Senior Basic Schools, 152049 High Schools/Higher Secondary, Intermediate, Pre-degree Jr. Colleges, 10377 colleges for General Education, 3201 Colleges for Professional Education, 407 Universities (Deemed University/and Institutions of National Importance) (See Table 1.1). As on 2004-2005, the dropout rates in Classes I-V is 29.00 percent (31.81 for males and 25.42 in girls), in Classes I-VIII, the rates is 50.84 percent (50.49 males and 61.28 for females).

(b) Growth of Students

As on 2004-05 the number of students, in Primary/Junior Basic (Class I-V) are 130763067 (69674543 boys, 61088524 girls) in Middle Upper Primary (Class VI-VIII) are 512245426 (28503657 boys, 22741769 girls), in Higher Secondary/Pre-degree 37075386 (21686880 boys and 15388506 girls) in the higher education, 11777296 (7135720 boys and 4641576 girls). See Table 1.2

(c) Growth of Teachers

As on 2004-05, the number of teachers for Primary Education is 2160666 (1318660 male and 842006 females), in Middle upper Primary the number is 1589200 (992407 male and 596873 females), in Secondary and Higher Secondary, the number is 2082900 (1281816 male and 80174 females) (See Table 1.3)

(d) Increase in Literacy Rate

The following Table 1.4 indicates the literacy rate in India and male and female literacy rates in the country from 1951.

It is evident that the gap in male-female literacy rates of 18.30 percentage points in 1951, increased to 26.62 in 1981, but has improved since then. In 1991 this gap was reduced to 24.48 and in 2001, it has

TABLE 1.1

Statement 1: Total Number of Recognised Educational Institutions in India, 2004-05 (Provisional)

Sl. No.	States/UTs	Primary/ Junior Basic Schools	Middle Senior Basic Schools	High Schools/ Higher Sec. Inter-mediate/ Pre-Degree/ Jr. Colleges	Degree and above levels: Colleges for General Education	Degree and above levels: Colleges for Professional Education	Univs./ Deem Univs./ Instts. of National Importance#
1.	Andhra Pradesh	61680	16667	17710	1340	406	25
2.	Arunachal Pradesh	1371	495	214	10	4	1
3.	Assam	30068	8143	5374	317	50	7
4.	Bihar	39347	10963	3639	743	45	19
5.	Chhattisgarh	33595	10799	2670	213	5	5
6.	Goa	1003	73	445	23	13	1
7.	Gujarat	16385	22623	7718	507	216	20
8.	Haryana	11800	2269	5222	166	113	9
9.	Himachal Pradesh	11178	2210	2341	89	33	7
10.	Jammu & Kashmir	12049	4239	1347	50	137	9
11.	Jharkhand	16572	4933	1196	117	22	8
12.	Karnataka	26645	26816	11818	930	360	27
13.	Kerala	6827	3049	5402	186	127	9
14.	Madhya Pradesh	96737	34641	8301	760	109	21
15.	Maharashtra	41669	26295	18717	1208	450	42
16.	Manipur	2552	831	706	58	5	2
17.	Meghalaya	5851	1759	711	54	2	1
18.	Mizoram	1481	939	512	26	2	1
19.	Nagaland	1520	480	379	37	1	1
20.	Orissa	45700	15893	8661	700	80	15
21.	Punjab	13352	2503	3980	212	100	10
22.	Rajasthan	55942	26201	10144	611	117	25
23.	Sikkim	684	185	161	2	4	2
24.	Tamil Nadu	33470	7111	9234	445	362	41
25.	Tripura	1776	1001	652	14	3	1
26.	Uttar Pradesh	129976	36874	12766	1009	224	41
27.	Uttaranchal	14663	3861	1855	86	4	9
28.	West Bengal	50397	1929	7971	374	139	26
29.	A&N Islands	213	58	95	3	1	0
30.	Chandigarh	25	8	118	12	9	4
31.	D&N Haveli	127	91	22	0	0	0
32.	Daman & Diu	53	24	28	1	1	0
33.	Delhi	2463	635	1712	63	41	17
34.	Lakshadweep	31	3	11	0	0	0
35.	Pondicherry	328	127	227	11	16	1
	Total	767520	274731	152049	10377	3201	407

#As on 31.3.05 (University Grants Commission Annual Report, 2004-05).

TABLE 1.2

Enrolment by Stages 2004-05 as on 30.09.2004 (Provisional)

S. No.	States/UTs	Primary/Jr. Basic (Classes I-V)			Middle/Upper Primary (Classes VI-VIII)			Sec./Hr. Sec./Pre-Degree (Classes XI-XII)			Higher Education		
		Boys	Girls	Total	Boys	Girls	Total	Boys	Girls	Total	Boys	Girls	Total
1	2	3	4	5	6	7	8	9	10	11	12	13	14
1.	Andhra Pradesh	3894649	3797762	7692411	1918363	1724667	3643030	1781072	1378977	3160049	659616	397103	1056719
2.	Arunachal Pradesh	100064	84609	184673	32698	26972	59670	24356	17163	41519	4226	2519	6745
3.	Assam	1794039	1716626	3510665	737094	652661	1389755	459818	339574	799392	125610	88732	214342
4.	Bihar	5938345	4103774	10042119	1430687	778302	2308989	923934	379050	1302984	414270	135423	553693
5.	Chhattisgarh	1776950	1628552	3405502	687761	522233	1209994	424603	275140	699743	193226	60028	163254
6.	Goa	55713	51115	106828	38836	34616	73446	31529	30637	61866	9074	12569	21643
7.	Gujarat	3702108	3850917	6553022	1431810	1041725	2473535	1012769	690912	1703681	371491	274198	645689
8.	Haryana	1097631	976308	3073939	656396	528418	1184814	511875	371859	883734	150392	113939	264331
9.	Himachal Pradesh	350760	320047	670017	219699	199103	418802	367716	322733	690449	54815	48813	10328
10.	Jammu & Kashmir	504792	464680	969479	253629	303268	456897	201480	153401	354881	44078	36327	80408
11.	Jharkhand	1911035	1535949	3446984	544507	379752	924259	236978	143778	380756	132617	76559	209176
12.	Karnataka	3040721	2843186	5883907	1549520	1396782	2946302	1137328	1001912	2139240	393039	313312	700241
13.	Kerala	1296261	1245161	2543422	850089	000341	1628030	684173	696777	1380650	128985	184170	313155
14.	Madhya Pradesh	5491292	4859801	10351093	2156596	1670352	3826948	1292618	729396	2022014	521054	237364	758418
15.	Maharashtra	5918639	5466844	11385483	3277661	2910891	6188552	2590608	2081424	4673032	956721	577892	1534613
16.	Manipur	180660	168237	348897	72315	64985	137300	50445	46298	96743	21257	17422	38679
17.	Meghalaya	232537	235418	467955	65594	71246	136840	36873	37336	74199	16432	14284	30716
18.	Mizoram	64803	58902	123706	36301	25213	51514	18574	18504	37078	7855	4325	12180
19.	Nagaland	117054	107192	224346	44547	41073	85620	25093	22578	47671	7506	6139	13644
20.	Orissa	2718222	2500346	5218568	997910	843023	1840933	8380016	544482	1382498	293855	73332	367187
21.	Punjab	1010079	891329	1901408	555492	486602	1043094	458266	395032	853298	136385	143422	279707
22.	Rajasthan	5063707	4266085	9329792	2003374	1153437	3156811	1261080	531945	1793025	262492	131986	394478
23.	Sikkim	43337	45812	86149	13529	15154	28683	8934	9049	17983	3885	2711	6596

(Contd.)

TABLE 1.2 *(Contd.)*

1	2	3	4	5	6	7	8	9	10	11	12	13	14
24.	Tamil Nadu	3321365	3082051	6403416	1934301	1763557	3697858	1521320	1431034	2952354	429873	379493	809366
25.	Tripura	240599	220610	461209	99196	88394	187590	64764	54145	118909	12956	9491	22447
26.	Uttar Pradesh	13241089	11338549	24579638	4168396	2929636	7098022	3757509	2168550	5926059	926531	581460	1507991
27.	Uttaranchal	616672	574833	1191506	287620	264632	552252	266550	204068	470618	69295	62447	131742
28.	West Bengal	5065416	4815936	9881352	1945462	1676564	3622026	1280474	922458	2302932	470211	276298	746509
29.	A&N Islands	20852	19422	40272	12442	10987	23429	9581	9056	18637	1227	1479	2706
30.	Chandigarh	34233	28678	62908	20257	17459	37716	22592	30599	43191	25980	25329	51309
31.	D&N Haveli	18085	15539	33624	7192	4665	11857	4474	2926	7400	0	0	0
32.	Daman & Diu	8696	7625	16321	4345	3815	8160	3430	2829	6259	294	325	619
33.	Delhi	744712	716602	1460714	422128	400364	822492	346082	322901	668983	366700	342469	709169
34.	Lakshadweep	3736	3317	7053	2298	1812	4110	2198	1942	4140	0	0	0
35.	Pondicherry	53593	50306	103999	35018	32078	67096	29768	30351	60119	9873	10326	20199
	Total	69674543	61088524	130763067	28503657	22741769	51245426	21686880	15388506	37075386	7135720	4641576	11777296

Source: Annual Report, Ministry of HRD, 2006-07.

TABLE 1.3

Enrolment by Stages 2004-05 as on 30.09.2004 (Provisional)

S. No.	States/UTs	Primary/Jr. Basic			Middle/Upper Primary			Sec./Hr. Sec./Pre-Degree		
		Male	Female	Total	Male	Female	Total	Male	Female	Total
1	2	3	4	5	6	7	8	9	10	11
1.	Andhra Pradesh	91782	75153	166935	60900	43085	103985	116326	68033	184359
2.	Arunachal Pradesh	2518	1112	3630	2164	905	3069	2760	796	3556
3.	Assam	53811	29077	82888	55734	17328	73062	56461	30792	77253
4.	Bihar	59187	14015	73202	43550	12191	55741	36202	4876	41078
5.	Chhattisgarh	49712	19107	18819	19762	6296	26058	30110	8776	28886
6.	Goa	398	1806	2303	123	361	484	2925	5085	8010
7.	Gujarat	16928	19111	36029	92845	89461	182306	52874	18774	71648
8.	Haryana	25085	24806	49891	6136	3760	9896	37176	27728	64904
9.	Himachal Pradesh	15596	13605	28301	8752	4995	13747	18678	11711	30389
10.	Jammu & Kashmir	19697	12213	31910	16707	11572	28279	15362	8936	24297
11.	Jharkhand	23858	6244	30102	19523	8719	28242	8490	1855	13345
12.	Karnataka	39371	24900	64271	83836	108582	192418	63555	29856	93411
13.	Kerala	11125	30333	41458	14435	30961	45396	39526	94814	134340
14.	Madhya Pradesh	176011	62857	238868	111198	182939	129437	43147	51196	94343
15.	Maharashtra	75393	115080	190473	109218	83264	192482	190874	87571	278545
16.	Manipur	4939	3094	8033	5181	3572	8753	7183	4950	12133
17.	Meghalaya	7300	6445	13745	4317	3090	7407	3512	3692	6204
18.	Mizoram	3015	2954	5969	4777	2200	6977	3043	1894	4437
19.	Nagaland	5159	2968	8127	3921	2375	6296	4760	3424	8184
20.	Orissa	63709	85370	99079	23419	7974	31393	60383	17321	77704
21.	Punjab	14771	23906	38676	6336	6870	13206	29256	37748	67004

(Contd.)

TABLE 1.3 (Contd.)

1	2	3	4	5	6	7	8	9	10	11
22.	Rajasthan	86981	32988	119969	115456	44967	160423	85596	33001	118597
23.	Sikkim	2559	2562	5121	755	417	1172	929	468	1397
24.	Tamil Nadu	37390	82579	119969	26217	30741	56958	81940	129487	211427
25.	Tripura	6145	1891	8036	6566	2315	8880	12201	5369	12470
26.	Uttar Pradesh	286888	113569	399457	124097	33750	157847	154858	29852	184710
27.	Uttaranchal	20741	22974	43715	11274	6165	17439	22343	8791	31134
28.	West Bengal	110096	41569	151665	11303	4171	15474	85722	34781	120503
29.	A&N Islands	414	510	954	340	383	723	1423	1418	280
30.	Chandigarh	46	212	258	15	176	191	918	4008	4923
31.	D&N Haveli	259	282	541	167	111	278	161	135	296
32.	Daman & Diu	90	327	426	133	148	281	193	119	312
33.	Delhi	7714	17030	24744	2473	6737	9210	30064	39082	59146
34.	Lakshadweep	180	143	323	87	61	148	363	116	379
35.	Pondicherry	783	2186	2969	691	931	1622	2602	3223	5825
	Total	1318660	842006	2160666	942407	596873	1589280	1281816	801174	2082990

Source: Annual Report, Ministry of HRD, 2006-07.

TABLE 1.4

Literacy Rate in India from 1951-2001

Census Year	*Persons*	*Males*	*Females*	*Male-Females gap in literacy rate*
1951	18.33	27.16	8.86	18.30
1961	28.30	40.40	15.35	25.05
1971	34.45	45.96	21.97	23.98
1981	43.57	56.38	29.76	26.62
1991	52.21	64.13	39.29	24.48
2001	65.38	75.85	54.16	21.70

Source: Census of India, 2001.

further gone down to 21.70 percentage points. These decline according to the Department of Education and Literacy are bound to be slow initially as a result of the continuing past legacy of a large number of adult illiterate women, but will show accelerated trends in the coming decade.

The following table indicates the number of literates and illiterates in the population aged 7 years and above, and their change from 1991 to 2001:

TABLE 1.5

Number of Literates and Illiterates in the Population aged 7 years and above, and their change from 1991 to 2001

Literate/Illiterates	*Persons*	*Males*	*Females*
Literates 1991-	358,402,656	228,983,134	129,419,492
2001	562,010,743	336,969,695	225,041,048
Increase in 2001 over 1991	203,608,117	107,966,561	95,621,556
Illiterates 1991-	328,167,288	128,099,211	200,068,077
2001	296,208,952	106,654,066	189,554,886
Increase in 2001 over 1991	-31,958,336	-21,445,145	-10,513,191

Source: Census India, 2001.

It is seen from the table that out of the 203 million added to the literate population during 1991-2001, 107 million were males and 95 million were females. On the other hand, during this period the contribution to the total decrease of 31 million among illiterates is dominated by males (21 million) as compared to the females (10 million).

(e) Mounting Expenditure on Education

The finance increased from 153 crores in First Five Year Plan to 24,908 crore in IX Plan. The percentage of expenditure on Higher Education out of total Education expenditure is low, i.e. varying between 9 to 25. In IXth Plan, it was 10.0 percent

TABLE I.6

Expenditure on Education in the Five Year Plans

Five Year Plans	*Elementary (%)*	*Secondary (%)*	*Higher (%)*	*Total expenditure*
I	85 (56)	20 (13)	14 (9)	15,300
II	95 (35)	51 (19)	48 (18)	27,300
III	201 (34)	103 (18)	87 (15)	58,900
IV	239 (30)	140 (18)	195 (25)	78,600
V	317 (35)	156 (17)	205 (27)	91,200
VI	8023 (30)	736 (25)	530 (18)	2,04,000
VII	2849 (34)	1829 (22)	1201 (14)	8,50,000
VIII	40066 (47)	1538 (18)	10558 (12.4)	8,52,190
IX	16,364.6 (47)	2,603.5 (10.5)	2500.0 (10.0)	24,90,850

Source: Five Year Plans, Annual Plans and MRHD Reports.

The outlay approved for Tenth Plan for Secondary and Higher Education is given in Table 1.7

TABLE I.7

S. No.	*Name of the Scheme*	*Ninth Plan Tenth Plan Anticipated*	*Ninth Plan Allocation Expenditure*	*Tenth Plan approved outlay*
1.	Secondary Education	2,603.49	2,323.66	4,325.00
2.	Univerity and Hr. Education	2,520,05	2,270.92	3,607.00
3.	Technical Education	2,375.51	2,109.54	4,300.00
4.	Langauge Development	324.45	298.40	434.00
5.	Scholarships	25.32	3.23	52.00
6.	Book Promotion	16.25	26.06	67.00
7.	Planning and Admns.	65.38	21.46	65.00
	Total	7,809.40	7,052.29	12.850.00

Source: Tenth Five Year Plan (Draft), p. 65.

(f) Growth of University and Higher Education

There were only 20 universities and 500 colleges at the time of Independence. There are 369 Universities at present comprising 222 State Universities, 20 Central Universities, 109 Deemed Universities, 5 Institutions established under States Legislations and 13 Institutions of National Importance established by Central Legislation. Four new Central University

Acts are in the process of being brought in to force. In addition, there are 18,064 colleges including around 1902 women's colleges. At the beginning of the academic year 2006-07, the total number of students enrolled in the Universities and colleges was reported to be 110.28 lakhs—14.27 lakhs (12.94%) in University Department and 96.01 lakhs (87.06%) in affiliated colleges.

The enrolment of women at the beginning of the academic year 2006-07 was 44.66 lakhs, constituting 40.40% of the total enrolment. Of the total enrolment of women, 12.35% were enrolled in professional courses. Enrolment of Women as a percentage of total enrolment in a State is the highest in Kerala (66.00%) and the lowest in Bihar (24.52%). In terms of absolute number of women enrolled, Maharashtra tops the list of States.

The number of doctoral degrees awarded by various universities (position as on 1.1.05) was 17,898. Out of which, the faculties of Arts had the highest number of 7532 degrees, followed by the faculties of Science with 5549 degrees.

The regular faculty strength in universities was 0.79 lakhs (16.15%) and 4.09 lakhs in colleges (83.85%) totaling 4.88 lakhs.

(g) Education through Distance Education

In recent years, there has been a great expansion of the Universities and institutes running post-graduate and under-graduate courses through correspondence (Distance Education). Students through Distance Education account for 24 percent of total enrolment in Higher Education. In 11th Plan, it is going to rise significantly.

(h) Diversification

Education at school, college and University level is highly diversified. There are large number of vocational Courses at school and college level. In sciences, arts, many new specialisations have been started.

(i) New Directions

The Education Policy of 1968 has been replaced by New Policy of Education (NPE) 1986 and Plan of Action (POA) to meet the changed requirements. Besides, the review of its policy has been undertaken. Based upon review, A New Policy Document of New Education Policy 1986 with modifications taken in 1992 has been issued.

A brief overview suggests a great gap between achievements and requirements. There is a need to examine the issues and problems which stand in the way of educational development. This would help in taking remedial action and prompt us to move faster to attain the goals of education.

Unfortunately, the process of expansion has been an unplanned one. New institutions have sometimes been started just to satisfy misplaced demands. This has had its enviable toll as far as quality is concerned. Mediocrity is now seen in most places and excellence prevails only in islands. The major challenge is how to balance the demands for access to higher education and equality of opportunity with the overwhelming need for excellence. The matter has been rendered difficult in the face of the ever-increasing financial stringency specially in the context of globalisation and privatisation of all sectors of economy.

Culture is an integrating force that binds the nation and it is reflected in people's daily life and should be treated as an integral part of all development programmes. Given the continental size of the country, the monumental diversity of its people and their languages, the plurality of faiths and beliefs systems, conservation and promotional activities of cultural heritage call for ensuring dissemination of our composite culture. Special efforts are required to promote all regional languages, to sustain the folk and traditional art, and to maintain, document, research and propagate dissemination of the intangible cultural heritage. Also a system need to be evolved (with involvement of PRIs) to protect monuments not protected by ASI.[6]

(C) MEANING OF EDUCATIONAL ADMINISTRATION

Educational Administration comprises of two words—Education and Administration. Let us define these two words and then attempt the definition of Educational Administration.

It is very difficult to define education as it permeates every aspect of individual's life and is a life long process. The contents and process of education would depend upon the status and need of the country concerned. Education is a process to develop the personality and creativity in the individuals so that they can in turn help in promoting healthy Society and national development.

Education thus is a process which influences individual capabilities, Social environment, economic development, ethical environment and above all cultural adaptability. The Ministry of Education in one of its documents has mentioned the contents of education. To quote the documents[7], the system of education is expected to generate new knowledge in all fields within the reach of the human mind. In addition, it has to evolve principles, methodologies and guidelines for the application of knowledge for benefiting Society. It is also expected to provide knowledge and skills for solving the problems of development. It must also enable the students to develop an understanding and a perspective of the physical and Social environment. Research and development and extension, therefore, have to be accepted as essential ingredients of the educational process. Secondly, emphasis has to be laid on the socio-economic well-being, competence and creativity of the individual, which encompasses:

(i) physical, intellectual and aesthetic development of personality;
(ii) inculcation of a scientific temper and democratic, moral and spiritual values;

(iii) development of self-confidence to innovate and face unfamiliar situations;
(iv) creation of an awareness of the physical, Social, technological, economic and cultural environment;
(v) fostering a healthy attitude to dignity of labour and hard work;
(vi) a commitment to principles of secularism and Social justice;
(vii) dedication to uphold the integrity, honour and foster the development of the country; and
(viii) promotion of international understanding.

Education thus is a process to shape the quality of the life of the individual and through him of the Society and the World. Let us define now Administration:

Administration is at the centre of all human affairs. Its principal aspects are formulation of policy and its implementation for the attainment in an optimum manner of stated ends in the shape of services or products. Administration is an activity which demands correct analysis and accurate orientation. According to Simon, "In its broadest sense, administration can be defined as the activities of groups cooperating to accomplish common goals."[8] In the words of Marx:

> "Administration is determined action taken in the pursuit of a conscious purpose. It is the systematic ordering of affairs and the calculated use of resources aimed at making those things happen which one wants to happen and forestalling everything to the contrary."[9]

Pfiffner and Presthus define administration as "the organisation and direction of human and material resources to achieve desired ends:"[10]

In simple words, administration may be defined as the management of affairs of Education with the use of well thought-out principles and practices and rationalised techniques to achieve certain objectives.

Administration consists of a structure or an organisation of various institutions essential for its functioning; the processes, procedures and interaction of various constituents; and the techniques and skills of human relation. It is the management of human affairs concerned with the needs of carrying out specific objectives; administration is involved in all fields of human endeavour where there is a planned effort. It is a force which lays down the objectives which an organization and its management are to strive for and the broad policies under which to operate. Administration provides the means whereby the most effective use can be made of the knowledge and skills of those giving the service. It is a way of conceptual thinking for attaining pre-determined goals through group efforts.

Administration is the comprehensive effort to direct, guide and integrate associated human strivings which are focused toward some specific ends or aims. Administration is conceived as the necessary activities of those individuals (executives) in an organisation who are charged with ordering, forwarding and facilitating the associated efforts of a group of individuals brought together to realize certain defined purposes.[11]

Let us now define the term Educational Administration. It is a branch of Public Administration which provides educational services to the people with economy and efficiency. Efficiency in Educational administration can be ensured through proper policy formulation and its implementation. Educational Administration is the force which can help the education system in the formulation of sound Education Policy and its implementation.

"Educational administration approaches statesmanship when there are clearly formulated long-term policies and objectives, and when day-by-day activities and problems are dealt with under the guidance of the perspective given by such long-term policies."[12]

Since the resources for education are limited, therefore Educational administration has to maintain the economics of educational services. From this angle Educational Administration may be defined as that branch of knowledge which seeks to optimise Educational action, that is to study ways of spreading the available resources so as to ensure the best possible state of education for the population within the limited means.

Educational Administration aims at developing Human creativity and personality which in turn generate Social, Economic, Political and Cultural Development leading to the creation of a society where democratic values are respected and individuals find a respectable place.

It is the process of planning, implementation and evaluation of Educational services that both maintain and improve the Educational facilities of the Society.

In a broader sense authors feel that Educational Administration is the Art and Science of Planning, Implementation and Evaluation of educational inputs by preserving, producing and disseminating of knowledge for the physical, intellectual and moral and aesthetic development of individuals to achieve a higher quality of life, social cohesion, social justice, Environmental adjustment and International understanding. (Refer Chart 1.1)

Educational Administration need to apply the principles of administration specifically developed in the context of Education through research and experience to ensure best results.

These principles coined by Luther Gulick and L. Urwick are summed up in the words "POSDCORB." These stand for:

- Planning: the working out in broad outline the things that need to be done, the method to be adopted to accomplish the purpose set for the enterprise.
- Organisation: the establishment of the formal structure of authority, through which the work is sub-divided, arranged, defined and co-ordinated for the defined objective.

CHART 1.1

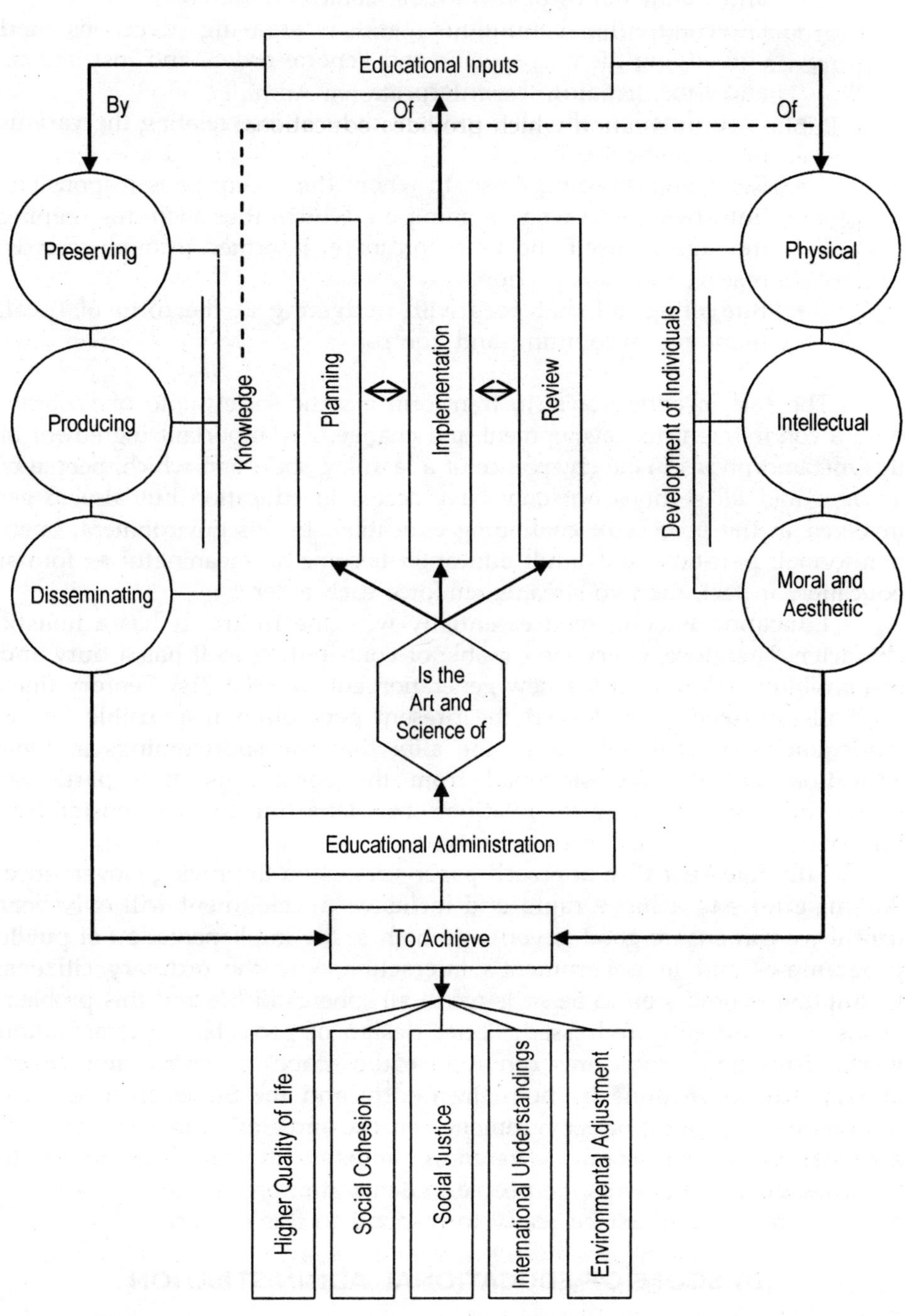
Educational Inputs
By
Of
Of
Preserving
Producing
Disseminating
Knowledge
Planning
Implementation
Review
Physical
Intellectual
Moral and Aesthetic
Development of Individuals
Is the Art and Science of
Educational Administration
To Achieve
Higher Quality of Life
Social Cohesion
Social Justice
International Understandings
Environmental Adjustment

- Staffing: the whole personnel, bringing in and training the staff, and maintenance of favourable condition of work.
- Directing: the continuous task of making decisions and embodying them in specific and general orders and instructions and thus, guiding the enterprise.
- Co-ordinating: the all important duty of interrelating the various parts of the work.
- Reporting: keeping those, to whom the executive is responsible, 'informed as to what is going on, which, thus includes keeping the' agency itself and its subordinates informed through records, research and inspection.
- Budgeting: all that goes with budgeting in the form of fiscal, planning, accounting and control.

The role of educationist to transform a static society into one vibrant with a commitment to development and change. An important ingredient of this metamorphosis is the emergence of a learning society in which, people of all ages and all sections not only have access to education but also to get involved in the process of continuing education. In this environment, open, non-formal, part-time and adult education become as meaningful as formal education; in fact, the two streams reinforce each other.[13]

Education is concerned essentially with the future. It has a holistic character. Therefore, everyone capable of contributing to it has a duty and responsibility to do so. If the new generation entering the 21st Century finds itself ill-equipped, it will hold the present generation responsible for its inadequacies. It will not accept the alibi that the shortcomings in their education and training stemmed from the constraints of a particular framework of Centre-State relations or departmental responsibilities. Education is a national responsibility.

11th Five Year Plan approach paper stresses on Improving Governance. All our efforts to achieve rapid and inclusive development will only bear fruit if we can ensure good governance both in the implementation of public programmes and in government's interaction with the ordinary citizens. Corruption is now seen to be endemic in all spheres of life and this problem needs to be urgently redressed. Better design of projects, implementation mechanisms and procedures can reduce the scope for corruption. Much more needs to be done by both the Centre and the States to lessen the discretionary power of government, ensure greater transparency and accountability, and create awareness among citizens. The Right to Information Act empowers the people to demand improved governance, and as government we must be ready to respond to this demand.[14]

(D) SCOPE OF EDUCATIONAL ADMINISTRATION

The scope of Educational Administration can be viewed from different angles as Education has many dimensions.

A. Types of Education—We can divide this into three recognised types, that is:

(i) Elementary Education	Pre-Primary, Primary
(ii) Secondary Education	Schools,
(iii) Higher Education	Colleges, Universities

B. Orientation of Education—We can divide this into three broad categories which can be further sub-divided, that is

(i) General Education	Humanities Science Arts Engineering
(ii) Technical Education	Medical Agriculture Management
(iii) Distance Educations	

C. Levels of Education—We can divide this into the following four aspects:

(i) Local Levels
(ii) State Level
(iii) Union Level
(iv) Inter-Governmental Level

D. Educational Technology—We can divide this into the following two categories:

(i) Formal	
(ii) Non-Formal	Adult Education Distance Education

E. We can also look at education on the basis of agencies supporting the education. These can be:

(i) Governments—Union and States
(ii) Local Governments—Urban and Rural
(iii) Voluntary Agencies
(iv) Private agencies (Aided and Unaided)

F. We can also look at education from the point of view of the contents:

(i) Personnel Administration.
(ii) Financial Administration.
(iii) Curriculum.
(iv) Examination

We can thus say that Education is a complex process having multiple dimensions. There is a need to go into all aspects of Education by Educational administrators to formulate policy and plans for Education. To quote one of the documents of Ministry of Education:

"The role of education is to transform a static society into one vibrant with a commitment to development and change. An important ingredient of this metamorphosis is the emergence of a learning society in which, people of all ages and all sections not only have access to education but also get involved in the process of continuing education. In this environment, open, non-formal, part-time and adult education become as meaningful as formal education; in fact, the two streams reinforce each other."[15]

Education is concerned essentially with the future. It has a holistic character. Therefore, everyone capable of contributing to it has a duty and responsibility to do so. If the new generation entering the 21st Century finds itself ill-equipped, it will hold the present generation responsible for its inadequacies. It will not accept the alibi that the shortcomings in their education and training stemmed from the constraints of a particular framework of Centre-State relations or departmental responsibilities. Education is a national responsibility

(E) NATURE OF EDUCATIONAL ADMINISTRATION

Educational Administration as a Science and an Art

Educational administration is becoming complex day-by-day. Man is acquiring undreamt of powers, for scientific progress makes him everyday more capable of shaping the world and his destiny. He has the potentiality to bring about socio-economic revolution for the harmonious and healthy development of the people. The world has the resources and know-how to achieve a significant improvement in Educational Development which will not perocolate to the majority of the people as a natural consequence of economic growth. It requires an efficient administrative and managerial system to translate the benefit of science and technology to people. Unfortunately, developing countries have failed to produce the expected system. The weakness, ineptitude and general inefficiency of their governmental systems are massive obstacles not only in their development but even in their survival.[16] These deficiencies prevent the vast flood of money, talent and material from achieving their objective. It is accepted that inability to manage efficiently or utilize effectively the available potential resources is the common ill of all the less developed countries. It follows that successful development demands a sound programme for managerial improvement.[17] Thus, the administrative inadequacies in a national government have a retarding influence on socio-economic development. Charles F. Nicklas, Public Administration Adviser to the Philippines Government, remarked:

"The success of management improvement efforts and indeed the quality of public administration depends to a very great and undeniable extent upon the concepts, philosophies, interests and characteristics of key officials at the top echelons of the government hierarchy. Without the proper attitude and impetus at these levels, the cause of improved management and operation in government faced constant frustration. It is, therefore, essential in the interest of progress that the individuals be endowed with the desire to see that the public service is administered in the most efficient, effective and economic manner possible and possess the knowledge and breadth of understanding necessary to fulfil that desire."[18]

Educational administration is an area of activity which calls for specialised knowledge and techniques which can help to achieve the educational development. Until and unless, we understand all the implications of such an administration, we may not be able to reap the potential benefits of educational organisations. This is a definite art which can be learnt and practised to produce predesigned output. Educational administration is an art as it can help to direct and guide the efforts of those involved in such an enterprise towards some specific ends or objectives efficiently. There is a great need to make this art perfect and professional. A professionally efficient and competent administration is able to serve the people better. Besides, the educational personnel must be dedicated to their profession.

Now the question arises whether educational administration is a science or not. It is definitely not a science like the physical sciences as it cannot claim certainty. It is a science similar to other Social Sciences like Economics, Sociology, etc. We are applying scientific methods in educational administration for careful planning, analysis and design of the procedures. We can make the instruments of Educational Administration more perfect through careful practice and research and thus reach definite universal principles. We should be clear here that the universal principles in human organisations would differ to a great extent depending upon the ecological differences prevalent in different areas. We can say that scientific societies and the exchange of knowledge and hypotheses by natural scientists have advanced the exactness of knowledge in the domain of natural science, so we may expect administrative societies, and the exchanges among administrators to advance the exactness of knowledge in the domain of administration."

Thus educational administration is both a science and an art. In order to advance the cause of this budding discipline for the present and the future academic scholars and practitioners, we may concentrate on its principles, philosophy and practice. The developing world is faced with the problems of limited resources, infinite needs and competing demands in the domain of education. In order to provide the educational services

(Elementary, Secondary and Higher) to the total population, the developing world would have to provide an effective system of educational administration. If these components are combined fruitfully, it is sure that the educational administration can deliver the desired goods and services to its constituents.

(F) SIGNIFICANCE OF EDUCATIONAL ADMINISTRATION

Educational administration is the vehicle which can translate educational policy and planning into action. Words written or spoken are of no use if not put in action. Educational Administration can optimise educational action to achieve economically and efficiently the predetermined objectives and goals. A good educational administration can ensure the achievement of educational targets in time. Educational administration can help in the following ways:

(i) To make available the services required to meet the demands not only of those who have easy accessibility but also the demands of those most in need, who are usually too poor or too geographically or socially remote to benefit from existing facilities.

(ii) Ensure the implementation of Educational Policy which has been designed to meet the aspirations of the people of the country.

(iii) Devise ways and means for mobilisation of existing and untapped resources—Community, Government (local and National) bilateral, multilateral, and non-Governmental to provide decent educational facilities and services to all.

(iv) Need of Manpower development through training, research, consultancy for different areas of Education.

(v) Encouraging integration and co-ordination through vertical and horizontal linkages among all levels and types of education.

(vi) Improving research and development capacity to solve educational problems and issues.

(vii) Encouraging decentralised planning involving the participation of beneficiaries in the process of educational development.

(viii) Designing educational technology to suit the field and environment.

(ix) Encouraging innovation and creativity in educational administration. Educational administration can help the nation in achieving the targets, goals and objectives set in policy-documents of education economically and efficiently within the time frame and resource constraints.

(G) CHALLENGES OF EDUCATIONAL ADMINISTRATION

We mention here some of the challenges facing Educational Administration in the developing world especially India. We would do them here briefly as some of these and others would be discussed in Chapters that follow.

1. Lack of Equity of Distribution and Adequacy of Coverage

There has been increase of educational facilities since independence. For example, the literacy rate has increased from 18.33 per cent in 1951 to 52.11 per cent in 1991 and 65.38 per cent in 2001. A close examination would reveal that literacy rate for females is still 54.6 (2001). This needs to be removed to make use of the female potential for development. The New Education Policy rightly stressed this need, "The removal of women's illiteracy and obstacles inhibiting their access to, and retention in, elementary education will receive over-riding priority, through provision of special support services, setting of time targets, and effective monitoring:" Ministry of Education also suggested many lines of action like mobilisation of women's groups around basic issues of women's empowerment and girls' education and enhancing access of girls to vocational, technical and professional education at all levels, breaking gender stereotypes.

Education is the most potent factor for changing women's position in Society. It equips them to contribute in different fields more meaningfully. Late Dr. (Mrs.) P.K. Devi, Professor of Gynecology, at P.G.I., Chandigarh stated on the basis of her critical examination among the various states of the Indian Union, "Literacy of women seem to be a significant factor in differences in the mortality and morbidity rates as these coincide with a very low female literacy rate." Educated women can become good mothers who can make a good nation with Solid foundation.

The percentage of the share of education for Scheduled Castes and Scheduled Tribes is low as compared to the total reflecting inequality. New Education Policy 1986 has also stressed that the central focus in the SCs' educational development need be their equalisation with the non-SC population at all stages and levels of education, in all areas and in all the four dimensions—rural male, rural female, urban male and urban female. There is also inequal distribution for some minority groups and handicapped. Further, there is rural and urban imbalance. It was also voiced emphatically in a document of the Ministry of Education, "Challenge of Education." To quote, "Though our achievements have been substantial in quantitative terms, these have not been enough to provide access for all. For a country like India with aspirations of developing into a highly productive and Modern society committed to the distribution of the resultant benefits to all, this is an occasion for a serious introspection."[19]

The Government need to serve the millions of people who suffer from chronic, ignorance, disease and inequality of opportunity. The Government must fulfil the aspirations of the people enshrined in the Constitution.

Austin summed up the Constitution of India in the following words:

> "The Indian Constitution is first and foremost a social document. The majority of its provisions are either directly aimed at furthering the goals of the social revolution or attempt to foster this revolution by establishing the conditions necessary for its achievement. Yet despite the permeation of the entire constitution by the aim of national renaissance the core of commitment to the social revolution lies in Part III and IV, in the Fundamental Rights and in the Directive Principles of State Policy. They are the conscience of the Constitution."[20]

Have we lived up to the expectations and aspirations of the people? The answer is plain and simple: certainly not. What can we do in future? We can devise technology and organisational objectives and structure which would benefit the largest number of the people and if possible reach the last person as desired by Mahatma Gandhi. What is required is change of ideology, philosophy and priorities in favour of the poor people.

There is a need to draw an index to monitor the progress. UN report on Education (p. 48) for all released in 1993 has developed Basic Education Index involving five elements—adult literacy, the male-female literacy gap, the proportion of enrolled children who reach grade four and the pupil-teacher ratio in primary education. Such index needs to be developed at the union and state levels to monitor the progress of educational developments.

2. Lack of People's Participation

Merle Fainsod remarks: "The most favourable setting for progress in development administration exists where a politically influential and dynamic modernizing elite strongly desires development and can successfully project this attitude into both the bureaucracy and the population at large."[21]

Many well-intentioned and technically sound programmes aimed at solving educational problems have been frustrated by a lack of popular acceptance and community participation. "It has been observed that such programmes are either not actively associated or passively ignored because they do not 'belong' to the population they are designed to help; they are rather seen by the population as imposed external programmes that belong to the government and consequently deserve and require little, if any, of the population's attention, action, or other response."[22]

The NPERC had rightly underlined the importance of involving educationists, teachers and educational institutions not only in educational improvement but also in the overall process of development. However, the concept of participatory educational order should go beyond involvement of educational institutions and should extend to the community itself. People's participation in education particularly elementary education and adult, literacy should be in the form of informed facilitation of achievement of educational goals, and through a well formulated system of overseeing the laxities and under-performance of the system.[23]

3. Poor Linkages between Education and Modernization

Modernisation aims at creating an environment of socio-economic development wherein all people can enjoy a decent standard of living. This is in addition to spiritual values and self-discipline. Education Commission (1964-66) has rightly said that, "The most important and urgent reform needed in education is to transform it, to endeavour to relate it to the life, needs and aspirations of the people and thereby make it a powerful instrument of social, economic and cultural transformation necessary for the realization of the national goals. For this purpose, education should be developed so as to increase productivity, achieve social and national integration, accelerate the process of modernization and cultivate social, moral and spiritual values."

The self-reliant and indigenous character of an economy can only be maintained when competent people are available to foresee, plan and execute research and development activity, necessary to keep India abreast of developments elsewhere in the world.[24]

It is a paradoxical situation that on the one hand there are large number of educated people without any job while on the other hand, there are many jobs without suitable manpower. The report of the Education Commission (1964-66) laid stress on this aspect in the following words:

> "Quantitatively, education can be organised to promote social justice or to retard it. History shows numerous instances where small social groups and elites have used education as a prerogative of their rule and as a tool for maintaining their hegemony and prerogative the values upon which it has rested. On the other hand, there are cases in which a social and cultural revolution has been brought about in a system where equality of educational opportunities is provided and education is deliberately used to develop more and more potential talent and to harness it to the solution of national problems. The same is even more true of the quality of education. A system of university education which produces a high proportion of competent professional manpower is of great assistance in increasing productivity and promoting economic growth. Another system of higher education with the same total output but producing a large proportion of indifferently educated graduates of arts, many of whom remain unemployed or even unemployable, could create social tensions and retard economic growth. It is only the right type of education, provided on an adequate scale that can lead to national development; when these conditions are not satisfied the opposite effect may result."

4. Poor Financial Allocation to the Educational Development and Improper Utilisation of Existing Resources

Resources allocated for education are very less, i.e. ranging between 3-4 percent of the total budget. More resources have been allocated in 11th Plan. Besides the resources are not being properly utilised (For details see a separate Chapter on Financial Management).

5. Very Little Emphasis on Character Building in Educational Institutions

The success of any government depends upon the effective collaboration of its citizens. All the books on civics would emphasize civic consciousness for the progress of the country. This is possible only if our educational system and mass-media are re-oriented to character building among the people. People's character is the ultimate source which can supply kinetic energy for modernization and development. Swami Vivekananda rightly says:

> "The national ideals of India are renunciation and service; intensify her in those channels, and the rest will take care of itself." What the world wants is character.

Thus, there is a great need to infuse civic consciousness, patriotism and discipline among the citizens through education, adult education and functional literacy. President Sanjiva Reddy while inaugurating the Silver Jubilee Celebration of Kurukshetra University on January 11, 1980 has rightly said that India is in need of a new educational system which will look upon the child as a bud that opens up petal by petal and which needs the sunlight of the ideals of truth, beauty and goodness. Only such citizens would be able to contribute to national prosperity in whatever field they may be engaged as it has been rightly said that not gold but only men can make a nation great and strong.

6. Lack of Administrative Capability and Competence

Educational administrators at all levels from top to bottom are engaged on the jobs without prior training or experience resulting in *status quo*. Administrative capability is the capacity to get intended results. It is high time that Union and State Governments may devise ways and means of appointing administrators of educational institutions purely on the basis of merit and aptitude. Administrators without requisite qualities produces degenerating effects on the organizations resulting into chaos.

Those who are not fit need to removed. *The Tribune* editorial has rightly commented that, if picking good men is the most important of them all, dumping the bad ones is the next most important.[25]

So we must find out the educational administrators who should possess the following qualities: First, there are certain specialised knowledge and skills which are programme relevant such as substantive knowledge of field of specialisation. Second, managerial expertise and skills are paramount in effective implementation, coordinating and scheduling work, planning and allocating resources and so on. Third, modern administrative leaders need human relations ability to deal with major resources in organisational life. Motivating people to perform beyond normal requirements to instill a strong sense of programme commitment and integrity and to incite programme personnel to unfetter the suffocating bonds *of* anachronistic administrative values, traditions and practices are additional requisite skills. Finally, there are certain 'political' skills required to sustain support and Cooperation from the volatile public (legislators and ministers), mass media, clientele, local, political notables, etc.[26]

7. Lack of Co-ordination and Linkages

Coordination means bringing about consistent and harmonious action of persons and programmes with each other towards a common goal. The first essential requisite to achieve co-ordination is to develop meaningful linkages with all sectors of development which can influence the promotion of educational development. There should be well developed linkages between all sectors of education, i.e. formal and informal, Elementary to University and so on. They should supplement each other rather than compete and downgrade. For example, there is no co-ordination between the Post-graduate Departments run through formal system and Distance Education system resulting into huge losses. How can we achieve effective coordination? According to Dr. White, its achievement may require,

> "The most delicate insights, the most mature wisdom, and perception of a truely artistic quality."[27]

It has to be achieved through formal as well as informal methods. The effective co-ordination and linkages would automatically result from 'effective planning, policy-making, manpower planning'. After planning and policy-making, the effective instrument to achieve coordination is to design a sound educational organisation. Dr. White says:

> "An organization characterized by clear lines of authority, adequate powers, well-understood allocation of functions, absence of overlapping and duplication of efforts and proper delegation of work in itself reduce the necessities of coordination."[28]

Besides, if the organisational boundaries are properly demarcated, there would be little scope of confusion and misunderstanding and coordination would naturally flow from this inherent structure.

8. Deteriorating Quality of Education

The quality of education is deteriorating. Even the Universities are engaged in routine teaching to post-graduate students. Research has been relegated to the background. In the system of rotation in the universities, such persons have come to occupy positions who themselves have not much academic attainments, thus, vitiating the atmosphere of higher education. Education based on quality and action is the answer to accommodate the channels that are bound to take place in 21st century. In the Eighth Report on the World Health Situation covering the period 1985-90, it has been rightly mentioned that "We cannot continue doing what we have always done. Tomorrow cannot be just more of yesterday. We need flexibility and pragmatism as much as innovation, but the stress must invariably be on action." Quality of education is difficult to define. The Challenge to Education, a policy document of the Ministry of Education states that, "a quality conscious system would produce people who have the attributes of functional and social relevance, mental agility and physical dexterity, efficacy and reliability and, above all, the confidence and the capability to communicate effectively and exercise initiative, innovation and experiment with new situation."[29]

9. Outdated Evaluation System

Assessment of performance is vital for any system of education as upon it depends the nature of curriculum and quality of teaching. There is a need to devise an examination system which is scientific and relevant. National Educational Policy suggest the following for improvement:[30]

(i) The elimination of excessive element of chance and subjectivity;
(ii) The de-emphasis of memorisation;
(iii) Continuous and comprehensive evaluation that incorporates both scholastic and non-scholastic aspects of education, spread over the total span of instructional time;
(iv) Effective use of the evaluation process by teachers, student and parents;
(v) Improvement in the conduct of examination;
(vi) The introduction of concomitant changes in instructional materials and methodology;
(vii) Introduction of the semester system from the secondary Stage in a phased methodology; and
(viii) The use of grades in place of marks.

IMPACT OF GLOBALISATION, LIBERALISATION AND PRIVATISATION ON HIGHER EDUCATION

Globalisation has come as a reality as the world has become a small place. It means that all nations must come together and sustain opportunities that enhance the good of all. In the Vedas we have already this philosophy, i.e. all people in the world should be happy. Francis Fanthome, Chief Executive and Secretary, Council for the Indian School Certificate Examinations gave an address at Education Victoria '96—an international education exhibition and conference-held at Victoria,

Australia recently. He said, "We view the challenges merging as a consequence of the globalisation of education, as opportunities to enable and enhance capabilities to effectively cope with the changing physical, economic and social environment of the planet the responsibility for attainment of 'shared aspirations' is dependent on the quality of the educational effort we can collectively sustain, on the threshold of the 21st century."[31]

Shri Atal Bihari Vajpayee, Former Prime Minister of India delivered the convocation address at the seventeenth convocation of Sri Sathya Sai Institute of Higher Learning. He said, "Thanks to globalisation, issues such as management of the economy, stability of national currencies, trade and investment, environmental protection, harnessing of natural resources, regional and global security, etc. are no longer exclusively national concerns. They call for increasing global cooperation among nations. As we all know, modern education especially that imparted in reputed universities in India and abroad is constantly upgrading itself, to understand these issues in a global perspective. We suggest appropriate responses.

However, there is another set of problems facing the world in the era of globalisation, which modern education has largely bypassed. These are problems arising out of the neglect of the ethical, cultural and spiritual upbringing of people. At no time in history has the world been so inter-connected and inter-independent as it is today in the age of globalisation. The problems being faced by people in different parts of the world are becoming increasingly common. These problems may show local forms and manifestations. However, very often they have global roots. Naturally, their solution also requires a global approach and a global effort.

"I must admit here that, even after five decades of freedom, India is far away from this model of education. Our biggest failure has been the ability of the formal education system to build the character of our students and strengthen their ethical and cultural foundation. In the words of Bhagavan Sathya Sai Baba, "Character is the hallmark of man. A life without character is a shrine without light, a coin that is counterfeit, a kite with the string broken."

Character-building comes with a careful and sustained nurturing of Samskaar—that is right thought and conduct. Our schools and colleges have, by and large, neglected the development of Samskaar of their pupils. They focus almost exclusively on imparting information and skills. They place little emphasis on value education, which alone can prepare our students to discern between right and wrong.

On this occasion, I can do no better than to conclude my speech by recalling the stirring words from the Convocation Address delivered by Dr. Mookerjee at the Nagpur University in 1936, when he was only 35 years old:

An Indian University must regard itself as one of the living organs of national reconstruction. It must discover the best means of blending together both the spiritual and material aspects of life. It must equip its alumni, irrespective of caste, creed or sex, with individual fitness, not for its own sake, not merely for adorning varied occupations and professions, but in order to teach them how to merge their individuality in the common cause of advancing the progress and prosperity of their motherland and upholding the highest traditions of human civilisation. That constitutes the perennial ideal of a university rooted in the Indian soil and expresses one of the greatest needs of the hour."[32]

Shri Yashwant Sinha said that Globalisation is not merely a challenge. It is also an opportunity. Globalisation has made it possible for us to become world leaders in the area of information technology where we have world class skills and world class strength. Education is another area where India can improve upon its skills and strength. Our institutes of technology are already famous for their excellence the world over. There is no reason why India, in the days to come, cannot once again become the university of the world where students will come from far and near, to study and excel. Bihar, with its tradition of Nalanda and Vikramshila, has clearly the potential to emerge once again, as an important centre of international learning.

We are living today in a globalised world. Technology has devoured distance. Every point in the world today is at the centre of the world, because it is linked to the rest of the world through air-waves and satellites. India also has opened up. Therefore, when we talk of competition, it is not merely competition within a city or within a state or even within a country. It is global competition that one has to face. It is in the global market place that one has to strive. We have to prepare ourselves for this global challenge.

The NPE suggest the following to meet the Education Challeneges:[33]

(a) Evolving a long-term planning and management perspective of education and its integration with the country's developmental and manpower needs;
(b) Decentralization and the creation of a spirit of autonomy for educational institutions;
(c) Giving pre-eminence to people's involvement, including association of non-governmental agencies and voluntary effort;
(d) Inducting more women in the planning and management of education, and
(e) Establishing the principle of accountability in relation to given objectives and norms.

Besides the above, there are many other areas requiring urgent attention for the qualitative improvement and restructuring of the education system. Of these, the most important pertains to the need for establishing a viable and effective infrastructure for education at the central, regional, state and district levels. Multi-level planning has to be recognized as a crucial process for formulating programmes, maintaining reliable data systems and evaluating the functional efficiency of the system on an objective basis. Besides planning; it is necessary to provide adequately for methodological research, innovation and experimentation in respect of the interfaces between knowledge, pedagogy, skills development and educational technologies for various aspects and streams of education. An appropriate institutional arrangement is also required for taking care of the horizontal and vertical linkages between education and other activities on the one hand and the centre-state cooperation, on the other.[34]

We may suggest the following approach to make Educational Progamme practical and useful for protection of Human Rights:

(a) The existing educational institutions and programmes need to be consolidated and put to optimum use to serve the goals of development in the community as a whole.
(b) Provision of suitable educational facilities in backward areas and for the deprived groups and promotion of non-formal and Distance Education programmes at all levels in a systematic way are important.
(c) Educational Planning need be linked effectively with man-power planning at all states and aspects of skill development. Adequate attention need be paid for optimisation of benefits from the existing investments and facilities.
(d) It is vital to transform the system of education qualitatively in terms of value content, standards and relevance to life. The role of education to promote humanistic outlook, sense of brotherhood and a commitment to cultural and ethical values need to be re-emphasized
(e) The importance of educational technology has to be adequately provided for greater efficiency and effectiveness and wider reach of the educational programmes economically.

Education, in its broadest sense of development of youth, including sports, is the most critical input for empowering people with skills and knowledge and for giving them access to productive employment in the future. The 11th Plan should ensure that we move towards raising public spending in education to 6% of GDP, which is an NCMP commitment. It must fulfil the Constitutional obligation of providing free and compulsory elementary education of good quality to all children upto the age of 14. This means we must ensure both access and good quality and standards in respect of curriculum, pedagogy and infrastructure irrespective of the parent's ability to pay.

"Swami Vivekananda defines Education as a process through which the divine possibilities lying latent in the man are brought out in its full splendour, meaning thereby that education is to make a complete man, competent to build up a strong nation. It is therefore, that he suggested a scheme of education completely different from the scheme followed by the university system. A healthy nation can be built up by the youth burning with the desire to serve the nation and ready to dedicate their energy at the altar of the nation. Unless education creates this type of youth it becomes useless and it is sure to prove itself futile."

G. Madhavan Nair, Chairman, Indian Space Research Organization delivered the Convocation Address at the XXXIX Convocation of the Indian Institute of Technology, Kanpur on June 1, 2007. He said, "We do know that many of the problems we face today cannot be simply solved by the current scientific understanding and technological knowledge. They may probably have to wait for the emergence and accumulation of new knowledge and newer technologies in the coming years. While it may be true that science and technology alone cannot solve all the problems we face, it is no denying fact that they have a direct relevance in the globalised age of the 21st Century. The 21st century is also perceived to be critical turning point for mankind in many sense—whether it is the depletion of fossil fuel, increasing global warming scenario and for that matter, the changing value system itself in a globalised village environment with improved intimate connectivity across the communities around the world. That is where there is a need to provide appropriate ambience for empowering the young creative minds to carry out research driven by curiosity, and find out newer knowledge and technologies." Excerpts.

The National Knowledge Commission (NKC) was constituted on 13th June 2005 as a high level advisory body to the Prime Minister of India. The vision for NKC was articulated by Dr. Manmohan Singh, Prime Minister of India, in the following words:

> "The time has come to create a second wave of institution building. and of excellence in the fields of education, research and capability building."

The Terms of Reference of NKC are:

- Build excellence in the educational system to meet the knowledge challenges of the 21st century and increase India's competitive advantage in fields of knowledge.
- Promote creation of knowledge in Science & Technology laboratories.
- Improve the management of institutions engaged in Intellectual Property Rights.
- Promote knowledge applications in Agriculture and Industry.
- Promote the use of knowledge capabilities in making government an effective, transparent and accountable service provider to the citizen and promote widespread sharing of knowledge to maximize public benefit.

Notes and References

1. GOI: The Second Five Year Plan, New Delhi, 1958,p. 501.
2. GOI: The Third Five Year Plan, New Delhi, 1961, p. 573.
3. GOI, Education Commission, 1964-66, p. I.
4. GOI: Ministry of HRD, Deptt. of Education, National Policy on Education, 1986, with modifications taken in 1992, pp. 4-5.
5. Dayanand Dongaonbar, Higher Education in India: The Varied Dimensions, *University News*, May 24-30th, 2004.
6. GOI, Planning Commission, Towards Faster and More Inclusive Growth: An Approach to the 11th Five Year Plan (2007-2012), Yogjna Bhavan, New Delhi, Dec. 2006, p. 65.
7. GOI: Ministry of Education, Challenge of Education, a Policy Perspective, New Delhi, August, 1985, pp. 68-69 (in this Book, this document is referred as: Challenge of Education) in later chapters.
8. H. Simon *et al., Public Administration,* New York, Alferd, 1950, p. 3.
9. Fritz Morotein Marx (ed.), *Elements of Public Administration,* New Delhi, Prentice Hall, 1964, p. 3.
10. John Ronald Pfiffner and R. Vance Presthus, *Public Administration,* New York, p. 5.
11. Ordway Tead, *The Art of Administration,* New York, McGraw Hill, 1951, pp. 3-4.
12. Grayson Kefauver, *The Forty fifth Yearbook,* PI. II, Chicago, The University of Chicago Press, 1946, p. 2.
13. GOI, Ministry of HRD, Deptt. Of Education, National Policy on Education 1986 with modification taken in 1990, pp. 4-5.
14. GOI, Planning Commission, Towards Faster and More Inclusive Growth: An Approach to the 11th Five Year Plan, New Delhi, 17th Nov. 2006, p. 8.
15. *Challenges of Education,* Foreword, p. ii.
16. S. David Brown, "Improving the Administrative Capability of the Aid Receiving Countries," *Public Administration Review,* June 1964, p. 64.
17. J.I. Iboko, "Developing the Administration in a developing country", *International Review of Administrative Science,* Vol. XXXVIII, No. 2, 1972, p. 293.
18. Nicklas E. Charles, in the book Approaches to Development: Policies, Administration and Change, Edited by Montgomery and Siffin, New York, 1966, p. 188.
19. Challenge of Education, p. 34.
20. Granville Austin, *The India Constitution: Cornerstone of a Nation,* Clarendon Press, Oxford, 1966, p. 50.
21. Merle Fainsod, "The Structure of Development Administration" in Irving Swerdlow, (ed.) *Development Administration: Concepts and Problems,* Syracuse, N.Y., Syracuse University Press, 1963, p. 1.
22. *WHO Chronicle,* 30 (1976), pp. 177-78.
23. GOI: Ministry of HRD, Department of Education, Report of the CABE Committee on Policy, New Delhi, 1992, p. 4 (In future, this document is referred to as only CABE Committee).
24. Challenge of Education, p. 6.
25. *The Tribune,* July 17, 1975, p. 4.
26. EROPA's Summary Report of the Seventh General Assembly and Conference on "Implementation, the problem of achieving results", Vol. II, pp. 1-8.
27. L.D. White, *Introduction* to *the Study of Public Administration,* New York, Macmillan, 1958, pp. 213-14.

28. L.D. White, *op. cit*, p. 214.
29. *Challenge of Education*, p. 111.
30. Ministry of HRD, Department of Education, National Policy on Education, 1986 (with modifications in 1992), New Delhi, p. 42.
31. France's Fanthome, Globalization of Education—India's Response to Challenges and Opportunities, *University News*, No. 11, 1996, p. 17.
32. Atal Behari Vajpayee, Education in an Era of Globalization, *University News*, January 25, 1999, p. 13.
33. *Ibid*, p. 45.
34. *Ibid*.

Distance Education: Meaning, Extent, Rationale, Issues, Problems and Suggestions

PART A

(a) Meaning

Since traditional education system was unable to cope with the current needs, therefore, Distance Education System took birth to cope with the current and future needs of the educational development. Dr. Bharat Bhushan Sharma has come out with some limitations of the formal system of Higher Education. To quote him:[1] "The formal system is essentially developed to educate younger generation mostly of the age group 17-24 for various technical, professional and vocational streams activities. The major constraining factors of the formal system are:

(a) Full time and long study periods leading often to uncertain achievements.
(b) Non-availability of seats in educational institutions.
(c) Non-availability of such institutions in geographically difficult terrains.
(d) Failure of having obtained the required qualifications for entering a particular university course.
(e) Courses and educational programmes not relevant to the existing social needs.
(f) The highest paid teachers are reaching fewer selected students.
(g) Benefits of higher and better education continue to be enjoyed by a privileged few.
(h) High per capita cost of education.
(i) Faulty examination system."

Distance Education Council in its Guidelines for support to State Open Universities (28th April, 1992) beautifully sums up the features of Distance Education Systems which made its impact in about 70 countries of the world. The council affirms that the Distance Education System augments opportunities for education; it ensures access to higher education, it is cost effective, it promotes a relevant, flexible and innovative system of education. The major characteristics of the Distance Education system are its high productivity, greater flexibility and above all its capacity to respond to varying demands. Analysis of cost incurred by the Distance Education system shows that it can offer education programmes of an acceptable quality at a cost which is somewhere between one-fourth and one-third of the cost incurred by the conventional education system. It is in this context that promotion and coordinated development of distance education system in India assumes significance.

Shri M.K. Kaw, former Secretary, Deptt. of Education, Ministry of HRD, Govt. of India also sums up beautifully the need and relevance of distance education system. To quote him: "Education is not something that is finished when a student leaves the portals of a University; it has to be continuing, life long education so that our system has to provide for a mix of formal and non-formal, open and distance modes of teaching, and we have to harmonise all the technological devices that science has evolved to take education to the drawing room of the students, so that he can learn when he has time, at a place of his choice, at his own pace, with a bit of teaching and a lot of self-learning with the audio tape, the computer and the internet, the TV and the VCR."[2]

K.B. Powar, Former Secretary General, Association of Indian Universities has rightly observed that, "The existing model of Higher Education, requiring selective learning over a specified period is being replaced by a model of life-time learning for all. This has become necessary because of the changing nature of jobs which now require continuous renewal and updating of knowledge and skills (UNESCO, 1995). Throughout the world higher education is undergoing a paradigm shift from an instruction centred college/university model to a learner centred integrated network model which is based on access to learning resources and on student initiative."[3]

Correspondence education means that aspect of education wherein education is provided to the students sitting at their places through well prepared study material based on course contents, supplemented by the audio visual technology keeping in view the needs and levels of students. The study material compensates the students the absence of the teacher in a class room. With the developing of electronic media, the correspondence institutes supplement the study material with radio-broadcasts and video-tapes. With these new developments, the name correspondence education is being changed to Distance Education which has wider implications.

In 1982, at its 26th Conference, the International Council for Correspondence Education changed its name to the International Council for Distance Education. Such a system of education enables the nations to provide equality of opportunities for education for a large segment of the population not covered by traditional system of education. V.C. Kulandaiswamy in his article, "Open University" in (ed.) Higher Education Reform in India by Suma Chatnis and Phillip G. Altbach, (Sage, 1993, p. 366) has observed that Distance Education is neither a supplement nor a mere alternative to the conventional system, but a new stage in the evolution of education which recognises the fact that in many situations, it is easier to transport knowledge to people than transport people to the place of knowledge.

Education Commission of 1964-66 headed by Dr. D.S. Kothari, observed: "The Correspondence or home study course is well tried and a tested technique. Experience of correspondence courses in other countries of the world such as the USA, Sweden, Erstwhile USSR, Japan and Australia, where they have been used extensively for a long time . . . encourages us to recommend fuller exploitation of the method for a wide range of purposes. There is hardly any ground for apprehension that correspondence courses are an inferior form of education than what is given in regular schools and colleges. Experience abroad and experiments in India have shown results which on balance tend to strengthen the case for correspondence education." The most important aspect of correspondence education is the need to develop links with the students through well established communication channels.

The UGC Scheme of Distance Education (1983) mentions the following rationale for setting up the Distance Education System:

(i) to provide a system of student-centred self-paced learning;
(ii) to provide a flexible, diversified and open system of education;
(iii) to develop by providing wider access to higher education to persons of all ages and sex particularly to working persons and to economically or otherwise handicapped and persons residing in remote areas;
(iv) to provide means of upgradation of skills and qualifications; and
(v) to develop education as a life long activity so that the individual can refresh his knowledge in an existing discipline or to acquire knowledge in new areas.

Daniel mentions that communication is the most vital feature of Distance Education which need special attention. To quote him:[4] "The most important feature for characterizing distance education is not its morphology but how communication between teacher and student is facilitated. Because the teacher and student are physically separated, distance education must rely on technology to mediate the communication process. While considerable attention has been given to the use of technological media, less attention has been paid to the nature of the communication process and the role of the technologies supporting it."

According to Michael Moore[5] the distance education system departs from the conventional system because of the use of a multi-media communication approach by it. To quote him:

"Distance teaching may be defined as the family of instructional methods in which teaching behaviours are executed apart from the learning behaviours, including those that in a continuous situation would be performed in the learner's presence, so that communication between the teacher and the learner must be facilitated by print, electronic, mechanical or other devices." Charles Wedemeyer[6] favours the term 'Independent study'. He points out that a learner learns in his own environment and through his own efforts. "Independent study consists of various forms of teaching-learning arrangements in which teachers and learners carry out their essential tasks and responsibilities apart from one another communicating in a variety of ways. Its purposes are to free on campus internal learners with the opportunity to continue learning in their own environments and developing in all learners the capacity to carry on self-directed learning, the ultimate maturity required of the educated person."

Dohmen stresses the use of media which enables the teacher to reach out to the learners and emphasises on self-study. To quote him:[7]

"Distance education is a systematically organised form of self-study in which student counselling, the presentation of learning material and securing and supervising of students success is carried out by a team of teachers, each of whom has responsibilities. It is made possible at a distance by means of media which can cover long distances."

David Seward looks at Distance Education as an industry. To quote him: "The description of distance education as an industrialised form of teaching and learning was first made by Otto Peters[8] in his seminar work. The importance of his definition is now widely accepted and he highlighted the relevant characteristics of distance education as follows:

- the division of labour in the teaching process itself which allows a rationalisation of the elements of the teaching process;
- the use of technical equipment to ensure a product of constant quality in theoretically unlimited volumes;
- the application of organisational principles to cut down unnecessary effort on the part of those teaching and those learning;
- the use of technical media such as television and radio to replace teachers and cater for volume;
- the testing of the product, the teaching package, to eliminate mistakes and guarantee a standard; and

- the monitoring of the teaching system by scientific methods to maintain quality and standards."

Hilary Parraton[9] highlights both the nature of learner and that of institution. "Distance education means an educational process in which a significant proportion of teaching is conducted by some one removed in space and/or time from learner."

The Programme of Action, 1992, however, speaks about a more modest target for enrolment in the distance education system in the Eighth Plan. It says that during the Eighth Plan period, the enrolment in the Open University/distance education system is expected to increase from about 11.5% of the total enrolment in higher education to about 16.5%. In absolute terms, this would involve a net addition of 4 lakh students to the enrolment in the open university/distance education system by the end of the Eighth Plan.

P.V. Narasimha Rao in his address at the opening ceremony of the New Campus of B.R. Ambedkar Open University, Hyderabad has said that Distance Education is not the cheap kind of education that it is said to be. It is education which is even more sophisticated, more difficult to achieve than ordinary regular kind of education, orthodox kind of education. I found that the large number of students who are spread allover the state, or the country, as the case may be, find it sometimes baffling how they can cope with this learning that is being imparted from a distance through several media, through several gadgets, and whether it is possible for them to understand the subjects as thoroughly as it is possible in regular education. We have found, however, after going into the experience of some other countries like Thailand, England, Canada, that this is as good and effective an education as any, if not better, and therefore, the credentials I think have now been established after a few years. I have no way of checking the quality of your products but I hope that some one is checking, someone is doing this checking and keeping track of the quality of these products. Please do not allow the Open University system, the Distance Education system, to languish behind and get a bad name for the system itself.

(b) Scope

The scope of Distance Education is far wider than traditional education which is mostly restricted to lecturing in a classroom. International Council for Educational Development refers formal education to the hierarchically structured, chronologically graded "educational system" running from Primary School through the University and including, in addition to general academic studies, a variety of specialized programmes and institutions for full time technical and professional planning. Erling Ljosa[10] rightly mentions the contents of Distance Education:

"Distance Education involves very specialized knowledge and competence in a variety of fields—such as curriculum development and the development and production of educational material, communication skills related to media, information, marketing, counselling of students, study support and tuition, distribution and delivery of materials and organisation of teaching activities often in collaboration with local partners. In order to cater to all these functions, which differ significantly from the parallel functions in a Conventional school or University, there is need for specialisation in distance education institutions or departments."

Thus, Distance Education is aimed at teaching, guiding and supporting the students in all locations through well designed lecturer scripts, supported by tutors, personal contact programmes, response sheet assignments and electronic media.

PART B

(a) Extent

The system of Distance Education has been adopted in a big way in both developed and developing countries. A Round Table Conference on Distance Education for South Asian Countries, the proceeding of which were published by Asian Development Bank (1987) indicate that Asia has witnessed growth of Distance Education. China, Hong-Kong, India, Korea, Japan, Pakistan, Sri Lanka, and Thailand have all well established national institutions dealing with Distance Education. For example, the Japan University of Air founded in 1981 after 14 years of Planning is catering to a large population. The Central China Television University set-up in 1979 is engaged in providing education to more than 5 lakh students through 44 Provincial Television Universities, 690 Branch Schools, 1600 study centres and more than 13,000 teaching classes. Many countries have adopted a dual mode also, i.e. adding a Distance Education Wing to their traditional formal system.

In Latin America, there are two well established autonomous distance teaching University in Costa-Rica; and the National University in Venezuela. African continent has adopted the system of creating Distance Education Department, in the existing universities, e.g. the University of Lagos in South Nigeria.

African countries like Burkeria Faro, Buruncto, Cameroon, Central African Republic Chad, Gambia, Ghana, Togo, Zaire, Botswdna, Kenya, Lesotho, Madagascar, Malawi, Somalia, Swaziland, South Africa, Tanzania, Uganda, Zambia have set-up distance education at various levels. T. Dodds[11] survey of the story of Distance Education in Africa reveals that it has been a story of hopes, successful experiments, inadequate resourcing and often disappointing long-term impact. It is essentially a story of hope deferred.[12]

In this way, Distance Education System has grown both in size and diversity especially during the last three decades. K. Murali Manohar[13] has summed up the developments as:

> "At present, over 300 DE Universities in 60 countries are found to be offering about 10,000 different courses to its learners. Out of about 50 institutions operating at the University level in India, except about ten institutions the remaining are found to be offering exclusively correspondence system of education while not venturing to get themselves converted into DE Centres."

R.C. Sharma in his Article "Distance Education in Global perspective" has provided the information in the Global Context. He mentioned that in Eight Regions having 106 countries, there are 1026 institutions of DE system offering 31,752 courses, the highest being in Europe (26) with 387 institutions."[14]

There is a Need of Evaluation alongwith expansion—Mary Thorpe has raised a pertinent question which need answer to make the DE system viable and efficient. To quote: "It is not a question either for congratulation or for blame that the developments heralded by distance and open learning are now expanding so rapidly and changing the conditions in which teaching and learning happens so radically. But it is a matter for crucial enquiry, for the evaluation of the effects of change so that our future decisions are shaped by what we know of the results of this previous developments."[15]

(b) Developments in India

Several Commissions recommended open education system as an alternative to the conventional education. The Kothari Commission (1961),[16] The Parthasarthi Commission (1971),[17] Ram Reddy Committee (1982),[18] State Education Ministers' Conference, New Delhi (1986),[19] have recommended the establishment of correspondence schools/open universities. Let us discuss in detail.

The establishment of the Open University in the U.K. in 1969 made the policy-makers in India to think about the proposal for establishing an Open University in early seventies. The Ministry of Education and Social Welfare, Ministry of Information and Broadcasting and the U.G.C., organised a seminar in December 1970. Professor V.K.R.V. Rao, the then Education Minister while inaugurating the seminar said:

> ". . . It must cover not only the comparatively limited number of university students, but should cover much large number of students who drop out from the school at various points, the neo-literates, and eventually all adults who desire to avail these programmes of continuing education. . . . The new interesting programmes of instruction based on modern science-oriented educational technology for students of higher education studying in the Open University should be made available to this much larger body of population which remains outside the so-called University system."[20]

Based upon these suggestions, the Government of India appointed a working group with Mr. Parthasarath, the then Vice-Chancellor of Jawahar Lal Nehru University, Delhi in 1971 to examine the feasibility of establishing an Open University in India. This Working Group in its report observed: "In the situation of this type, where the expansion of enrolments in higher education has to continue at a terrific pace and where available resources in terms of men and money are limited, the obvious solution, if proper, standards are to be maintained and the demand for higher education from different sections of the people is to be met, then there is need to adopt the Open University System with its provision of higher education on part-time or whole-time basis. The Group, therefore, recommends that the Government of India should establish, as early as possible, a National Open University by an Act of parliament."[21] A Committee to inquire into the working of Central Universities with Dr. Madhuri R. Shah as its Chairperson took the issue of open universities. This Committee made the following remarks:

> "To satisfy existing thirst for knowledge as well as degrees, admission to formal courses on the basis of merit requires that opportunities for off-campus studies should be created on a large scale, for a great variety of courses of high quality. We already have a number of Universities offering correspondence courses; we need to utilize and coordinate this expertise and infrastructure to create an effective system of distance learning. Mass media, such as radio and television, which are already beginning to be used in conjunction with correspondence education, and for which a greater potential is being created through the satellites should be employed in a systematic manner to enlarge the scope and enrich the quality of distance education. We could create with available know-how in software and hardware a highly proficient and attractive system of education for the whole country of which the present correspondence institutes could become focal points. Courses in new fields, particularly in science and some in technology could also be started, perhaps using college laboratories in off hours and some of the best teachers could be involved in delivering lectures. Libraries of audio and video cassettes could be created to enrich both formal and non-formal education. . . The Committee recommended that practical steps for creating a National Open University of distance education be taken up without delay."[22]

While the idea of establishing a National Open University was still in embryonic stage, there were some developments. In the state of Andhra Pradesh, the Government established Dr. Ambedkar Andhra Pradesh Open University in 1982. The system of Distance Education was first of all set-up in 1962 at Delhi University for under-graduate courses. Dr. K.L. Shrimali, the then Education Minister while inaugurating the First School of Correspondence Courses of Delhi in 1962 mentioned the following objectives of Distance Education:

"(i) To provide an efficient and less expensive method of educational instruction at a higher level in the context of national development in India;

(ii) To provide facilities to pursue higher education to all qualified and willing persons who had failed to join regular university courses due to personnel and economic reasons or because of their inability to get admission to a regular college; and

(iii) To provide opportunities of academic pursuits to educated citizens through correspondence instruction without disturbing their present employment."

The success of this experiment prompted many such institutes at different places in the country. The higher level Distance Education is channelised through two channels—Open Universities and the Departments of Correspondence Studies attached to the Universities. The school level Education is channelled through Open School set-up at the Union level and in some of the States.

As on 2005 there are 13 State Open Universities (SOUs) and 119 Correspondence Course Institutes (CCIs) in conventional Universities. The Council has extended technical and financial support for development of technological infrastructure, institutional reform, professional development and training, student support services, computerization and networking for improvement of quality of education.

We may mention briefly about Indira Gandhi National Open University which is the biggest and trend setter: IGNOU coordinates the functioning of exclusive 24 hour satellite based Educational TV Channels called Gyan Darshan (GD). It is a collaborative venture of various government agencies. It has potential to offer a bouquet of 6 channels. Gyan Darshan-1 is the 24 hours exclusive Educational TV channel of the country. Prasar Bharti has put this channel on DTH in 2005. The University has added Gulestan-e-Urdu under Bhasha Mandakini bouquet for teaching/ learning of Urdu and creating awareness about the richness of the language. Gyan Darshan-2 is being utilized as interactive channel for tele-counselling, tele-lecturing, teletraining of coordinators/counsellors. Gyan Darshan-3 'Eklavya' Channel is devoted to technical education for the benefit of engineering students in the county. Transmission of this channel has been fully automated. GD-4 is "Vyas" Channel; a curriculum based higher education channel. In the year 2005, the University established about 100 EduSat supported Satellite Interactive Terminals in its regional centers and study centers all over the country.

Gyan Vani: IGNOU is nodal agency for the implementation of radio cooperative of 40 FM channels dedicated to education and development. Seventeen FM stations are operational at Allahabad, Bhopal, Coimbatore,

Bangalore, Mumbai, Lucknow, Vishakhapatnam, Delhi, Kolkata, Chennai, Varanasi, Guwahati, Jabalpur, Mysore, Rajkot, Raipur and Shillong. In addition, every Sunday, Radio Counselling is provided for one hour from 186 Radio Stations of All India Radio (AIR). Toll free conferencing facility is also available to the learners in 80 cities, who interact freely with the experts.

IGNOU, at International level, is currently offering academic programmes in 32 countries. In collaboration with UNESCO and International Institute for Capacity Building in Africa (IICRA), Distance Education Programmes of the University are being offered in Ethiopia, Liberia, Madagascar and Ghana. Through an agreement signed with Commonwealth of Learning (COL), University is offering its Distance Education Programme in Lesotho, Swaziland, Namibia, Seychelles, Jamaica, Malawi and Belize.

According to Planning Commission, GOI in its report of 11th Five Year Plan, The Open University system is an important instrument for expanding higher education since it overcomes the infrastructure constraint. Until a larger network of accessible and well supported colleges is developed, the open supported colleges is developed, the open schooling programme should be strengthened and expanded. In case of subjects that do not require laboratory work, it will be helpful for students to access pre-recorded selections of lectures, tutorials, and standardized tests available at internet kiosks. Testing and examination centres where students can take standardized examinations in parts can reduce the pressure. For this autonomous institutions charge with the responsibility of testing and examination will have to be developed. The 11th Plan should pay attention to creation of electronically available content and testing mechanism so that the pressure on infrastructure can be eased.

The Open Universities all over the world have become increasingly popular on account of their flexible admission requirements, curriculum and pacing of learning taking education to the very doorsteps of the learner. As an agency developing human resources and imparting skills it has no parallel. By making proper tieup arrangements and establishing approrriate linkages with industry it has proved that quality education can be imparted through distance education methods. The studies made by the Open University system in China clearly indicate that the economic development and industrial advancement is possible if human resources can be carefully trained in the various areas ensuring that the quality of instruction imparted is kept up."[23]

(a) Virtual University and Networked System

A third approach to distance teaching is now emerging as virtual university. The Networked System mainly based on a cooperation between a number of open universities and correspondence course institutes, called "network" approach. The advent of electronic media and communication technologies have made it possible to pool intellectual and physical resources spread over number of people. The communication networks are examples of participatory and collaborative styles of functioning[24]

Prof. Dr. Ram Takwale, the former Vice-Chancellor, Indira Gandhi National Open University, delivered the Convocation Address at the fifth convocation of the North Maharashtra University, Jalgaon. He said, "The transition from the existing institutional pattern education *to* a networked system of education will open out learners at or near their home courses and programmes from the best of experts and educational institutions from India and abroad. . . . The roles of a learner, a teacher and an educational institution would change radically in the learner or customer-led system of education." Excerpts.

Distance Education is likely to become a major issue for discussion in higher education if number of conventional students fall again (as in Britain in the 1990s), if the costs of higher education become the subject of political debate or if wider access to higher education becomes desirable. Distance Education seems to offer solutions to all these problems separately and probably uniquely, to offer a single solution to each of them simultaneously, access can be widened to adult students or to other desirable target groups and at a most favourable set of costings.[25]

(b) Function-oriented Structure of Open Universities

A distance education institution is organized around certain core functions. These are:

- Planning
- Developing instructional material
- Production and multiplication
- Delivery of materials and services
- Infrastructural support services
- R & D activities
- Human Resource Development
- Quality Assurance[26]

(c) International Cooperation in Distance Education

The collaboration among the Institutions of Distance Education can promote pooling of resources and exchange of ideas for better planning and administration of these institutions. Recent years have also added the increased activity in international cooperation in distance education. These are visible through the creation of organisations like Commonwealth of Learning (COL), the European Association of Distance Teaching Universities (EADTU) and the European Distance Education Network (EDEN), International Council for Distance Education (ICDE), European Home Study Council, Canadian, British Associations of Correspondence, Distance Education Institutions and Distance Education Council in India.

(d) Pillars of Distance Education System

Distance Education system is run with the following facilities: (Refer Diagram 2.1)

CHART 2.1

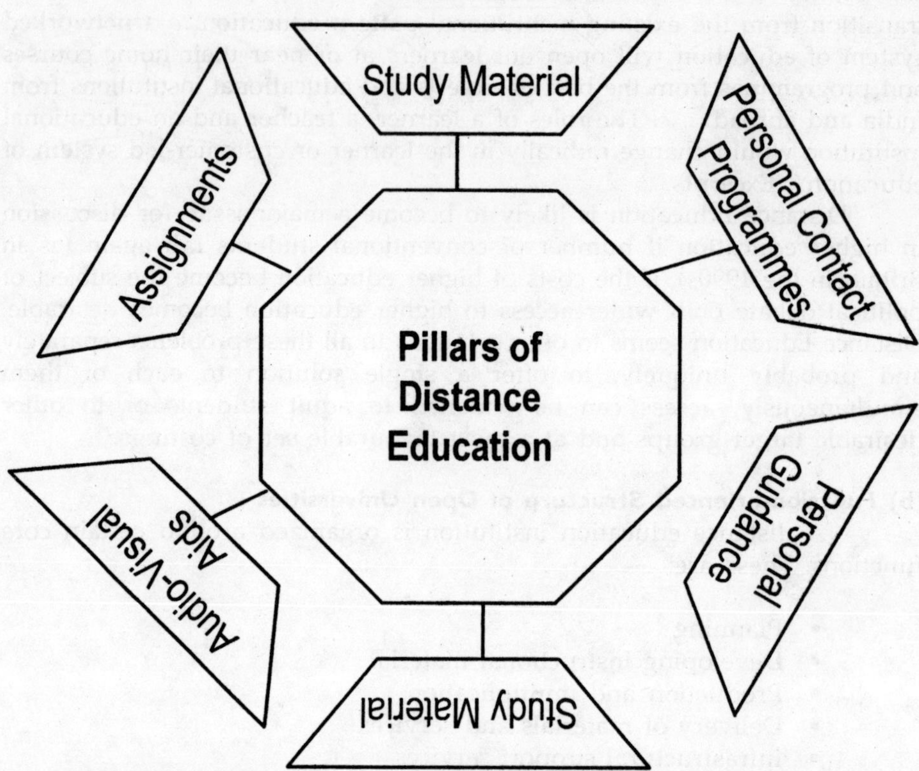

(a) Study Material popularly known as lecture scripts;
(b) Teaching for short duration to maintain personal contacts, i.e. Personal Contact Programmes;
(c) Student Assignment, i.e. Response sheet; 126
(d) Electronic media: Broadcasts on selected topics through Radio; Video, teleconferencing, computer, etc.;
(e) Study centres; and
(f) Personal guidance: Casual visit by the students to meet the faculty.

PART C

RATIONALE OF SETTING UP OF DISTANCE EDUCATION SYSTEM (See Chart 2.2)

There are many merits of distance education system which are reflected in the growth and diversification of the system. Let us analyse them briefly.

CHART 2.2

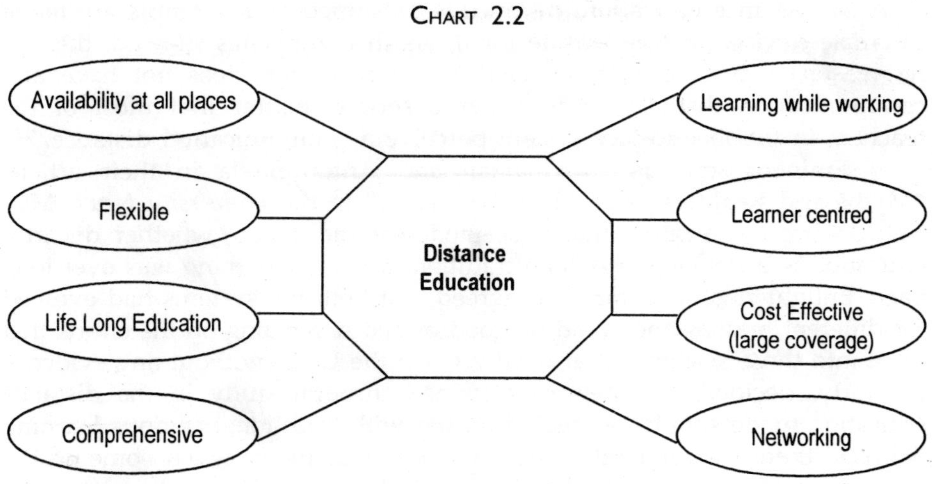

(a) Supplement the Efforts of the Traditional System in a Better Way

The student population is increasing. Traditional system has neither the capacity nor the resources to meet the needs of the growing number of students. Further expansion of formal education systems would not be possible because of mounting economic constraints. The Distance Education System can meet this need in more realistic way and at much lower cost. It also meets the needs of the students who had to discontinue studies owing to financial and other constraints. Eighth Five Year Plan has rightly visualised it for coming years. To quote the Plan, "The additional enrolment in higher education during the Eighth Plan is estimated to be around 10 lakhs of which 9 lakhs will be at the undergraduate level. This expansion in higher education, keeping in view the present resources crunch has to be accommodated in an equitable and cost effective manner mainly by large scale expansion of Distance Education, system and providing opportunities to large segments of population, particularly the disadvantaged groups like women and people living in backward and hilly areas and by measures for resources generation. The programmes of Distance Education should absorb atleast 50 per cent of the additional enrolment during the Eighth Plan."[27]

Besides the Distance Education System can help in improving the quality of formal education. A recent study by Suneeta Anil Pathak found nineteen factors which limit the communication in a formal system-document clarity, lime frame, Statement of the Objectives, Self-study, Text-book, Learner autonomy, Layout, Teacher Personality, Language, Interaction, Student peace, Teacher accessibility, Student individuality, facilities, library and laboratory systems, examination system, question papers, evaluation methods and technique and feed comments. The study concludes, "To compensate for this distance, one can look towards the Distance Education mechanisms. The face-to-face education has thus a number of lessons to learn from distance education.

In distance education, distance is presumed and attempts are made to create devices to compensate for it. As this study has showed, there is no reason to believe that the face-to-face education does not have any communication distance. It is rather a serious matter that most of the teachers in the face-to-face system perceive a communication distance."[28]

Eminent scholars A. Gnaman and Anton Stella in their article, "Myths and Realities in Distance Education" in the *University News*, May 24, 2004 rightly observe that it seemed that the debate whether distance education is better or worse than traditional campus learning was over long back. Enlightened academia had agreed that both the systems had evolved for different reasons and could be good or bad depending on the efforts that went into those systems. That is why when the UGC, without any evidence or study, decided that degrees obtained through study in the distance education mode should be treated on par with traditional campus learning degrees, there was not much hue and cry. But today when some of the academia and educational administrators who can shape public opinion as well as policies of the government make statements that defy the basic understanding about distance and open learning, it signals that the situation is becoming alarming and calls for a revisiting of some of the aspects of distance and open learning.

It looks as though now the distinction between distance education and campus education itself is a myth, if one considers the convergence between the two already happening in the major universities. When technology is integrated into formal educational processes and used for the 'distributed education' for both on- and off-campus students, the distinction between them gets blurred. This appears to be the general intention of the Indian UGC in diverting enormous funds for ICT ultimately to promote the distributed education in the traditional dual mode universities. That makes one wonder how the stand-alone distance education centers like the national and state Open Universities are going to uphold their relevance and distinct purposes they wish to pursue and how the Distance Education Council is going to steer them.

(b) Equality of Opportunity

There are many people who cannot pursue higher education due to poor socio-economic backgrounds and other limitations. These persons were denied the benefits of higher education. The Distance Education system offers them a second chance of updating and acquiring higher education. Prof. P.K. Ponnuswamy, Vice-Chancellor, University of Madras in his Presidential remarks in a Round Table of Directors of Correspondence Course Institute rightly observed that "Education gives opportunity for higher education, ensures access, is cost effective and promotes flexible and innovative system of education. Because of this thrust, the distance education system has now touched the peak of over 7 lakh learners who seek knowledge inspite of the fact that they may be really the economically weaker sections, dropouts from the conventional systems and even so far non-starters. It is expected that this growth would out-number the former system itself in the near future."[29]

We may conclude here our discussion by reasserting that distance education has a vast potential for growth in a developing country like India. It is much more cost-effective than formal system Distance Education Institutions should provide some financial incentives to the poor students in terms of fee concessions, scholarships. There is a need for raising the efficiency of the present organizational system for the improvement of the ODL programme. In this context, major emphasis is to be given on strengthening its financial position by raising the revenue through other sources than the students. Certainly, it would require a change in the central and state government's policy on DUs with regard to the financial management.[30]

Education contributes to development by providing and enhancing the skills, knowledge and attitudes needed for development. Distance education has been widely recognized as an alternative route for educating masses in the developing world. Conventional education at institutions could not achieve the target of democratizing education, especially in developing countries and distance education in these countries has taken the challenge of providing equality of educational opportunities despite time, place and economic constraints of the learners. Multimedia approach is the basic feature of distance education and with the help of modern communication technologies, it can overcome the barriers of time and space. In their efforts to democratize education and provide for life long education, distance education institutions need to collaborate among themselves and with the conventional educational approach so as to make the best use of educational resources, avoid duplicity of efforts and to reach the larger segment of the society. Collaboration will help in sharing knowledge and expertise, exchange courses, develop joint degree and diplomas and capacity building in institutions and nations.[31]

(c) More Structured Course Content Designed through Careful Analysis

Courses of distance education are evaluated at various levels. The Bias of the teacher in the class room is elimінded. The print materials as well as multi-media bearing packages designed by the institutes with the help of a number of experts and professionals of respective disciplines provide more structured and less flexible formats of course contents."[32] Thus, the distance education material is under great scrutiny as compared to the lecture of a teacher in a formal classroom.

(d) Expand the Capacity and Capability for Education in New Areas

Traditional system provides education within the time Frame. Scientific and technological changes are occurring at a fast rate. Distance Education System can meet the needs through fresh courses specially designed for the purpose.

It seems that the Open and Distance Learning system is in the process of redefining education and repositioning the objectives of educational institutions. It has great potential for transformation of an extensively large manpower into manpower skilled with knowledge under a tight time frame. We also understand that such a transformation will completely change the concept of viewing large population as a serious problem under resource crunch to an extremely useful human resource with significant and visible contributions for the cause of national development. There cannot be any dispute about the importance of the issue and the national priority that it deserves. We encounter this requirement in almost all areas of human development. As a first step, any process of implementation of projects and plans, we require as an essential prerequisite of training large number of master trainers who in their turn carry out the process to educate, motivate and create necessary awareness for further target groups of people. Several Institutions in the Open and Distance Learning system have already made a visible and successful dent in this direction. This is what I mean by redefining of education system leading to a very purposeful and directed education. The tailor made, prescription-based education which is often quite independent of the learners varying capacity, capability, aspirations and expectations is getting transformed to education for people as per their expectations and requirements, at their convenience, pace and place.

The purpose of highlighting the success and credibility of the Open and Distance Learning system is to assure our students about the quality and credibility of the Degrees and Diplomas earned by them through the Open University. You have to have confidence in you and I am sure you will successfully accomplish your ambitions and missions as you pass out from the system.[33]

(e) Education in Natural Environment

Education through Distance Education can be beautifully synthesized with family life and work environment. In this way, the students can learn while working as well as living in home environment.

(f) High Potentiality for in-Service Education at Lower Cost

With the fast change in science and technology, government functioning is under constant change. To reap the benefits of new developments, the Government has set-up training institutes to upgrade the skill and knowledge of the personnel working in the Government. The authors suggested to the Department of Personnel, Government of India to start training for the Government functionaries through Distance Education System. This can also standardise training. A patchy coverage during training through short duration does not help much in improving performance. The Distance Education System has a great potential for providing in-service training especially for technical personnel.

Traditional System can meet the limited needs of Training but Distance Education System can cover larger numbers in a better way. For example, training courses for Nurses leading to B.Sc. degree can be achieved at a fast rate through Distance Education System. National Institute of Health and Family Welfare, New Delhi is organising training programme of one year through Distance Education for District Health Officers.

(g) Flexibility: Learner Centeredness

Distance Education being a flexible system can meet the requirements of large number of people as per their needs. K.B. Pathak and S.K. Singh has rightly said that in the Distance Education system, students are placed at the centre and institutions function mainly as facilitator. Consequently, the programmes and different components of its modus operandi are prepared in view of potential learner's perception and needs.[34]

(h) Avoid the Evil Impacts of Privatisation of Higher Education

Privatisation of higher education would exploit the people and would reverse the attempt to equity, social justice, women education, etc. High level of fees and capitation fee would discourage the merit system. M. Venkat Reddy and Vijay Chandra Tenneti have rightly sensed the need of Distance Education to avoid the inherent dangers of privatisation of higher education. To quote them:

"Development and expansion of Distance Education is a world-wide phenomena and its popularity is due to its openness, flexibility, wider access, multimedia teaching and the wide range of course openings relevant to the social needs. Distance Education has not only ushered in an era of globalisation but is emerging as an effective tool to overcome the evils of privitisation and in providing wider access to higher education.[35]

(i) Entrepreneurship Development: New Experiments through Distance Education

It is a matter of fact and experience in India that the economy which is predominantly agrarian in character continues to remain backward economically. It is therefore felt that industrialization holds the key for rapid economic development. Industrialization, i.e. promotion and development of industries will involve entrepreneurship development. Therefore, it is recognized that there is no economic development without entrepreneurship development and they indeed form the two faces of the same coin.

However, it has been widely believed that entrepreneurs are not born but are made, therefore, a new educational development approach has been found to include entrepreneurship in the educational system to orient the youth towards developing entrepreneurial concepts and values in the school or college education. Training has been followed as a most sustainable and effective approach for Entrepreneurship development, the world over. Many institutions, both at central and state levels have been following this strategy of training to bring about entrepreneurship development in this country. The training is widely called as Entrepreneurship Development Programme (EDP) of usually 6 weeks duration. Entrepreneurship Development Institute of India (EDII), Ahmedabad, Centre for Entrepreneurship Development of Karnataka (CEDOK), Dharwad are some of the institutions engaged in Entrepreneurship development by conducting EDP's.

However, these programmes are conducted in training camps at a particular place, time and for a limited number of aspirants. This has posed a number of problems:

(a) Coverage of persons as compared to the need is negligible.
(b) Such courses are restricted to some city centres.
(c) Women do not come forward as they cannot find time to leave home for such a long time away from the family.
(d) Costs of developing entrepreneur is very high.
(e) It excludes the people living in backward areas and isolated places.

To meet the difficulties mentioned above Entrepreneurship Development Institute, Ahmedabad in collaboration with Friendrick Naumann Stiffung. Germany have brought out a novel programme called Open Learning Programme in Entrepreneurship (OLPE) which is being implemented in Karnataka by CEDOK. Unlike Conventional Entrepreneurship Development Programmes (EDPs), OLPE gives an opportunity to the learner (Prospective Entrepreneurs) to obtain the requisite inputs at his desired time, place and pace.

Advantages of OLPE

A. It provides opportunity for training in preparatory steps required for setting up of enterprises to multitude of adult learners.
B. It provides cost effective mode of training in Entrepreneurship to those living in remote areas and thus deprived of conventional education.
C. It provides flexibility to suit the needs and aspirations of different sets of learners.
D. It provides training to potential Entrepreneurs to start and successfully manage their own enterprise.

OLPE stretches over a period of 11 months inclusive of 9 months training and 2 months follow up. The package offers inputs mainly in

1. Business opportunity identification,
2. Market assessment,
3. Support assistance, and
4. Small Business Management,

The Package Provides three main Services Like

(i) Provision of self-instructional study material consisting of ten units of text comprising of about 90 modules, which are sent to the learners over the period of first 9 months of the package. The topics covered in this are:

1. Entrepreneurship Development,
2. Information on support system,
3. Business opportunity identification,
4. Market assessment,
5. Entrepreneurial motivation,
6. Business plan preparation,
7. Small Business Management, and
8. Statutory requirement.

Learners will also be given assignments as part of the course.

(ii) Personal counselling is given to the learners at the district headquarters in terms of resolving queries that they may encounter in the text and assignments throughout the programme. In addition, 2 contact sessions of five days duration are organized at a place and time mutually agreed upon by the learner and the counsellor to have one to one discussion on the topics learnt.

(iii) Providing follow-up support in developing and implementation of projects which include guidance for project report preparation, preparing loan application, acquiring loan sanctions, selection of location, getting legal approvals, etc. Since the objective of OLPE is to help the learner to set-up his/her own enterprise and manage it successfully, the programme envisages the involvement of the following components:

1. Motivation and reinforcement of Entrepreneurial traits through achievement motivation training.
2. Facilitating decision-making process to set-up new enterprise consisting of business opportunity guidance, information, project planning and technical inputs.
3. Facilitating successful and profitable operation of the enterprise containing management-related inputs such as production, finance, marketing, personnel and planning, etc.

This programme provides an opportunity to meaningfully execute university industry linkage by helping the students to finalize their career plans, while they are completing their academic courses. The escort services rendered by each district official of CEDOK ensure speedy execution of the projects so identified. Besides CEDOK has also trained the teachers of the colleges within the jurisdiction of Karnataka University, Dharwad in guiding students in this noble venture. The foundation of this ambitious programme has been laid by the then, Vice-Chancellor, Dr. S. Rame Gowda and efforts are on to make it a success.

The trainees of Entrepreneurship development programme have benefited a lot. It may not be out of place to mention that the performance of the students of the Distance Education System offering same courses as provided by traditional system has been equal and sometimes better than the students of the traditional system of education. Even sometimes top positions in the same examination and same period is attained by the students of Distance Education System. Authors were invited by CEDOK to lecture the potential entrepreneurs enrolled for the course in 1996 at Dharwad (Karnataka). Our discussion with the participants revealed great appreciation for such courses. They felt that they were immensely benefitted by this course through Distance Mode.

(f) Need of Diversification of Distance Education in New Areas

Distance Education may not be restricted to traditional courses but should extend to engineering, medical, agriculture, education. This would help our technical personnel in keeping them upto-date as well as improve their qualifications which would be beneficial both for the technical persons as well as the society. Anand Kumar in his article: "Open Medical University: Demand, Scope and Opportunities" in *University News*, Aug. 26, 1996 (p. 8) rightly suggests the need of equipping the medical personnel with the latest developments. To quote him: "A better educated and skilled doctor will be more of an asset to the community than a practitioner with no further growth after he finishes his "totipotent" initial training. Hence provision of degree and diploma courses for medical graduates through distance learning will only improve the quality of health care rather than ruin it."

The aims of an Open Medical University (OMU) in providing medical education could be to:

1. provide opportunities for those who missed post-graduate specialist training of their choice earlier;
2. provide continuing medical education (CME) to general practitioners and the specialists in this era of information explosion;
3. provide education in the area not covered by the traditional medical colleges but are the identified need of the society and professions such as Public Health and the training of the medical teacher; and
4. generate financial resources for sustenance of university activities.

In brief many trends in higher education are influencing the future of distance learning, e.g. student's enrolment are growing to surpass the capacity of traditional infrastructure, learner profiles are changing, and students are shopping for education that meets their needs. On the other hand, Traditional faculty roles, motivation and training needs are shifting while workload enhanced compensation and instructional issues continue to deter the faculty from participation in distance education. The institutional and organisational structure of higher education is changing to emphasize academic accountability, competency outcomes, outsourcing content, standardizing and adaptation to learner-consumer demands. The Internet and other information technology devices are becoming more ubiquitous while technological fluency is becoming a common expectation. Funding challenges are increasing and it is expected that with fewer resources, the increasing life-long learning demands would be fulfilled.[36]

Co-operative learning is evolutionary wedded to the economics of Distance Education, complex and an ongoing educational and consumerist process, diversifying into multichannels of delivery methods, keeping in view the broad spectrum of specialised target groups in a professionally oriented ambience. Beginning with the concept of a study centre the Open University now anticipates multiplicity, diversity and varied delivery systems especially in areas such as Business Management, Computer Education, etc. It aims to reach out to learners in all segments of the society cutting across barriers of age, sex and class divisions. This transcendental vision of Distance Education is replete with 'possibilities' and invests it with a concrete shape giving a definite impetus and thrust to the philosophies of continuing education, It is a total learning situation.

PART D

ISSUES, PROBLEMS AND SUGGESTIONS

S.P. Anand in his Editorial remarked:[37]

> "A look at the educational map of India reveals that while the northern and the southern regions of the country have a large number of these institutions, the eastern and the central regions are almost bereft of them. In the former two regions the Directorates are situated in close proximity to one another. More glaringly, these Directorates make provisions for identical types of study programmes. To illustrate, the Directorate of Shimla, Chandigarh, Patiala (located on one linear strip of 150 km) provide for Bachelor's and Master's degree programmes in literature (English, Hindi and Punjabi), Social Sciences (Political Science, Economics, History and Public Administration) and Commerce. This type of uncoordinated development of both the institutions and the study programmes has seriously told upon the health not only of the individual institutes but of the system of distance education at large."

The Distance Education system is developing very fast but there are many (A) external, and (B) internal limitations which need analysis and review for putting the Distance Education system on sound lines. Let us examine them.

(A) EXTERNAL LIMITATIONS

(a) Low Status of Distance Education Institutes

Leaving aside the Open Universities, Distance Education Departments are functioning within the framework of traditional Universities. The authorities in the Universities do not provide full facilities to these departments. In this way, the potential of the system remains unutilised. Bakshish Singh, an expert in Distance Education rightly mentions:

> "If Distance Education continues to be subservient to the traditional universities, then it will remain a poor relation of the traditional system of education with its wings of innovation completely clipped-off, and it would not grow beyond that. I strongly feel that if this sort of situation is allowed to continue, then the very purpose of adopting an innovative system would be defeated and it would become merely an economical alternative channel for imparting the traditional education. It would be impossible for this system to break any new ground and to give purposeful direction to our education."[38]

S.P. Anand has rightly observed:

> 'This dichotomy in the system which is there less by design than by the exigencies of the situation, seriously hampers its proper development. It shuts the system into two watertight compartments which though espousing a common objective, do not have much to do with each other. Not to speak of their working hand in hand with each other, their relationship is in fact strained with mutual suspicion and acrimony.[39]

What is required is the combined Planning of these Departments and Open Universities and forging developed networking among them to reap the benefits of the total system.

(b) Rigidity Imposed by University Regulations

Distance Education Departments have to function within the rules and regulations of the University thus leaving little scope for experimentation, the faculty in regular departments try to put hurdles in the working of these departments. For example, the frequent revision of syllabus is done to the disadvantage of such departments. Students of Distance Education Departments are denied the Campus facilities inspite of paying more fees than the regular students. However, the hold of regular faculty is loosening and may end with the passage of time. Both campus-based and Distance Education have much, to gain from fuller integration in terms of expanding the range of courses available to Distance Education Students, economizing on teaching functions; allowing campus-based students greater flexibility in choosing from a range of resources and strategies for learning; and in the case of part-time evening students removing the necessity of regular campus attendance. Moreover, in a dual mode institution these are the advantages of allowing academics to maintain contact with colleagues in their discipline to benefit from contact with post-graduate students and to continue to work in a research-oriented environment."[40]

Shamshad Hussain, the then Vice-Chancellor, Nalanda Open University in his Article, "Distance Learning—The Latest Attraction" rightly observes that "While talking about distance learning and conventional learning system, it is to be kept in mind that these two systems are not rival to each other. The two systems can move together in order to take benefit of each other in serving the noble cause of providing education to all."

However, distance education can achieve much more so far as widening access to education is concerned.

(c) Misconception about their Role as an Industry to Mint Money

University authorities and faculties of regular departments think that the main function of Distance Education Departments is to mobilize resources for meeting the deficit of the University. Some Departments are working in this direction. However, this is fallacious and wrong impression. Distance Education can provide services at less cost but cannot be like coaching academies. These departments of Distance Education must be the centre of higher learning in the same way as regular departments and should contribute to the academic excellence for which the University stands for.

(d) Discrimination with the Product of the Distance Education Departments

It has been seen in the University and outside that the products of Distance Education are not equated with the products of traditional system inspite of their better achievement in the same examination. Why is it so? This needs to be examined and discouraged. We may keep in mind that knowledge knows no boundaries and it is not the monopoly of anyone.

(e) Open Universities are unable to Supervise and Control the Expanding Number of Students and Study Centres

Open Universities have limited staff at the headquarter. The number of students and study centres are increasing at a fast rate. IGNOU has more than 2000 study centres. The Supervision and control over these centres cannot be done qualitatively resulting in low performance. Electronic gadgets, Library, etc. are not being used at study centres. There is a need to ensure supervision and control.

B. INTERNAL LIMITATIONS

The success of Distance Education Institutes depends to great extent upon its internal efficiency and effectiveness There are, however, many internal issues which need review and solution. Let us mention some of them here:

(a) The University Administration exercises administrative control through assigning staff in the administrative wing without any regard for the need of the department. Frequent transfers of the administrative staff hamper the functioning of Distance Education System.

(b) These departments depend for financial and other supports on University administration which is not given systematically and in time.

(c) Faculty members, once recruited, do not evince active interest leading to frustration, indolence and indifference.

(d) Lesson scripts, once written, are not vetted and updated minutely resulting in poor quality of lessons.

(e) Personal Contact Programmes are not planned in tune with the needs of the students.

(f) Response Sheets are not despatched promptly. K. Murali Manohar has summed up nicely the internal problems as: "An Analysis into the actual operationalisation of various Distance Education Programmes in India indicate several deficiencies in the existing system. Problems such as excessive enrolment of students, failure to use multi-media packages, poor quality of course material supplied, poor counselling and guidance, non-seriousness in offering students services, lack of innovations, absence of continuous student evaluation, etc., lead to the fall of quality of Distance Education. While the Distance Education units in conventional Universities are more to be blamed in this regard, studies are required to be undertaken on a large scale so as to not only identify the bottlenecks but improve the quality of programmes."[41]

With these problems, there is a danger of the system becoming stereotyped leading to inertia. Until and unless, this inertia is removed, the system of distance education may deteriorate.

Thus, Distance Education requires better planning and implementation as this system has to operate in a challenging and difficult environment of openness. Piet rightly says, "Open Higher Education as it differs from Conventional contiguous education is characterised by a range of flexible measures to make higher education more open or accessible for adults."

There is a need to devise ways and means to improve upon the external and internal environment of Distance Education system to avoid stagnation and generate dynamism and development to reap the potential of this system. We may say in the words of Fred Jevons, "Distance Education should no longer be written-off as second-best. It has a different pattern of advantages and disadvantages from campus-based education but it is not intrinsically inferior.

Distance Education has some advantages which should be recognised more widely. Easier access; independent learning opportunities, a more intimate interface with employment; better quality controls over course materials, the possibilities of cumulative improvement in pedagogic quality; the staff development effect and under certain circumstances, lower costs."

There is a need of computerisation and net working. The vice-Chancellors' Conference recommended the following: Every DEI should have a good computer centre with LAN facilities for the purpose of computerising students' records, administration, production of learning materials, development and use of multi-media packages, etc. These centres should also be used for providing learning support to students enrolled in programmes of computer applications. Efforts should be made to evaluate student assignments by the computer. All the open universities are being networked for the design, development and delivery of programmes and courses. Eventually, the DEI of traditional universities are also expected to join this network. The reorganisation and development of these Institutes should therefore, be taken up with a view of their eventually becoming part of the Open University Network (OPENEl). The advantages of such networking are that the students will have a wider range of programmes and courses to choose from; sharing of programmes will make for greater efficiency and economy by avoiding duplication of efforts; good quality material will be available to all students; and they will have the advantage of mobility among institutions and programmes.

Dr. A.S. Desai, Ex-Chairperson, U.C.C., in her inaugural address has come out with important suggestions to improve the quality of Distance Education. To quote her,[42]

1. Improve the quality of our course material.
2. Share/jointly develop lesson units within the state, the region and ultimately at the national level. This will pave the way for collaboration at the international level.
3. Adopt a multi-media approach for imparting education.
4. Increase outreach to ensure that the CCIs and Open Universities can really take education to the disadvantaged sections of society in villages and tribal areas.
5. Organise effective student-support services through good study centres and mobile study centres for remote areas.
6. Provide suitable library facilities at the study centres including public libraries which should have a cell for distance education students.

7. Provide equipment at the study centres for the play-back of audios, videos and recorded radio and TV Programmes.
8. Organise an adequate number of orientation and personal contact programmes at places where CCIs have a reasonable cluster of learners or, several CCIs can share the cost of one centre if their geographical areas overlap.
9. Computerise students' profile, and other records evaluation of some of the tests, and maintain computerised administrative records.
10. Encourage staff development of teachers and administrative staff in the CCIs.
11. Ensure the mobility of students from CCIs to the conventional teaching departments of universities and colleges, and vice-versa as also from one CCI to another.
12. Diversify courses to make education relevant to the needs of learners and the society, by liaisoning with employers, and identify self-employment opportunities, urban and rural. Diversification should also mean enrichment and updating courses for persons engaged in different vocations/professions.
13. Organise the feedback from the students for improvement of the programme.
14. Organise an effective monitoring system for monitoring the various processes involved in the efficient working of CCIs.

Distance education can be a particular boon for women, especially since parents are unwilling to send them beyond their immediate locale for education after the completion of primary or middle school. Our programme must have a special gender bias towards the girl child and women so that they can benefit from education.[43]

Distance education has the potential to make equity and access to education a reality and, thus, increase opportunities for a population in a vast democracy like ours. It has great potential for meeting the requirements of the varied demands for human resource. In doing so, our programmes should not be so stereotyped in their urban context, that students in rural areas get no benefit from them. We often forget that a majority of our youth live in rural areas and a substantial number of our colleges are located in district headquarters and taluka towns. They need courses more appropriate to their local context in upgrading their household occupation, agro-industries, and rural enterprises such as cooperatives, rural banks, rural development and panchayati raj institutions, as also the vastly developing rural service sector, especially in the fields of transport, storage and communication. We have a vast potential for reaching out to this sector which has been largely left untouched by our urban-based universities and teachers who develop the syllabi. We need to have open universities and schools in every state of the country to nurture this vast sector for human resource development leading to a productive India of the future. Hence, we need the growth of distance education to reach out to this vast country and its diverse needs, and especially for developing competency for various occupations and careers.

"Educationists will have to ponder over major system-wide and product-related issues of more relevant Distance Education products, networking, faculty development, level of fees and remission and constant updating of programmes. Open communication among learners, potential learners, faculty, Distance Education Institutions and administrative wings on the one hand and funding agencies, employees, mass media, and Government on the other will be the critical factor that will facilitate the success of EDPs in India."[44]

S.V.R. Reddy and G.M. Reddy on the basis of the research study of the profile of students in Dr. B.R. Ambedkar Open University from 1988-89 to 1994-95 concluded: "The Open University system has made a niche for itself and has, established itself as an independent system of its own. There is no exaggeration in the statement that the Open University System is a second string to the bow of higher education."[45]

However, while talking about distance learning and conventional learning system, it is to be kept in mind that these two systems are not rival to each other. The two systems can move together in order to take benefit of each other in serving the noble cause of providing education to all. However, distance education can achieve much more far as widening access to education is concerned. This system has the advantage of flexibility in designing and developing course materials relevant to the aspirations of learners and it makes different media available to carry the torch of education to even remote rural and tribal areas which have all along remained neglected. Thus, this innovating system of education will fulfil the aim towards achieving social justice. However, this system needs concerted efforts, good team work, dedication, open mind and broad thinking. Much more requires to be done for achieving the goal of distance education which is not only correspondence education but utilizes higher technologies.[46]

Education being an investment in the future, the state and the society can't be permitted to abdicate their two-fold responsibility of ensuring first, that nobody spreads and permits fundamentalism, obscurantism, intolerance, ideological factionalism and such other vices in the name of privatisation of higher education and second, that merit and not money, caste or creed is the sole criterion of selection to any institution. Democratic values, social equity are too precious to be sacrificed for economic pragmatism. In this backdrop, distance education system, is undoubtedly, an effective alternative system, given the social-economic conditions prevalent in the country.

However, for the DE system to be fruitful in its mission of providing a wider access to education, to all section of society, there is an urgent need to strengthen its hands and develop it on sound and healthy lines. In this direction, following suggestions may be considered:

1. DE institutes need be granted independent status and should not function as subservient to the traditional universities.
2. The DE institutes should not come under the grip of the traditional rigidity in the shpere of rules and regulations, imposed by the universities.
3. The DE system should not be made a tool for resources generation for the universities.
4. The DE institutes should avoid, as far as possible, the bureaucratic style of functioning and should adopt simplified procedures.
5. To raise the work efficiency and to instil morale, more attention should be paid to the staff training and development.
6. The state should provide liberal financial assistance.
7. Autonomy should be granted to the DE institutes.[47]

Distance education system is a device to provide education to distant students as well as reduce communication gap between the distant student and the teacher.

We may end with a warning, given by *The Hindu*, a leading Newspaper of India that the ballooning enrolments in almost all the CCIS in the country point to the great urge among the middle class youth (both urban and rural) to acquire a degree or a post-graduate status. By itself this trend is good but the CCIS almost invariably bite off more than they can chew. They take in too many students, much more than they could manage. Infact, this had led to the criticism of the universities looking at the CCIS as "milch cows" for generating funds through the collection of a plethora of fees.[48]

Notes and References

1. B.B. Sharma, Dynamics in Distance Education: Some Innovative Approaches—In Academic XII, Directors' Meet, Special Number (April 22-24, 1993), Academic Staff College, HP University, Shimla, Vol. V, No. I, April 1995, p. 41.
2. *University News*, 37(35), Aug. 30, 1999, p. 16.
3. K.B. Power, Globalisation of Distance Learning System-Implications for Developing Countries, In *University News*, January 27, 1997, AIU, New Delhi.
4. J. Daniel and Marquise (1979), Interaction and Independence, getting the mixture right, *Teaching at a Distance*, (14), pp. 29-44.
5. M.G. Moore (1973), "Forwards a theory of Independent Learning and Teaching", *Journal of Higher Education*, 44, p. 664
6. C.A. Wedmeyer (1977), "Independent Study" in A.S. Knowles (ed.) The International Encyclopaedia of Higher Education, S. 2114-2131. Boston, CIHED.
7. G. Dohmen, (1976), Das Femstudium. Einneues Padagogisches Forschungs-und Arbeitsfeld, Tubingen: DIFF, p. 9.
8. David Sewar: Student Support System in Distance Education, p. 4.
9. Hilary Parraton, 1981: "A theory for Distance Education", Prospects XI, 1: 13, 24.

10. Erling Ljosa, "Distance Education in a Modern Society", *The Journal of Distance and Open Learning*, Vol. 7, No. 2, June 1992, p. 30.
11. T. Dodds: Distance Learning for pre-tertiary education in Africa, in Thorpe, M. and Grugeon, D. (eds.) *Open Learning in the Mainstream*, Longman Group Ltd., Harlow, 1994, pp. 319-331.
12. Henderik, Piet, Management and Promotion of Quality in Distance Education, in Open Learning, *The Journal of Open and Distance Learning*, Vol. 7, No. 3, Nov. 1992, p. 3.
13. K. Murali Manohar, "Distance Education in India: Problems and Prospects", in *Kaktiya Journal of Distance Education*, Vol. I, No. I, January 1992, pp. 23.
14. R.C. Sharma: Distance Education in Global Perspective, *University News*, AIU, Nov. 17, 1997, p. 12.
15. Mary Thorpe: The expansion of Open and Distance Learning—A Reflection of Market Forces, in *Open Learning*, Vol. 10, No. I, February, 1995, p. 29.
16. Kothari Commission, A report 1964-66, Manager Publications, New Delhi.
17. "Towards An Open Learning System", Report of the Committee on the working of an Open University, Government of India, Ministry of Education and Social Welfare, 1976 (popularly known as G. Parthasarthi Committee Report.)
18. Govt. of A.P., "Towards an Open Learning System", Report of the Committee on the establishment of an Open University in A.P. (G. Rama Reddy Committee), 1982.
19. *The Times of India*, 31st August, 1985.
20. Quoted in A. Biswas and S.P. Agarwal (Eds.), Indian Educational Documents Since Independence, the Academic Publishers, New Delhi, 1971, p. 606.
21. Report of the Working Group on National Open University, New Delhi, GOI (unpublished).
22. Development of Distance Education in Asia—An Analysis of Five Case Studies, *op. cit.*, p. 115.
23. K.A. Judipillai, Member Secretary, TN State Council for Higher Education in "Open Universities" in *University News*, July 3, 1995, AIU, New Delhi.
25. Harris, 1987, p. 1 quoted in *Open Learning*, Vol. 10, No.1, Feb. 1993, p. 47.
26. R.R. Rausaria and Bharat Bhushan, Institutional Models for Distance Learning in India, *University News*, July 2-8, 2001,p.10
27. GOI, Eighth Five Year Plan (1992-97), New Delhi, 1992, p. 295.
28. Suneeta Anil Pathak, Distance in Physics Education: A Study of Factors, in *University News*, October, 27, 1997, p. 8, AJU, New Delhi.
29. Proceedings of the Round Table of Directors of Correspondence Course Institutes, Organised by UGC in association with IGNOU, Hosted and Published by the Institute of Correspondence Education, University of Madras, 15 Oct., 1995, p. 5.
30. Ashok Kumar Gaba and Bharat Bhushan,, "Funding of Open and Distance Higher Education in India: Quality and Policy Issues", *University News*, Feb. 23-29, 2004, p. 21.
31. Darshana Sharma, "Promoting National Development through Distance Higher Education: Scope, Initiatives and Challenges, *University News*, April 2, 2007, p. 15.
32. K.B. Pathak and S.K. Singh, Distance Education Programmes in Population Studies, *Journal of Higher Education*, Summer 1998, Vol. 21, No. 2, New Delhi, UGC, p. 243.
33. H.P. Dikshit, Open University System and International Presence in *University News*, Aug. 15-21, 2005, p. 17.
34. *Ibid.*, p. 242.
35. M. Venkat Reddy and Vijaya Chandera Tenneti, Distance Education and Privatisation of Higher Education, *University News*, 36(3), August 3, 1998, p. 12.

36. Beena Shah, Distance Education *vs.* Flexible Learning: Pressures, Practices and Perspectives", *University News*, March 1, 2007, p. 7.
37. S.P. Anand, Editorial, in India, *Journal of Distance Education*, Chandigarh, Directorate of Correspondence Studies, Panjab University, Vol. I, January 1992, pp. 2-3.
38. Bakshish Singh, The Need for a National Institute/Open University for Distance Education, in *Distance Education—A Reappraisal,* National Council of Correspondence Education, 1984, p. 3.
39. S.P. Anand, Editorial in *Indian Journal of Distance Education*, Vol. IV, DCS, PU, Chandigarh.
40. Mavis Kelley, "Barriers to Convergence in Australian Higher Education," in *Distance Education and Mainstream*, edited by Peter Smith and Malvis Kelley, London, Cross Helen, 1987, pp. 175-76.
41. K. Murali Manohar, *op. cit.*, p. 6.
42. Fred Jevons, "Distance Education and Campus-based Education: Parity of Esteem", in *Distance Education and the Mainstream* (ed.) by Peter Smith and Movis Kelley, London, Cross Helm, 1987, p. 12.
43. Round Table of Directors of Correspondence Course Institute, *op. cit.*, pp. 8-10.
44. P.V. Desai and P.R. Shah, "Distance Education Progamme—A Marketing Approach and its Implications," in *University News*, January 20, 1997, AIU, New Delhi.
45. S.V. Rajashekhar Reddy and G. Mallu Reddy, Profile of Distance Learners: A Case Study of Dr. B.R. Ambedkar Open University, *University News*, 35(4), January 27, 1997, p. 27.
46. Shamshad Hussain, "Distance Learning—The Latest Attraction", *University News*, Oct. 28,1996, pp. 15-16.
47. M. Venkat Reddy and Vijaya Chandra Tenneti, "Distance Education and Privatisation of Higher Education", *University News*, Aug. 3, 1998, p. 14.
48. *The Hindu*, Nov. 14, 1995, Tamil Nadu.

Good Governance Essential to Maintain Standards in Distance Education System

Distance Education system is comparatively new to traditional education system. Distance Education grew out of the needs of the society. It has grown so fast that no one can believe it. However, it has not deep roots and that is why its credibility is in doubt. Why? The Institutes and Universities set-up to impart distance education are not properly equipped in terms of infrastructure, personnel—both teaching and administrative leading to mismanagement. In addition the existing set-up in distance education system was not put to the best use resulting in wastage of resources in terms of human, material and financial resources. Students are the last priority of a distance education system. What can be the impact of distance education system in such an internal environment? We would realize later that distance education system has become a liability rather than asset. On discussion with students undergoing distance education, they felt that Distance education is a passport to get degrees of higher education. They further remarked that teachers in distance education is being run getting paid holidays. In this way Distance Education may pose threat to higher education quality. It is high time for the policy-makers, planners and those responsible for running the DE Institutes to inject improvements through Good Governance otherwise it would be too late. (Chart 3.1)

Good Governance is of paramount importance in these times of far reaching changes. In this backdrop of major changes, we need to re-orient ourselves to devise ways and means to promote, good governance. No DE System of course can hope to survive without a strong and effective good governance nor can any DE System exist without the support of those it was established to serve.

It is this human transformation that must come to all in our distance

CHART 3.1

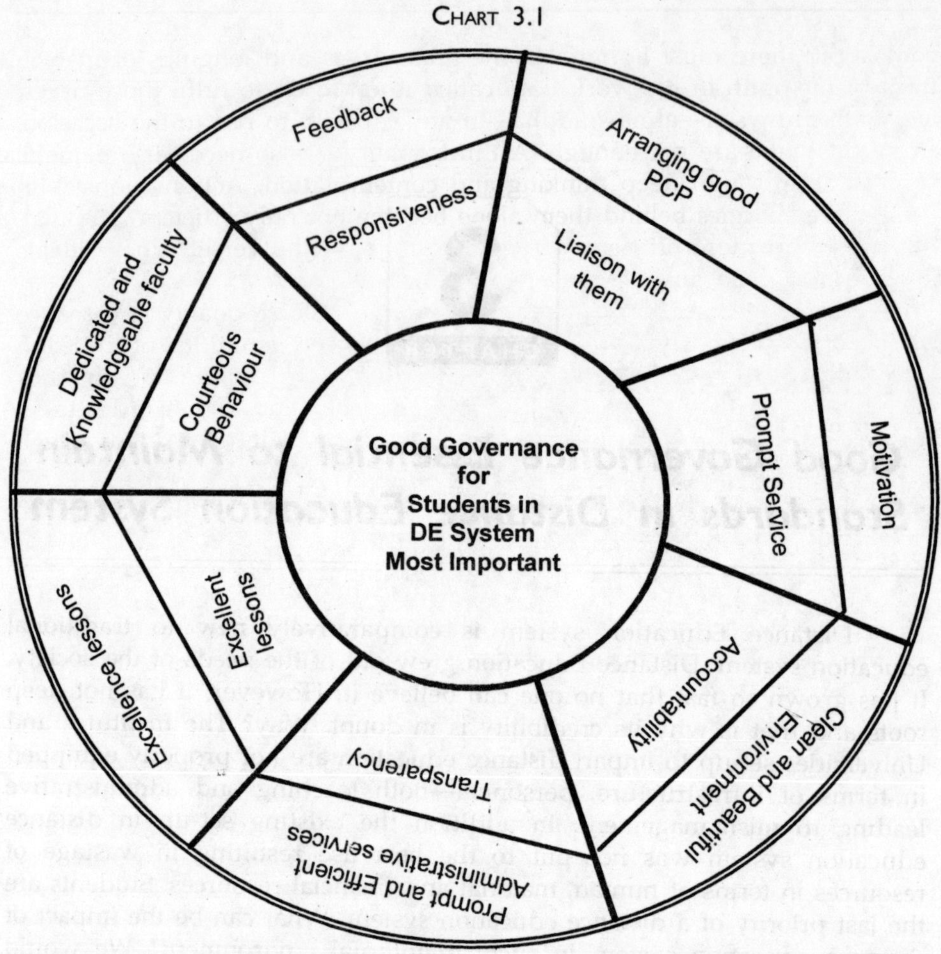

education administration, to ensure good governance. We have a great message on this subject in a verse of one of our Upanishads, namely, the Chandogya Upanisad, only next in importance and size to the greatest among all the Upanisads, the Brhadaranyaka Upanisad. These are between three thousand and four thousand years old. What inspiring and profound ideas come out of this great literature of so ancient a period of human history! What is the source of human work-efficiency? That is the question, to which the Chandogya verse gives the following answer (1.1.10): which is the essence of good governance.

Yadeva vidyaya karoti, sraddhaya, upanisada, tadeva viryavattaram bhavati.

It is a very simple Sanskrit utterance. Yadeva Karoti—whatever is done; vidyaya—through knowledge—what we call today the 'know-how'. The first thing to acquire is the 'know-how' of a task. Is that enough? No, says the Upanisads, and add: sraddhaya—through sraddha—faith or conviction; there must be faith in the great urges and longings of man in front of me, faith in the work I am called upon to do to fulfil those urges, and faith in myself—atma-sraddha—in any capacity to rise to the occasion. Even these two are not enough. A third quality is also necessary, namely, Upanisada, through deep thinking and contemplation. Actions done with these three energies behind them alone become not only efficient, viryavat, but more and more efficient, viryavattaram, says the verse.[1] These ideals give birth to good governance.

R.S. Tiwari mentioned that a future model of high quality governance has been discussed and endorsed by the Executive Committee of the Club of Rome, need attention. It mentions that "the minimum qualities governance need for adequately fulfilling ordinary and higher order tasks in the twenty first century so as to avoid very costly failure, take advantage of fleeting opportunities and influence the future for the better, are far superior to what we have now or had in the past. Following facets may be considered crucial for high quality governance:

- *Morality*: Governance should observe certain basic norms like freedom, Democracy, neutrality, human rights values and ethical behavour.
- *Knowledge Intensive*: It should strive for knowledge society with vigor which is neglected by many.
- *Committed to future*: There should be will to influence the future and be considerate towards future generation.
- *Consent-based*: Governance should be founded on the consent of the people and really democratic in spirit. It also permits alternative forms of consent appropriate to different values, cultures, societal traditions and situations.
- *High energy but selective*: The DE System must perform tasks leading to weaving the future for the better rather simply a night watch. It suggests that spontaneous processes and zero governance institution cannot deliver the goods. High energy is an essential attribute of that governance with its long-term responsibilities. This does not mean more but effective governance.
- *Deep thinking*: The need for action-oriented thinking directed toward fundamental issues rather than focusing on symptoms.
- *Holistic*: The governmental thinking, choice and action must be holistic.
- Learning in context of rapid change and need of creativity and innovation.
- *Pluralism*: it refers to providing for multi-level, multi-skill and multi-culture-oriented governance.
- *Decisiveness*: It requires that the various elements of governance reinforce yet correct one another and result in a clear choice, rather than neutralising each other. This requires workable rules for decision-making, controlled hierarchical authority and democratic power concentration.

Students in distance education are located at different places and thus cannot approach distance education institute to get their grievances removed while the students in the formal education are present on the campus with little difficulties. To ensure good delivery of services to distance education students Good Governance in the distance education institute is essential. Students in distance education face a number of problems because the delivery of services by the administrative staff is poor. The administration in distance education works on adhoc basis causing irritation and lack of interest among students.

Let us discuss the problems of administration in a distance education system institute attached to a formal university. The administrative staff is on deputation from the main university office or registrar's office, who exercises control over them. They are transferred resulting into a void of experienced personnel. The entire staff is not trained and they work like any other office. In order to maintain Good Governance we suggest the following: (See Chart 3.2)

1. Staff in the distance education institute

It may not be transferred without the consent of Chairman of the Department of Distance Education . It is a tendency of the main office to send persons who are not fit for the job causing inefficiency. The head of the distance education system occupies a position with too much interference by Vice-Chancellor or Registrar office.

2. Training may be imparted to the staff engaged in distance education institute or university in the art and science of distance education

Training connotes that the trainers can influence the performance of the trainees. The influence takes the form of knowledge, attitude and action. The ultimate success of the training depends upon the change in behaviour of the trainees, who in turn can inject efficiency and effectiveness in their services. Action training is aimed at creating a situation in which employees can act optimally. Morton R. Davies rightly mentions the need of Action Training. To quote him, "Action training is training designed to achieve explicit, predetermined results which will enhance attainment of an objective of an enterprise in a recognizable, preferably quantifiable way. Action Training is designed to solve a problem, to effect change, to implement a policy or to arrive at other observable and predictable results."[2]

One of the key factors in the effort of the DES to accomplish its development goals in the area of management is to enhance its administrative capability for development at all levels of administrative hierarchy, which is very much a part of the development process. Such complex problems call for a multi-disciplinary solution, to which concerned people at all levels must apply their technical skills, general knowledge and understanding. The education and training of all responsible staff engaged in DES are absolutely essential, if worthwhile results are to be obtained.

CHART 3.2

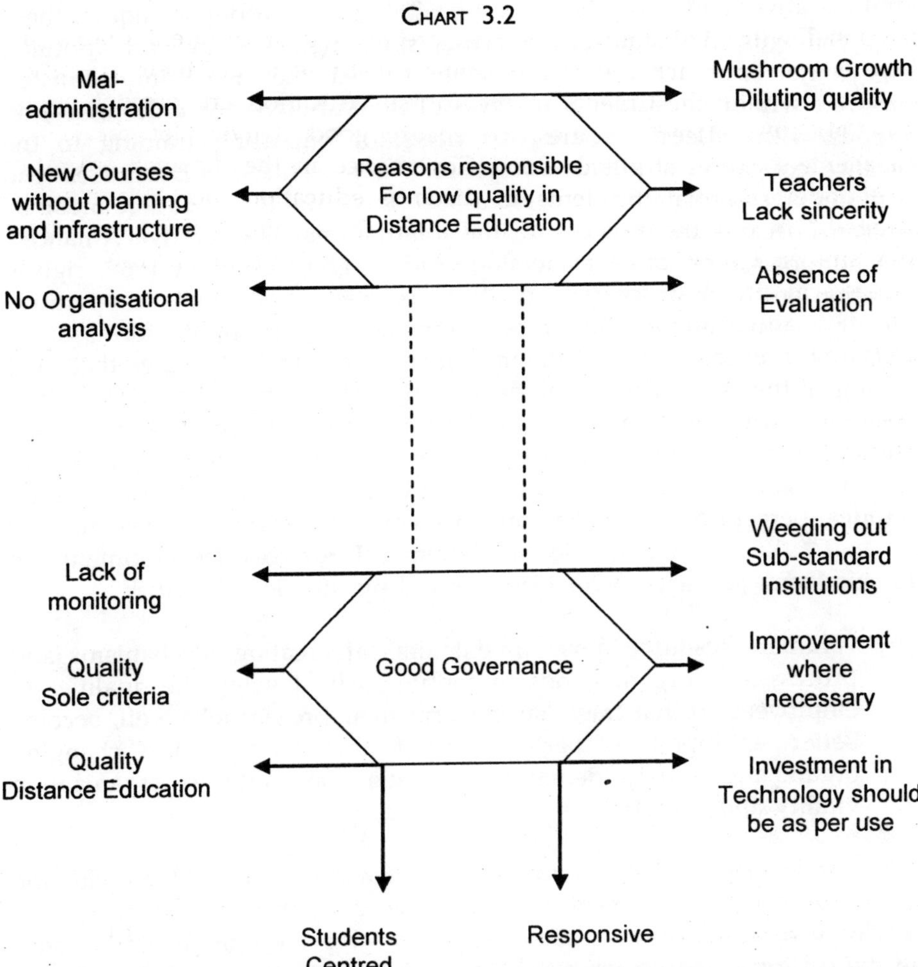

This is true whether they are, administrators, executives, technical people or clerical personnel. But, our experience during the last three decades has demonstrated that the DE plans have not been satisfactorily implemented, because of inadequate administrative performance. The reasons for the low level of administrative performance include: organizational defects, lack of coordination, complex and cumbersome administrative and financial procedures, etc. these defects and deficiencies need to be corrected in order to bring about a sharp reduction in the administrative obstacles to DES and bridge the gap between aspirations and performance. Simultaneously, the level of competence of DE personnel directly involved in providing Distance Education can be raised by training them in modern concepts and techniques of DES administration and management. This category of personnel at the senior or intermediate level, comprising both technocrats and generalists, is constantly called upon to discharge increasingly heavy administrative and managerial responsibilities. In order to equip these personnel with the required expertise, skill, methodology and aptitude, there is a need to train such personnel. In fact, the then Prime Minister, while addressing the Chief Executives of the Public Sector Enterprises) on May 29, 1985 stated, "There was need for imparting training to the management cadres of public enterprises. The percentage of Executives who have undergone training at present was low and the situation must be changed." In this context, one of the International Cooperative Alliance's Seminars on Cooperative leadership held in New Delhi in 1960, rightly declared in the first sentence of its recommendations that "cooperative education and training should be organized in appropriate forms at all levels and in every branch of the movement's activity."[3] All agree that right training is the first priority for developing DE system. The most fruitful investments are not in material supplies, but in efforts undertaken to train men and women who, through their own development and initiative, can in turn be catalytic in transforming students' outlook and change their attitudes, perception and behaviour in favour of a better DE system.

TV Rao in his article on "Human Resources Development" in *Business India*, January 13-26, 1986 has rightly mentioned that:

> "Human Resource development aims at creating mechanisms and processes in organizations to continuously develop the qualities of employees so that they can perform their present jobs well, become better equipped to perform the future roles of the changing organizations may demand and thus contribute to organization vitality and growth."

The objective of the training is to Provide an individual with the knowledge of the environment or ecology under which he is to function; the knowledge of administrative management to achieve optimum performance and cultivation of necessary attitudes.

Training is essential for building confidence, commitment and competence among DE personnel. Mahabir Singh Kasana, rightly observes, "Training is very important component of Human Resource Development. It is, perhaps the most cost effective method of improving competencies amongst the manpower of any organisation. Training has been defined as a planned process to impart knowledge, develop skills and modify attitude of the work force through learning processes to achieve the effective performance in any activity or range of activities. The right mix of knowledge, skills and attitudinal components in a training course or a training programme is essential for performance improvement. Performance calls for upgrading confidence, competence and commitment of the persons to enable them to handle the situation and show the results on the ground. Whereas, increase in knowledge, arguability imparts confidence, the skills contribute to enhancement of competency of individuals. The attitude primarily leads to commitment to job. Possessing of the right attitude, combined with appropriate knowledge and skills is required to be assured through training efforts. It is, therefore, necessary that a systematic approach to training linking it with performance is necessary. Developing confidence, competence and commitments require enriching learning experience consisting of Tell, Show, Do, Check and Act through systematic approach to training."[4]

3. Administrative Staff

They must understand the art and science of public relation so that DE students are attracted and not repulsed by employees of DE institutes. They must treat the students with respect and dignity. This would create harmony which would promote efficiency. This would create a chain effect for future development of the DE institutes. One of the important functions of personnel in a distance organization should be the development of cordial, equitable and harmonious relationships with the DE students to ensure their welfare and participation. The role of public relations is the establishment of a climate of understanding. It means interpreting the programme of an organization to the students and *vice versa*. The purpose of public relations is not only to supply information, but also to encourage an understanding and ensure co-operation between the students and DE Institutes. Its objectives should be to increase prestige and goodwill, and to protect the organization by safeguarding it against unwarranted attacks as well as to remove the genuine complaints and grievances of the students. This creates confidence in the minds of the students regarding the competence, fairness, honesty, impartiality and sincerity of the DE institutes.

4. Cultivating Work Culture

Work culture in Distance Education University or Institute is of a very low standard as they do not keep themselves alert with the latest developments in their area of specialization. Even the administrative staff take the work in a casual manner. Top personal in DE institution must create work culture and not psycho-fancy. Work culture is at the lowest ebbs. Bata K. Dey in his Article, 'Work Culture in India—Achievements and Failure' rightly says that culture is not something which can be imported or transplanted; it must grow from within; it grows, and it does, in fertile soil and congenial climate. Gap in capital equipment or technology can be filled by import. You can even buy management, but not dedication, commitment, culture. How to create work culture that is a million dollar question. An inexpensive answer to such a costly question is that, work culture tends to be congruous with, and is an extension of the societal, indeed national culture. And the latter, at the moment, is the elusive commodity, despite this country's ancient civilization and old culture. The search is on. And we shall succeed.[5]

The greatest efficiency and productivity will flow from the efforts of those who find satisfaction in their work and conditions of service, who sense an awareness of usefulness of their functions, who feel encouraged to move ahead and to meet new challenges, who perceive their working environment as one in which high standards of performance are maintained and rewarded and not one in which indolence and incompetence can be ignored or even protected and rewarded. Motivation can do miracles, as a motivated worker can achieve more than an expert with no motivation. Leaders must, therefore, devote considerable time and effort in planning for, and achieving, high levels of motivation and morale. In such a situation, we would achieve goal congruence, i.e., identity between the individual goals and the organisational goals.[6]

We may follow the following:

(a) Care for the DE students;
(b) Craze for creativity;
(c) Concern for DE students;
(d) Democratic culture in contrast to authoritarian and paternalistic culture;
(e) Empowerment of the DE students;
(f) Enlighten visionary and dynamic leadership;
(g) Synergistic team;
(h) Top quality in production and services not only by removing the students annoyance but providing them unmitigated pleasure;
(i) Quick action and prompt response;
(j) Effective management of change;
(k) Creating competitive advantage in products and services;
(l) Creating climate of achievement;
(m) Linking reward with the excellence; and
(n) Investing in DE employees to realize their full potentialities to be harnessed for services of the DE students.

All these result into improvements, creativity, and innovation which provide organizations competitive edge and coping capabilities by reviewing, revising, renewing, revamping, rejuvenating and re-inventing their systems and procedures. Organizational culture ensures this climate and motivates its members to be proactive, positive and committed than to remain reactive, negative and casual. Organization creates conditions wherein the basic goodness in men gets released and exhibited in their actions. Their worth gets manifested for their own growth and for others. In the organizational context, this would mean creating conditions (in terms of rewards, opportunities, etc.) wherein employees willingly come forward together to do their very best, enjoy doing so and continue to grow.[7]

5. Administrative Reforms

The DE institutes are working haphazardly. There is no well designed strategy to serve the students. Preparation of lessons are defective and there are delays in sending them to students. Response sheets are either not evaluated or sent as these were received. There is a need of reforms both in academic and administrative activities. Administrative improvement means the act or the process of improving the administration. As stated in a United Nations Report: "Management improvement comprises of planning, implementation and evaluation of various measures conducive to the increase of organizational effectiveness and efficiency."[8]

Simple commitment by management is not enough. The improvement process must become as basic and continuous as our concerns. There is no magic approach or solution to be gleaned from either a text-book or a consultant, although either of these can help management discover an effective programme for carrying out its required responsibility. But, the manager remains the key to tapping the most underutilised resource that is people.[9]

Administrative reform is still widely regarded as a special type of improvement activity, even when it is often closely connected with other activities. The concept of the 'administrative reform', as it is applied in practice, also has its weaknesses.

Efforts at administrative reform too often stop with the preparation of reports or promulgation of laws. Unless administrative reforms encourage macro-level improvement of performance and their micro-level self-evaluation with a view to providing a managerial feed-back loop for bringing about further improvement in performance, any elaborate machinery for external evaluation can only degenerate into evaluation for evaluation's sake. In fact, performance itself often becomes a casualty. It also helps to "pass the buck" upwards and reduce accountability from those who should perform to those who supervise.

Administrative reforms are not only to be planned but implemented as well, with sincerity at all levels, to achieve the desired results. There has to be a genuine desire to ensure just and impartial administration. Making improvements in procedures and practices, form and techniques of administration are only partial remedies. These alone may not give the desired results unless the human elements in charge of running the administrative machinery show genuine commitment to bring about good governance. Unfortunately, the deteriorating quality of leadership has adversely affected the quality of administrative machinery as well. For, unless the top is clean and truly dedicated to the well-being of the people, other layers of administration are unlikely to behave any better. The lower ones generally follow the footsteps of the higher ones.[10]

6. Promoting Human Resource Development

The basic objects of HRD in DE System can be as under:[11]

1. To equip the academic and administrative staff of DE system with precision and clarity in transaction of business;
2. To attune the DE personnel to new tasks which they will be called upon to perform in a changing world;

3. To develop resistance to the danger of becoming mechanized by visualizing what he is doing in wider setting and by preserving his own educational development;
4. To develop his capacity for higher work and greater responsibility;
5. To develop and maintain DE personnel morale, particularly because large number of people have to deal with tasks of a routine nature;
6. To inculcate right attitude towards the students, never foregetting that the DE teacher is the guide and not the master of the community; and
7. To sustain the human touch not only in direct personal contact with the students but also in handling correspondence which demands a proper sense of urgency and due consideration of the "student at the other end."

L.P. Singh has given a beautiful definition of HRD. To quote him, "HRD refers to the improvement in the capacities and capabilities of the personnel in relation to the needs of the particular sector. It involves the creation of a climate in which the flower of human knowledge, skills, capabilities, creativity can bloom . . . Human Resources Development seeks to provide a package of systems and process through which these can be cultivated and enhanced among the people forming part of the network of roles in that sector."[12]

The HRD represents an intervention strategy with, *inter alia* the following overall objectives, namely:

1. Arresting obsolescence, both individual and organisational (preventive);
2. Bridging pro-active insufficiencies of knowledge and professional skills (curative);
3. Shaping adjustments with socio-technological, environment changes (adaptive);
4. Developing new outlook, an ethological version of quality excellence and accomplishment (promotive); and
5. Making a total man with new cultural attributes (transformative).[13]

7. Proper Reception to Students Visiting DE Institution and Prompt Removal of their Grievances

Students visiting the Distance Education Institutes are not treated well. They are not offered seats to sit comfortably. Generally, bevaiour of Administrative staff of DE system is rude and not decent. The officials would not attend their problems and advance one excuse or the other to postpone the work. What should be done? How can we improve their behaviour?

Human Resource Accounting and Audit are the latest terms to evaluate personnel in an organisation. Human Resource Accounting is the term used to describe the accounting methods, systems and techniques, which coupled with special knowledge and ability, assist personnel management in the valuation of personnel in financial terms. This term has been defined by different scholars. Human Resource Accounting is the measurement of the cost and value of people for the organisation. It is based on the presumption that there exists a great difference among personnel in their knowledge, ability and motivation in the same organisation and from organisation to organisation. There are some individuals who are able to produce more as compared to others in terms of goods and services. It means that there are some who may be a liability. Human Resource Accounting would provide all this information to facilitate decision-making about the personnel either to keep the personnel or dispense with their services or give promotion or to provide training.

The Manpower Audit is conducted to ensure that the manpower implementation plans are being executed and the objectives achieved. If these are not being achieved, it becomes necessary to 'flag' that important assumption and analyse it to take corrective measures. Human Resource Auditing is the continuous and systematic process of ascertaining whether personnel policies are being put into action as designed. The objects of such auditing are:

(a) To confirm that the policies of personnel management are being properly executed and to draw attention to those areas where policies appear to be inadequate.
(b) To verify that the information used by personnel management to control human resources is both adequate and accurate.
(c) To conduct a systematic survey and analysis of all operative functions of personnel with a summarized statement of findings for correction of deficiencies.

S.A. Sapre says that an organisation should be built on the strength of the people, not on their weaknesses . . . trees die from the top, so do the organisation, for want of integrity in the manager (*Financial Express*, July 7, 1992).

There is a real need to reform the current personnel polices in DE organisations through intellectual and idealistic approach. The day-to-day personnel administration is the responsibility of the personnel department, but, the major policy decisions in the form of rules or regulations would require the approval of the chief executive. Most of the personnel in an organisation agreed that the personnel administration is passing through a crisis caused by the antiquated procedures backed by unwillingness and incapacity to introduce the desired reforms.

The performance of the personnel functions by the personnel department is limited in practice because of the following drawbacks:

(a) Inadequate understanding and appreciation of the basic and the essential problems of personnel management;
(b) No future personnel planning resulting in the absence of timely corrective measures;
(c) Lack of control and supervision over the personnel especially of the field personnel;
(d) Lack of effective decentralisation to substantive departments resulting in delays and confusion;
(e) Absence of effective participation of the employees resulting in a gulf between the management and the staff;
(f) Lack of a manual setting out all the rules and regulations clearly and fully in a single document; and
(g) Lack of effective communication between the staff and management.

If one visits a distance education institute/university, one is wonder struck to see:

(i) Teachers and administrative staff absent themselves without any leave.
(ii) Late arrival is a standard practice.
(iii) Taking the work casually is a usual phenomenon.
(iv) Faculty does not concentrate on improving lecture scripts or video-tapes. They sign previous years lessons with mistakes and do not correct them.
(v) Clerks and other staff are also not available in their seats.
(vi) Students do not get their lessons regularly and in time.
(vii) The cleanliness is poor. Even the lavatories are stinking.
(viii) Chairman of DE has no control over teachers and administrative staff.

Schools of correspondence courses or Distance Education Institutes in formal universities, are viewed more as resource-generating channels, generating income much above the corresponding costs, rather than as ones that offer effective education. On the whole, the effectiveness of open learning systems in terms of quality and efficiency—specifically external efficiency—is yet to be established beyond doubt. Until then, the open learning modes will naturally be treated as inferior or second-rate quality institutions.

There is a need to introduce Good Governance which can set right the functioning of DE institutes. This would involve the laying down of priorities for students centric approach, transparency, accountability. In addition, the personal of DE must build administrative capability and capacity to serve the students earnestly, with zeal and enthusiasm. In this way we can inject Good Governance in these institutes. Good Governance would be automatic marketing for distance education institute as the image of the DE institute travels fast. We must always keep in mind that:

- The student is the most important in distance education institute.
- The students is not dependent upon us.
- We are dependent on him.
- The student is not an interruption of our work.
- He is the purpose of it.
- The students is not an outsider to our business. He is our Business.
- The student is a person and not a statistic.
- He has feelings, emotions, biases and wants.
- It is our business to satisfy him.

To achieve the above, the employee of the DE system may keep the following in view:

(i) Extent of loyalty to the institution and identification with it and its objectives;

(ii) Extent to which the goals of units and individuals facilitate the achievements of the organization's objectives;

(iii) Level of motivation among members of the organization with regard to such variable as:

 (a) Performance including both quality and quantity of work done.

 (b) Concern for elimination of waste and reduction of costs.

 (c) Concern for improving the product.

 (d) Concern for improving processes.

(iv) Degree of confidence and trust among members of the organisation in each other and in the different hierarchical levels.

(v) Amount and quality of the teamwork in units and between units of the organisation.

(vi) Extent to which people feel that delegation is effective.

(vii) Extent to which the members feel that their ideas, information, knowledge of processes, and experiences are being used in the decision-making processes of the organisation.

(viii) Upward, downward, and sideward efficiency and adequacy of the communication process.

(ix) Leadership skills and abilities of supervisors and managers, including their basic philosophies of management and orientation towards leadership processes.

NOTES AND REFERENCES

1. Swami Ranganathananda, "Democratic Administration in the light of practical Vedanta, Madras, Sri Ramakrishna Mission, 2003.
2. Morton, R. Davies, Organising for Training, *IJPA*, January-March, 1992.
3. ICA: The Role of Co-operation in Social and Economic Development (edited), Asia Publishing House, New Delhi, 1966, p. 159.
4. Mahabir Singh Kasana, "Systematic Approach to Training for Rural Industrisation" in *Management in Government*, Janaury-March 2000, pp. 56-57.
5. Bata K. Dey, *IJPA*, April-June 1989, p. 175.
6. Jawaharlal Nehru and Public Administration, *IJPA*, New Delhi, 1975, p. 88
7. B.D. Singh, "Role of Organisational Work, Culture in Optimising Human Performance in P.P. Arya and R.P. Gupta (Edition)—Human Resource Management and Accounting, New Delhi, Deep & Deep, 1999, pp. 282-83.
8. UN: "Inter-regional Seminar on Administration of Management Improvement Services", Vol. I, Copenhagen, Denma, K., Oct. 1970, p. 24.
9. UN: "United Nations Programme in Public Administration", pp. 11-12.
10. U.C. Agarwal, Good Governance Cutting Edge of Administration, in *IJPA*, July-Sept. 1998, p. 436.
11. UN: A Study of the Capacity of the UN Development System, Vol. 1, Geneva, 1969.
12. L.P. Singh, HRD Perspective for Agricultural Marketing Sector in India, in the *Indian Journal of Commerce*, Vol. 52, No. 1, January-March, 2000.
13. Batat, K. Dey, Training in the Civil Services—Plan for a Holistic Construal, *IJPA*, Oct.-Dec., 1982, p. 4.

Instructional Material: Lecture Scripts for Distance Education System: A Critical Review

(a) Meaning of Instructional Material

Satyapal Anand rightly says that "the backbone of correspondence teaching is the material in print which is sent to students in regular instalments and without any oral supplementation. . . . It is also sometimes called "lecture script" or "a lesson unit."[1]

It must guide the student's studies, aid him in the assimilation of knowledge and skills, give him practice in the use of this knowledge and skill and test his understanding and attainment to find out where he needs additional help.[2]

Savita Kaushal in her article, "Making Distance Education Work" in *University News*, Nov. 27, 1995, p. 7, rightly stresses the need of good instructional material. To quote her, "The quality of distance education depends essentially upon the learning material provided to the learners. The economic constraints of our country make it difficult for us to use audio video inputs to a large extent. In such a situation, good quality self-instructional material is the answer. Unless the quality of distance education material is substantially improved and media mix incorporated to the extent feasible, the reputation of performance of distance education will remain under threat.

Now the basic question which needs answer is "What is a lesson unit." Whether a lesson unit is a chapter of a book or a class room discussion topic or a small material of the total course? It may be answered that the lesson constitutes a set of interconnected notes covering a topic. It is written in such a style that it is self-explanatory and does not need the help of the teacher. Lessons should be intelligible, comprehensive, simple and thought-provoking and motivate learning.

The backbone of Distance Education is the lesson units which are sent at regular intervals of time indicated in the prospectus. These lecture scripts cover the entire course in such a way that the students can depend entirely on them or supplement with other material depending upon the ability and interest of the students.

Instructional material is one of the basic tools of distance education. The day, the student of distance education receives the instructional material he goes into action and start preparing the course. If instructional material is not dispatched in time students personally come to ask about the instructional material or write reminders. Most of the students feel that the receipt of right instructional material make them secure and motivate them to learning. Some students put blank papers either at the end of the lesson or in between the pages of the lessons to write on them additional information from books, journals, newspapers, etc. to update them or expand them as per their requirements.

(b) Importance of Instructional Material

The quality of distance education depends essentially upon the quantity and quality of instructional material provided to the learners in regular timely instalments.

The most important input in the Distance Education system is the course material since more than half of the students depend mainly on printed material. Since the students are geographically located far away from the teacher, it is the course material which transfers the ideas of experts to the learners. These lessons therefore, constitute the thrust of the system and are more crucial to the success of a Distance Education Programme especially in a developing country like India. Post-graduate students may be provided extra material as well in the form of extracts from journals, reference books, etc. to keep them abreast with latest developments. In the words of Holmberg, "By far the most important medium in distance education courses is the printed word. This applies to conventional correspondence study, as well as to highly sophisticated multi-media presentation like courses of Open Universities." He mentions four essential requirements to ensure utility of instructional material.

The four major requirements of instruction referred to by Bruner (Holmberg, 1981) are equally applicable to distance teaching. They are:

(i) Developing in the learners a predisposition toward learning by specifying experiences;
(ii) Simplifying information for the learner to generate new propositions and to manipulate a body of knowledge;
(iii) Specifying the most effective sequence to present the material; and
(iv) Specifying the nature and pacing of extrinsic and intrinsic reinforcement.

As stated in a UGC document, the preparation of instructional material is crucial to the success of the entire programme of Distance Education and would require adequate preparation for the division of the course into integrated units and for the supply of lessons to the students well in time. Lessons should be written by the best available persons individually or in teams of 3-4 selected on an all-India level or at least the state level from among those who have experience of teaching the subject for at least five years including the courses of correspondence courses. The panel of lesson writers should be drawn up by subject committees.

Lesson should be revised and made up-to-date at least once in every three years and at more frequent intervals whenever necessitated by changes in syllabi, comments of reviewer and feedback from students.[3]

It is a boon for Distance Education students to get first rate ready-made study material which saves his time and energy and make him concentrate directly on genuine lecture scripts.

(C) ESSENTIALS OF A WELL PLANNED INSTRUCTIONAL DESIGN

Gordon has suggested the following salient features of a well planned instructional design:[4]

1. Internal consistency
2. Explicit boundaries and limitations
3. Not contradicted by empirical data
4. Parsimony
5. Usefulness
6. Comprehensiveness
7. Optimality
8. Breadth of applicability
9. Cost estimates
10. Time
11. Decision-making.

An analysis of above points reveal that the decision about well planned instructional design should ensure the production of a lesson which meets the needs of the students is, comprehensive and inspire creativity, interest, enthusiasm among students. Besides, it should be the product of the best efforts and talent of the academic community. Such a lesson would provide confidence in the student and make him to go ahead as per his interest. Many students have approached the authors after the receipt of the lesson as to what more they can read to get more material which can help them in securing high marks.

CHANGE OF INSTRUCTIONAL MATERIAL INTO SELF-INSTRUCTIONAL MATERIAL

We may also mention some of the recommendations made by UGC and DEC to change the lessons into Distance mode of teaching. Printed course material is the mainstay of providing instruction to the distance learners. Since students have to study mostly on their own and away from their teachers, they have to primarily depend upon the printed course material supplied to them. It is therefore very necessary that the course material should be carefully planned and developed in the Self-instructional distance education format. A serious attempt should be made to build the teacher into the course material. The course lessons/units must be presented in personal style and simple language to match with the comprehension level of the target groups. The content of the lessons should be of good quality, relevant to the topics and presented in an easily comprehensible manner. The staff of distance education institutions should therefore have a look at their printed course material lessons and take immediate steps to transform them into self-instructional distance education format. The course content also should be got evaluated by outside experts and revised and edited accordingly. Good course material is bound to enhance the reputation of the institution.

(a) Essentials of Self-Instructional Material

Self-Instructional material is unique in the sense that it differs from the chapter of a text book or a lecture in the class room. Its main thrust is on the development of the ability of the learner. Its main essentials are:

(i) Comprehensive

Lecture script should encompass comprehensive material so that the learner need not search for other sources. All the essential elements need be incorporated in the lesson.

(ii) Self-Motivation Generation

The Materials of the lecture script may be designed in a way that it promotes or encourages the learner to learn more and more. Since there is no teacher with the student, only the quality of lecture script can generate the necessary motivating force among the learners.

(iii) Self-explanatory without outside help

Contents of the lessons need be designed in a way that the learners can seek explanation themselves without any outside help.

(iv) Self-learning and Evaluating

The lecture script should inspire the learners to do self-learning to move from one point to the other. Along with it, the learners should be able to evaluate themselves to assess their capability and capacity.

Some of the special features of the open learning materials are:

- clearly stated objectives,
- user-friendly you and I style of writing,
- shortish, manageable chunks of learning,
- plenty of helpful examples,
- preference to the learners' experience,
- use of illustrations where they are better than words,
- headings to help learners find their way around,
- links to other media where appropriate,
- obvious awareness of different learners' needs,
- exercise that get the learners to use the material,
- space for learners to write down their own ideas,
- feedback to help learners check their own progress, and
- suggestions about getting help from other people.[5]

Networked education will be developing a new paradigm of education appropriate to the 21st century society. It will transform education quite radically. Changes will occur:

From	*To*
• Teaching	To Learning
• Teacher/Institution prescribed courses	To Learner demand
• Synchronous teaching-learning Process separate	To Asynchronous and teaching/ tele-teaching and learning process
• On Campus 'Classroom' education	To Home, workplace and community-based Education
• Single Institution	To Consortia of institutions networked togather by electronic communication
• Traditional students	To Non-traditional students

And Promoting symbiotic learning the new paradigm will be a working relationship leading to the learning society of the information age.[6]

(b) Essentials for Developing Independent Learners

The important criteria identified by experienced and distinguished distance educators (Ross Paul, 1990; Maca Skill, 1988; Brigetta Willen, 1988) to make instructional material relevant.

- making the learners fully aware of the challenges they will face in Distance Education,
- developing self-confidence among the distance learners to become independent learners,
- motivating the students to opt for distance learning more actively rather than passively. The implication is removing the negative views/biases towards D.E. system by explaining the advantages of D.E. system, and
- developing the students ability to learn independently by equipping them with effective reading, writing, and study skills and time management skills which are prerequisites for independent learning-providing the facility for interactive learning situations inculcating the habit of answering the assignments regularly which form the primary channel of two-way communication in distance tuition between the teacher and the learner and also regularising the study schedule of the learners.[7]

(c) Measures of Quality Assurance in Distance Education Material

It is crucial to be explicit about the purpose(s) of learning encounters which are designed to:

- deal with individual queries and problems encountered by students in working through the materials;
- help deepen the student's understanding of the topics covered in the materials (i.e., reinforcing learning);
- test knowledge and skills to check whether or not students have achieved the outcome;
- update issues covered in the learning resources particularly with respect to new ideas and recent developments;
- utilise and share the responses of students to the activities within the materials;
- counsel students;
- provide students with opportunities for utilising ideas and techniques from the materials, thereby developing their skills and competencies; and
- provide a forum within which the efficacy of the materials and the encounters can be evaluated.[8]

Self-instructional material would sustain the interest of learners, ensure quality and keep the learners absorbed in studies. Moreover, the self-instructional material would generate creativity among learners-an essential objective of higher education and would make them independent. This would also encourage them to make use of library and other electronic media. It is not easy to design self-instructional material. It requires hard work, knowledge of the subject matter as well as the art of designing self-instructional material. We have to arrange staff development programmes for this purpose. Besides, it should be a continuous exercise. If we examine the instructional materials of prestigious institutions, we do not find them perfect attempts—these are only partial efforts in the direction of self-instructional material.

(a) Strategies in Designing Lesson Units

(i) Splitting of the Course into Lesson Units Numbering between 20 to 30

The course is divided into lecture units in an intelligible fashion so that adequate attention may be paid to that portion thoroughly. This can be done either by the teacher teaching the course or by the group of teachers. It is important as the foundation is laid for the actual drawing up of a lesson unit in its logical sense.

(ii) Dovetailing of the Lesson Units in Blocks

Lecture scripts should appear to be integrated chain in the entire course especially the block. Block means grouping of lessons so that span of control becomes easy and this helps in sorting and mailing. It may be noted that each succeeding unit should be seen as a logical extension of the succeeding and preceding unit without being a part of it. It should have an independent existence of its own with backward and forward linkages.

(iii) Specifying the Objectives and Parameters of each Unit and Block

Since lecture scripts are to be written by different persons and not by the same person, therefore, there is a need to define parameters so that the writer can remain within the defined area and this can avoid duplication, overlapping and confusion. The writer can write the lecture script with clarity and can also provide the link to the entire block. It is suggested that efforts need to be made to get a single expert who can write the whole block so that continuity can be made and a compact block can be designed.

(iv) Identification of Script Writers Based on Experience, Qualifications and Aptitudes

There is a need to prepare a roaster of experts to get those lessons written. While selecting the writer care may be taken to select not only on the basis of qualifications but also on the time he can devote. We got some lessons written from eminent persons but they could not do justice for want of time.

(b) Stages and Steps in Writing a Lesson Unit (See Chart 4.1)

Let us now explain briefly the important stages of lesson writing.

(i) Pre-Planning

It means to take a decision before a line of action is taken instead of improving after the action has started. This involves a judicious selection of lesson writer based on academic excellence coupled with experience.

CHART 4.1

Work Model for the Preparation of Instructional Material (Lecture Scripts)

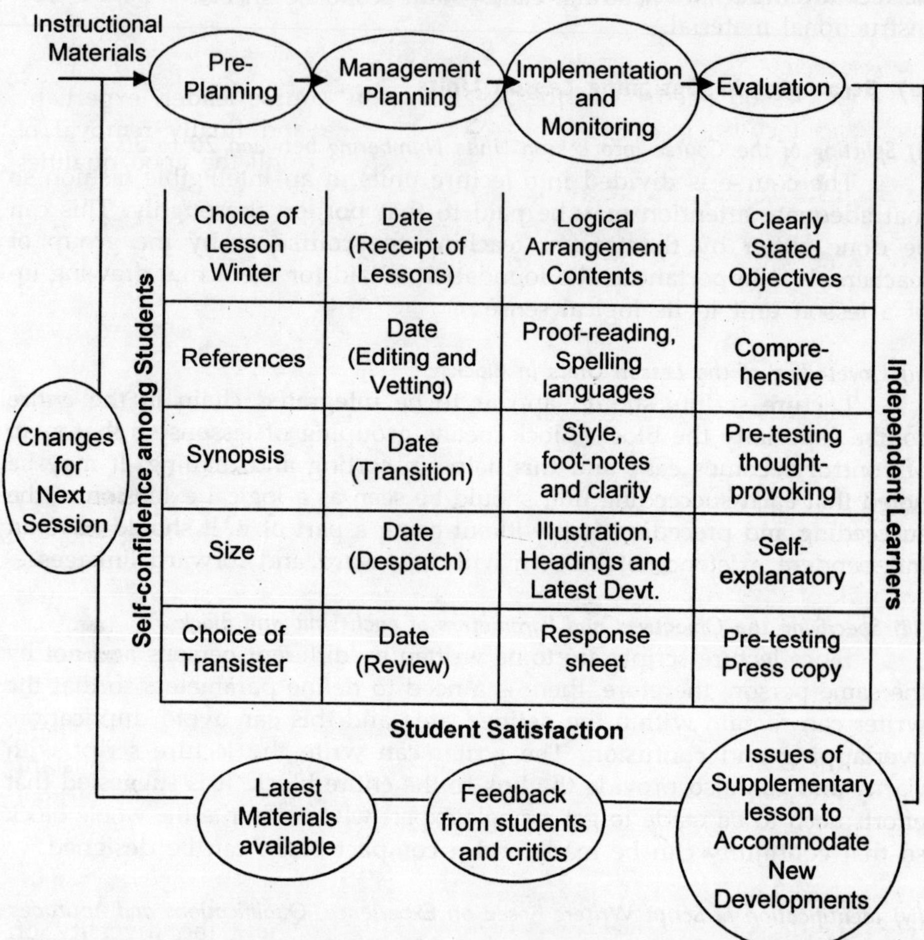

Those who are engaged in teaching or research in the area, would be more suitable and such selection would ensure availability. We may be careful to set our design concerning references, synopsis of the lesson unit, size of the lesson, faculty choice about the lesson and roll in plan to keep the lesson upto date. All these decisions may be taken before hand. We may also plan for translation if the lessons are to be supplied in more than one media.

(ii) Managerial Planning

These are to be decided before we act to ensure delivery in time. These includes fixing of dates for receipt, vetting, editing and despatch dates.

(iii) Implementation and Monitoring

We may now check the actual lesson script from the point of view of contents, style, time, footnotes, spelling, logical arrangement, language, illustration, uptodate, heading, clarity, and response sheets.

(iv) Evaluation

The lesson need be further evaluated by course leader, expert, by concerned faculty, pre-testing on some students and finally removal of queries by writer and editor. We must ensure here all the good qualities essential for self-instructional material.

(v) Press Copy

Based upon above, press copy need be prepared.

(vi) Printing and Mailing

Press copy may be printed into desired number of copies and mailed to students.

(vii) Supplementary Changes

If there is any change required later on, a supplementary lesson may be sent incorporating the changes. This may be followed by continuous feedback of PCP and whenever students come to meet you. The difficulties expressed by students may be taken care while printing for next year.

(c) Contents of Lesson Script

What points need to be kept in mind while writing a lesson? There are no set lines or guidelines which can direct our efforts. Our constant endeavour towards excellence can improve the quality of lessons. We may keep the following in view:

(i) Neither Over-Simplified nor Complicated

The lessons should be written keeping in view the diversity of clientele, i.e. difference in age, qualifications and environment. It should be written in a way that it can serve the purpose of this heterogeneity. We should neither write simply research-based or text book type material but we should present the material in a way which can be comprehended by all, i.e. neither too complex nor too simple.

(ii) Use of Illustrations

In order to make the students understand the lesson, there should be illustrations, references, cross-references, examples, tables, charts, graphs, etc. to make the lesson interesting. A good lesson should help and promote understanding and motivation rather than overwhelm the student by its enormity and volume.

(iii) Use of Simple and Clear Language

Language should be as clear and simple as possible. If technical words, phrases or other concepts are introduced, these may be defined to make better comprehension. The purpose is not to complicate the language but to understand the subject matter.

(iv) Contents

Contents must be clear. We must check whether any point has been missed or left so that it can be included.

(v) Editing and Vetting

Editing and vetting is very important to improve the quality of the lesson. Editing is not merely a technique of removing spelling and grammatical mistakes in a lesson rather its main thrust should be on the content of a lecture script. This is possible only if the vetter is expert in the area and takes pain in improving the lessons by incorporating the missing links and latest developments.

Vetters should be free to add or subtract from the lecture script to make the lecture script interesting.

(d) Aspects of Editing and Vetting

(i) Need of effective relationships' among different paragraphs.
(ii) The grammatical structure of each sentence.
(iii) Elimination of errors of spellings, punctuations, etc.
(iv) Harmonious linkages and tone throughout the script.
(v) Making sentences clear by removing vagueness.
(vi) Removing duplications and inconsistencies.

(e) Updating the Lesson

If the lesson is already written, there is a need of incorporating changes which have come after the lesson was written. UGC had suggested that steps should also be taken by the institutes to set-up review teams which should assess the lessons periodically taking into account the students assimilation on the basis of feed-back provided by them in the from of response sheets, etc. The review team should also ensure updating of the lesson content wherever necessary.

While it is necessary for lessons to be updated and given a new shape in every new session, the exigencies of the Indian academic climate, shortage of staff in the correspondence courses institutes, tightness of the printing and mailing schedule and a host of other allied constraints do not allow a major overhauling of each lesson. Only marginal vetting and correction of the previous year's misprints are done unless wholesale revision is necessary on account of a change in the syllabus of a particular subject. Even when syllabus or a part of it undergoes a change, mostly on account of academic reasons which govern the functioning of Boards of

Studies and Academic Councils in our universities, the lesson is not scrapped as a whole. New topics are written and added to the old material, taking due precaution that there should be no repetition or redundance. Further economy is effected in some subjects and lessons are printed in bulk for two or more years, and only the print-line and the year of print is rubber-stamped in the new session. This is indeed possible in case of English and Indian language courses where no change in syllabus and course of reading is stipulated for atleast three years.[9]

The Conference of the Directors of Correspondence Courses held at New Delhi in October 1974 recommended:

> "The correspondence courses institutes should get their old and newly written lesson, reviewed by competent reviewers and improve them in the light of suggestions made. But all lessons need not be reviewed. Only such lessons should be sent to the reviewers which in view of the concerned subject department in the institute need this exercise. The original writer should be requested to incorporate the suggestions of the reviewers without being paid any extra remunerations for this.

The UGC guidelines on the running of correspondence courses also require the lessons to be reviewed every alternate year. This is done in most of the cases by appointment of a panel of reviewers who are experts in the subject. A complete set of printed lessons is sent to this panel, the members of which are required to go through the lessons individually and then discuss their suggestions, separately, amongst one another and with the faculty members of the institute of correspondence education. The latter present their point of view which may be at variance with the suggestions of the reviewing panel, but finally the suggestions in the modified form are supposed to be incorporated in the lessons for the next session.

We may keep in mind that many Distance Education institutes have to supply lecture scripts in more than one media. For example, DCS, Panjab University, Chandigarh is supplying instructional material in English, Hindi and Punjabi. Now the question arises as to whether the instructional material should be written independently in all the languages or written in one language and later on translated. The weightage is in favour of translation because of: (i) uniformity of contents, (ii) cheaper, (iii) comparability, etc.

Rita Rani Paliwal in her article, "Translating Distance Teaching Materials" in the *Indian Journal of Open Learning* (Vol. I, No. 27, pp. 27-32) says:

> "The translation of distance teaching materials requires one to keep in mind the material to be translated is self-instructional. Not only does it have to fulfil all that is expected from a translation in general—to be faithful to the original, and to look like an original

piece in itself—but it should also serve as a companion to the learner in the process of learning. Care has to be taken to ensure that those students who study through a medium other than English are not deprived of even a fraction of the content which the English medium students receive. So the material prepared through translations should be communicative, informative, interesting and easy to comprehend. For this, it is necessary that the idiom of the language into which it is translated should be maintained without fail. A congenial atmoshphere to foster the culture of translation, which is obviously missing, needs to be created in the various fields of learning. Indian languages need to undertake the task of developing and enriching themselves in new discipline and areas of learning. If positive steps to achieve these objectives are taken, the translator's task would become smoother and comparatively easier.

FACTS AND SUGGESTIONS

Based upon personal experience and discussions with the students let us mention the major recommendations for improving the quality of lessons.

I Clear-cut Demarcations

A lesson should have a clearly demarcated parameter within which it must find a frame of reference for itself. A frame of reference would help the lesson writer to keep within clearcut limits and it would make his job easier and scientific. There should be no place for digressions, lengthy quotations and out of the way references not in tune with the lesson. Examples to illustrate points should be taken, as far as possible, from the text prescribed for the student's course of study. No lesson should normally draw upon non-textual sources for examples in the form of illustrating quotations at the undergraduate level. In social sciences, examples from daily papers may be used.

2. In Consonance with the Level of the Students

'Highbrow' lessons defeat their own purpose. A lesson should make the students curious to know more about the subject, instead of making him afraid of the enormity and intricacy of a topic. He should be motivated properly and guided step by step. The lesson-writer should keep in mind for whom he is writing, with what purpose and to what result. Though in distance education, there is too much heterogeneity among students but still the purpose of the topic can keep them together. The writer should ensure that all categories of students can take advantage out of it.

3. Manageable Length

A lesson, to be more 'acceptable' to the students should be of a manageable length, written in a lucid and easy style without being 'commercial' or 'cheap'. It should neither be unnecessary lengthy which may waste a lot of time of the students nor too short to make the students run after completing the gaps.

4. Pre-testing of Lesson

Though pre-testing of a lesson is quite desirable, under the existing circumstances, it is difficult to do so. However, individual teacher if he so desires, can pre-test a few lessons. We should depend more on feedback from the students for effecting improvement in various lessons at the time of PCP or the students visiting personally to sort out their difficulties.

5. Faculty Improvement Programme

There is a danger of the faculty becoming outdated since the faculty does not keep in touch with actual teaching. Correspondence teachers should be permitted to participate in the faculty improvement programme started by the UGC. Transfer of the teacher from the Directorate to the Departments in the University and, *vice versa* need be encouraged. Exchange programmes for correspondence teachers among different Directorates should be encouraged. Facilities for faculty seminars in the Directorate should be provided. Orientation programmes and workshops need to be organised for training teachers in writing/transforming course material lesson/units in the self-instructional distance education format, evaluation of students Response Sheets, Personal Contact Programmes. Such orientation programmes and workshops should become a regular in-house feature in all the Distance Education Institutes/Open University.

6. Division into Lesson Units Need be Logical

More flexibility should be given for dividing the syllabus into lecture units. At times, just to get the requisite number of units, a unitary topic is broken into two or more units, thus affecting the unitary character of the topic.

7. Pre-Planning

A right planning means more than half success. We should choose our lesson writer in advance carefully and design the parameters of the lesson carefully. The lesson writer must have good academic background coupled with experience. It is very essential in social sciences as their scope is expanding fast. Those writers who are in touch with the subject through teaching and research may be assigned such work. This would solve half of the problem.

In addition, if there were changes of a peculiar nature and it was necessary to update the material, the institute might issue supplementary instructional material to the students.

We can safely say that the course leader is the king-pin in the whole exercise of lesson writing. He knows best his students as he is experienced and has previous reactions of students in his mind. He can guide the lesson writer. In the end, he can fill in the gaps through the process of editing and vetting. The course leader, can put life into the lecture script through his knowledge and deep understanding of the clientele.

CONCLUSION

By far the most important medium in distance education is the printed word. This applies to conventional correspondence study as well as to highly sophisticated multi-media presentations like courses of an open university. Although the choice of media depends on the nature of subject-matter, print media has been found largely effective in each of the cognitive, affective and cognitive domains. In fact, a medium is just a support for course for course material in form of print. Care must always be taken that this existing and fundamental medium should not be overlooked. Research done in the area of 'learning from text' reveals that the written word is more effective in certain domains than the other. If the objective is cognitive, involving analysis as in philosophy, the printed word will probably be more effective.

Thus, it is evident that the logical structure of the written material and provision of opportunities for 'search' in it, contribute to the improvement of learning. Adroitly presented 'orienting instructions' also play an important role in disposing the reader to respond to certain aspects of text. General instructions to learn, advance organizers, various cueing strategies, questions and tutorial letters are some of the important categories of orienting directions. In order to make distance learning more lively and effective these strategies and 'aids to study' should be integrated into the learning material and study guides.[10]

However, in practice, we find that the quality of lecture scripts are highly unsatisfactory from majority of the distance education institutions. These scripts appear dull in getup and poor in contents. These scripts are the same for the last one or two decades without any change. Even the figures and facts about changing socio-economic phenomenon are not updated causing great harassment to students. Some institutes only complete the formalities of giving few pages in the name of the lecture script. There is a need and responsibility of Distance Education Council to enforce standards through its infrastructure. We talk of high technology without providing even the basic facilities, i.e. an excellent lecture script. A distance education institute should plan the use of electronic media only when it can meet the basic requirements. DEC may set-up a section which can review the lecture scripts of these institutes and help them in taking remedial measures. Until and unless DEC takes corrective steps, quality of distance education institutes and open universities may go down and bring bad name to the system.

Lecture script should be a reflection of the pooled wisdom and spirit of course faculty and support from available experts.

Notes and References

1. Satyapal Anand, University without Walls, New Delhi, Vikas, 1979, p. 76.
2. Rene F. Erdos; Teaching by Correspondence, UNESCO Source Book, Orient, Paris, 1957, p. 14.
3. Summary of the Observations of the UGC Sponsored Conference of Directors, New Delhi, 10-2 October, 1974, Stencil.
4. Quoted in V. Usha Sri, Implementing Instructional Design in B.Ed. courses in *Journal of Higher Education*, Vol. 19, No. 2, Summer 1996, New Delhi, UGC.
5. Derek Rowntree, Preparing Materials for Open, Distance and Flexible learning, Kogan Page Publishers, 1985, p. 4.
6. Professor Ram Takwale, Vice-Chancellor, IGNOU in Convocation Address of the Amravati University, *University News*, April 27, 1998. p. 13.
7. Vijaya Lakshmi Pandit, Development of Independent learners in Quality Assurance in *Distance Education*, M. Satya Narayan Rao (Ed.), Dr. Ambedkar Open University, Hyderabad, 1995, p. 162.
8. Peter L. Jennings and Roger Otter Walls, "Integrating Open learning with face-to-face tuition: Astrology for Competitive Advantage", p. 16.
9. Satyapal Anand, University without Walls, New Delhi, Vikas, 1979, p. 84.
10. Umrao Singh Chaudhari, "Distance Education and Print Media—Some Instructional Strategies", *University News*, Oct. 23, 2000.

Instructional Material: New Educational Technology

PART A

"Today success in the global market place means creating and applying new knowledge—which is to say new technology—faster than one's competitors. That is the fundamental law in this competitive world."[1]

(A) IMPORTANCE OF ELECTRONIC MEDIA

Until the invention of the electronic media-aids, the institutes of distance education the world over exclusively depended upon the printing press for providing instruction to their distantly located students. Such a mode of education is considered passive, devoid of interest and enthusiasm leading to bordom. It creates apathy and indifference in the minds of the learners. Realising the fact that Distance Education has come to stay in this country, there is hardly a need to elaborate its role. Instead, we look at the limitation of Distance Education, particularly with regard to the existing facilities to distant students. These may be spelled out, as under:

(a) A majority of students do not attend Personal Contact Programmes organised for them, the reasons being:
  - (i) Long distance between their homes and the institute;
  - (ii) Non-availability of leave from offices;
  - (iii) Unsuitability of programmes;
  - (iv) Inability to complete the whole course of study even in a capsuled form in the short duration of the PCP programme;
  - (v) Unsuitability of the programme-hours (these generally are held in the late afternoon by which time the students get completely exhausted in their offices and other work places); and
  - (vi) Monotonous nature of the programmes.

(b) The limited range of radio stations from where broadcasts are made and consequent inability of the students to listen to the talks properly.
(c) Isolation-lack of company of students which motivate learning.
(d) No guidance, persuasion, coercion to study independently.
(e) Lack of confidence, enthusiasm, etc.

Thus, there is a need for taking the help of new technologies that are available in this modern age so that Instruction through, distance education are made more effective and the limitations mentioned above can be overcome.

Ram Takwale, ex-Vice-Chancellor, IGNOU has rightly stressed in his article "IGNOU's Challenges of Quality, Quantity and Equity" in *University News* (May 27, 1996). He rightly says [Modern Communication Technologies (CTs)] are costlier and may not be available and accessible in rural and hilly areas and to poorer people. However, with a little political will and appropriate national policies, communication, technologies have a great capability to reach the unreached and to bridge the gap of disparities. The process of education with a conventional approach of dominantly of a "diffusion" or "cascading nature", with best educational facilities being available at metropolitan cities and lesser and poorer facilities available in towns, districts, blocks, and, villages, in the order.

Now with the employment of CTs, the best expertise and learning facilities could be made accessible and available to all the disadvantaged learners where-ever they might be located.[2]

K.K. Bajaj in his Article "Student Support Services for Interactive Communication in Distance Education" rightly foresees the future. To quote him: 'There is no doubt that the self-instructional printed lessons are the foundation of any academic course to sustain it but the quality, comprehensiveness level, context, applicability and outreach of the printed material are now a matter of greater concern to our distance education management effort. While the distance education institutions have been thriving on the unidirectional supply and flow of information to students through printed lessons because of the small reach of technology in India "yet in the time to come the demands and requirements of students will necessitate a complete conceptual and practical overhaul in its delivery system and call for a more articulate and systematic, contextually relevant student focused support system to supplement the quality and context of such courses."[3]

(B) MEANING

"Modern Science and Technology have placed at the disposal of the educators and learners a variety of electronic based instructional aids. These have a highly significant role to play for a developing country like that of ours in reaching out to the distant students. These can further be helpful in improving the quality of instruction both in the classroom and in distance teaching." Communication media and technology is the application of modern techniques and resources to meet educational needs of the learners to adjust according to their environment to make subject matter more comprehensible, attractive and at the same time ensure the retention factor.

It is a systematic way of designing, implementing and evaluating the total process of learning and teaching in terms of specified objectives based on research in human learning and communication and employing a combination of human and non-human resources to bring about effective instruction. Its primary role is to increase the efficiency and effectiveness of the entire teaching-learning process through a systems approach putting to use modern communication technologies and the media."[4] The main aim of new technology based on electronic media is to supplement the instructional material with electronic media to keep the learners motivated, well informed and move towards self-learning practices which would make him slowly and slowly into an independent learner.[5]

Modern technology has the potentiality to make available to the distant learners the knowledge and study material in a comprehensive and intelligible manner. It is the capacity and capability of distant learner to select the matter that suits him and appear interesting to him. The responsibility of the Distance Education institutes is to guide the distant learners in the choice of new technology and how to operate it. However, at present, even the faculty of distance education is not making use of this technology in preparing instructional material.

(C) HISTORICAL DEVELOPMENT

With the coming in of the radio, Distance Education institutes began to supplement their printed lessons with radio scripts. The combination of the old and the new mediums brought about a good deal of qualitative improvement in the whole concept and methodology of distance teaching. Though radio could only establish an impersonal contact between the teacher and the taught and that too one-sided, yet the students were able to listen to the live voice of their teachers. That gave them a considerable amount of psychological satisfaction. As a result, their reservations against this system were mitigated to some extent. It stirred their feelings and created interest in them.

Then came the invention of television which caused the beginning of the second phase in the use of electronic aids in the field of distance education. With the help of Television, the students were now in a position not only to hear the voice of their teachers but could also see them in action. In other words, the actual scene of the class-room could now be demonstrated on the TV screen. Invention of the video stimulated the potential and popularity of these modern technologies. The developed countries which had plenty of resources with them adopted . . . in a big way to educate their students. Highlighting the popularity of television, one study discloses that in 1978-79, more than 1800 colleges and universities were using television, and almost half a million students were enrolled in 6884 television courses.[6] Another study reports that in 1979, 71 per cent of colleges and universities in the U.S.A. used television instruction. "Many of these instructions used closed circuits on-campus television, but open broadcasting has been a leading vehicle for reaching the off-campus students."[7]

Summing up the importance of television in distance education, Marian Craft observes: "New emerging technologies such as TELIDON, direct broadcast satellites, NABU and video disc will all have significant impact on the field. Several ongoing community-based experiments in interactive video, like QUBE in Columbus, Chio and Hi-OVIS in Japan have illustrated the outstanding potential of television as a tool to provide increased opportunities for lifelong learning."[8]

Therefore, opportunities have to be extended to all. With the explosion of knowledge there also arises the need to introduce innovations in both teaching and learning. "Modern communication technologies have the potential to by-pass several stages and sequences in the process of development encounter in earlier decades. Both the constraints of time and distance at once become manageable. In order to avoid structural dualism, modern educational technology must reach out to the most distant areas and the most deprived sections of beneficiaries, simultaneously with the areas of comparative affluence and ready availability."[9]

In Australia and a few other countries, the distance educators have also been using telephone to impart their instructional programmes. But it has not been able to replace audio and video cassettes. It is employed largely in such distance teaching programmes as have smaller number of students.

At present, the use of these electronic aids in developed countries has been switching to its third phase. However, it does not mean that these two media have now been totally removed. Instead, the distance educators make a simultaneous use of all the available media, and have thus adopted a multi-media approach. They combine the print and the post with radio broadcasting, television, audio and video cassettes, video discs, and telephone, thereby making an effort to overcome the obstacles of distance education which have thus far been standing in the way of this system. This multi-media approach has been quite successful.

A number of universities and colleges in the advanced countries have adopted this approach. The important among them are: the British Open University (it has been delivering multi-media non-traditional study programme since 1971), the National Open University, Vanezuela and the Open University of Maryland (U.S.A.).

The situation in the developing countries is, however, saddening and handicapped in various ways as the institutes of distance education of these countries still depend on the printed lessons. Wherever radio/

television network is available, they try to get time from them. Radio-broadcasting has of late begun to catch, the imagination of distance educators and they are now making an increasing use of it. Television and video technologies, by and large, are inaccessible to them. As far as telephone is concerned, it is a facility, available only to the elite sections of society. The question of their having been put to the use of distance education does not, therefore, arise at all.

(D) EDUCATIONAL TECHNOLOGY IN DISTANCE EDUCATION IN INDIA

India has its own communication satellite in space and a large network for radio and television broadcasts having potential to produce educational programmes. Making best use of the existing facilities to a large number of people can be brought into the fold of education and teaching-learning process therein can be optimised. Let us discuss the types of technology and their utility.

(i) Radio

It was in the year 1932 when AIR started broadcast for education. Radio is used as an indispensable components of multi-media as it is within the reach of common man and can be transported easily. It is being still preferred by most countries of the world in their multi-media package. The number of users of a radio broadcast may range from those within the radius of a few kilometers in the case of FM transmission to several millions in the case of national broadcasting. Educational broadcasts is a part of the programmes of several AIR stations. For example, AIR Jullundur broadcast daily for Distance Education students of Northern India. On personal discussion with the students registered for studies through distance education in Panjab University, Chandigarh, it was revealed that most of them do not find time to listen to these broadcasts. Some mentioned that the scheduled time is not free with them. Some informed that some isolated talks in a course do not serve any purpose and even the talks are not interesting and well prepared. In developed countries, Radio is rarely used as a medium of instruction because of its inherent limitations. However in developing countries, Radio can be used as an educational media through proper planning. Largely, the radio broadcasts are for listening at the time it is broadcast or recorded tapes can be stored in the library for the students to refer at a later stage.

However, distance education institutes in India are not taking radio broadcasts seriously. Faculty members do not take interest in preparing radio talks. It is generally speaking only what is written in lecture script. Students are not, therefore, interested in such programmes in India.

(ii) Television

TV is very effective medium as it is highly expressive and powerful.

TV broadcasting is an important component in the open universities especially IGNOU. Directorate of Correspondence Courses, Kurukshetra University has entered into an agreement with Zee-Education (ZEE TV) for its educational programmes. This is proving to be a great success. With the acquisition of its production technology and falling prices, home receiving sets of TV broadcast are now available in large number of Indian households and the number is increasing day by day especially in the urban areas. The specific value of TV broadcast will vary according to the context in which it is used. But there is no doubt that it can provide distance learners with unique resource material. Demonstration of complex or expensive experiments, field visits, advanced technical equipments, industrial techniques, social and interpersonal interaction are just some of the experiences that can be offered to students in their own homes through broadcast television.

Television programmes have their strength in generating, stimulating thinking. C.V. Ranga Rao in his article, "Reaching the Unreached-Experience of an Open University" in *University News*, Oct. 18, 1999 rightly says that Audio-visual media in general and Television in particular is extremely rich and expressive in its nature. Television programmes can attract the attention of students because moving pictures make the learning process lively and enthuse the learner's imagination. Further, moving pictures present few problems of understanding too. Television programmes are particularly useful explaining past events, exotic places or other things that can be seen. It can show objects, that are too small to see with the naked eye. Thus, these programmes can be an invaluable aid for the students to understand their subjects. However, in developing countries like India, these are still costly and there is lack of adequate software. It is very difficult to reach the rural people. UGC is doing a good service in this area.

K.B. Powar has some genuine reservations. To quote him: "the mere existence of a technology in a country is not enough. It is difficult to use the technology for distance education unless it is integrated in the life style of the public at large. Even in advanced countries like the United States, Japan, U.K., and France the promises held out by the TV and Computer technologies have not been fulfilled (S.M. Pottiez, Distance Education and the New Technologies, 1994). TV Broadcast is often presented as having vast possibilities; even as a panacea for problem relating to mass education and training. The accumulating evidence allover the world, however, suggests that one way broadcast television is one of the least effective media of learning, though it is useful for raising awareness and spreading information."[10] Indian Programmes for distant learners are not tailor made to meet the requirements of their study. These programmes are generally based on foreign models which do not suit the requirements of students and hence they do not feel interested, rather some of them say that this is a wastage of time and money. Hence, there is a need of serious efforts to make the programme useful and interesting. This should not be like a movie for entertainment, rather, its focus should be instructional, educative and interest generating.

Jagannath Mohanty and Susandhya Mohanty in their Article, "IGNOU Educational Television Programmes: An Appraisal" concluded that an Educational Programme on TV without objectives is like a letter without address. They found that knowledge objectives was given more emphasis in 100 per cent of the programmes, whereas due importance was not given to other objectives like application and understanding. They suggested that the instructional objectives like understanding, application and skills should be given more emphasis while producing the programme. Besides, various formats, particularly dramatisation, role playing, etc. need be used in more programmes.[11] TV is still used in a big way in UK, China, Thailand and Japan and other countries for their distant students. Their programmes are well planned and meet the needs of the learners. However in our country, there are number of problems.

(a) Programmes are not well prepared;
(b) Programmes may be little bit entertaining but have not much, thrust on educational contents;
(c) Timings are not suitable;
(d) Most of the students cannot afford TV especially Cable TV;
(e) In most of the places electricity remains off for most of the time; and
(f) Students prefer to have good instructional material rather than watch TV programmes.

(iii) Audio-Cassette

These are cassette already stored with the required information. Most of Distance Education Institutes have a library where these cassettes are made available. These can be used again and again through duplication. However, there are many problems like lack of continuity, limited coverage, uninteresting voice of the speaker, etc. DEC can create a cell where these cassettes can be stored and sold to other distance education institutes, thus providing mobility and networking. There is little progress so far in this direction in India except by some elite open universities.

(iv) Video Cassette

Video cassette is more recent and an evolving educational medium. Video-cassettes are like broadcast television in the sense that they combine moving pictures with sound. These are still very costly and programmmes recorded do not meet the requirements of the students.

(v) Computer

Computer provides personalised education service to learners as he can take the advantage of the huge material stored in it. Sitting at home, he can screen the material available in the computer. Personalised computer can make the learner learn at his convenience with latest material. However, till now, it is not possible for an average Indian student.

(vi) Satellite

Satellite provides abundant potentialities and can help the distant learners sitting in any remote areas. Telephone and Teleconferencing are some of its manifestations Teleconferencing is just like a class room where students interact with the faculty face to face. However, it provides unnatural environment and not a class room like environment. Some reservations come when students and experts feel that they are being watched thus creating an artificial environment.

We have discussed the different media available for imparting education to distant learners. Which is the best? Which would be more suitable? The decision would depend upon the need, resources, circumstances and availability of trained personnel in a particular distant education institute. Therefore, we have to depend on a media-mix to suit the requirements. Blend of media in right direction would give maximum benefits to the students.

Tele-education Delivery System

Dr. A.P.J. Abdulkalam narrates his personal experience. To quote him: I would like to narrate my experience in the development of a Tele-education delivery system. I had a dream; a good mathematics teacher teaching mathematics in a remote village in West Bengal should be able to teach a number of schools located in different parts of the country including Konkan villages in Maharashtra, interact with the students in sequence and be able to clarify the doubts. Also the teacher must be able to draw the knowledge from various sources, such as internet, digital library, generated creative content and the lectures given by various experts in the same field and deliver to all the students as if they were in the same simulated class room in a cost effective manner. Such a system has been implemented in Rashtrapati Bhavan.

Characteristics of System

This universal tele-education delivery system works via heterogeneous network platform through IP protocol. It provides virtual classroom in a multi-class and studio environment with seamless two-way interaction between the teachers and students in a collaborative framework. It provides seamless, one-to-one, one-to-many connectivity, through the broadcasting network in a multi-casting mode of delivery. It seamlessly enables a remote teacher to become a teacher to all the students in a session. Unlike the other video conferencing system and multimedia tools currently in use for tele-education purposes, this Interactive Universal Tele-education delivery system creates a virtual classroom. It enables the teacher to take the student on a live virtual tour of the subject.

This provides a cost effective solution for interactive content delivery. On a comparative basis we can create 250 nodes tele-education system for interactive delivery at a cost of establishing four multi-station video conferencing systems.

IGNOU had started its Training and Development Communication Channel (TDCC), in 1993, with collaboration and support of ISRO. Every year, nearly more than 500 hours of tele-conferencing activities have been conducted through this one-way video and two-way audio satellite based channel. On the Republic Day of the year 2000, the Gyan Darshan—Educational Channel of India—was started, with IGNOU as the nodal agency. The purpose of conducting tele-conferencing through TDCC and Gyan Darshan are:

- Tele-counselling with learner groups.
- Extended Contact Programmes (ECP) with learners.
- Training of Study Centre Counsellors and Coordinators.
- Administrative interaction with Regional Centre functionaries.

As an academic support service, IGNOU providers two-way audio and one-way video communication channel for live and interactive tele-counselling sessions through Satellite Communication technique. In a Face-to-Face (F-2-F) classroom teaching-learning situation, the transactional distance between the teacher and learner is just negligible due to their close proximity with respect to physical distance too. Although the academic resource person is delivering his/her inputs from a remote teaching end, as far as physical distance is concerned, the learner at the receiving node feels as close as F-2-F environment. The 2-way telephonic live and real-time interactive process diminishes the real distance and creates a negligible virtual distance due to the easy accessibility. In other words, the tele-education is at a call (telephone call) distance only. The technology shrinked the physical distance between the Distance Tutor and Distance Learner, with no delay response.

The distance between the Distance Learner and Distance Tutor is technically reduced to just a hand distance that is, the distance between "ear phone" and "mike" in a telephone handset: Due to which, 40% of tele-counselling time has been devoted to presentation and 60% to discussion arising out of telephonic/fax interaction (Sanjay, 1999).

By providing a "Tell-Free" number, the receiver will make payment for calls received for academic interaction purpose, exclusively to have live interaction with resource person at IGNOU studio, New Delhi. With this facility, the learners are motivated further for interaction. At present, the toll-free number for Tele-Counselling is available at 80 Cities in the country.

With the support of Tele-Counselling channel, IGNOU organizes Extended Contact Programmes for Post Graduate Diploma in Higher Education learners. During the 10 days long ECP, the tele-counselling mode provides 40% of input and remaining portion is conducted at local level. Similarly, for Information Technology programmes (ADIT), the tele-counselling provides a regular academic support on weekly basis, besides local F-2-F; counselling sessions; Once again, with technology merger, it proves to be a mode of Distance Education at Call Distance. An empirical analysis of Tele-counselling is presented in terms of interactive component.

PART B

IGNOU'S PERSPECTIVE

(a) IGNOU has suggested the following in its document vision about the future thrust on new technology:

(i) Promote the use of educational technology to support students, and develop resource centres and multi-media learning centres throughout the country.
(ii) Develop and evaluate strategies for large scale applications of audio-visual, computing and multi-media material in teaching-learning processes.
(iii) Consider, in collaboration with the concerned national agencies, the close involvement of the national networks of telecasting, broadcasting and computer communication for learning purposes.
(iv) Explore the possibility of launching distance education networks, knowledge networks, multi-media learning networks, digital library networks, open education networks, etc.
(v) Complete transformation of all programmes of correspondence education into distance education programmes and ensuring their compatibility with new delivery technologies."[12]

Policies about new technology mentioned in the Document vision are not practical. What is required is to make use of that technology which can be used by all the learners. The emphasis must be on use and applicability and not only on accessibility and availability. IGNOU should make the best use of its resources to benefit poor distant learners and not always planning to have higher jumps on new technology, which may be first rate from all angles but till the students can be benefitted out of it, we should not flaunder our resources on such technology.

Dr. Murli Manohar Joshi, former HRD Minister in his convocation address at IIT Bombay informed that an operation knowledge will see the installation of computers with internet access in every school, University and public hospital by 2003, networking of all centres of higher education, spread distance education and making it compulsory for all degree courses."[13]

Anand P. Srivastava has urged the need of digital technology in higher education. To quote him:

> "Higher education is bound to go for the unavoidable shift from the culture of print to a culture of digital technology, which affects not only teaching, learning and research but the whole of university life."[14]

S.K. Gandhi has rightly suggested the need of new technology; "Electronic-based technologies will dominate the education scenario in the developed countries. We have also noted some of the limiting factors in their wide-spread use in the less developed countries. The need of the 21st century will be to exploit the information highways to the fullest possible extent. Economic development will depend to a large extent on creating and optimal use of the technological infrastructure. Countries which would harness the power of multi-media communication for education and training purposes will be the economic powers of the next century."[15]

A great success story in this connection is the "UGC country-wide class room" which was started in 1984 for tertiary level education covering all discipline—arts, pure sciences, management, social sciences, and applied sciences. Educational Programmes are produced in 17 media centres set-up by UGC (7 educational media Research Centres and 10 Audio Visual Research Centres). These are being transmitted by the Doordarshan. A list of institutions having Educational Media Research Centres (EMRCs) and Audio Visual Research Centres (AVRCs) is given below:

EMRCs

1. Jamia Millia Islamia, New Delhi.
2. University of Pune, Pune.
3. Central Institute of English and Foreign Languages, Hyderabad.
4. Gujarat University, Ahmedabad.
5. St. Xavier's College, Calcutta.
6. Jai Narain Vyas University, Jodhpur.
7. Maduari Kamaraj University, Madurai.

AVRCs

1. Osmania University, Hyderabad.
2. Roorkee University, Roorkee.
3. Anna University, Madras.
4. Manipur University, Imphal.
5. Devi Ahilya Vishwavidyalaya, Indore.
6. Punjabi Univesity, Patiala.
7. Kashmir University, Srinagar.
8. Dr. Hari Singh Gour Vishwavidyalaya, Sagar.
9. Mysore University, Mysore.
10. Calicut University, Calicut.

Presently, about 85 per cent of the programmes transmitted on TV are produced indigenously. These cassettes are viewed not only by students but by others concerned as well. These have been designed very nicely and perfectly.

(b) UGC Perspectives on Communication technologies and their impact- UGC has identified the role of communication technologies under the following categories: (See Chart 5.1)

"Mass communication and personalised communication technologies available at present, and in the near future, are offering increasingly intimate facilities of interactivity through text, voice images and data communications. Existing and future technologies are of three types:

CHART 5.1

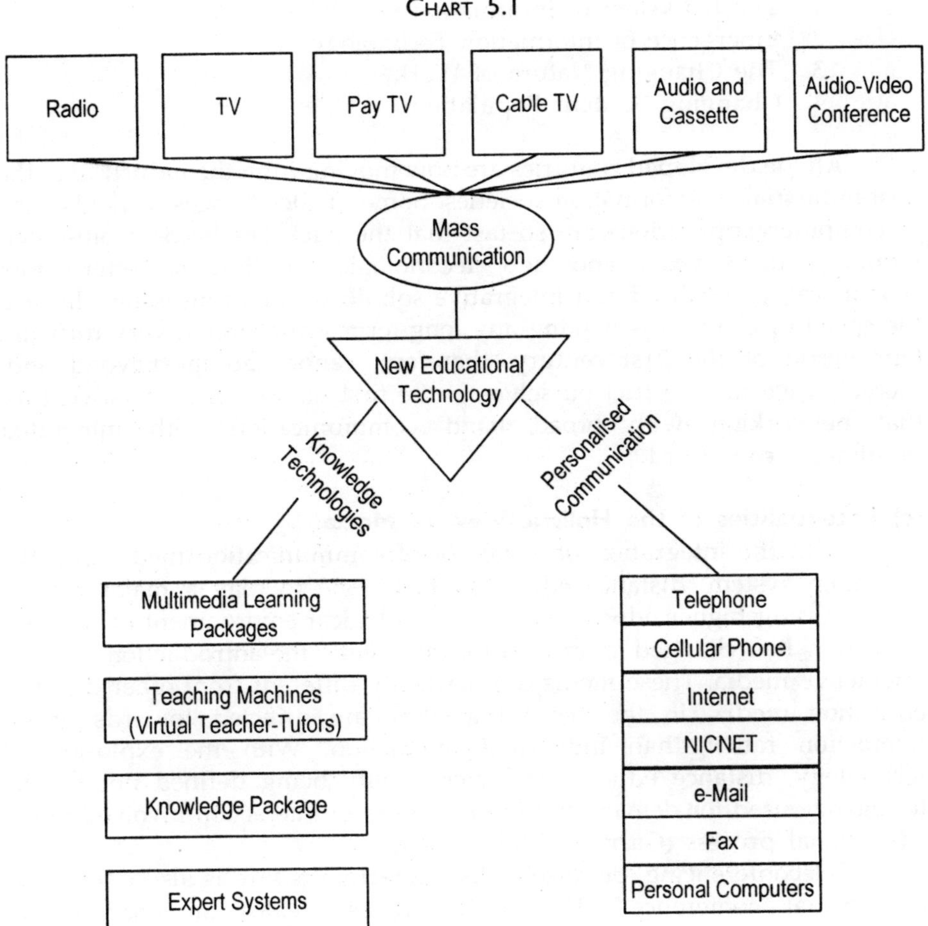

(a) Mass communication type: This category includes radio and TV broadcast, pay TV, Cable TV, audio and video cassettes, audio and video teleconferencing.

(b) Personalised communication technologies, such as telephone, cellular phone; INTERNET, NICNET, mail, fax and personal computers.

(c) Knowledge technologies developed by using artificial intelligence, such as expert systems, multi-media (integrated media) learning packages, teaching machines (virtual teacher/tutor), and knowledge packages.

While considering the educational paradigm shift, the Report of the Task Force of International Council on Distance Education (1996) identifies four major factors as drivers of educational change:

1. The Explosion of Information
2. Emergence of Information Technology
3. The Changing Nature of Work
4. Changing Student Population

All the developed countries are now moving from the industrial to the post-industrial or information societies. Some of the changes in fields such as computer applications are so fast that the packages become out-dated within 2 to 3 years and new technologies/applications offer more economical, generalised and integrative solutions to current issues. In fact, the speed of changes is making any long-term visualization very difficult. Our vision of the 21st century, therefore, cannot go far beyond and, therefore, we may restrict ourselves to the first quarter of the 21st century that networking with broad band communication with integrated multimedia can afford.[16]

(c) Potentialities of the Holistic View of Media

With the integration of a variety of communication media into the education system, distance education has come to play a major role in universalising higher education. The technological environment of distance education has changed more significantly with the introduction of live, interactive media. These media are markedly different from other distance education media, in the sense that they are directed towards group interaction rather than individual interaction. With the explosion of technology, distance education is increasingly being defined not by the technology used for delivery but by the nature of interaction involved in the educational process (Garry E. Miller, 1994).

Teleconferencing, because of its interactive nature is also referred to as "virtual conference." Virtual conference creates an analogue of communication forms that typically occur in a face-to-face conference, including paper presentation, discussion, moderation, questioning and answering, etc.[17]

IGNOU has been using Interactive E TV for its students and counsellors. Many experiments have been conducted to experiment the utility of these interactive technologies like CEC-ISRO-UGC-IGNOU Teleconference (Dec. 1524, 1994), NOS, DECU-ISRO Talk back Experiment, (Dec. 17, 19, 1996), etc. Based upon these experiment D.R. Goel and D.

Sarang made the following observations which need analysis. To quote them:

(i) The technical, instructional, economic feasibility, legal viability and social acceptability was established and it proved the operational possibilities of an interactive Distance Education system.
(ii) Potency of teleconferencing as an instructional tool in direct classroom, enrichment education and professional training was realized through the experiments.
(iii) In most cases technical coordination among the technologists and pedagogists was very successful.
(iv) Except in few cases of improper use of media-materials due to technology unfamiliarity on part of the academicians and learners, occasional technological shortcomings and personnel management, the experiments were successful in preparing for the operational level.[18]

However, it may be added that its large scale use needs caution, advance preparation and financial resources availability, pooling of resources, understanding the environment of the country, and the needs of the learners.

An Indian distant learner is not studying to enhance his ability, capacity and expertise in a particular area. His interest is to earn degrees to get a good job. So, he pursues one course after another without having any direction. In such a situation, the technology cannot help. Distance Education Institutes can ascertain the interest of the students and make admissions accordingly. In such a situation, new technology can have a thrust only if we keep the objectives of learners in our mind.

(d) Use of New Technology in Training

Training in Government, Banking, public sector undertakings, multi-nationals is becoming necessary because of the fast changes in the environment, technology, procedures, etc. but is becoming difficult due to shortage of funds, availability of expertise, infrastructure, etc. Earnest Dale and L.C. Michelon rightly sense that today's manager lives in a world of rapid change, yet the rate of change is likely to increase in the years ahead. Unless he can keep up with this change, he is likely to find himself obsolete perhaps unpromotable or even unemployable."[19] All agree that right training aims at an action process by which capabilities of the personnel can be improved to meet the organisational needs in terms of their knowledge, skills, and attitudes required in performing organisational tasks and functions within relatively short period of time. To come over this new challenge, training through distances education with new technology can be achieved with great success.

Conventional classroom training is considered to be too slow and inefficient to keep pace with change. Moreover, administrative hurdles, which include setting up infrastructure and finding tutors, have stymied the growth further. Traditional distance education modes like postal coaching have also failed, as these are non-interactive.

Front-running global corporates have now opted for interactive Distance Learning. A notable exponent of distance learning tools is Ford Motor's Fordstar Network, a VSAT-based satellite system connecting 6,000 dealerships around USA for providing a range of information from repair updates to technicians to product information for sales people. This system overcomes time and distance, turning any enterprise network-satellite or Internet into a powerful, interactive learning resource, incremental cost of setting up a new centre is low once the investment on the uplinking the network hub is made.[20]

Mr. Ranganath Misra, former Chairman National Human Rights Commission in his convocation address at the Seventh Convocation of the IGNOU in New Delhi rightly mentioned the need of distance education in industry (*University News*, May 27, 1996). To quote him: To attain global and national competitiveness, industry and business needed a workforce with the latest knowledge and skill. Distance education offered a unique possibility to the adult learners in the workforce to meet this challenge. Industry and business, which would benefit from this enterprise, must fulfil their responsibilities, academically and financially. "The marriage of distance education and continuing engineering education has many benefits to confer on both systems", he said. However, it may be added that its large scale use needs, caution, advance preparation, financial resources availability, pooling of resources, understanding the environment of the country and the needs of the learners

Dr. M.N. Kulkarni, Programme Officer, UNICEF, Chandigarh in his article, "Communication for Social Development: Some Issue" has rightly issued warning to those who are in a great hurry to use new technology at any cost which is highly damaging. To quote him:

> "Mass media can play an effective role in human development programme, provided the software experts understand the vast millions who are caught in poverty situations, who have no time to listen to Radio or can afford to see TV in their life time. In the words of Peter Drucker, "It is the recipient who communicates. The so-called communicator, the person who limits the communication does not communicate. He or she utters. Unless there is so new one who hears, there is no communication. There is only noise."[21]

R.S. Mahajan and P.K. Rangole in their paper "Training and Technology Absorption for Developing Country" maintained that Planning, designing and implementation of specific Programmes of studies need to take into account cultural, habitual and economic constraints and incidental and environmental excellences. Besides we should take planning of specialized studies with due regard to national priorities and requirements of human resource on short-term and long-term basis. [22]

Thus, there is a need today for designing self-learning packages. A self-learning package is a document containing all that is necessary for a student to attain one or more educational objectives independently of the teacher. Using these packages, a student can cover a large part of his education while the teacher remains available only when needed.

PART C

(a) Introduction

The technology scene seems to be exploding, and the result, instead of desired improvements in productivity, seems to be confusion. What they are often not prepared for are the overwhelming managerial problems involved in the implementation of these new technologies. There is an urgent need to re-orient the system of management to cope with changes in technology and social behaviour and maximise opportunity for improving quantity and quality of education. By goals or objectives is meant the end towards which action is directed. Since a policy is a guidance for action it is reasonable to expect that a policy indicates the direction towards which action is guided either explicitly or implicitly. Before taking advantage of new technologies based on electronics for supplementing and improving the educational system, we may keep the following administrative implications in mind to optimise the use of such costly devices otherwise all our resources would be wasted.

(b) Spelling out clear-cut Objectives about New Technology

Before we introduce any modern technology for the Students of DE System, we must first define the objectives or purposes of our endeavour. We should adopt a definite criteria before using any technology otherwise our whole exercise can be a futility.

Though the spelling out of educational objectives has become almost a fashionable subject of conversation defining them is becoming a mark of modernity through the spelling out of educational objectives there is a danger that we may get used to them without understanding their purpose, their nature, their advantage, their limitations and the risks involved in them. In drawing up educational objectives, what counts is not their formal definition but their relevance to the professional task of the personnel to be educated. Hence, there is a need to state in clear terms the objectives of the use of the modern technology particularly with regard to: (a) whether the subject covered is of independent nature and can be grasped thoroughly without any extra reading, (b) is it in the nature of a supplementary and, i.e. to add to the already provided literature, (c) the boundaries of the subject to be covered, (d) clientele for which it is intended, (e) extent of better understanding that it would generate than the written material, and (f) temporal dimension, i.e. the time upto which this would be relevant, etc. All these issues must be critically examined.

(c) Policy-making and Planning about New Technology

Policies may be thought of as the main system which provides the framework for the accomplishment of intended objectives. It involves making explicit the various assumptions which are made with respect to the basic premises and the priorities of needs and allocating the finances accordingly. In this context, the following policy issues need to be thrashed:

(a) Whether each university would develop its own communication technology or the resources of all universities in India can be pooled together. I think that there should be centralisation of policy-making in the context of educational technology. Production of cassettes etc. may be distributed among various institutes according to some criteria. This would reduce duplication and save a huge cost of production.

(b) There is a need to define the areas in each subject which can be best taught through this technology.

(c) Appointing the team of experts for writing and production of the material through this new technology from within and outside the Institutes. Thus planning is in essence, an organised, conscious and continual attempt to select the best available technology to achieve specific goals, i.e. to meet the needs of the students.

(d) Good Organisation to Deliver the Benefits of New Technology

Most of the new ventures in DE institutes in developing countries including India are started with great enthusiasm but these schemes do not operate regularly and the resources employed are generally wasted. No administrative performance is possible without a suitable organisation. According to Simon, organisation is a planned system of cooperative effort in which each participant has a recognized role to play and duties and tasks to perform. The key to the whole process is effective cooperation among the persons engaged in the operation. In this context, the following issues need to be examined:

(a) availability of space;
(b) appointment of competent people;
(c) purchase of best equipment;
(d) expertise to repair the apparatus;
(e) relationships of the staff with the chief executive;
(f) awareness to make use of the resources by students and teachers;
(g) availability of recurring budget; and
(h) training to the staff in fast changing technology.

An analysis of the working of EMRC in DE System reveals that many institutions have failed to utilise properly all the equipments at their disposal because of the lack of availability of all the inputs. It means that either we should provide all the inputs or may not provide at all to any DE Institute.

(e) Evaluation of the Programme of New Technology

Evaluation is a continuous process based upon criteria, cooperatively developed, concerning such aspects as the measurement of performance of learners, the effectiveness of teachers and the quality of the programmes. We should devise in advance the tools that would be used for getting the feedback from the users about the utility of the new technology as the ultimate purpose of this technology would be the injection of better learning through it.

(f) Coordination with Mass Media

These institutes must establish active liaison with mass media as this would facilitate the use of the latter for the benefit of the students. The material thus produced can be telecast.

Some of the administrative issues have been mentioned here. We must be clear that without proper planning of the details of implementation, we would not be able to transmit the benefits of this technology to the students programmes fail in the developing countries not because of resources, financial or technical, but because of the poor implementation machinery.

(g) Need of Creating Awareness

It is very difficult for the distance education students to locate the information. There is a need of some training to them. To quote Sanjay Mishra:

"With the proliferation of information technology and electronic access to information, the availability and accessibility of information has undergone profound changes. Though print still forms the common learning materials for distance learners, because of the E-mail, Internet, World Wide Web (WWW) and easy access to remote data bases, they now have new opportunities to find information at the press of a computer key. But distance learners shall have to be taught the skills associated with information literacy to help them use information judiciously and become deep learners. Let me conclude with a Chinese proverb.

If you give a man a fish;
He will have a single meal;
If you teach him how to fish;
He will eat all his life.[23]

While technology opens the doors it does not compel us to enter. We cannot use technology just for the sheer pleasure of it. Before embarking upon any new technology a number of criteria must be given due consideration.

They are:

(1) *Availability*: The technology must be well established in the local environment.
(2) *Accessibility*: Ideally the chosen technology must be available to all the students or at least in the study centres.
(3) *Acceptability*: The attitude of the teachers and students must be favourably disposed towards the technology.
(4) *Validity*: It must be appropriate to the instructional objectives and contents that constitute the courses.
(5) *Economics*: The results must justify the cost incurred.

No one technology can satisfy all the criteria mentioned nor all the developmental needs of the Indian Distance Education.[24] We may add to this list some more criteria, i.e. Quality, Specificity, and Sensitivity.

PART D

(a) Research Study: Students' Responses to Radio Broadcasts

The authors interviewed 100 undergraduate students of DCS, P.U., Chandigarh based on the following questions (Refer Table 5.1) for the year 2005-06 about the use of new Educational Technology, Students were 10 (Sanskrit), 10 (Psychology), 10 (Philosophy), 30 (Political Science), 20 (Public Admn., Sociology 20, Hindi 10). Their replies are mentioned in Table 5.1

The study suggests that 80 per cent of the respondents were aware of the new educational technology. They mentioned that a special booklet sent by the D.CS., P.U., Chandigarh kept them well informed. However, 90 per cent of them said that they do not remember the dates and topics as the talks are broadcasted intermittently as well as there is no continuous flow. It is strange that only 10 per cent listened to the talks specially designed for them. They said that arranging 2-3 talks per subject makes no sense and that too only from the lesson itself. Respondents mentioned that they listened only 10 per cent of the talks as they either forgot or did not feel interested. 70 per cent find that the quality of talks in terms of contents were not well designed. However, 70 per cent of the respondents appreciated the voice of the speaker. 60 per cent did not want + more talks as these do not help them in preparing for their examinations. All the respondents felt that instructional material is more useful than radio talks. The conclusions is that the Radio broadcasts has not made much impact on the study of students. Ranga Rao has nicely summed up the experience of an APOU. He stated that as on to date there are 117 study centres providing academic counselling to the students of the University. A handful of studies have revealed that in most of the cases the students are not aware of the availability of Audio/Video lessons. Some studies, stated that they are aware of availability to watch/listen them. Another reason is that the number of video lessons in each course is not adequate and the technical quality of the tapes is not upto the mark. The presentation techniques are not motivating. Yet another reason is that Audio and Video lessons are not integrated with the counselling schedule. Watching or listening of Video/ Audio lessons is optional and left to the sweet will and pleasure of the coordinator and students. The net result is Audio/Video components is not taken seriously by one and all. This calls for a serious rethinking to multi-media approach.

TABLE 5.1

Students' Responses to Radio Broadcasts

S. No.	*Items*	*Yes*	*No*
1.	Are you aware of the Radio-Broadcasts by AIR, Jalandhar specially designed for you?	80	20
2.	Do you keep yourself alert about the date and topic of the talk to be broadcast by AIR, Jalandhar?	10	90
3.	Have you listened to talks on AIR Jalandhar	10	90
4.	Would you like additions of more talks?	10	90
5.	Were the quality of talks in terms of contents good?	30	70
6.	Was the voice of the speaker clear and attractive?	70	10
7.	Is the time allotted sufficient? (about 15 minutes)	90	10
8.	Do you find Radio Talk more useful than instructional material?	40	60

On random discussion with students who came to attend PCP in 2005-06 at Correspondence Deptt., P.U., Chandigarh, it was revealed that they were not interested in the new technology as they are interested in preparing according to syllabi to get good marks. Many of them remarked that New Technology is not well planned and do not cover the topics they are interested. They felt that we want only excellent lecture script and excellent PCP. They complainted that on telephone, no person is available, what to talk of high technology like Tele-Conferencing etc. It may be added that radio-broadcasts have also been discontinued. Whatever is taught through education technology is beyond their comprehension. There is a need to use educational technology keeping cost-benefit in mind.

(b) Facts and Suggestions—Based upon Experience, Research Study and Discussions. We give here Facts and Suggestions

(1) Educating the Learners on the use of New Technology

Most of the learners except those living near the Open University/ DEI, do not have the knowledge to operate these electronic medias. They think that these are simply wastage of time and resources. It is our duty to educate them about the availability and use of new technology.

(2) Educational Material through Electronic Media not well Prepared

We have not been able to prepare new educational material to suit the needs of our distant learners. It is mostly either borrowed or prepared on the model of the foreign material. In order to sustain interest, Open Universities/DE should come out with innovative materials required in the context of our country. What to talk of material prepared through electronic media, even intructional material is based on the writings in foreign books, the contents of which are not relevant to our students.

Dr. S. Bhatnagar in his Article, "Electronic Mass Media and Distance Education" has also stressed the above points. To quote him: "As regards the future, only such technologies will earn popularity with the teachers and students of distance education as assure: (a) control of the teacher over the production of the instructional programmes, (b) accessibility to the students in the sense that they are in a position to play these programmes in their homes and as many or as few times as they wish to, and (c) cost efficiency both from the institutes and students' point of view. Audio and Video technologies alone fulfil these conditions and thus the future appears to be with them. To derive the maximum benefit from these technologies adequate planning needs to be made particularly with regard to the development of their software parts. Also precious resources may not be frittered away on the creation of these facilities in a reckless and unplanned manner. These may be created on regional basis and proper coordination among various beneficiary institutes be properly effected.[25]

(3) Efficient Design and use of New Technology

Success of distance education depends largely on the efficient use of alternative media available to us. There could be several other media not discussed here but of relevance to distance education such as telephone teaching, tele-conferencing, computer-aided instruction, teletext and videotex systems, etc. What is important is not just using these media but properly organising them into a well defined instructional strategy, which is the essence of educational technology.

(4) Need of Assuring Availability: Use of Different Technology at different Study Centres

It may be difficult to reach all the learners with all the media mainly because many of them are inaccessible to several learners. This probably requires that local study circles and local media resource centres are available to all learners within easy reach.

(5) Need of Planning for the use of Radio and TV in a Big Way

With growing access to radio and television serious efforts need be made to include them in every distance education course. A suitable system of using audio/video cassettes and the large network of telephone facility needs to be evolved. As utilisation of radio and TV transmission network is concerned the targets identified in the Programme of Action in the National Policy of Education 1986 are promising. They include expansion of the existing network, establishment of radio stations in teaching universities, provision for a educational TV channel, and in the long-run creation of a satellite system for educational needs.

(6) Need of Strengthening various Technologies through Proper Policy and Plans

In the words of K. Gopalan: Indian basic infrastructure and supportive sub-systems need considerable strengthening. The rapid developments now taking place in information technology call for revolutionary changes not only in our methodologies and concepts relating to education, but also in our policies regarding teaching, research, and educational administration. With our teeming millions who have not only to be educated, but also kept updated on a continuing basis, we have no other way except to use modern information and communication technologies for the delivery of education services in as many manifestations as possible. We need to make full use of the future generation. INSAT systems with exclusive and separate channels to meet the educational and training demands in various sectors. New experiments, creative innovations, and appropriate strategies, have to be developed and tried out to improve access to education and to reorient the content and process of education at all levels."[26]

COL, UGC and DEC have rightly come to the following conclusions to improve the educational technology in the DE system.

Electronic media are of great importance in making distance education a multi-media teaching-learning system. Audio-visual components make learning more effective and interesting for the students. With the advance of communication media, distance education institutes all over the world have adopted very sophisticated communication media as an integral part of their teaching process. We may not be able to use all those media because of our limitations, but media which are readily available to us should be used to supplement instruction imparted through the printed lessons.

The CCIs should therefore, plan to develop multi-media packages of teaching-learning materials—

(i) To begin with, the CCIs/DDEs should make use of the existing audio and video cassettes of IGNOU and the UGC country-wide class room.

(ii) CCI/DDEs within the same region can share radio-talks and telecast etc.

(iii) Now that Insat 2 has become operational and Doordarshan has 4 more channels, the Ministry concerned should allot a good chunk of time slot on the enrichment channel for educational programmes of DDEs and Open Universities. TV Programmes can be very helpful in supplementing instruction provided through the printed course material.

(iv) The Directorates of distance education and their study centres should be provided necessary equipment and facilities for the playback of audio/video cassettes, recording and playing back to radio broadcasts and telecasts. Universities may put up their proposals to the DEC for financial assistance.

(v) In the long-run the EMRCs in the States should help in the development of video/audio cassettes for distance education institutes. Meanwhile, service of some private studios could be hired for this purpose.[27]

Sameer P. Narkhede, quoting Koumi (1994) rightly concludes: "There are in fact significant Pedagogic reasons for choosing one medium over other. . . . Each medium has its, distinctive presentational attributes, its own strengths and weaknesses . . . these distinctive must be fully exploited by choosing different treatments of the topic for different media which may address different teaching functions and perhaps even by choosing different topics.[28]

Anurag Saxena and Monika Jouhar have rightly concluded: "Educational Planners have to rethink about their existing media package, i.e. the combination of presented text supported by Radio, TV, Audio, Video-casettes and teleconferencing. They have to switch over to a combination that makes them less "distant" and more interactive, reduces the delivery cost and remains accessible to students."[29]

(c) Conclusion

There is a lot of potentiality in new Educational Technology but the problem is to harness this technology for the benefit of Distance Education learners. There is a lot of difference in theory and practice. Only a selected few with a huge financial resources can plan such services. Even, in these institutions these are more a prestige issue of the institution with little benefit to the students. Therefore, we must provide only that technology which can really benefit the students and not a glamour to the institute. At the moment, more attention need to be paid to written material which may be provided in a decent quality. This would be a real great service to the students of DE system. Side-by-side, we must prepare material in the Indian context to be used through electronic media. Besides, a regular evaluation and monitoring is required. We should not use resources on electronic media beyond a certain level.

We may keep in mind that merely electronic media can create passive attitude and make the learners dull. We can overcome this through well arranged Personal Contact Programme.

Naturally the introduction of technology obviates the need of teachers or instructors. A teacherless classroom with Computer-aided learning may take time to strike roots in the Indian context. Learning is not merely a process of storing the mind but one of scocializing the individual in the backdrop of the society. It is doubtful whether IT can address itself to the needs of the creation of . . . "A humane and enlightened society" as visualised by Professor Acharya Ramamurthy (NPERC). Teleconferencing and interactive technology may give the necessary fill in. But sensitization is as much a part of socialization as acculturation.[30] The essence of use of New Technology should not ensure merely availability, accessability but also utilisation

NOTES AND REFERENCES

1. Quoted by B.M. Malik, Technology Management, Making India More Competitive, in *University News*, 37 (5), Feb. I, 1999, p. 4.
2. Ran Takwale; IGNOU's Challenges of Quality, Quantity and Equity, in *University News*, (May 27, 1996), p. 14.
3. K.K. Bajaj, "Student Support Services for Interactive Communication in Distance Education" in *University News*, AIU, New Delhi, Vol. 5, February 3, 1997.
4. K. Gopalan, "Education Technology, New Horizons" in *University News*, Feb. 10, 1997, p. I, AIU, New Delhi
5. Study Programme: An overview, Distance Education Bulletin in International Council of Distance Education, Vol. 12 (September, 1986), p. 43.
6. C.H. Shulman, Instructional Television: Higher Education Without Commercial Interruption, American Association for Higher Education, May 1981, (33, S), p. 711, quoted, *Ibid.*, p. 43
7. *Ibid.*, p. 43.
8. Marian Craft, W.L.U. Telecollege; Distance Education by Television, International Council for Distance Education Bulletin, No. 11 (May 1986), p. 26.
9. NPE, 1986, pp. 15-16.
10. K.B. Power, Globalisation of Distance Learning System, Implications for Developing Countries, *University News*, 35(4), January 27,1997, p. 4.
11. Jagannath Mohanty and Sushandhya Mohanty, "IGNOU, Educational Television Programmes: An Appraisal", *University News*, July 31, 1995, pp. 13-14.
12. IGNOU, Planning and Development Decisions, Distance Education Vision and Strategies, New Delhi, 1986, p. 20.
13. Quoted in *University News*, 36(34), August 24, 1998, p. 14.
14. Anand, P. Srivastava, Information Technology and Higher Education, *University News*, 36(33), Aug. 17, 1998.
15. S.K. Gandhi, Distance Education: Role of New Technologies in the 21st Century, *University News*, 36(33) Aug. 17, 1998, pp. 11-12.
16. UGC: Contribution of Education in National Development, Ninth Five Year Plan and Future Perspective, New Delhi, 1996, pp. 47-48.
17. N.D. Ushadevi, Virtual Conferencing Hearing through Mediated Technologies, *University News*, Sept. 29, 1997, AIU, New Delhi, p. 6.
18. D.R. Goel and D. Sarangi, "Interactive Distance Education: A Sununative View of Indian Teleconferences" in *University News*, 35(42), Oct. 20, 1997, p. 11.
19. Earnest Dale and L.C. Michen, Modern Management Techniques, New York, Pengiu, 1974, p. 3.
20. Shashi Ulah, "Distance Learning Tools" in the *Indian Express*, Chandigarh, Sept. 13, 1999, p. 9
21. M.N. Kulkarni, "Communication for Social Development: Some Issues", National Seminar in Communication Technology, DCS, P.U., Chandigarh, Nov. 57, 1986, p. 17.
22. *Ibid.*, p. 8.
23. Sanjay Mishra, Teaching Information Literacy To Distance Learner, *University News*, May 19, 1997, p. 5, AIU, New Delhi.
24. Saraswati Rao, Sophisticated Technologies: Their relevance to the Indian Distance Education, In M. Satya Narayan Rao (Ed.) p. 196.
25. S. Bhatnagar, Electronic Media and Distance Education, National Seminar on Communication Technology, Nov. 5-7, 1986, DCS, P.U., Chandigarh.
26. K. Gopalan, *op. cit.*, p. 4.
27. COL/UGC/DEC Round Table Conference on quality assurance in Distance Education: Action Plan Agreed upon on 2 July, 1994, Appendix C.

28. Sameer P. Narkhede, Education and Technology in *University News*, 36/24, Aug. 24, 1998, New Delhi, AIU, p. 1.
29. Anurag Saxena and Monika Jauhar, Communication: Quantifying Interactive Learning, in *Indian Journal of Open Learning*, Vol. 8, No. 2, May 1999, New Delhi, IGNOU, p. 168.
30. S. Abdul Kareem, Information Technology and Knowledge, in *University News*, Oct. 18, 1999, p. 19.

Personal Contact Programme

PART A

NATURE AND MEANING

Personal contact programme is an ideal activity where meeting of minds take place among students and the faculty. In formal system of education, students meet their teachers throughout the academic session in the classroom and beyond the classroom which create confidence, motivation and satisfaction among the students and Faculty. However, students in DE System being geographically scattered cannot avail of this facility and advantage resulting in many social and psychological problems. What is the way to come out of this chaos? How to bridge this gap between the students and their faculty members? How to ensure their association though limited to remove their apprehensions and other academic problems? The answer is the institution of Personal Contact Programme which are designed to narrow the gap between the aspirations of the students and the faculty and make them feel a sense of belongingness to the institution to which they belong.

Personal Contact Programmes, as is clear from the very nomenclature, are designed to meet the needs of the students of DE system for purposeful social contact and intellectual confrontation between the Faculty and the students of DE system.

Satyapal Anand rightly mentions that "Personal Contact Programme, as is very clear from the very nomenclature are designed to unreveal the mystery of elusive identities through purposeful social contact and intellectual confrontation between the faculty and the students of correspondence studies."[1]

UGC rightly mentions that "The provision of personal contact programmes should be regarded as an essential feature of correspondence through lectures, tutorials, seminars and discussions. The personal contact programmes through intensive classroom instruction, individual guidance and counselling help in giving a proper orientation to the students, add to their motivation, encourage regular study habits and instill confidence in them."[2]

In the Indian context a distance student has to complete the given course in a specified period of time and has to take the same examination alongwith the regular university students. However, the open university has its own schedule being autonomous and flexible. Not only this, the UGC guidelines also categorically emphasize that "the provision of contact programmes should be an essential feature of correspondence education in order that the mind of the student is exposed to the mind of the teacher lecturers, tutorials, seminars and other forms of discussion" and recommends that "a contact programme of 20 working days at the undergraduate level and at least two programmes of 15 working days each at the post-graduate level should be organised in different places, wherever there is a reasonably good number of students besides Sunday classes which should be regularly organized for correspondence course students at the headquarters. This may be done by the staff of the directorate at the headquarters and by staff engaged specially for the purpose from local institutions in other areas. There should also be an orientation programme of two days for post-graduate students. The programme at the post-graduate level should be compulsory for each student. Thus, the UGC guidelines have not only set the aims of PCPs but have also reflected the modus operandi of these programmes.[3]

The term Personal Contact Programme (PCP), as used in Indian context, denotes the assembly of distance students and representative teachers of the supporting institution or other teachers employed especially for the purpose at a predecided place for a specific period with the intention of teaching, motivating, creating a sense of belongingness and supplement distance learning material already sent. Generally during this period, there is a face to face encounter between the two which generates the atmosphere of the classroom teaching of the conventional system, only with the difference that in the later the teacher tries to unfold the similar course content in one academic year whereas in the former its unfolding is attempted within a period of two to three weeks in an innovative way generally styled as capsuled programme. On top of this, academics of these institutions provide sufficient time during the PCPs for removing individual learning difficulties of the students and other psychological and administrative problems. H.C.S. Rathore has added another dimension to PCP on the basis of his research. He concluded that the student population in distance education be distinguished as part time and full time students and PCPs be planned and organised for these two groups of students, taking into account their differing needs and expectations.[4]

The teaching at personal contact programmes has to be quite different from classroom teaching provided in the colleges or universities as these lectures aim at revision of syllabus already covered through lessons, supplementing material provided in the lessons and introducing students to the portions still to be covered so as to motivate them to read further. These programmes provide a good feedback from the students to the teachers and enable them to understand the requirement of students as also the shortcomings that may be there in the reading materials supplied by the institute. In case of science/commerce/professional courses both at PG and UG levels, attendance should be compulsory.

PART B

MERITS OF PCP

The following benefits result from personal contact programme:

(a) Generates Harmonious Relationships between DE System and Students

It creates a climate of understanding. This creation of awareness is integral to liberate the minds and potential of the DE students. Besides, the DE students also feel elated in the company of their fellow students which were earlier unknown. They develop many permutations and combinations among them keeping in view their nature, proximity and interest, which help them substantially later on, i.e. after the PCP. Such contacts generate many informal relationships which help them to come out of academic drudgery or mechanical life.

(b) Psychological Motivation

The research theory in social and organizational psychology has suggested that participation in classrooms would enhance students satisfaction and remove many of inherent and self-created tensions. PCP becomes a morale booster and generates a feeling in him like a student in a formal system.

(c) Better Understanding of DE Students

PCP provides opportunities to understand the profile of DE students. This is a challenging and interesting task for the DE faculty. The DE students come with different aspirations, perceptions and attitudes. PCP provides the opportunity to fulfil their needs.

(d) Development of Loyalty to the DE System and Institutes

DE students attending PCP are the messengers of DE System. They will carry the impressions of the PCP with the and later on exchange with the potential users. This chain reaction can generate good will and ultimately raise the status of DE institutes and the system.

Problems

Let us discuss the problems inherent in the conduct of PCP.

I. Poor Attendance

It has been found that only 25-30 percent students come to attend PCP classes since attendance at PCP is not compulsory. Seeing this trend, it makes many person think as to what is its utility? Why not to abolish it? Besides, there is no correlation between the attendance at PCP and their performance in the examination. Many students and experts suggested that there is a need to create more awareness through mass media and the prospectus about the utility of these programmes. A discussion with students revealed the following reasons for not attending PCP.

(1) Long distance between the place of PCP and residence;
(2) No leave available from the office;
(3) Wastage of time;
(4) Lack of proper stay arrangements;
(5) Very big classes;
(6) Teachers not well prepared; and
(7) No time for personal discussion.

2. Better Teachers not Attracted to Teach because of very Low Honorarium

Honorarium paid to outside teachers is very low. In these days of high salaries, good teachers are not available at odd hours for a meagre sum. There is a need to revise rates or the university may motivate the regular departments to take up this work as a part of their duty.

3. Contents not decided in Advance

It is left to the individual teacher to teach the topics he/she likes. In this way some topics which are difficult are not taught. Students listen to any topic taught to them. There is a need to design the contents before the start of the PCP.

4. No time to meet Individual Teachers to sort out their difficulties

PCP schedule is so tight that students do not find time to meet their teachers and discuss their problems personally. There is a need to provide half an hour break when the students can meet the concerned teachers.

5. Overcrowding

Even with 25 to 30 per cent students attending the PCP of the total admitted, there is over crowding in the classroom. We may divide the students into sections to ensure that there are not more than 50 students in one classroom.

6. Unsatisfactory Environment at PCP

The daily paper "Hindu" mentions that there has been a spate of complaints from students of several CCIS all over the country that the classes are held in ill-ventilated halls, often without fans, the choice of the institutions for holding such classes must be done carefully with an eye on the comfort and the convenience of the learners.[5]

7. Teachers Teaching at PCP Lack Enthusiasm and Interest

Another grievance raised by the students relate to the selection of teachers for contact classes. Evidently the teachers must have an appreciation of the difficulties experienced by the learners, if not an empathy with them. The idea of contact sessions is to enable the learners to have their doubts cleared and competent pedagogues can alone do the job well.[6]

8. Lack of Infrastructural Facilities

Most of the students were sore over not providing good lavotary arrangements, availability of goods drinking water and arrangements for tea on payment. They feel that they get tired after 2-3 periods and need some refreshment. There is a need to provide all these facilities.

Satyapal Anand though skeptical about the utility of PCP but still prefers the holding of PCP. To quote him: "In the final analysis, therefore, it seems irrelevant to consider that (a) only a fraction of the total number of correspondence students attend the PCP organised by the sponsoring institutes, (b) that their final results have very little to do with their attendance at a PCP, (c) that their reactions to the teaching/seminar/counselling/difficulties, resolving sessions (DRS), are favourable or unfavourable, and (d) that teachers relate or do not relate their PCP teaching to the course-material already received by students. However, this should sound like a cynical approach to the problem. Even if PCPs are necessary only in terms of their psychological value, they should be retained as an important component of correspondence teaching."[7]

Another serious thinker, Bade A. Agboola[8] has challenged the basic premises of Personal Contact Programme on the basis of his research. However, he feels in his concluding remarks that PCPs is essential.

An assessment of what takes place at the contact session also reveals a mixture of desirable and undesirable trends. Research results indicate that tutors are not good at identifying and explaining problems and often lack personal interest; that extensive feedback and increased personal and supporting comments do not necessarily increase student achievement or decrease withdrawal rates, (Coldway, 1982). Difficulties of employing reliable tutors and the lack of dedication and professionalism in quite a number of tutors inspite of the supply of guidelines (Idrus, 1992) too constitute bottlenecks. It has been observed that face-to-face components of short duration have limited positive effect on learning.

Consequently, over the last decade, there have been experiments in various distance teaching institutions to diversify student support services with the object of cutting down on face to fact contact sessions in order to economies as well as to take advantage of the developments in telecommunications. Idrus (1992) did not mince words when he stated that tele-tutorials have been introduced at the University Sains Malaysia so as to greatly reduce the expenses on tutorials. This is only one instance of many such world-wide attempts. This essay therefore concludes that the advantages of the contact sessions give meaning and an identity to distance education, although at some substantial costs. Thus, contact sessions are both an asset as well as a burden which distance teaching institutions have to cope with in order to achieve desirable educational goals.

PART C

ORGANISATION OF PCP: PROCEDURE AND CONTENTS (Refer Chart 6.1)

In principle, as per the UGC guidelines, a PCP is required to be held at places wherever there is a concentration of more than 200 students. Most of the institutions reported that they do keep in mind this principle while deciding the venue for the PCPs. But they are often unable to stick to it for reasons like: unavailability of an institution willing to host the programme; lack of funds; lack of expertise in the city in question; lack of accommodation for students and faculty, etc., let us talk in detail about the procedure.

The success of the PCP depends upon micro-planning so that the benefits can be optimised. What should involve in planning a PCP programme? How to go about it? What constraints may be kept in mind? We suggest here the procedure based on our personal experience and discussion with DE students and other colleagues. We mention here important steps.

(a) Advance Planning of Dates and Venue

The DE faculty should decide in sufficient advance about the dates of the PCP keeping in view the needs of the students, availability of the faculty and despatch of reading material. Venue should be in the proximity of large number of students. Venue should have nice classrooms with blackboard and electric fittings for use of audio-visual aids. It is better if these dates are published in the prospectus to avoid expenditure on post later and also ensure the knowledge of PCP to students. It is advantageous to both. The DCS, Panjab University, Chandigarh adopted this practice a decade ago.

(b) Advance Planning of Contents to be Taught

We should prepare in advance the topics to be covered during the PCP. We may select the topics in which DE students can face difficulty in comprehending from the lessons or in the areas where more light can be thrown on the topic. Books recommended in the topics must be checked from the Library so that the students if they want to consult them, these are available to them. It has been seen that faculty members teach the topics without telling in advance which make the students non-participative. Advance decision would make the students come prepared for better understanding and appreciation. This would also keep the faculty well prepared.

CHART 6.1

Conduct of PCP Programme

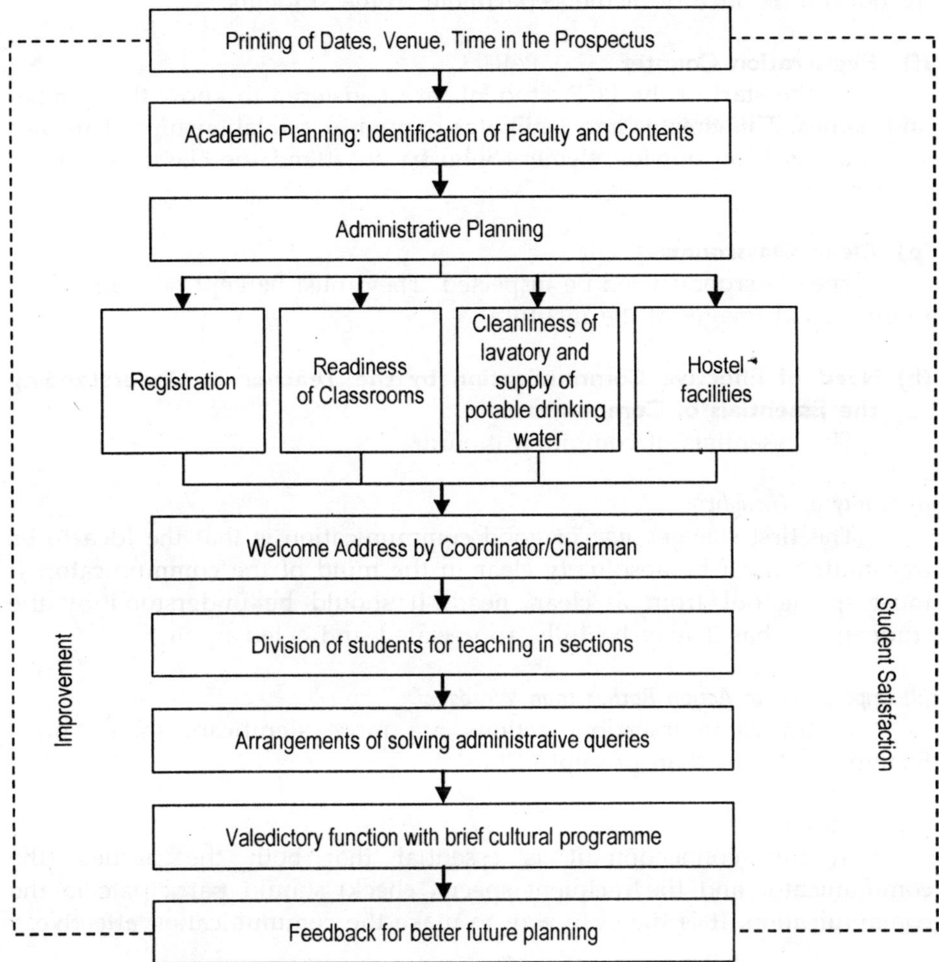

(c) Deciding about the Faculty keeping in view the Topics to be covered

We must decide as to who would teach, which topic so that he can prepare well in advance. While allocating the topic to an outside teacher we must be sure of his capability and competence.

(d) Keeping the Infrastructure Well Planned

The coordinator of the PCP must see that those persons who are to assist in the conduct of PCP are told in advance. The Audio-visual aids may also be booked in advance.

(e) Introductory Lecture

The coordinator may give introductory lecture to familiarize the students about the institute and the course. It would be better if he also introduces the faculty of the department to the students.

(f) Registration Counter

At the start of the PCP, students are registered to know the number and names. This creates and facilitates harmonious relationships. This also keeps a check on outside element who try to attend the classes or create problems.

(g) Clean Classrooms

The classrooms need be inspected. They must be kept neat and clean to give good image 'of the institute.

(h) Need of Effective Communication by the Teacher in Understanding the Essentials of Communication

The essentials of communication are[9]:

(i) Clarity of Thought

The first *sine qua non* of good communication is that the idea to be transmitted must be absolutely clear in the mind of the communicator. It must spring out from a 'clear' head. It should be understood by the students so that it may be fully appreciated and acted upon.

(ii) Importance to Action Rather than Words

In all communication, actions are more significant than words. Example is better than precept.

(iii) Participation

In this connection it is essential that both the parties (the communicator and the recipient special check) should participate in the communication. It is the only way to make the communication effective.

(iv) Transmission

The communicator must plan carefully what to communicate and how to communicate. The success of this would depend upon the understanding of the students.

According to Terry, eight factors are essential in making communication effective:

(a) Inform yourself fully;
(b) Establish a mutual trust in students;
(c) Find a common ground of experience and slowly raise their level;
(d) Use mutually known words already sent in lecture script;

(e) Have regard for context;
(f) Secure and hold the receiver's attention;
(g) Employ examples and visual aids; and
(h) Reinforce the main points.

According to Millet, seven factors make communication effective. It should be clear, consistent with the expectation of the recipient, adequate, timely, uniform, flexible and acceptable.

PART D

(A) STUDENTS RESPONSES TO PCP—A RESEARCH STUDY (B) SUGGESTIONS AND RECOMMENDATIONS

In order to ascertain the views of the students about the Personal Contact Programme, the authors, asked the following questions to about 100 undergraduate students who came to attend the PCP in 2005-06 at DCS, P.U., Chandigarh.

The study suggests that the students were happy about the programme. The study suggests that 95 percent of respondents were aware of the dates of PCP. However, 90 percent were not aware of the topics to be covered in the PCP. 80 percent were satisfied with the regular conduct of classes. 90 per cent were satisfied with the coverage of the contents at the PCP. 80 per cent were satisfied with the duration. 50 per cent did not like the taking of the classes by outside teachers as they were not well versed with the style of teaching to Distance Education students. 95 per cent were highly enthusiastic about the quality of teachers at PCP. Besides, they enjoyed their stay and termed the PCP as fruitful. It is a lively scene to see the heterogeneous group of students at work.

The reactions were different by students of different subjects. Students mentioned that where teachers teach with good preparation and interest, most of the students do not miss the classes in PCP. They wanted that all the teachers must be present at the PCP dates as they can get their difficulties cleared.

(B) FACTS AND SUGGESTIONS

Based upon the experience of 30 years, in teaching DE students at P.U., Chandigarh and the Students of other DE institutes as guest faculty the authors found the following facts and suggestions to improve Personal Contact Programme. These are based upon the reactions of the students as well.

(a) Need of Increase in Duration as well as Coverage of Course

Most of the students wanted that number of days and frequency for holding PCPs should be increased. This is a demand from those who are not employed. However, there are others who are too busy and feel happy with the existing arrangements.

(b) Need of Deciding Convenient Time and Place for PCP

The time and place of PCPs should be decided in a way that these are within easy reach of students. We can also arrange PCP during Sundays or other holidays.

(c) Need of Allocating Time for Discussion as Well

Subject specialists/experts be deputed to conduct PCPs and they should give more time for discussion than teaching alone. Time at the disposal of the students is very short which need be utilised profitably.

(d) PCP Need be Held Sufficiently in Advance of Examinations

All PCPs should be completed atleast two months before the commencement of the examinations and students should not be disturbed by asking them to participate in the PCPs just before the examinations. This would provide sufficient time at their disposal for the preparation of the examination.

(e) Need of Small Sections

More number of teachers should be involved and students should be divided into small groups according to their needs and assigned to teachers separately, so that individualized tutoring is possible. The number of students in some classes is very large and the students feel like sitting in a crowd and not a class room. There should not be more than 50 students in a class.

(f) Need of Hostel Facilities

Necessary accommodation for out-station students be arranged and if possible at subsidized rates. Accommodation should be such where they feel comfortable.

(g) Need of Despatch of Lessons

Before the conduct of PCP necessary steps be taken to ensure that all the lessons are mailed to the students before the PCP so that the students should come fully prepared for the PCP.

(h) Preference for Teachers from Parent Institution for Teaching at PCP

The institution of part-time tutors engaged to teach at the PCP should be abolished and of the faculty members of the parent institution should share the full responsibility of running the PCP among themselves.

(i) Need of Advance Planning of Contents to be Covered at PCP and Communicating the same to Students

The faculty members of each department would identify at least one month in advance of the commencement of the PCP at a particular station, the topics that they would be covering in the course at the PCP and would communicate the same to the students so that the latter may also be able to spell out their difficulties in writing to their teachers (the student may in fact be encouraged to do so.) When both the teachers and the students go adequately prepared to the PCP, the Instructional content of the PCP would get strengthened considerably which in its turn would make the PCP much more effective and popular.

(j) Need of more Emphasis on Discussing Examination-related Topics

During the PCP emphasis should be on the preparation of the students for the examination and not merely academic orientation.

(k) Need of Spreading the Benefits of PCP to More Places

When the DE institutes find convenient efforts may be made to extend its coverage to a larger number of stations, so that more and more students may be able to get benefit from this programme.

(l) Need of Organising Sunday Classes to Keep the Students in Continuous Touch

Besides Sunday classes should be regularly organised for correspondence course students at the headquarters. This may be done by the staff of the directorate at the headquarters and any staff engaged specially for the purpose from local institutions in other areas. There should also be an orientation programme of two days for post-graduate students. The programme at the graduate level should be compulsory for every student.[10]

(m) Need of Courteous Behaviour to Socialise Students to Values and Ideals of the Institute

Courtesy on the part of academic and administrative staff can make the students comfortable and self-confident. This can generate a climate of shared understanding and creativity. Tarun Bahl in his Article "Courtesy as a Habit" in the *Daily Tribune*, Oct. 10, 1999 rightly stresses the value of courtesy. To quote him: 'The good thing about practising courtesy is that while it costs nothing, it can bring rich dividends. No one is too big or too busy to be courteous. It enhances others self-worth and prods them to be good in return. Many brilliant and talented people were obnoxious, pig-headed, insolent, ungrateful and ill-mannered. Their pomposity clouded their judgement and they forgot that they had to treat others with respect and humility before they can be accorded the same regard."[11]

(C) CONCLUSIONS

PCP is the most important aspect of a Distance Education system to bring together students and faculty face to face. A well organised PCP has tremendous potentialities for a distance learner. After attending PCP, he feels secure, comfortable, and motivated to learn and move ahead. Based upon personal experience, it has been noticed that those students who took keen interest have performed well in examinations as well.

NOTES AND REFERENCES

1. Satyapal Anand, University Without Wall, New Delhi, Vikas, 1979, p. 127.
2. UGC, Scheme of Distance Education, New Delhi, 1993, (Appendix D3).
3. *Ibid.*
4. H.C.S. Rathore: Personal Contact Programme of Correspondence Institutes in India: An Evaluation, in *Indian Journal of Open Learning*, New Delhi, IGNOU, January, 1995 (Vol. 4, No. 1), p. 15.
5. *The Hindu*, Nov. 14, 1995.
6. *Ibid.*
7. Satyapal Anand, University Without Walls, New Delhi, Vikas, 1979, p. 147.
8. Bade A. Agboola, "Contact Session in Distance Education: An Asset as well as a Burden" in *Indian Journal of Open Learning*, Vol. 2, No. 1, pp. 17-22.
9. S.L. Goel, Advanced Public Administration, New Delhi, Sterling, 1994, pp. 188-89.
10. UGC., *Ibid.*
11. *The Daily Tribune*, Oct. 10, 1999, p. 2 (Sunday Reading).

Students Assignments: Response Sheets

PART A

(a) Meaning and Objectives (Chart. 7.1)

Response sheet creates a climate of shared understanding between the faculty and the students. Teaching through response sheets is very important to the activity of teaching through distance education. Here we develop a continuous link between the teacher and the student. Possibly the faculty in DE spend more time checking response sheets than doing anything else. The student too spends a considerable amount of his time writing out the answers to the questions set in the Response Sheet Assignments at regular intervals. The technique of teaching through response sheet, therefore, calls for special attention.[1] H.C.S. Rathore views that students believe that assignments help them in the process of learning and their preparation for examinations.[2]

RSA is a question-sheet which is attached at the end of all or some of the lesson-units. The questions included in this sheet are based on the material either already provided to the students in the preceding lesson-units or in the unit with which it is appended. On top of the page, the student has to write his name and address on a perforated chit, in clear and legible hand. This chit is detached by the Mailing section of the institute at the time of sending back the "Tutor Marked Assignment (TMA)" and pasted on the face of envelope so that there is no mistake in writing out the address of the students, as also effecting economy in time and labour. Response Sheet Assignments comprise exercises, questions, problems, etc. which are made for the student by his teachers to enable them to evaluate students' performance on the basis of his 'preparation' of the course material already with him. These exercises are helpful to ascertain the following:

CHART 7.1

Parameters of Response Sheet Assignment

Distance Education System

Conceptual Skill | Response Sheet Assignments | Understanding of the subject

Analytical ability | | Creative Thinking

Extra-Reading ← Student Send Back Response Sheet → Through study of Instructional material

Record Keeping and Store ← Receipt at DE institute (Sorting and distributing to tutors) → Distribution

Genuine Comments | Evaluation by Tutors | Grading

Prompt Assessment | | Responding to querries

Ensure Uniformity ← Monitoring by Course Leader (Simple Checking) → Keep the Tutors responsive

Mailing Section of the Institution

Dispatch to Student

Feedback

Student Satisfaction

Student Satisfaction

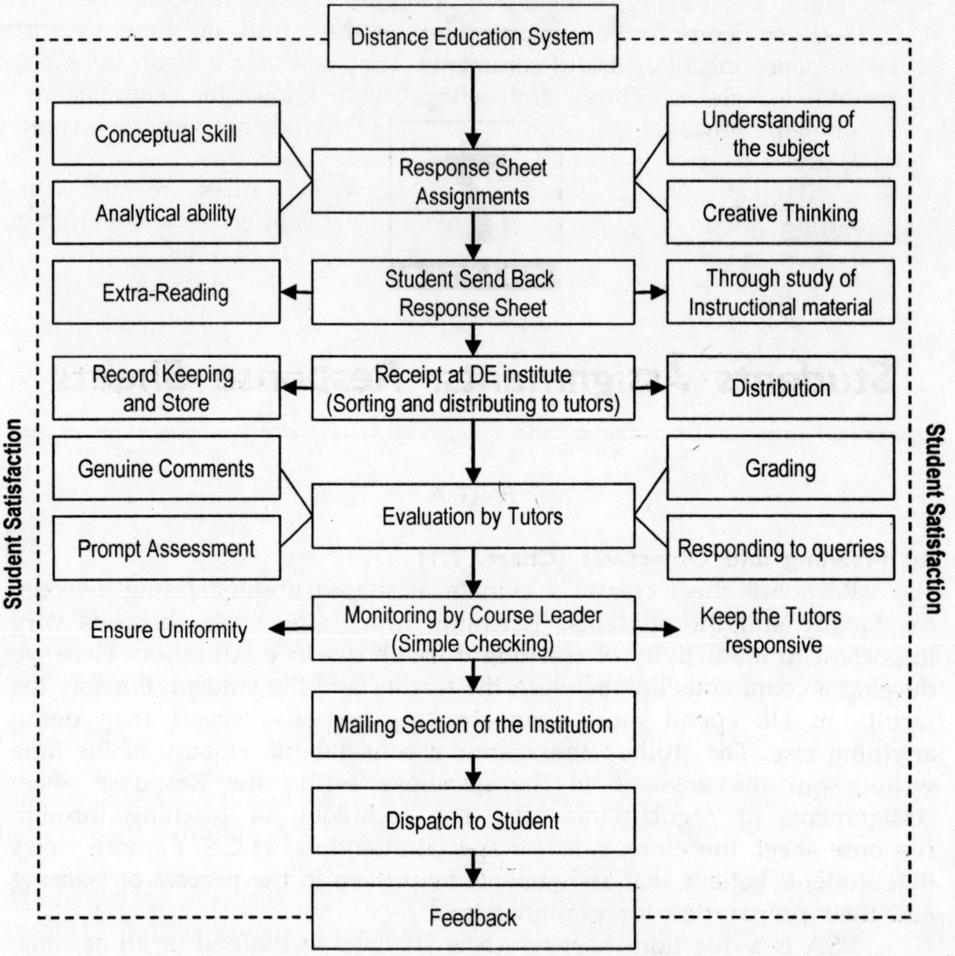

(a) the student has understood and absorbed the course units sent to him;

(b) he knows how to organize the material involved;

(c) he gets a prompt evaluator feedback which enables him to improve continuously through the comments/suggestions for revision, etc. that he received; and

(d) that he studies continuously throughout the year.[3]

Assignments form an important part in distance education since they assess the progress of the learner at different stages of the course. These also facilitate comprehension of the learner and his success in the course.

However, both the faculty and the learners are unmotivated in realising the beneficial nature of the assignments. Many students take it easy and are rarely prompt in submitting the assignments for regular evaluation. Even many of them do not submit a single response sheet as the counsellors Seem to be unconcerned as they find no time to correct assignments and offer useful comments. They consider it as an unnecessary burden on them. Those counsellors who know the significance of assignments offer valuable tutorial comments which are very well received by learners in several cases.

If the physical requirements of the study centres are met with by providing adequate staff a separate wing to supervise evaluation and analysis of assignments to check the progress of the students much of the present non-compliance may disappear. Once the students realise the benefit of submitting honestly completed assignments they certainly will put in the necessary efforts in that direction.[4]

The UGC has suggested the following requirements for submission of Response Sheets:

(i) Every student at the undergraduate level should be required to do at least a total of 20 home assignments in all the subjects put together before he qualifies for the examination to be held at the end of that particular academic year.

(ii) The student response sheets should be properly evaluated and promptly returned to the students with corrections, remarks, grade and suggestions for improvement. It must be ensured that all response sheets are returned within a stipulated period and the system must be notified in advance so that students know what to expect.

(iii) It would motivate the students to send their response sheets regularly if the time-lag in marking and returning their response sheets could be kept to the minimum.

(iv) At the Post-graduate level, in lieu of response sheets, students may be required to write at least five essays/Projects on each paper during the year.

PART B

(a) Designing of Response Sheet Questions

Framing questions is a scientific technique which requires hardwork, experience and training of the teacher. While framing the questions for the response sheet we must bear in our mind that the questions are not the 'tricks of the trade', or the 'rules of the thumb.' The success and efficiency of our teaching depends on the skill with which we formulate questions than any other single factor. In practice, teachers do not apply their mind while formulating questions.

Questions in the response sheets dealing with humanities and social sciences are generally worded vaguely. The familiar words used are: discuss, describe, critically examine, elucidate, etc. There is a casual attitude in designing response sheets.

(b) Essentials of Designing Response-Sheet Questions

(a) Questions should be thought-provoking and generate mental activity in the minds of the students.
(b) Questions must be framed in such a way as to stimulate thinking. It is to make students rearrange and restructure as well as modify the material being studied by them. He should not find answer in a simple way but should apply his mind which would be training in creativity.
(c) Questions should be set keeping in view all types of students, i.e. mediocre and intelligent. Some questions should be simple and some thought-provoking. The aim is to cover heterogeneous population.
(d) Questions should be styled to judge the grasp of correct knowledge or content of the subject. Questions should not be vague.
(e) Questions should be framed so as to increase the analytical and creative faculties of the students.
(f) Questions should be such as to develop conceptual skill and intellectual ability in the use of various concepts or tools.

PART C

(a) Evaluation of Response Sheets

It is a process of continuous evaluation. The Distance Education institute receives massive number of completed students assignments from different courses. On receipt, these are sorted at the level of the institute and distributed to the concerned teacher of the institute or outside tutor. After evaluation, these are dispatched back. In most of the Distance Education institutes, there is no weightage given towards pass marks on the basis of evaluation of RSA. However, in IGNOU, the assignments submitted by students get 25 to 35 per cent weightage and are of 2 types—the computer marked and the tutor marked. There is one assignment for every 2 credit course subject to a maximum of 3 assignments for an 8 credit course. Evaluation of Response Sheets is an important activity. The students will get their feed-back only if their response sheets are evaluated properly. We may discuss here various aspects of evaluation.

(b) Comments

What type of comments may be given on the Response Sheets. These may relate to the subject matter, language, interconnection of paragraphs, new developments, etc. On the comments would depend the seriousness of the students. Tutors should give constructive suggestions, which should be concrete, pointing to exact mistakes rather than just saying that one's performance was not upto the mark. The comments should inform the students exactly about what they are specifically required to do and which materials they should refer to[5] Based on a seminar, sponsored by UGC and British Council Division of the British High Commission, organised by DCS, P.U., Chandigarh, we mention below the consensus arrived at in the seminar on the nature of comments on Response Sheets evaluation.[6]

(a) Clarify expression;
(b) Clarify comprehension;
(c) Encourage the student;
(d) Help him achieve consistency of structure/content;
(e) Encourage extra reading;
(f) Elucidate or elaborate points;
(g) Relate to earlier lessons and future links;
(h) Help him achieve relevance;
(i) Encourage critical thinking; and
(j) Assess logical order, etc.

In another workshop, the participants identified the positive and negative comments which may be kept in mind by Response Sheet evaluators.[7]

1. Comments that clarify expression.
2. Comments that clarify comprehension
3. Comments that suggest further reading.
4. Comments that elucidate difficult concepts.
5. Comments that distinguish between different shades of meanings.
6. Comments that bring out the structural weakness of the argument.
7. Comments that encourage the student.
8. Comments on style.
9. Comments that encourage independent thinking.

Comments to be avoided were listed as follows:

1. Comments that discourage the learner.
2. Comments that are too general and vague.
3. Comments that confuse the student.
4. Comments that are not legible.
5. Comments that are at variance with the grades.
6. Comments that may upset the student, e.g. a warning, a rude censure and so on.

Dr. Ronald Carr in collaboration with participants of the workshop identified the following types of comments which may be given to students on their assignments:

1. Comments which indicate that the assignment as a whole has been received and considered by the tutor; comments that establish and maintain a two-way communication dialogue.
2. Comments which correct straight forward errors of fact or simple misunderstandings which students make. The student should receive precise reference in these comments to the corresponding context or the 'other set' reading material so that he can make his own corrections.
3. Comment about the relevance and appropriateness of approach of the answer to the particular assignment. Often the irrelevance or in appropriateness in his work can be fully explained to the student in writing only if the tutor provides a number of written examples of the relevant content or method. Example: Mathematics tutors can use specimen solutions.
4. Comments which Support and Encourage the Students: Even where an assignment is poor, a tutor may yet find some silver lining in a cloud. Some positive virtue might be found in an assignment to deserve a word or two of praise. Discourage comments such as: "extremely poor", "atrocious work", "improve your English" are extremely harmful and kill the enthusiasm of a student who looks forward to receiving sympathetic comments and remarks.
5. Comments on Assignment and Study Techniques: Technical defects some times are generated because of problems concerning the student's handling of the course material. Students, in such cases, should be advised properly regarding their errors of study technique. Where there are repeated problems of presentation and structure, the tutor should indicate points of weakness or strength in the margin of the assignment and then tackle these in a more generalized form at the end. Suggestions for improvements should be made in a precise manner.
6. Comments which Explain the Grade: This is a ticklish problem because a typical student normally looks up his grade in his assignment even before he has read the comments. If a tutor explains why a student has been given low, average or high grades (marks), it should be a well reasoned out explanation for the student's satisfaction. It will also give to the student an overall view of his performance. This should be particularly adhered to when the grade of the student is poor.[8]

Let me narrate here a personal example. A Brigadier from army was registered for M.A. Public Administration. He sent response sheets in all the papers. The departmental clerk gave his all response sheets to me. (one of the author) I found that the student has taken great pains from all angles. I wrote a note to him saying that "You are doing very well. In this way, you can secure some position in the University." When these response sheets went back to him he got excited after reading the remarks. He showed it to his wife who was an eminent gynaecologist. He came to me after two days and said that he had decided to stay in Chandigarh and prepare for the examination with more hard work. He got a high first class. It may be of interest to quote another example. The student sent his Response Sheet of B.A.-III Sanskrit. One of the authors wrote very good remarks saying that you can do very well. He later on competed for services and got into Indian Revenue Service. We may conclude by saying that we must encourage students through our notes and not discourage them.

Umesh Madhukar Rajderkar has also supported this view based upon his experience as lecturer Yashwant Rao Chavan Maharashtra Open University, Nasik. To quote him: "Counsellor's remarks are very necessary as they motivate and activate learners. Distance tutor should make use of constructive, positive, global and personal type of comments extensively as they will motivate the learners. Distance learners are adults, they could not take benefit of the conventional educational facility system and are always doubtful whether they can complete a programme for which they have registered. It is, therefore, necessary that distance tutors, or counsellors should provide them proper guidance and motivate in their study. There should be wide scope to supplemental communication between the learners and the counsellor which will break the barriers that are created on Psychological grounds on the part of the students. This will help learners get success in the programme they have taken up through distance mode of education."[9]

(c) Grading

Another problem in evaluation is of grading. There is no need of grading until and unless there is some system of internal assessment. Since response sheets are evaluated by different evaluators both from inside and outside, it is advisable to avoid to give marks as these response sheets may not be their own attempt. It is better to evaluate them by correcting and giving suitable remarks.

(d) Compulsory or Optional

Response sheets may not be compulsory, why? This increases unnecessary load of work without any purpose. In order to fulfil the requirement to appear in the examination, the students send small notes or get them typed from the lessons. We must encourage genuine interest in writing of response sheets. Their evaluation would be useful for the students in such cases.

(e) Time Dimension: Time Required for the Assignment to Reach back to Students

In order to sustain the interest of the students, response sheet should reach the students back within 15 days of the receipt in the institute. For this, we will have to plan the evaluation and despatch so that there may be no delay at any level. The students would be motivated to send the next assignments also. Students have been coming to me to ask about their response sheets sent 1 month or 2 months back as they needed them for the preparation of their examination. On search, they were found on the tables of the evaluators. This is highly damaging and need action. We should impress upon the teachers the urgency of sending back marked response sheets.

PART D

(a) Response Sheet and Students: A Research Study

In order to ascertain the views about RSA, the students numbering about 100 were asked about the utility of RSA in 2005-06 from undergraduate classes of DCS, P.U., Chandigarh. Their replies are tabulated below (refer Table 7.1).

TABLE 7.1

Response Sheets and Students: A Research Study

Sr. No.	*Area of Response Sheet Activity*	*Yes*	*No*
I.	Are the Response Sheets well designed in terms of contents and language	80%	20%
II.	Do you find the answers of questions easily available from the lecture scripts	60%	40$
III.	Do you find time to write these RSA	50%	50%
IV.	Should RS submission compulsory	20%	80%
V.	Do you find these useful	50%	50%
VI.	Do you get them back within 15 days	10%	90%
VII.	Are you benefitted by comments	50%	50%
VIII.	Do you receive constructive comments by your evaluators	20%	80%
IX.	Do you submit your response sheets regularly	30%	70%
X.	Do you get the answers to querries	30%	70%
XI	Any other comments/suggestion		

The study suggests that students feel (80%) that the response sheets are well designed and 60 per cent of them feel that they can easily locate the answers to the questions from the instructional material. However, 50 per cent of them feel that they are short of time to write these response sheets. 80 per cent feel that there should not be any compulsion in writing response sheets. 50% say that these are useful in their study. However, 90 per cent say that they do not get back their RSA within 15 days. 50 per cent say that they are benefitted by comments, 80 per cent feel that quality of comments are very bad, 70 per cent do not submit their RSA regularly. However, 70 percent state that they do not get answer to their querries. Faculty members mention the following difficulties pertaining to RSA:

(a) Students generally copy from the Lecture Scripts and try to complete the quota of assignments.
(b) Some students do not evince any interest in writing their assignments. They take it very casually.
(c) A large number of students do not submit their assignments and as per the normal practice, they are exempted and allowed to appear in the examinations. This has its chain effects.
(d) Outside evaluators, if engaged, do not do full justice.
(e) Response Sheets of the same student is evaluated by different teachers in the same subject resulting in confusion. It should be preferred if the same teacher evaluates the response sheet of the student to ensure proper monitoring.

N. Pardhan and Pabla Ranjit Kaur have found out the reasons for not submitting the response sheets. To quote them: "Students are not motivated to do the assignments as they are not provided with proper feed-back, guidance to carry out the assignments, and study materials are not made available to them in time. A large majority of students do not give any assignment in some of the courses. The assignments have the drawbacks of not covering the whole syllabus, questions not being clear, and the study materials and reference materials not being available. Sufficient time is also not available to students for preparing assignments."[10]

Lakshmi Chander rightly suggests that there is need of monitoring of the response sheet marked by outside evaluators (Tutors) by a fixed permanent faculty member (Monitor). This would promote control over the tutors who do not do the work seriously. Monitoring is nothing but sample checking like the system of head examiners used in evaluation of answer books. To quote: "Monitoring if done properly can add more meaning to the DE system. It can lower the drop out rate, help in uniformity in marking; maintain high standards of tutor comments; prevent delays in returning assignments; give students access to re-evaluation and it can reduce student, tutor isolation. . . . If monitors and tutors work in harmony, the distance students will definitely benefit."[11]

(b) Suggestions and Recommendations

The following recommendations are suggested:

(i) Both from the 'examination point of view' and general questions should be included in the Response Sheet Assignments. This would help them in scoring better marks in the examination as well as improve general ability to tackle any question.

(ii) The first lecture script could contain a list of typical questions that may appear in the final examination, in order to give the student an idea of the type of questions he should expect in the final examination.
(iii) Response sheet assignments should ensure that a student has grasped the necessary concepts, skills, etc. of the previous lesson script before he proceeds to study the next lesson script.
(iv) Questions should be so framed that students be discouraged from reproducing entire extracts from the lesson script, and should instead arrange necessary information (from the lesson script and other sources) to organize the material and develop the argument logically. This would develop mental faculty.
(v) Questions leading to self-study and self-assignment could be included within the lesson script wherever necessary.
(vi) Submission of Response Sheets should be made compulsory for all the students. These should be submitted in a phased manner and the time limit for the submission of a Response Sheet should be strictly adhered to.
(vii) Marked Assignments should be returned to the students promptly.

We can also encourage personnel presentation of response sheets on suitable occasions like PCP, etc. Kenneth Chav Chee has suggested the following to promote submission of Response Sheet:

(a) Good relationships and trust encourage communication. Tutors would be more willing to provide useful and honest feedback on 'course materials, students' performance and reactions and other matters related to tutorials, without the need for defensive behaviour or fear of being seen as offensive.
(b) Tutors would also be more self-disciplined (in keeping of time, marking of assignments, etc.) and motivated in the course of carrying out their duties. The rapport/relationship established between the tutors and their supervisors, would be an effective internal driving force for the conscientious tutors to carry out their duties in a professional manner so as not to betray the relationship established between them.
(c) Tutors would also be more willing to help and take up additional work in case of emergencies. An example being the case of sudden and unexpected absence or delay of a particular tutor in attending tutorial session, other tutors holding another class at the same venue and time would be happy to take over the group of students of the particular tutor although without additional benefits, financial or otherwise. The satisfying relationship established with tutors may facilitate or contribute to better relations amongst tutors themselves. On the other hand,

it may also lead to the development of a culture where self-monitoring and mutual cooperation is a norm which undoubtedly is helpful to their supervisor.

(d) Less time and effort will be required from the administrator for closely monitoring the tutors (or 'policing' the tutors in another word) when self-monitoring and peer-monitoring have become the 'norm' or accepted practice among tutors.[12]

UGC has suggested the following for making RSA attractive:

1. The evaluation of student response sheets must be done very carefully and thoroughly. The teachers should give detailed comments on the student's written work and explain the faults and lapses in unambiguous terms. It would motivate the students to send their response-sheets regularly if the timelag in marking and returning their response could be kept to the minimum. The submission of response-sheets by the students and their correction by the teachers go a long way in establishing a useful rapport between the pupil and the teacher and in mitigating the feeling of isolation that a correspondence course student may otherwise suffer from.
2. Some of the questions in the response-sheets (say 1/4 to 1/3) sent to the students could be of the multiple-choice type and solutions provided later so that the students may themselves ascertain their progress and grasp of the subject.
3. At least 10 per cent of the response-sheets should be sample-checked in the institute to ensure that these are being properly evaluated by the staff. The system of sample-checking should be clearly defined, and the help of an outside expert may be taken for this purpose, whenever necessary.
4. The institute should maintain a systematic record of lessons sent, response-sheets received and sent back, and the grades given, for each student, along with the date of each step referred to above.
5. The correspondence course institutes must educate their students about the importance of written assignments because one of the major advantages of the correspondence course methods over the other study methods is in the quantity of exercise and test materials available to the students. It would probably ensure good response if the awards scored by the students in response sheets are counted in lieu of internal assessment.
6. At the post-graduate level, in lieu of the response sheets, students may be required to write at least five essays/project in each paper during the year. In universities which have introduced internal assessment for regular students, essays written by correspondence course students, should be assessed and the marks/grades shown separately in the mark sheet.[13]

(c) Conclusion

Response sheet assignments are essential both to students as well as to the faculty. It has been realised by both and they consider this exercise as an indispensable element of DE system. However, in practice, this is more neglected than adhered to resulting in casual attitude on both the students and the faculty. There is a need of educating the students about the utility of these RSA at study centres, during PCP and through written words. Besides, faculty should take this seriously and once they are convinced, they would state that the students also would start taking keen interest in RSA. This would benefit both and ultimately promote Distance Education system on right course.

Notes and References

1. D.C.S., P.U., Chandigarh, Report of the Series of Faculty Workshops in Distance Education), (26th March to 21st April, 1979), p. 13.
2. H.C.S. Rathore, Treatment given to Assignment Responses at the Correspondence Institute: A study of Students' Reactions, in *Indian Journal of Open Learning*, Vol. 2, No. I, p. 26.
3. UGC, Scheme of Distance Education, New Delhi, 1993.
4. K. Raghunath, Management of Distance Education, A Case Study of APOU, Delhi, Ajanta, 1994, p. II.
5. H.C.S. Rathore, "Treatment given to Assignment Responses at the Correspondence Institutions: A Study of Students' Reactions", in *Indian Journal of Open Learning*, Vol. 2, No. 1, p. 26.
6. Report of the Proceedings of the Workshops in Distance Learning, Oct. 13-21, 1978, OCS, P.U., Chandigarh, p. 28.
7. D.C.S., P.U., Chandigarh, Reports of the Series of Faculty Workshops in Distance Education, 26th March to 21st April, 1979,
8. D.S.C., P.U., Chandigarh, Reports of the Proceedings of the Workshop in Distance Learning, Oct. 13-21, 197R, Sponsored by UGC and British Council Division, British High Commission, pp. 26-27.
9. Umesh Madhukar Rajderkar, Tutors' Comments in Distance Education in *University News*, 36(10), March 9, 1998, New Delhi, AIU, p. 8
10. N. Paradhan and Pabla Ranjit Kaur, Researches on Management of Instructional System in Distance Education and Open Universities A Meta Perspective, *University News*, 37(9), March 11, 1999, p. 4.
11. Lakshmi Chandra, Tutor Grading by Monitoring in the Distance Education Scenario in *Indian Journal of Open Learning*, Vol. 3, No. 1, p. 26
12. Kenneth Chav Chee: Strategic Tutor Monitoring, Open Learning, June 1996, p. 4.
13. Conference of Directors of CCI, *op. cit.*, p. 90.

Students Support Service

PART A

(A) INTRODUCTION

Student support services promote equitable and harmonious relationship between the students and the Distance Education System. The Distance Education System and students are intimately related to each other as the existence of one without the other is not possible. Since students of Distance Education are handicapped and do not have easy access to educational facilities, therefore, they need extra support, extra help to make them feel secure and stable.

The harmonious relationship depends upon the sincerity, earnestness and cooperation between the two. The achievement of good relations between the Distance Education System and the students is a matter which does not by any means depend solely on the conduct of faculty and administration of Distance Education Institute alone. It depends equally on the interest and attitudes of students and their keenness to learn. Moreover, we must normally assume that they for their part will behave well since Distance Education Students depend solely on the facilities provided by the Distance Education System, and they are spending money on this education from their own hard earned money.

Therefore, there is a great need to pay thorough attention to their problems, genuine demands, genuine needs, etc. to ensure benefits of the Distance Education System to them. Dr. P.K. Mehta, Director (RSD) IGNOU has rightly said, "Student support services underpins the entire teaching and learning philosophy of an open university. Provisions of student support services, is in someways, a reflection of the institution's commitment to distance learner who are virtually invisible and are rarely able to speak for themselves when decisions are taken."[1] "He also cautioned the need of ensuring human element to reduce learners sense of Isolation."

CHART 8.1

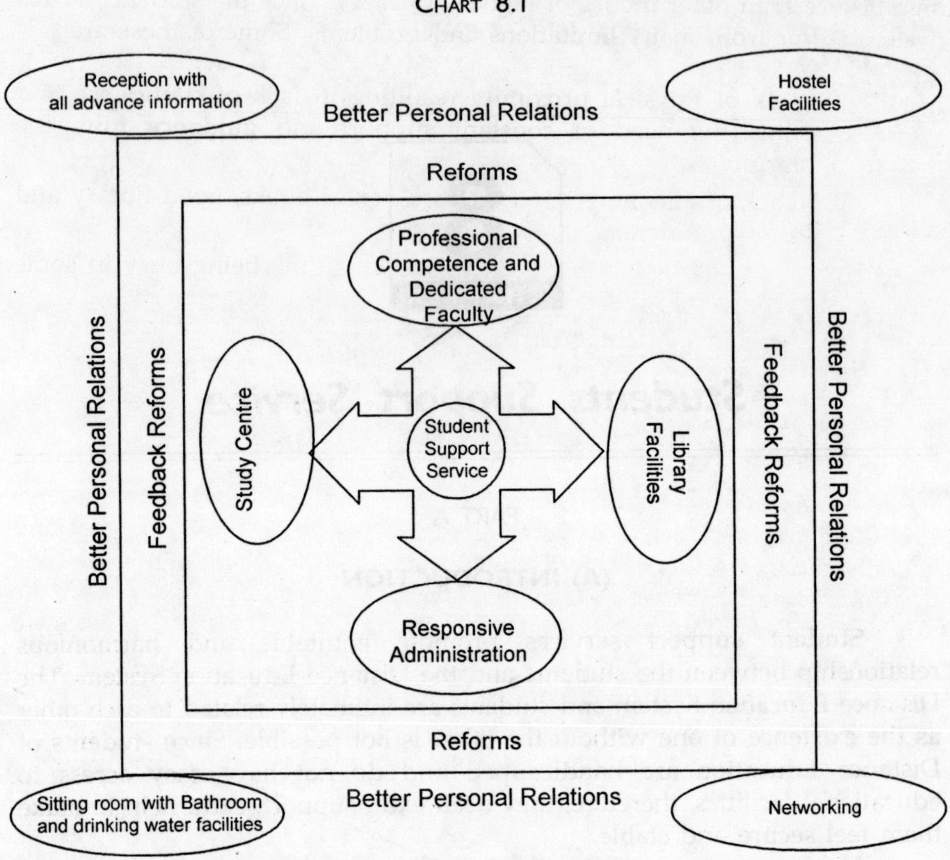

(B) BENEFITS AND NEED

Good student faculty relationship would:

(a) Encourage student participation a *sine qua non* for the success of distance educational system.

(b) Kindle the potential energy of the students into kinetic energy to accelerate their potential for educational development.

(c) Supplement the efforts of the Distance Education system in the conduct of its affairs.

(d) Strengthen the values of responsibility in the minds of the students.

(e) Enlist respect in the practices of Distance Education institute.

(f) Develop bonds of friendship and goodwill between students and faculty and *vice versa*.

(g) Avoid social unrest, tensions, violence and other social upheavals which have become the order of the day on the campus.

Student support services in Distance Education System are of greater significance than other modes of higher Education since the students in this system suffer from many limitations and problems. Some of these are:

(a) lack of Physical proximity resulting in lack of confidence and thus the need of constant support and guidance from the faculty.
(b) Lack of adequate infrastructure—extra books, good library and fellow students.
(c) Lack of adequate time as productive time being busy in some occupation or service.
(d) Lack of guidance from any source.
(e) Fear of examinations.

(C) MEANING AND CONTENTS

Distance Educational system is never something apart from students and their needs: rather it is the means by which these needs are met and the Distance Education system which thinks of its existence as something apart from the students will fail to recognise significant problems of the students and the Distance educational system will not be in a position to deliver the goods.

A number of elements are proposed as universal components for a Student support system, which include:

- providing clear information as to what was expected from students;
- publicising a procedure for dealing with student complaints;
- guaranteeing that the mode of delivery would not affect the award or credit;
- guaranteeing timely and effective feedback and commentary on assignments;
- guarantees provision of library services where these are necessary;
- provision of academic pre-study counselling before selection of courses;
- access to tutor on a regular basis;
- the publication of clear information regarding administrative regulations;
- the right to complete a programme of study within agreed time scales; and
- the charter should be related to the institution's mission statement.[2]

PART B

(A) INTRODUCTION

Student Support services have now become an integral part of most of the good distance education institutes. It is now internationally recognised that adequate student support services must be provided to the distant learners who are most of the time studying in isolation, away from their institution, teachers and the course mates. The purpose is to help these students to overcome the feeling of isolation and to facilitate learning. It is therefore, necessary that Distance Education Institutes should organize proper student support services.

There is a great competition among Distance Education institutes relating to the attraction of students to their courses. Better student support services would automatically spread the reputation and prestige of the institution. It requires that the Distance Education institutes must ensure:

(a) Academic excellences through faculty.
(b) Administrative responsiveness.
(c) Sound financial health.
(d) Orientation of media to the needs of the students.
(e) Relevance of the programme.
(f) Liaison with Industry and business.

An efficient functioning of a distance education institute is a self-generation exercise and students would be attracted automatically:

1. Reception and sitting room with bathroom and potable drinking water facility.
2. Responsive administration.
3. Professionally competent and dedicated faculty.
4. Library facilities.
5. Functional study centres.
6. Hostel facilities with nominal charges.
7. Net working.
8. Feed-back.

(B) RECEPTION AND SITTING ROOM WITH BATHROOM AND POTABLE DRINKING WATER FACILITIES

In the main building of the Distance Education Institute or Open University, there should be a reception office staffed by; a dynamic receptionist well acquainted with the functioning of the institute. There should be room with proper sitting arrangement, lighting, fans, etc. where the students coming from outstations can sit comfortably. The main purpose of the receptionist should be to establish a climate of understanding between the students and the Institute. Most of the problems of the Distance students pertain to some information which can be supplied by the receptionist, for other, the student can be referred to the concerned sections after informing the section concerned through PBX. There is also a need for sign boards and playcards to guide the students. Besides, a comfortable sitting room with bathroom and potable drinking water facilities need to be provided where a student coming from outstations can relax and sit comfortably. Such small facilities would add substantially to the prestige and good will of the Distance Education institutes. However, in practice, we do not pay attention to such facilities which lead to unwarranted attacks against the DE institute. Small facilities for students can build bridges of understanding between the students and Distance Education institute.

(C) RESPONSIVE ADMINISTRATION

Distance education students need a lot of clarifications for which they either write letters or come personally. The administrative set-up of the Distance Education institute must be designed in a way that it can solve their difficulties/problems promptly and efficiently. Since the programmes of study are time bound, therefore, the administration cannot delay the decisions. The people in administration must do all this with a sense of purpose and devotion. The head of the institution must ensure good administrative support to students. Jawaharlal Nehru, while delivering the inaugural address at the Indian Institute of Public Administration rightly said: "Administration like most other things is, in the final analysis, a human problems, to deal with human beings, not with some statistical data. There is the danger that pure administration at the top (not so much at the bottom, because they come in contact with human beings) may come to regard human beings as mere abstractions. The administrator may think in abstract of the people he deals with, come to conclusion, which are justifiable, but which miss the human element. After all, it is ultimately a problem of human beings and the moment we forget them, we are driven away from reality."

In Distance Education system we need to apply total quality management (TQM) which is designed to create student focused, high performing organization by involving all employees in process improvement efforts. In this way Distance Education institute can improve products and services, increase job satisfaction and enhance student satisfaction. This would automatically result in growth and development of Distance Education institute.

All this mentioned above would be possible only if there is transparency and accountability in the system. To quote V. Natarajan: "Transparency indicates straight forwardness; it stands for clear visibility, it shows openness in thought and deed; when there is transparency nothing is hidden, there is no secrecy or conspiracy. All problems arise only when there is secrecy or suspicion. Sometimes frankness may lead to misunderstanding and quarrel but it may not last long, once the cloud of misunderstanding passes and the sun of good will emerges, transparency pours its benefits."[3]

However, in practices, the administrative system is not effective resulting in drop outs, incurring expenditure by students to visit personally to get their problems solved and wastage on postage, etc. The heads of these institutions can help in removing most of the difficulties by injecting administrative improvements and keeping a constant watch on key issues. Administration has not to be only good but also appear to be good. The test of any good system of administration of a Distance Education system is to promote satisfaction of the distant students and create motivation and energy to excel in their pursuit of higher education, forgetting the inherent limitations in their stride.

A Case Study

A foreign student was studying in Semester III Public Administration. He was not informed of his result of Semester II. When he visited personally, he was surprised that he had passed Semester III examination for Semester IV was due after 15 days. He contacted the Assistant Registrar and then the Director who showed their inability to do anything at this stage. He approached me as Head of the Public Administration. I could persuade the Director that there was no fault of the student and we should allow him to appear. He was allowed to appear and the student passed in good 2nd class. Thus a minor rethinking can make or mar the career of a student.

(D) PROFESSIONALLY COMPETENT AND DEDICATED FACULTY

Faculty members are the life and blood of a distance education system. However, in the present scenario, we find that the faculty of higher education in general and of distance education in particular is least interested in discharging their duties honestly, earnestly and with devotion. Even in many cases, they do not come punctually and remain absent without leave. Most of the teachers have lost the identity with the profession. Dedication, enthusiasm and zeal are missing. Even the basic values are being eroded over a period of time. They are autonomous to the extent that they are their own masters. They never bother about the students interest. Library has become foreign to them. Some of them have kept it as a part time hobby with full pay while their permanent job is somewhere else. One feels sad, irritated and starts reflecting on these disheartening developments. What has happened to this noble profession? What has made them forget the ideals of a Guru? All this happening even when teachers in a University are being paid handsome salary and is not less than any other profession.

It is very difficult to adopt negative attitude of punishment or disciplinary action. There is a need to appeal to their inner conscience through HRD activities.

UGC through its Academic Staff Colleges and other programmes can inject skill and commitment in the faculty of higher education. It has been rightly said in "A study of the Capacity of United Nations Development System" that the "Human rather than capital is the key to development."[4]

Development is not a mechanical process. It is a human enterprise and its success will depend ultimately on the skill, quality and motivation of the persons associated with it. There is a need to plan, execute, and monitor HRD activities conduced through Academic Staff Colleges earnestly. ASC can create motivation among faculty trainee. Motivation can do miracles as a motivated worker can achieve more than an expert with no motivation. Educational administrators must, therefore, devote considerable time and effort in planning for and achieving high levels of motivation and morale. In such a situation, goal congruence would be achieved, i.e. identity between the individual goals and the organizational goals. My association with ASC has disappointing experience and to my mind, there is a colossal wastage of crores of rupees as we are running our ASC in an haphazard and unplanned way. ASCS have been started without any infrastructure, without any planning, monitoring and control over quality. Teachers attending these courses are forced to stay in unhygienic places where there are poor arrangements for bath rooms, lavatories, drinking water. How can one learn under such conditions? All are attending to complete a formality for promotion requirement. We must inject innovation and excellence in them which in turn can promote excellence in faculty of Higher Education.

S.K. Mukelji in his lecture, "Challenge in the Management of Higher Education in India" (Zaheer Science Foundation Lecture, 1978), rightly stresses the role of teacher. To quote him: "He is the central figure in whom the University sees its past glory and around him it builds its future dignity. A teacher must be constantly searching, researching, criticising and learning and making himself fit for his calling. A failure on his part can mar all other grandiose structures of the university. If he fails to understand this and its importance, nothing can save a University from stagnation and degeneration."

There is a need of accountability of the faculty to ensure the success of higher education. Besides, the following factors would determine the efficiency of the faculty of the Distance Education Institute:

(i) Extent of loyalty to the quality of distance education institution and identification with it and its objectives.

(ii) Extent to which the goals of units and individuals facilitates the achievement of the Distance Education institutes objectives.

(iii) Level of motivation among the members of the distance education institute with regard to such variables as:

  (a) Performance including both quality and quantity of work done.

  (b) Concern for elimination of waste and reduction of costs.

(c) Concern for improving the student services.
(d) Concern for improving processes.

(iv) Degree of confidence and trust among members of the Distance education institute in each other and at the different hierarchical levels.

(v) Amount and quality of team work in administrative and academic wing and between units of the organisation.

(vi) Extent to which the members feel that their ideas, information, knowledge of processes and experiences are being used in the decision-making processes of the distance education institute.

(vii) Upward, downward and sideward efficiency and adequacy of the communication process.

(viii) Leadership skills and abilities of key officers of the Distance education system.

We have to develop all these qualities among the faculty of the Distance Education Institutes.

(E) LIBRARY SERVICES

Distance education has been described more attuned to learning than teaching. Library and other information technology has a central place in the process of Distance Education. Therefore there is a need of:

1. Setting up a good library in the institute with proper borrowing facilities for students. It would be ideal if students are supplied library books, by post, on demand. The postage should be borne by the institute. Students may return the books personally or by post (Regd. Post) in which case the postage will be borne by the students.
2. DEs should try to set-up a Book Bank for providing text books to students belonging to economically weak and other backward classes and scheduled castes.
3. Distance Education Institutes should make arrangements for supplying text books on payment to the students residing at distant places.
4. To aid and activate faculty members, writers, editors to design, revise and uptodate reading material, library according to D.K. Gupta and S.L. Jain, should perform the following functions[5]:
   - To motivate all category of learners to get benefit from open learning-the most suitable form of imparting education to them;
   - To inform learners regarding educational opportunities through open university, its educational programmes and components of each programmes;
   - To make information available regarding tools and sources, learning packages in print and non-print form;

- To assist learners to make the effective use of library services available to them;
- To share resources with other agencies involved in educational guidance;
- To support consellors/tutors in successfully completion of counselling/tutoring sessions; and
- To motivate all category of learners to get benefit from open learning.

Neelu Jagannathan describes the functions of IGNOU library and its structures which may be adopted by other DE institutes.[6]

- to develop appropriate collections in various disciplines for satisfying the needs of the diverse clientele of the libraries of the University, regional and study centres;
- to provide reading, lending, reference, information and documentation facilities to all categories of staff and students;
- to develop special collection of distance education books and journals at the libraries of the Headquarters as well as Regional centres; and
- to provide documentation and comprehensive reference/information services in areas related to distance education to other open universities of the world, and of India in particular.

Net Work Pattern of Libraries at Open Universities

Some libraries of the distance teaching universities, such as IGNOU, operate through the three-tier system; the main university library and the branch libraries at the regional and study centres. The two-tier system, functional in universities such as Bhimrao Ambedkar Open University of Andhra Pradesh in India and Sukhothai Thammathirat Open University, Thailand have the supporting libraries at study centres, directly responsible to the Central Library at Headquarters. These libraries comprise two distinct categories:

(a) Central Library at the University Headquarters.
(b) Libraries at the Regional and/or study centres as the branch libraries.

The central library combines the features and functions of both, a general academic library as well as a specialist library. This dual responsibility increases the complexity of library policies regarding the development of collections and provision of library and information services.

In practice, we find that the students do not make use of the library as they should do. The faculty members at PCP and through letters, must motivate the students to take immense benefits of libraries. The students must also be given the lesson in information literacy so that they may know the methods of using library and other information facilities. The objectives of bibliographic instructions are:

(i) to increase student awareness of the library as primary source of recorded information and as an agency to which students might turn with their information needs;

(ii) to educate students to make effective use of the services and facilities of the library systems;

(iii) to develop student's skills in finding information and in identifying and locating bibliographic references for specific purposes;

(iv) to teach effective methods of approach to information searching tasks in such a way that the skill learned can be adopted by the students to other library search situations; and

(v) to encourage a sense of enjoyment in information searching and in becoming acquainted with various sources of information.

We must also ensure the appointment of a dynamic librarian who can motivate and guide the learners. No machine can compete with a creative, knowledgeable, flexible, professional librarian, one who provides interpersonal interaction, information evaluation, communication, synthesis and judgment. The role of librarian is to distinguish between data and information, between facts and knowledge. Libraries must be concerned not only with the what and the how but with the why also. Our challenge is not just to provide more information, or even the right answers, our challenge is to help people formulate the right questions to receive their answers.

Inspite of the inherent advantages of libraries, distance education institutes are not in a position to provide full facilities because of the financial constraints and lack of interest. A study on University Library system highlights the following problems:[9]

- The meagre budget allotment poses a threat to the very existence of the study center libraries;
- The holdings of libraries are insufficient to meet users requirements;
- Periodicals subscribed to are very few and need to be increased;
- Physical facilities are not available;
- Users need better access to the resources of the library and improvement of services offered;
- Audio-visual materials in the study centres are not sufficient;
- Book lending services are not available; and
- Staff of the study centre libraries are less cooperative.

Distance education libraries to be useful must be equipped with facilities like satellite communication, computer networks, audio and visual facilities, text and reference books, foreign and national journals, photostat facilities, etc.

(F) FUNCTIONAL STUDY CENTRES

Every CCI should have adequate number of study centres in the ratio of one study centre per 500 students. Every study centre should act as an information, publicity and guidance cell.

The study centres must be well organised with proper facilities of library, personal contact programmes and playback of audio and video cassettes, radio broadcast and TV telecasts. Besides academic support, study centres can also serve the following functions:

(i) It can help in assessing the local requirements which can help in designing new programme.
(ii) It can serve as a place of meeting of students where they can develop friendship for mutual support.
(iii) It can serve as a meeting place for interaction between the students and the tutors which can lead to socialization.
(iv) It may act as a centre for social and cultural activities to reduce the boredom of the learners.
(v) It serves as a place for socio-psychological satisfaction.
(vi) It serves to make distant learners at ease.

All Open universities have set-up study centres so that the students can take the benefit of proximity and avail of all facilities near them. For example, IGNOU has setup more than twelve hundred study centres to cater to the various needs of the students. The Kota Open University functions through 26 study centres, Andhra Open University functions through 117 study centres. Most of the Distance Education Institutes have also set-up these study centres at selected places, e.g. Panjab University, Chandigarh, Department of Correspondence Studies has also set-up 7 study centres since the staff posted in these study centres is paid a meagre salary, students are not looked after properly. There is a need to act as follows:

(i) Networking of Distance Education Institutes to create a study centre with full time staff and adequate facilities and infrastructure to attend to a large clientele.
(ii) Staff at study centres must be attuned or regularly trained to understand the needs of the students.
(iii) A good library may be set-up with latest books and journals to cater to the current needs of the students.
(iv) Visit of the staff of the headquarters to ensure thorough effective supervision and proper functioning of the study centres.

The library at the study centres is essential to meet the needs of the Distance Education students. There must be multiple copies of relevant books to ensure availability. Library may also keep audio and video-cassettes for the needy students. The procedure of borrowing by distance education students must be simple so that they can get them issued easily.

Except the study centres of some good Open Universities, they are not functioning nicely because of the following reasons:

(a) Persons appointed in study centres are on part-time basis with a meagre allowance.
(b) They have neither the training for the work nor any motivation.
(c) Study centres are poorly equipped in terms of books.
(d) No modern information technology is available.
(e) Students rarely make use of the study centres.
(f) There is no supervision over them and regular feed-back from them.
(g) PCPs are not held at the study centre.
(h) TV and Video supplied are watched by peons and chowkidars of most of the study centres.

N. Pardhan and Pabla Ranjit Kaur have also stressed these factors. To quote them:[10] "The studies on utilisation of facilities at study centres revealed that the existing facilities are not managed properly and that has resulted in under-utilisation and even non-utilisation of facilities. To maintain the equipments there are no technicians and the audio-visual materials although available and of good quality cannot be traced for their utilisation easily. The staff are also not trained for the maintenance of equipments and facilities."

(G) HOSTEL FACILITIES

Students of distance education have to come to attend PCP and for other academic work. It is necessary to reserve some rooms for them. They may be given the accommodations on nominal rents for PCP days or some other urgent work. This is especially important for women students. Students can participate in large number if such facility is provided near the PCP venue.

(H) NET WORKING

Networking means pooling of resources and sharing of benefits by Distance Education system. This would improve the quality of services as an individual institution cannot afford the quality required to implement distance education programmes. IGNOU has already established more than 400 study centres which can be further strengthened to provide services to the institutes of other distance education system.

We would suggest that Distance Education Council may take over the management of study centres so that these can be managed by an independent agency catering to the needs of all the institutions. Resources can be pooled and some parameters may be fixed to set-up the study centres. In this way, study centres can be dispersed even to the block level and the real purpose of development can be achieved. These centres can be used even by conventional students on payment, i.e. by becoming a member. The whole issue of Networking has not been studied scientifically so far. It requires to be implemented earnestly and sincerely.

Distance Education has immense potentialities in Networking. In 1993, efforts were made to link Regional Centres through a communication network by commonwealth of learning by means of Fax and Audio Conferencing. IGNOU introduced tele-counselling. This facility is also shared by some other open universities. R.C. Sharma has rightly put as: "The trend globally indicate that the student support services in open and distance education can be made more scientific, standardised and systematised through proper networking. New technologies will play a key role in the future development of DE making it more economical, accessible, and efficient.[11]

(I) FEED-BACK

The faculty and administrative staff of the Distance Education institutes must get the feed-back from the students on a continuous basis to know their problems and provide them better services in future. This endeavour will keep the system alive otherwise it becomes mechanical and outdated after some time.

PART. C

CRITICAL APPRAISAL

A general survey of the student support system reveals pathetic state of affairs. Students are admitted without looking to the capacity and capability of the Distance Education Institutes. The financial crises in most of the universities has compelled the universities to make money through distance education students. This is quite unfair. On the one hand, we are subsidizing regular students and providing them all the facilities while we are charging heavily from the Distance education students and providing poor services. Besides, the library, study centres are used only by 10-20 per cent of distance education students. Even their querries are not attended promptly. Therefore, there is a need of great improvements and reforms to make distance education institutes provide quality services. What can be done to restore quality services to distance education students? How can we protect their interest? How can we create confidence in them? How can we remove discrimination between regular and distance education students? What is the role of Distance Education council in it? How can we weed out sub-standard institutions? We need to answer all these questions, so that Distance Education system can be put on sound footing.

PART D

(A) FACTS AND SUGGESTIONS

To help the students to overcome the feeling of isolation and aloofness, what can be done to facilitate good learning, motivation and interest in the area of student support services? We may suggest here methods to promote good relationships between the Distance Education System and their students.

A GENERAL SUGGESTION

(a) Infusing Competence and Dedication among Distance Education Faculty and Administrative Staff

The success of educational administration depends upon the quality of its constituents, i.e. the ability, intelligence and competence of administrative personnel and academic faculty appointed in the distance education organizations or associated on part-time or contractual basis. It has been found that a large number of faculty working in distance educational organizations are unfit for the assignments they perform. Most of them occupy the positions because of political patronage, corruption, favoritism, etc. Most of the positions at higher levels are occupied by personnel promoted on the basis of seniority, irrespective of their suitability for the job. How to ensure the competence of the personnel in an organisation for optimum performance? It can be done through strict tests of recruitment, promotion based on merit, rigorous training, retraining and refresher courses.

Andrew Carnegie has laid great stress on the organization based on the competent people. "Take away all our money, our great works, our mines and coke ovens but leave our organisations, and in a few years, I shall have re-established myself." All the personnel in an organisation must attend seriously to the task of distance education development.

(b) Expansion of Distance Educational Activities must Match with the Availability of Resources

The administration needs to be equipped with adequate resources to meet the needs of the distance education students. In this context authors found that these problems also emanate from a number of constraints, e.g., shortage of staff at all levels, absence of proper accommodation to provide space to the ever increasing number of students, shortage of funds, shortage of equipment, etc., which need to be attended to by the universities to provide satisfactory educational services. Besides, the students must cooperate with educational authority to make the best use of the available resources. Thus, we shall have to have a three—pronged attack-increasing internal efficiency, mobilising university support and enlisting students cooperation to ensure the reputation, prestige, credibility and viability of the distant educations system. For example, in professional courses, like B.Ed., thousands of students were enrolled by many distance education institutes without matching facility and resources for them.

(c) Designing of Orientation Programme for Students

A two-day orientation programme may be initiated at the commencement of the session. This can pinpoint major issues and ideas to be kept in mind by distance education students to gain their confidence, interest and creativity. This may be done both at the headquarters and at the study centres. This can also solve many of their potential problems resulting in a good start. We all know the proverb, "Well begun is half done."

(d) Prompt Reply to the Queries of the Students

Students develop many problems relating to Distance Education Programme. It is very difficult for them to approach the Distance Education Institutes. What is required is prompt attention and positive reply to the students? It is suggested that teachers in Distance Education System can be allocated students according to enrolment numbers. Students may be asked to approach that teacher or correspond with that person whose name may be mentioned to the students in advance.

(e) Creating Availability of Time for Students to meet Personally

The Distance Education Institutes must provide time in their daily work for meeting the students to solve their academic and administrative problems. This can facilitate positive relationships.

(f) Need of Review of Structure of DE System

It is the duty of personnel in Distance Education system to review the structure for quality with specific quality indicators to meet the requirements of 21st century. They should encourage thinking and innovation. Cost and benefit of the quality process must be kept in view.

Dr. Taiseer Zaid Kailani has stressed upon the need of motivating the students of Distance Education Systems to make them feel comfortable through the following methods:

- By providing help when the students meet difficulties in their studies.
- By being good at explaining facts.
- By taking a personal interest in the students and their study progress.
- By adopting appropriate behaviour towards the students.

- By telling them that the university is interested in their progress and their study problems.
- By taking the best possible care of the students at the beginning of the course.
- By trying to follow up the students work.
- By writing to passive students or telephoning them.
- By promoting students' motivation through establishing and encouraging personal contact.

Further to these approaches, tutor's qualities such as, competency, warmth, enthusiasm and sympathy can indeed strengthen the students' motivation and enhance their perseverance to complete their open learning programme.[12]

(B) CONCLUSION

Distance education students need be provided essential support services. It has become a fashion with open universities and institutes of correspondence studies to spend most of the money on new technology while missing the basic minimum facilities. We should think of costly technology only after we are in a position to provide basic minimum essential support services to all. We should not blindly follow or come under the influence of foreign affluent countries to set-up the system for distance education students which we are not in a position to maintain for all.

All those engaged in Distance education system must keep the following definition of the students in their minds to provide decent student support services.

- The student is the most important person in the Distance Education institute.
- The student is not dependent on us, we are dependent on him.
- The student is not an interruption of our work.
- He is the purpose of it.
- The student is not an outsider to our business.
- He is our business.
- The student is a person and not a statistic.
- He has feelings, emotions, biases and wants.
- It is our business to satisfy him.

Notes and References

1. P.K. Mehta, Performance indicators in student support services, In IGNOU, Distance Education Council, Performance indicators in Distance Education National Seminar Report, 1996, p. 62.
2. Conference Report: Seminar on student charter. For Distance Education, May 25,

1993. Laurentien University Sudbury, Ontario, Canada, quoted in *Open Learning,* 1994, p. 64

3. V. Natrajan, Transparency and Accountability, in *University News,* Dec. 2, 1996, (Vol. XXXIV, No. 49), p. 1
4. U.N.: A study of the capacity of the UN System, Vol. 1, Geneva, 1909, p. 10.
5. Dinesh Kumar Gupta and S.L. Jain, Open University and Library: Concept and Relationship, *University News,* July 22, 1996, p. 10.
6. Neelu Jagannathan, Libraries in Distance Education, *Indian Journal of Open Learning,* Vol. I, No. 2, July 1992, p. 33.
7. J.C. Binwal, Bibliographic instruction: Objectives, Strategies and Evaluation in N.R. Satyanaryana (Ed.) User Education in Academic Libraries Ess Publishers, New Delhi, 1981, Quoted in Sanjaya Mishra, Teaching Information Literacy to Distance Learners, *University News,* 35(20), May 19, 1997, p. 4.
8. Patrica Glass Schuman, Quoted in, P.N. Kaula, Information and Communication Technology: Impact and Challenges, in *University News,* 30(35), Sept. 1, 1997, p. 5.
9. Tony Convangh and Bemacodete Lingham, Library Services for External Post-graduate and Overseas Students, Distance Education, Vol. IV, No.7 , p. 69. Quoted in Dinesh Kumar Gupta and S.L. Jain, Open University and Library, Concept and Relationship, *University News,* July 22, 1996, p. 11.
10. N. Pradhan and Pabla Ranjit Kaur, "Researches on Management of Instructional System in Distance Education and Open Universities", *University News,* 37(9), March, I, 1999, pp. 56.
11. R.C. Sharma, Networked Distance Education in India, in *Indian Journal of Open Learning,* New Delhi, May 1999, p. 156.
12 Dr T.Z. Kailani, "Quality assurance in the off campus delivery of Professional Development Opportunity" in *Open Learning,* February, 1993, p. 42

Quality Control in Distance Education System

Set and Raise your Quality Standards continuously to reach the best possible—Quality only happens when you care enough to do your best.
—Chinmaya

MEANING:

Defining Quality in DE

Apriori, quality cannot be considered as an absolute concept but is a multi-dimensional dynamic entity. It is also not a unitary concept but a phenomenon determinable by relating with the excellent or the best in the field. Consequently, for judging quality, a yardstick or standard needs to be established which is otherwise called 'benchmark'.

In general, quality is also a holistic view of an organization by which all the activities require active consideration, careful planning and implementation. In a nutshell, the quality concept in DE at the macro-level can be identified with the following:

1. Achieving the intended goals;
2. Satisfying the learners' needs and expectations;
3. Continuously improving the performances in the key areas; and
4. Total quality management (TQM) encompassing all activities and functions.[1]

Quality is of great significance to both the providers of Distance Education and the receivers of distance education and in the process builds a solid foundation of Distance Education institutions. Press Reports, personal discussions and observation reveal the poor functioning of DE services as there is no emphasis on quality. Such situations create unnecessary Problems to Students and even become cause of dropping in many cases. The situation can be improved by injecting quality in DE system rigorously and meticulously.

Quality in DE should also be students focused and should emphasize meeting the students with most effective and efficient manner. Quality, however, does not have to be luxurious or expensive. It should also be the responsibility of everyone involved and should be based on a learning environment rather than a disciplinary environment. Quality is simply a process of continuous improvement of the *status quo*.

Quality is of great significance in a distance education as the students have to depend upon the teachers who are far away from them. Quality and excellence can only make distance education system relevant to the needs of students. We are expanding both in magnitude and direction to promote distance education without caring for Quality. The main aim of starting distance education by traditional universities is to earn money for the sustenance of formal system. Distance education, by and large is being run without teachers, thus saving at the cost of quality. Whenever Vice-Chancellors have to accommodate influential persons sons/ daughters he appoints them in distance education department. Lesson scripts written 20 years ago are being signed and sent to students, fulfilling the formalities. Response sheets are not evaluated properly. Only 20 percent students attend PCP as teachers take no interest. When there are large number of teachers with 20-30 years experience in distance education are available, Vice-Chancellors are generally appointed from formal system. How can we expect efficiency and Quality from such Vice-Chancellors? In order to attract talented students to distance education and run distance education on sound principles, we have to determine norms and standards. Moreover, the new technology, which is being harped again and again, is nothing but a fraud as huge money is spent on these gadgets without any advantage. These are only show pieces. These have not become common use in the Indian context. These are used only rarely for specific purpose. Distance education system must be put in sound health before expecting too much from it. Knowledge commission, Distance Education Council, Policy-Makers and planners should not be under the wrong impression that Distance Education can be a good alternative source of education until and unless standards of quality are maintained. Based on our 30 years experience, one can say with a sense of truthfulness that distance education institutes may not be set-up any more till the existing institutions are ensured to impart quality education. Even the advisors to the Knowledge Commission, or Ministry of HRD have not much experience of distance education. Only those experts who have in-depth experience of theory and practice may be associated to overhaul the system of Distance Education to maintain quality.

Quality is described as having eight dimensions: effectiveness, efficiency, interpersonal relationship, safety, technical competency, access, continuity, and amenities. Each of these dimensions should be met at least minimally to meet the definition of quality.

The concept of quality has been defined as "The totality of features and characteristics of a product or service that bear on the ability to satisfy stated or implied needs." The features or characteristics may be: (1) Meeting well defined purposes; (2) Satisfying students and job satisfaction to DE personnel; (3) Complying with applicable standards; (4) Reliability of products/services; (5) Excellence; (6) Complying with safety requirements; (7) Complying with Environment requirements, and (8) Improving Educational status. (See Chart 9.1)

CHART 9.1

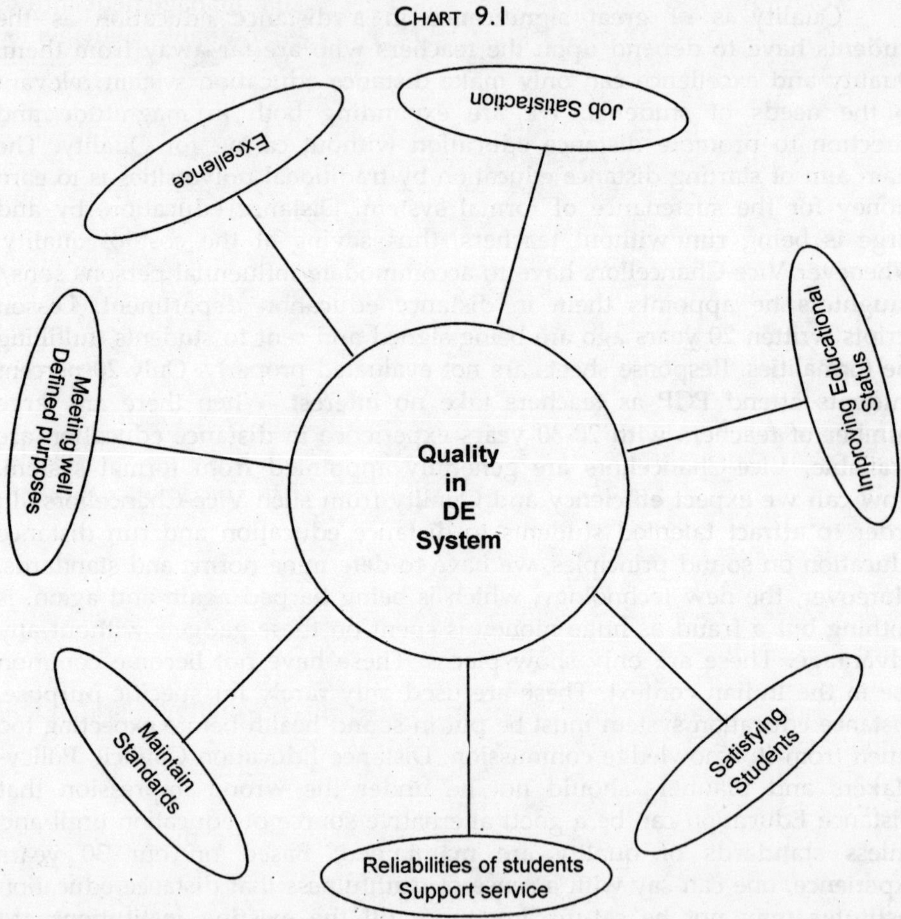

Quality is not obtained by chance. Efforts must be made by everybody at every level and at various phases of DE delivery system. In this context, the concept of total quality management (TQM) which is being adopted by almost all excellent institutions throughout the world appears to be the only hope for establishing quality standards.

TQM may be thought of as a way of organizing and involving the whole DE institution—every department, every activity and every single personal at every level towards achieving excellence. TQM can work well where culture and environment in the institution reflects academic quality as a way of life for all its employees.

Sri R. Venkatraman, former President of India, delivered the Convocation Address at the sixteenth convocation of Gandhigram Rural Institute, Gandhigram. He said,[2] "A quality conscious system has been described as one which produces people who have the attributes of mental agility, efficacy and reliability and, above all, the capability to take initiative and innovative measures to meet situations."

Dill (1992) grouped Deming's fourteen points management into six basic themes in providing a framework for academic quality management (Williams, 1993).[3]

- The imperative of continuous quality improvement of an enterprise is to hold or enhance its place in the market,
- The emphasis on obtaining consistent quality in incoming resources through careful management of suppliers,
- The active participation of all members of an organization's productive work force in the improvement of quality,
- The importance of meeting customer needs as the fundamental basis for the improvement of goods and services,
- The need for co-operation and coordination as the basic way in which an enterprise can improve its quality, and
- Quality improvement comes not from inspection but design, that is the establishment of procedures which make it impossible for bad quality to be inducted and encourage the primary aim of continuous improvement.

Murgatroyd and Morgan (1993) defined three quality related terms:

Quality Assurance

The determination of standards, appropriate methods and quality requirement by an expert body.

Contract Conformance Quality

Some quality standard has been specified during the negotiation of forming a contract.

Customer Driven Quality

Those who are to receive a product or service make explicit their expectations.

Quality assurance means delivery of efficient and effective delivery of distance education in accordance with the professional standards. The DE system need to develop standards of quality in a comprehensive and scientific manner. They should not refer only to the technical aspects of effectiveness but to other aspects as well, like compatibility of service and work environment, communication with students and promotion of collective responsibility for DE.

In the context of DE system quality assurance has to be understood in terms of entire DE system. The concept of quality assurance should not be fragmented for the different aspects of DE system rather the totality of the DE provided to the students should be kept in view.

In Public Administration quality control is also equated with Good Governance. Quality of DE system can be achieved only by efficient administration of DE services that is by optimising the use of DE resources.

NEED

Quality control is essential to make the efficiency of DE institutions possible through:[4]

(a) Improvement of existing obsolete processes and procedures.
(b) Improved layout of office and working environment.
(c) Economy in human effort.
(d) Suggesting the best use of money and material.
(e) Improved design of the goods or services provided by the organization.
(f) Improved performance.
(g) Job satisfaction.
(h) Improved flow of work
(i) Standardization of processes and products.

In brief, it aims at optimisation of resources which are:

- *Manpower*: Brain, skill, morale and effort.
- *Materials*: Inventory, Quality, Standards.
- *Equipment*: Design and Operation.
- *Services*: Communication and Information Systems.
- *Space and Building*: Availability, design, utilization.
- Environment of Quality Control.

Quality control cannot be initiated in isolation. It depends upon a number of factors both internal as well as external to the DE system. Let us analyse some of them.

However, when we see around the functioning of DE system in the country, leaving aside 2-3 open universities, we find, hear and see very sad commentaries on their functioning. Why these DE institutes are not adopting standard practices to maintain the standards of higher education? Why are we diluting the quality of higher education? Why are we creating a bad image of the system? The answer to all these questions is that we have designed these institutes well and worked hard in the initial stages but over a period of time, our inaction resulted in a pathetic scenario. We have become very slow in action. We always talk about the big strides about the DE system but we do not see its hollowness from inside.

Words written or spoken are of no use unless put to action. Robert Chambers has rightly observed, "It is action that matters. But knowing does not guarantee a change of feeling and a change of feeling does not guarantee a change of behvaiour. So we come to the final paradoxical reversal to start by acting. . . . Not everything can or should be foreseen. It is often best to start, to do something, and to learn from doing.

Parameters of Quality in a Distance Education:

1. *Excellent Lecture Scripts*: Most of the students depend primarily on the lecture scripts prepared by experts. These lectures must be of high quality in terms of contents, linkages, no spelling mistake, clarity in language, good quality of paper, well defined headings and sub-headings. The quality of lecture scripts would prompt the students to take interest in lessons and read them again and again. What has been observed in actual practice is the availability of low quality of lecture scripts leading a loss of interest among distant learners. A study of lecture scripts of 20 institutes reveal the following:
   (a) Lessons are written by outside expert without understanding the need of distance education students;
   (b) The remuneration paid by distance education institutes is very less leaving aside a few institutes like IGNOU.
   (c) Proper editing is not done by internal faculty and lecture scripts are not kept upto date with latest changes.
   (d) Cover design and paper is of very poor quality causing repulsion in the minds of readers.
   (e) It is high time to monitor the quality of lecture scripts.
2. *Regular Dispatch of Lecture Scripts*: Regular dispatch of lecture scripts is essential to maintain the interest of students. This will improve quality of services and students would remain motivated.
3. *Quality Assignments* must be prepared so that students apply their mind in answering the assignments. Assignments well prepared can judge the quality of students.
4. *Quality of PCP* should be of very high standard so that students take interest and attend the classes seriously. It has been seen that students do not feel serious and very few attend these classes as they find PCP of not good quality in terms of accommodation, teachers, topics, etc.
5. *Arrangements for drinking water*, tea, sitting arrangements, etc. are necessary to provide essential services.

ESSENTIALS OF QUALITY CONTROL

1. An Urge and Desire on the Part of the Personnel in the DE Organization to Find Better Methods of Quality system through Analysis of Existing Practices

Dr. M.K. Mani, Chief Nephrologist, Appolo Hospital, Chennai, delivered the convocation address at the third annual convocation of NTR University of Health Sciences, Vijaywada on Thursday the 4th Feb., 1999. He said,[5] "What we get by reading is the distilled wisdom of others. It is necessary, and we must do it, but there is something more important, and that is to learn from our own experience. Reason, Observation and Experience are the Holy Trinity of Science. Why do we not trust ourselves? An important reason is that we do not really know what we are doing.

2. Need of Initiative and Creativity among DE Faculty and Administrative staff through Critical Examination

The critical examination is the crux of the quality control as it helps us to arrive at the true basis underlying each event and to draw up a systematic list of all possible improvements for designing of the most efficient, economic and practical way in which the job could be done. As stated in the report of the Secretariat Training School, Ministry of Home Affairs, Government of India (p. 91).

> "Critical Examination is a disciplined questioning technique. The questioning technique attacks the governing considerations of a specified activity under study in a systematic, logical and objective manner." The questioning technique is the means by which the critical examination is conducted, each activity being subjected in turn to a systematic and progressive series of questions.

In short, we can say that critical examination challenges the existing purpose, the resources used, the processes employed, environmental considerations of DE organizations, etc. to improve quality DE system.

The critical examination is an intellectual exercise and must be used cautiously. It is perhaps worth-mentioning a few points which should be borne in mind:

(a) Facts must be examined as they are, not as they appear to be, or should be, or said to be.
(b) Preconceived ideas, which often colour the interpretation of facts, must be allowed no play.
(c) All aspects of the problem must be approached with a challenging and sceptical attitude. Every detail must be examined logically and no answer accepted until it has been proved correct.
(d) Hastly judgements must be avoided.

(e) Experiment resulting from 'hunches', which should have been immediately committed to paper as they occurred, should be reserved to the appropriate place in the investigation.

(f) New methods should not even be considered until all the undesirable features of the existing method have been exposed by systematic examination.[6]

(g) Details must have persistent and close attention.

We can thus say that the critical examination for its success presupposes the existence of the following ingredients—an analytical mind, freedom from prejudice, absence of pre-conceived notions, willingness to learn, strength of mind to avoid going off a tangent in pursuit of bright ideas, and concrete evidence.

EXAMINATION PROCEDURE

The examination is conducted by means of the sets of detailed questions: the primary questions to indicate the facts and their underlying reasons, and the secondary questions to find the alternatives and the best methods of improvement. The questions pertain to the purpose of the operation, the place where it is carried out and the means by which it is carried out. Both primary and secondary questions are asked for each aspect before passing on to the next.

In order to carry out the critical examination in a scientific way, a sheet of standard layout is used. The outline format of this sheet is reproduced on the previous page.[7]

While examining the factors impinging upon the operational efficiency of purpose, means, sequence, place and person, there is no set sequence to be followed. However, we must initiate with the purpose, as other factors would be considered only provided the study of purpose is justified.

The success of the critical examination depends upon the scientific attitude of the investigating team. The aim of all critical examination is the furtherance of the work study philosophy—there is always a better and effective way.

Let us cultivate the valuable resources of creativity to creatively respond to the changing situations and become the 'Masters of Change' in every field.

C = Customer satisfaction leading to students' delights,
H = Honour and dignity to all the students,
A = Accountability from every area of service,
N = New ideas and commitment to innovation,
G = Growth as a continuous discipline, and
E = Excellence expressed as yardstick for performance and evaluation.[8]

Factual data			Creative Thinking	
Facts	Reasons	Alternative	Implications Development	Selection for
1	2	3	4	5
Purpose				
What is being achieved?	Why is achieved?	What else can be achieved?	What are the advantages and dis-advantages of each alter-native?	What can be selected for development?
Means				
How is it achieved?	Why that way?	How else can it be achieved?	What are the advantages and disadvantages of each alternative?	What can be selected for development?
Sequence				
When it is achieved?	Why then?	When else can it be achieved?	What are the advantages and disadvantages of each alternative?	What can be selected for development?
Place				
Where is it Achieved?	Why there?	Where else can it be achieved?	What are the advantages and disadvantages of each alternative?	What can be selected for development?
Person				
Who achieved?	Why that person?	Who else can achieve it?	What are the advantages and disadvantages of each alternative?	What can be selected for development?

The DE institutions that will survive and thrive in the future, are those that foster creativity today among their DE professionals. Without creativity, professionals would become junk after a decade or so and would be a liability for the DE system and even on themselves. Creativity only can keep professionals alive in the true sense.

3. Need of High Quality Research both in the Area of DE system and Human Behaviours towards their Education.

According to P.V. Young, "Social Research may be defined as a scientific undertaking which by means of logical and systematized techniques, aims to:

(1) discover new facts or verify and test old facts;
(2) analyse their sequence, inter-relationships and casual explanations which were derived within an appropriate theoretical frame of reference; and
(3) develop new scientific tools, concepts and theories which would facilitate reliable and valid study of human behaviour.

As stated in the Encyclopedia of the Social Science, Social Research is systematic method of exploring, analysing and conceptualizing social life in order to "extend correct or verify knowledge, aids in construction of a theory or in the practice of an art."

The purpose of research is to discover answers to questions through the application of scientific procedures, i.e. Research Methods. There is no guarantee that any given research undertaking actually will produce reliable, relevant and unbiased results. But scientific research procedures are more likely to do so than any other method known to man. According to Young, "A researcher's primary goal, distant or immediate—is to explore and gain an understanding of human behaviour and social life."

Quality is more important than quantity in research. What is required is an increased quantity of quality research. The institutions must realize that high quality of work is a permanent asset which builds the foundations of science. A healthy climate is necessary for quality research. Openness, enthusiasm, trust, independence and team spirit is essential for the development of a scientific culture.

Successful application of research therefore depends upon the interest and commitment of both researchers and users. It cannot be achieved by individuals working in isolation (Bircumshaw, 1990). If the ultimate benefits must be understood and implemented by DE system at all levels of the system. This does not happen rapidly. It requires commitment and willingness to learn because this process is cyclical as well as continuous.

Research utilization is an organizational responsibility. It is best accomplished if there is real commitment to apply research findings at the organizational level. Therefore, translating DE research into DE practice is neither easy nor quick (Sheehan, 1986). It remains an enormous challenge.

4. Need of Commitment and Empathy

Quality DE system needs team work and mutual understanding. DE personnel must work in a team to achieve quality DE. S.S. Maricodoss mentions two ingredients of team work—commitment and empathy. To quote him:

> "Commitment is a deep and profound value of emotional intelligence. It means aligning oneself with the goals of a group or organization. It is applying oneself completely for a cause. People possessing this competence readily make sacrifice to meet larger organizational goals. Hence more than the individual interests, the group's mission or

interest takes priority. It is very deep to the extent of sacrificing oneself. It also involves taking sides or taking stance. Emotionally balanced and committed people don't yield to any pressure or threat. Instead they courageously proceed whatever may be the consequences.

Emotionally balanced people are generally empathetic and not sympathetic. Sympathy perpetuates oppression and makes people dependent. Sympathy is a form of judgement. We should therefore avoid being sympathetic towards others. Empathy means understanding the issue or concern that lie behind another's feeling. It is an ability to look at things from others' point of view or to read another's emotions or to put oneself into other's shoes and think from their angle. Avoiding pretension, it enables sensing and responding to a person's unspoken concern or feelings. It can be called the foundation skill for all the social competencies. Empathetic listening is a tremendous deposit in the Emotional Bank Account. Empathy includes understanding others, service orientation, developing others, leveraging diversity and political awareness.[9]

7. Outstanding Leadership and Strength of Character

DE services must also develop the normative linkages, i.e., they must develop professional standards which should help them in their performances. Standards are contagious. Standards depend upon the quality of Leadership.

Eminent Industrialist, Mr. Rahul Bajaj, Chairman and Managing Director, Bajaj Auto Limited and President, CII, delivered the Convocation Address at the 49th annual convocation of the SNDT Women's University, Mumbai. He said, "To realize our goals and aspirations, we need outstanding leadership in every field and at every level. Leadership means that there is no substitute for excellence, no tolerance of mediocrity and no compromise with integrity. Leadership is not just charisma, not public relations, not showmanship. Leadership is performance, consistent behaviour and trust-worthiness.[10]

Leadership depends upon strength of character

Honourable Mr. Justice A.M. Ahmadi, Former Chief Justice of India, delivered the Convocation Address at the thirty-ninth convocation and special convocation of Sardar Patel University. He said, "In the final analysis, what really matters is one's character and not the outward signs of achievement. It requires character to face the unending tests that life constantly puts one through; when faced with a crisis, it is only a person possessed of true character who is able to keep his head steady whilst others around are losing theirs.[11]

Samuel Smiles says in Self Help:

Character is the noblest possession of an individual. It exercises a greater power than wealth and secure all the honour without the jealousies of fame. . . Men of character are not only the conscience of society but in every well-governed State they are its best motive power. The strength, the industry and civilization of nations—All depend upon individual character. Mind without heart, intelligence without conduct, cleverness without goodness, are powers in their way, but they may be powers only for mischief. We may be instructed or amused by them. But it is sometimes as difficult to admire them as it would be to admire the dexterity of a pickpocket or the horsemanship of a highway man.

Measures of Quality Assurance in Distance Education Material

It is crucial to be explicit about the purpose(s) of learning encounters which are designed to:

- deal with individual queries and problems encountered by students in working through the materials;
- help deepen the students' understanding of the topics covered in the materials (i.e., reinforcing learning);
- test knowledge and skills to check whether or not students have achieved the outcome;
- update issue covered in the learning resources particularly with respect to new ideas and recent developments;
- utilise and share the responses of students to the activities within the materials;
- counsel students;
- provide students with opportunities for utilising ideas and techniques from the materials, thereby developing their skills and competencies; and
- provide a forum within which the efficacy of the materials and the encounters can be evaluated.)

Self-instructional material would sustain the interest of learners, ensure quality and keep the learners absorbed in studies. Moreover, the self-instructional material would generate creativity among learners—an essential objective of higher education and would make them independent. This would also encourage them to make use of library and other electronic media. It is not easy to design self-instructional material. It requires hard work, knowledge of the subject matter as well as the art of designing self-instructional material. We have to arrange teachers' development programmes for this purpose. Besides, it should be a continuous exercise. If we examine the instructional materials of prestigious institutions, we do not find them perfect attempts—these are only partial efforts in the direction of self-instructional material.

CONTENTS OF QUALITY

DE quality encompasses many attributes. It is very difficult to enumerate all of them. Let us discuss the important ones.

I. Effectiveness and Efficiency

Effectiveness is an expression of the degree of attainment of the predetermined objectives and targets of a programme, institutions, or activity seeking to reduce a problem or improve an unsatisfactory situation. This factor depends on whether the various activities and measures undertaken work (efficacy) and the degree to which they are accepted by those for whom they are intended.

Efficiency is an expression of the relationship between the results obtained from a programme or activity and the efforts expended in terms of human, financial, and other resources, the processes, technology, and time. The reason for assessing efficiency is to improve implementation and gain a better idea of the progress made.

Both effectiveness and efficiency came at the top of the list stressing the fact that quality can only be achieved if processes are performed appropriately and in a cost conscious environment. Only appropriate and necessary care should be provided. Waste, duplication and re-work should be eliminated. Only most economical ways and most effective ways to provide DE should be stressed. In a system of higher demands for quality care coupled with the reality of limited resources, prudent decisions regarding best possible combinations of effective and efficient DE are required and expected.

2. Equity

Equity considers the coverage of population groups and geographical areas, distribution of resources and facilities, and effectiveness of services in different areas. Equity in the distribution of DE depends on the extents to which different geographical areas and population groups, according to age, sex, or wealth, have access to essential services.

Emphasis in development has for too long been on economic advancement alone, based on a simplistic belief that an increase in national income would, of itself, result in social improvements including education. In effect the world has reverted to a latter-day trickle down theory of development, an approach that was already discredited 30 years ago. Furthermore, the promise of more money for social development, following the end of the Cold War, has not materialized.

There is a need to redirect our efforts to ensure social development, equity and justice in 21st century and remove the imbalance accumulated in 20th century otherwise, this would be a danger to peace and prosperity on this globe.

3. Students' Satisfaction in the Quality of DE System

DE is manned by teacher and meant for students whose interest and satisfaction must be ensured through quality Education care.

R.B. Jain in his article, "Citizens' Charter—An Instrument of Public Accountability" has nicely explained the key elements in setting of citizens' charters. These are:

(i) Standards

Setting, monitoring and publication of explicit standards for the services that individual users can reasonably expect. Publication of actual performance against these standards.

(ii) Information and Openness

Full, accurate information, readily available in plain language, about how well they perform and who is in-charge.

(iii) Consultation

There should be regular and systematic consultation with those, who use services. User's views about services and their priorities are to be taken into account for final decisions on standards.

(iv) Courtesy and Helpfulness

Courtesy and helpful service from public servants who will normally wear name badge. Service available equally to all who are entitled to them and run to suit their convenience.

(v) Putting Things Right

If things go wrong, an apology, a full explanation, and a swift and effective remedy to be offered. Well published and easy to use complaint procedures with independent reviews, wherever possible to be introduced and maintained.

(vi) Value for Money

Efficient and economical delivery of public services within the resources, the nation can afford. And, independent validation of performance against standards.[10]

The citizens have to have faith in the efficacy of the administrative system so that the distance between students and the DE System is reduced. The administration for good governance has to be accessible.[12]

4. Need of Positive Role of Functionaries of DE System

DE functionaries have developed negative attitudes which has damaged the reputation and prestige of DE system. M.K. Gaur has rightly said: Goodness of governance emerges from positive developmental roles of functionaries, underpinned with a summation of positive values—including morality, ethics, accountability, transparency, etc. in a Weberian model of public administration operating in a democratic context.

Advances in the patterns DE System cannot proceed unless the human resources that lead, plan, monitor and evaluate DE related services and programmes are enlightened and enabled to define and respond to societal needs. Given the evolving understandings of DE problems and the changing dynamics of DE system development, there must be a close and continuous interaction between educational, research and DE system development to ensure relevance of education to need.

5. Need of Change of Attitudes of DE Functionaries

Time has come for a strong message to be conveyed that administration is for the Students and not for the DE System. There has to be a change of attitudes, and teachers should realize that efficiency will be measured not in terms of what the services purport to offer, but in terms of students' satisfaction. Simultaneously, there has also to be a cleansing of the services and codification of the ethics and value systems.

There is a need for:

1. Making DE System accountable and citizen-friendly,
2. Ensuring transparency and the right to information, and
3. Taking measures to cleanse and motivate DE teachers and administrative staff.[13]

6. Need of Developing Positive Values for DE Functionaries and Ensure their Practice

Employees in DE services should avoid wastage and extravagance, ensure effective and efficient use of public money within their control, and endeavour that the benefits of schemes for disadvantage and poor sections of society are not wasted or diverted for the benefit of others. They should avoid ostentation and set examples of austerity for others.

All employees in DE system should promote and exhibit public and private conduct in keeping with the appropriate behaviour and standards of excellence and integrity. They should support the juniors in the latter's efforts to resist wrong or illegal directives and in abiding by the Code of Ethics. At the same time, they should reward good work and punish any dereliction of duty or obligations, based on objective and transport criteria.

7. Setting up of Work Improvement Teams

Another innovative measure designed to achieve higher productivity in Distant Education organizations is introduction of Work Improvement Teams (WITs). Adapted from the Japanese experience of Quality Control Circle, the WIT is essentially a small group of employees in the same work area or doing similar type of work who voluntarily meet regularly for about an hour every week to identify, analyse and resolve work-related problems. Thorough participation of the students the scheme seeks to generate higher employee morale, improved productivity and reduction in cost.

8. Need of Congenial Environment to Provide Quality DE Services

Good governance, however, is not a finished product. It is a dynamic concept. It encompasses fast-changing political, social and economic milieu, along with international environment and conditions of operational governance. Hence, the need for periodical rethinking on and even remodelling of the concept and institutions of governance. The search for good governance has to be a continuing exercise.

9. Need to have Transparent and Honest Administration to have Good Quality DE Administration

We mention here some ingredients of quality administration which can help in providing decent DE services:

1. Openness in the sense of having wide contact with students and their problems.
2. A sense of justice, fair play, impartiality in dealing with students and their matters.
3. Sensitivity and responsiveness to the urges, feelings and aspirations of student.
4. Securing the honour and dignity of all students, however humble he or she might be.
5. Humility and simplicity in the persons manning the DE machinery and their easy accessibility.
6. Creating and sustaining an atmosphere conducive to development, growth, and social change and honesty and integrity in thought and action.

THRUST OF DISTANCE QUALITY EDUCATION

For maintaining quality, the essential criterion is to satisfy the learners so that they gain rich learning experience and transferable knowledge and skills through distance learning. In order to achieve these goals, it is imperative to priorities the significant areas in the DLIs, improve the functioning of those areas and plan to produce the right output (successful learners). Finally, the effectiveness with which these goals are met has a major impact in moving towards the path of quality and excellence.

CONCLUSION

However, we should not forget that we should not alienate the student from the teacher. S.L. Mahajan in his article "Alienation of Students in Higher Education."[14] rightly cautions that distance education is a product of students-teacher alienation and gives solution to alienation of both. It is high time for the system to lift the students from depths of despair to heights of ecstasy to seek better outcome. Same feeling is expressed by

R. Natrajan in his article, "Emerging Trends in Technology, Education and Economy"[15] in that non-traditional education has, evolved from correspondence courses to video-based classes taught in a remote location, to online Internet classes which do not meet at a specific time. Different models of Distance Learning share the common feature of a remote place, but are distinguished by pace (scheduling), time (synchronicity), and interactivity. Although faculty can easily create a web-page for their course, incorporating new technology, and converting a class to the distance-learning environment, it requires rethinking the way the course is delivered.

We should endeavour to promote better and good relationship between teachers and students through PCP, personal visits and response sheets assignments.

To conclude with the words of The National Knowledge Commission (NKC) which believes that a radical reform of the system of Open and Distance Education (ODE) is imperative to achieve the objectives of expansion inclusion and excellence in higher education. The significance is obvious. For one more than one-fifth of the students enrolled in higher education are in the ODE stream. For another, ODE has an enormous potential to spread higher education opportunities beyond the brick and mortar world. But there are reasons for concern. First, the quality of higher education provided in large segments of ODE, particularly in correspondence courses in universities, leaves much to be desired. Second, it is not sufficiently recognized that ODE provides educational opportunities not only to those who discontinue formal education on account of economic or social compulsions, but also to young school leavers who are simply unable to secure admission in the formal stream at universities. It is time to address these problems. There is a clear need to improve the quality of ODE and to make it more appropriate to the needs of society. It is just as important to expand opportunities in higher education through the use of technology in ODE. It would not be possible to attain a gross enrolment ratio of 15% by 2015 without a massive expansion in ODE. In this endeavour, we must not forget that ODE is seen as inferior to conventional classroom learning. This perception. and the reality, both need change. We must realize that ODE is not simply a mode of educational delivery. but an integrated discipline engaged in the creation of knowledge.

It is hoped that some facts and suggestions mentioned above would help the policy-makers, planners, decision-makers of higher education system especially distance education system in ensuring excellence, responsiveness and rationalisation of student support services and facilities. Besides, the inherent potentialities in the distant education system can be optimised and potential energy of the personnel involved in the system can be changed into kinetic energy through well designed distance education system.

We may briefly conclude with the following pointed suggestions:

(i) A closer focus on results in terms of efficiency and effectiveness and service quality to distance learners.

(ii) The replacement of highly centralised organisational structure with decentralised management environments where decisions on service delivery and resource allocation are taken closer to the point of delivery and which provide feedback from distance learners and personnel engaged in the delivery of distance education system.

(iii) Flexibility to explore alternative methods and technology to provide better services to distance learners economically and efficiently.

(iv) Devising new personnel management policies to provide greater flexibility and motivation to ensure higher productivity and excellence in DE system.

(v) Creating incentives to improve performance through enabling organisations to retain a portion of savings for better student support services.

(vi) Creating greater accountability and transparency through requirements to report on results.

(vii) Equipping policy-making bodies with really eminent educationists visible from their Bio-data.

(viii) The distant learners interest and satisfaction must be at the centre of all policy-making, planning and decision-making in the area of DE system.

(ix) Constant monitoring and evaluation of the DE system against the norms and standards fixed by DEC should be a regular feature.

Distance Education system has the potentiality, capability and expertise to promote higher education in diverse fields. However, we have to be careful in ensuring quality and effectiveness from the institutions engaged in distance education systems. Inspite of these problems, distance education has developed both in magnitude and direction and need be perfected. R.K. Singh and Harish Kumar[16] in their article, "Distance Education: Maladies and Remedies" have rightly concluded as follows: it can be said that distance education has established its relevance and efficiency across the globe. development and expansion of distance education/learning is a world-wide phenomenon. It is cost effective and provides with the benefits of large-scale economy. Distance Education is flexible in nature and able to cater to the needs of innumerable that could not be blessed with the education provided in conventional temples of learning. There are many problems, currently being confronted by distance learners. These problems affect the process of learning and it ultimately defeats the basic purpose of the existence of the institutions imparting education/learning through distance mode of education. If the required measures are taken timely and seriously these problems can be resolved and the quality of distance education can be improved in a purposeful manner.

Standards of quality DE system are not fixed as these would vary from organization to organization depending upon the quality of inputs. However, efforts should be made to reach standards which are international so that people can get the quality DE system in their own country. Government and private resources are wasted in getting DE from advanced countries which can be made available within the countries themselves through the application of quality standards in our DE institutions. This is not going to be expensive but only require hard work and dedication on the part of the DE experts.

Method Study is one of the techniques of work study to improve on 'How' of doing work. It is a technique to improve method of work, with a view to increase efficiency and effectiveness of resources—men, money and material. In common parlance, 'Method' stands for the means of accomplishing an end while study means application of mind to a problem or an exercise. Method Study, then traces the cases responsible for poor administrative performance so that appropriate remedial action may be taken. In broad terms, it may be said that the Method Study approach can help in successfully grappling with a view to find solutions to all problems which face the working of an organization. In sum, we can say that the Method Study is like an autopsy interested in eliminating the disease rather than the symptoms of ailment. The scientific and technological advancements are affecting the functioning of governmental machinery and thus there is a corresponding need to adjust the methods of Public Administration to suit the changing conditions for optimum performance. Method Study can be of immense value to the administrators through its help in adjusting the procedure of work to the changed conditions. Method Study is a continuous activity to ensure that the methods of work in an organization are in tune with its objectives and are helping in accelerating the progress of the organization rather than retarding it. Method Study must be used when a new organization is created or when an alteration is made in the existing organization or when the problems arise in the existing organizations.

Notes and References

1. S. Kishore, Quality Perspective in Distance Education, *University News*, Sept. 28, 1998.
2. *University News*, March 11, 1996, p. 14.
3. G. William, Total Quality Management in Higher Education, Panacea or Placebo, *Higher Education*, 25, 1993, pp. 223-37.
4. S.L. Goel, Modern Management Technique, Deep & Deep, New Delhi, 1995, pp. 375-76.
5. *University News*, Aug. 2, 1999, p. 18.
6. R.M. Currie, Work Study, 2nd Ed. London, Pitman, 1963, p. 92.
7. Secretariat Training School, *op. cit.*, p. 92.
8. S.J. Mariadoss, Creativity—Competitive Resource and Core of Excellence, *University News*, p. 29, 1999, p. 13.

9. S.L. Maricodoss, Emotional Intelligence: Tool of Credibility in *University News*, March 20, 2000.
10. *University News*, March 13, 2000, p. 17.
11. *University News*, Feb. 17, 1997, p. 8
12. Quoted in R.B. Jain, "Citizens Charter—An instrument of Public Accountability, in *IJPA*, July-Sept. 1998, No. 3, (Special Number on "Towards Good Governance", p. 367).
13. Action Plan for an Effective and Responsive Government, Document-1.
14. *University News*, June 14, 1999.
15. *University News*, Oct. 14, 1999.
16. *University News*, January 28 and Feb. 2002.

Financial Administration in a Distance Education System

PART A

(A) INTRODUCTION

Finance is the fuel of administration and Distance Education system is impossible without adequate finances like any other activity. Financial Administration can help a distance education institute in the management of financial resources through the application of well thought out principles, practices and rationalised techniques of raising, allocating and utilising financial resources for the fulfilment of organizational objectives systematically and scientifically. It is the art and science of planning, organising, implementing and evaluating the financial resources to ensure their best use for the achievement of the objectives, goals and targets of DE programmes, i.e. excellent student support services. According to Prof. M.J.K. Thavraj—

> "Finance is the life blood of all monetised socio-economic formations ranging from simple nuclear families to complex national and international organisations. Financial administration relates to the system which generates, regulates and distributes the monetary resources needed for the sustenance and growth of an organisation. In this respect, financial administration is similar to the circulatory system in complex living organism."[1]

(a) Since the cost of education through distance mode is less as compared to formal system, there is a need to allocate more resources to this mode to meet the growing demands of Higher education. To quote Bakshish Singh, "In view of the comparatively low cost of educating students through the distance mode, its utility for large scale application, the need for qualitative improvement and innovations to make education relevant to the needs of society and the nation, need for diversification of education towards vocational, technical, Professional, the Central and State Governments should adopt a liberal policy of funding the flexible and innovative system of distance education."[2]

"In educational planning, the determination of the costs of alternative methods of realising set objectives that are feasible is the first step towards working out the economies of a system. When the costs are compared with the benefits that are likely to accrue to the society after the given resource are invested, an idea about the alternative choices of development paths is obtained, which, in turn, form the basis for taking an appropriate decision about a policy choice. Such an exercise is essential because in every country, irrespective of its stage of development, financial constraints do exist since the budget is never unlimited."[3] Prof. G. Dhanarajas, President, the commonwealth of learning, Vancouver, Canada in his inaugural address rightly mentions: "The cost of higher education is escalating and this includes the distance education sector as well. These escalating costs are unavoidable in the context of the volume to be educated and in the diversity of products, without compromising quality. This, therefore, requires the management of institution to be both effective and efficient; it must be efficient in the case of human and physical resources; and effective in providing the best framework for teaching and learning to take place, research to be sustained and students allowed to develop their full potential. Satisfying all these needs has become a much more complex challenge, especially for those of us who are functioning at the cutting edge of educational delivery, as distance educators do."[4] This makes out a case for Distance Education system as here we can achieve the goals of higher education with less resources. However, there is a need of caution in proclaiming that DE system is cheap. "It is important to note that long held claim that distance education is cheaper than conventional forms of education ought to be taken with caution." As Jevons stated: "selling distance education on the basis of cheapness is a two-edged sword because, if the system once established has to run inexpensively, the quality of the materials and richness of students support are bound to suffer."[5]

(b) Norms of Quality in Distance Education Institute and Finances

There are many misconceptions about financing of Higher Education relating to Distance Education system in India. Some institutes/universities are asked to fleece money from the students in the name of Distance Education systems while others run Distance Education systems without any regard to finance resulting in many wastages. There are Distance

Education institutes running with a skeleton staff while there are institutes running with surplus staff. Many of the Distance Education institutes start professional courses and sell those courses in a way to make crores of rupees. This makes many experts doubtful about the locus standi of these Distance Education institutes. Osmania University Organised a seminar on "Resource Mobilisation" and set-up three groups on different aspects. The first group came out with the suggestion that "Universities should start distance education courses in such subjects, which are in high demand—in market terms by using the services of existing faculty members. This would to some extent ease resources pressure . . . the regular faculty members or retired ones may be involved in teaching" (*University News*, Sept. 27, 1999, p. 20). Such recommendations are highly deterimental to the quality of distance education system as the main objective is to earn money and not service. Such efforts must be discouraged, rather critised by the distance Education Council.

These institutes, become the dens of earning money for the universities through exploitation of students and their parents. Therefore, the machinery of Higher Education especially the recently created Distance Education Council should devise ways and means to maintain standards of Distance Education system and ensure the best use of resources, i.e. students must get the full advantage of this system of education. There is a need to fix criteria of staffing, services, facilities before an institution may be allowed to run these programmes through distance education mode. Let us discuss different aspects of financing of Distance Education system.

PART B

MOBILISATION OF RESOURCES

(a) Fees Charged

The structure of fee charged from students differ from Institute to Institute and University to University. Distance Education Council should carry out a review of fee structure so that minimum and maximum fee structure can be recommended keeping in view the cost and services provided. Fees charged should be based on factors like:

(a) Cost incurred both recurring and non-recurring in running the course.
(b) Utility of the course—General or professional.
(c) Fees charges for such courses in formal systems and other informal systems.
(d) Paying capacity of the students.
(e) Infrastructure engaged in running the course.

There is a need to examine the fee structure otherwise these institutes of Distance Education would become fleecing places. For example, an

Institute of Distance Education in Southern part of the country is contributing about 10 crores annually as earning to the University exchequer which leads to exploitation of the students. However, we can take advantage of economy of scale within limits.

Studies on economics of distance education have revealed that there are economies of scale in Distance Education (DE) system:

(i) the average recurrent cost per student at the Open University (OU) was only 25 per cent of that of the Conventional University (CU);
(ii) the capital cost per student in terms of infrastructural facilities of (OU) was only 6 per cent of the Conventional University (CU);
(iii) distance education system have potential for effecting economics of scale; as the number of students increases, average cost declines since the fixed costs get distributed over large number of units;
(iv) for subjects/courses which are limited to a smaller number of students, conventional universities are cost efficient, but providing instruction to higher numbers, distance education is more cost-efficient;
(v) design and production costs are generally much higher than costs of transmission and reception;
(vi) transmission and duplication costs are very high for video systems;
(vii) the cost of distributing print and audio-visual materials depends on the means of distribution used, population and dispersal of students, and the difficulty of access to target groups; and
(viii) to take advantage of the economies of scale, a critical minimum enrolment of students is necessary.[6] On the other hand, here are statistics from some DE institutes where the cost is higher because of the employment of all norms of UGC Staff, Quality of Lessons, etc.

(b) Allocation

The Ministry of HRD is now allocating money to Distance Education Council to provide funds to Open Universities/Institutes of Distance Education. Previously this work was being done by the UGC. UGC had set the following guidelines for financing Distance Education Programmes. Fees from students from distance education courses should be realistically prescribed so that the distance education wing of the university does not go into deficit. In view of this, no large non-recurring or recurring assistance should be needed from the university/UGC.

A seed money of Rs. 10 lakhs for the first 5 years would be considered by the UGC for the distance education wing of the University. The University has to make a project proposal and submit it to UGC for such sanction. Condition of UGC assistance is that the distance education courses should involve availability of contact centre facility to students at least once in a fortnight. After 5 years assistance is given by the UGC to the extent of Rs. 5 lakhs every 5 years period if the courses are at graduate level and Rs. 7.5 lakhs for 5 years period if the courses are at post-graduate level also. Such assistance would be considered if on evaluation it is established that:

(i) there are at least 5000 students enrolled in DE,
(ii) the quality of teaching material is found to be good,
(iii) the despatch of teaching material to students has been regular and timely,
(iv) the system of evaluation of student responses is efficient and feedback is provided to them systematically,
(v) the university has set-up an adequate system of contact programmes and it works satisfactorily, and
(vi) the university has harnessed audio and/or audio visual cassettes for DE.

The University has to make a project proposal to claim such assistance. The UGC assistance both in the beginning and subsequently, is essentially meant for improving instrumentation and furniture in the department and contact class facilities and for getting prepared for procuring the audio visual or audio progarmmes. The UGC assistance should be utilised for arranging preparation of audio or audio visual material but the UGC assistance is not available for creating audio or audio visual production facility. The University should use the Indira Gandhi National Open University, EMRC/AVRC or the facilities with professional agencies for this purpose. The UGC assistance is not available at any stage for creating any post.[7]

The Universities would be financed by DEC as was done by UGC for their development programmes. DEC has devised guidelines for financing correspondence courses institutes in IXth Plan. These are mentioned below. The basic features of the development of the Open Learning System by DEC in the Ninth Plan would be:

(i) establishment of an Open University Network (OPENET) in which IGNOU and all the State Open Universities will be networked. In other words, each open university will be networking, as well as a networked institution;
(ii) programmes and courses produced by open universities will be pooled for sharing by all open universities through adoption, adaptation and/or translation;
(iii) delivery systems will be established and strengthened with a view to develop a national technology support system that can be drawn upon by all open universities;

(iv) provision of support to facilitate effective networking rather than creation of assets and facilities specific to individual universities;
(v) institution of quality assurance mechanisms for a range of concerns from programme design and development to delivery of all services and student evaluation systems; and
(vi) introduction of programmes of continuing and extension education of a massive scale.

INFRASTRUCTURE DEVELOPMENT

A. Existing State Open Universities which are Already getting DEC Support

Three state open universities in Andhra Pradesh, Maharashtra and Rajasthan will continue to receive support for the programmes which are already recommended by the DEC and which have not been completed so far. In particular, the areas in which they will receive support are: development of audio/video production capability; computerisation of operations; and provision of multimedia learning facilities.

B. State Open Universities which are still to become Eligible

Four state open universities in Bihar, Gujarat, Karnataka and Madhya Pradesh which were established by the State Governments concerned have still to be declared fit for central assistance under the UGC Act. Pending revision of the rules for declaration of fitness such universities as fulfil the existing requirements may approach the UGC to expedite the consideration of their cases. The remaining universities may take early steps to provide the initial infrastructure as per the revised DEC guidelines. These include:

(i) preparation of the detailed project report;
(ii) establishment of delivery system including provision of staff;
(iii) provision of Rs. 5 crore in the Ninth Plan for infrastructure and securing the commitment from the State Government to strengthen the OLS; and
(iv) though financial assistance to these universities may have to wait till the formal declaration of fitness by the UGC, the DEC may provide them with technical/consultancy support for preparing the project report and in putting the systems and procedures in place. They can also obtain some programmes from other open universities and commence their operations.

C. New State Open Universities

In order to ensure the development of effective open universities network with country-wide coverage as early in the Ninth Plan as possible, the DEC should vigorously pursue with the remaining State Governments the proposal to establish open universities. The establishment of such a network is necessary to extend the outreach of the OLS and also to ensure that worthwhile progrmmes and courses are available to large numbers of people in all major languages in the country. It is only when such a network is established that the system can penetrate all regions and areas. In the establishment of these new open universities, the DEC may provide the technical/consultancy services in the preparatory work—including project formulation.

As a general principle, and on the basis of the suggestions made by the UGC in its Plan of Action, we recommend that a CCI should fulfil the following criteria to become eligible for DEC support in the nurturing phase:

(a) the aggregate enrolment in the Institute should be not less than 10,000;
(b) any programme with enrolment of less than 1000 shall not be supported for transformation into distance education;
(c) programmes of a highly specialised nature which are not generally offered by the CCIs, and which fulfil a specific national purpose will be considered for support in irrespective of the enrolment; and
(d) any programme which will enrich the common pool of programmes of the open university network will be considered for support.

Within this broad framework, the DEC will provide support to CCIs during the Ninth Plan on the following basis:

(a) all programmes should be formulated as specific projects indicating the activity, its purpose and duration, specific inputs required, dates of commencement and completion, and also the outcome;
(b) the DEC will provide assistance to meet 50 per cent of the inputs required for each project activity the remaining 50% being shared by the CCIs from their own resources;
(c) in exceptional cases, where a project contributes to the enrichment of the network, a higher level of assistance from the DEC may be considered; and
(d) all manpower inputs required will be provided in terms of man months for each project. In other words, no supports will be provided by the DEC for creation of posts on permanent basis and/or for their maintenance.

Keeping these broad parameters in view, we recommend the following guidelines which are based on the UGCs Plan of Action for providing development support to CCIs during the nurturing phase provided they carry out the following institutional reforms:

1. The existing CCIs should be upgraded to DEIs. The organisational structure should provide for efficiency in functioning with strong and effective academic and administrative structures.
2. The governance structure should provide for an Advisory Committee for overseeing programme development, innovations and performance. The Advisory Committee's recommendations will be considered only by the Syndicate/Academic Council/Senate.
3. There should be a separate Board of Studies in distance education responsible for designing and developing programmes and courses. This board could work jointly with other Boards of Studies of the University.
4. The DEI should be headed by a Director (who should be a Professor). It should have a core faculty comprising of Professors, Readers and Lecturers whose recruitment and terms and conditions of services shall be at par with other teachers in the departments.
5. Each DEI should have adequate physical facilities (building, library, conference rooms, students hall, etc.) and should have sufficient functional autonomy in all academic, administrative and financial matters.
6. The Institutes should ensure that surplus funds available are utilised for the development and upgradation of their programmes, courses and services.

Distance Education Council in its meetings and sub-committee meetings has come out with norms for funding Distance Education system. This has been divided into three parts:

(a) Established Open Universities,
(b) Newly established Open Universities, and
(c) Distance Education Institutes.

Since the system of Distance Education is in its initial stage, there is a need to help them in a big way in a judicious manner so that the base of the Distance Education System can be established on sound basis. DEC must take care that this money may not be used for less useful purpose. The funds spent must promote student support services in a qualitative manner.

A research report rightly sounded a warning to policy-makers and university authorities to allow DE system function efficiently, rather than making them a milch cow for the University systems. To quote: "It is surprising that while conventional university system is highly subsidised by the central and state governments, distance education institutes are erroneously expected to be self-financing. The worst thing is that some DEI which generate surplus funds due to massive enrolments, and not in a position to utilise them on improvement of the institutes, as their surplus is diverted to the general revenues of the university concerned to cover the deficit. This has adversely affected the CCIS resulting in unsatisfactory quality of their course materials, laxity in the evaluation of students assignments and student support services including library services. Another serious repercussion of this situation is that such CCIs are unable to develop need-based, application-oriented or vocational courses relevant to the aspirations of the learners."[8]

Distance Education system can get sufficient resources only if there is more allocation to higher education in Five Year Plans. S.L. Azad in his article, "Educational Finance in India: Progress, Problems and Perspectives" has rightly summed up the present scenario. To quote him,[9] "In spite of exhortations, repeated adnauseam, about the role of education in accelerating economic development and social change, education sector, along with other social services sector, continues to be regarded, as a 'residual' sector and gets a back seat in the allotment of resources. Even the meagre resources that are allocated do not get fully utilised because of various reasons."

It has also been found that in spite of the constitutional amendment investing the Central Government with larger authority in education, the Central contribution for education, particularly, for non-tertiary education has been minimal. The state government's investment in education has been somewhat erratic, bordering on *adhocism*. It seems that the state GDP has no relevance for state inputs in education. The NPERC made an exhaustive study of several reports and documents and made valuable recommendations for augmenting resources for education.[10]

The recommendations are, in brief, as follows:

(i) Public investment in education should exceed 6 percent of GNP.
(ii) All technical and management education may be made self-financing with appropriate support to the students by way of student loans.
(iii) Increase by higher education institutions of tuition fee and fees charged for specific purposes such as laboratory fee, library fee, etc.
(iv) Mobilising institutional finance for promotion of research in universities and for creation of educational infrastructure such as buildings, hostels and staff quarters.
(v) Increase in funds provided for scholarships by the Central Government.
(vi) Mobilisation of community contribution.
(vii) Efforts to be made by higher, and technical and management institutions to augment their income by way of consultancy and other services.

It is high time that the Union and State Governments must realise that sufficient funds need be allocated for the development of education.

(c) Consultancy

A large number of government and private organizations wish to get their employees trained. It is very difficult to carry out this work through regular training institution which is highly costly and would take years to complete the work. Distance Education institutes can take up consultancy from Departments like Rural Development, Ministry of Health and Family Welfare, etc. to train their personnel. There is an abundant scope in these areas. IGNOU is doing some work in this direction.

(d) Community Contribution

Distance Education system can raise resources from the community and provide services in exchange.

PART C

INJECTING ECONOMY THROUGH THE CURTAILMENT OF WASTEFUL EXPENDITURE

Wasteful expenditure especially in institutions run by government is very high. A serious problem in this area is of inefficient use of expenditure and non-utilisation of actual and potential resources judiciously and properly. In the distance education institutes, huge resources are being wasted because of the selection of inappropriate technology, inefficient management, and unsatisfactory control mechanisms.

> "It is necessary that public revenue should be raised in an equitable manner and spent economically so that the tax-payers may get full value for their money."[11]

Dr. Hari Om Gautam, Chairman, UGC said that: "It is true that, the funds are not adequate, but the beauty is to make the utmost of the resources available than to circle about what is not available."[12]

The objects of financial control are to ensure, (i) that no wastage of resources occurs; (ii) that public money is not misused; and (iii) that intended results are obtained with the money spent. We can exploit the potential resources through careful planning and management.

A lot of expenditure at all levels results from slackness, apathy and indifference on the part of educational administrators. Let us explain with examples. Illustration Same courses are being carried out in neighbouring institutes without pooling their resources which can help in reducing expenditure, e.g. M.A. in Public Administration is being run by P.U., Chandigarh, Kurukshetra University, Kurukshetra, H.P. University, Shimla without any coordination.

Many DE institutes are running such courses where the strength is very less or we can say uneconomical. We may either not offer such courses or run them with the faculty of the Department of the University.

How can we improve resource management wherein resources are properly utilised and full impact made? The answer is to make use of the techniques of performance budgeting and Zero-base budgeting through well trained educational administrators and financial experts to husband our resources carefully to accomplish as much as possible with what is available. Performance budgeting is very useful as it facilities better programming, decision-making, review and control distance education activities.

Zero-Based Budget requires that distance education Organizations while preparing their budgets should not take earlier years expenditure for granted and therefore should start afresh. In this process, the examination of existing programmes and activities has to be done in the same manner as would apply to newly proposed ones because the demands of the courses are to be kept in mind.

The following steps can also inject economy:

(i) Make the Distance Educational Administrators conscious of the Cost of Education through training and circulars and inject in them the art of achieving efficiency through economy.

(ii) There is a need to appoint an economy committee which may suggest the ways and means of cutting wasteful expenditure.

(iii) Since 80 per cent of expenditure in Educational institutions relate to expenditure on personnel, there is a need to make use of Personnel optimally through Manpower Planning, Development, Utilisation, and Human Resources Auditing and Accounting.

(iv) Financial sections of educational institutions at all levels need be staffed by experts in cost accounting and financial management. These can ensure the following for educational administrators at all levels:

  (a) to feed management with timely information on the utilisation of resources,

  (b) to make statistical analysis to bring out what the performance data truly signify,

  (c) to explore and recommend possibilities of reducing costs, with due regard to the maintenance of efficiency and quality, and

  (d) to ensure the full impact on the main objective—Promotion of Distance Education.

(v) A constant attempt need be done to improve General Administration which would automatically take care of financial administration as well.

Systems approach to budgeting and financing (Noviek, 1965; Cutt, 1974; Horey, 1972) suggest the following to ensure optimisation of finances:

(a) to identify, who (action agent) needs how much money (cost) and for what (activities);
(b) to define criteria for, and priority in, allocation of budgetary resources among different activities and different organizations responsible for performance of activities;
(c) to provide flexibility in budgeting and financing, if necessary, beyond bureaucratic control; and
(d) to ensure the timely availability of funds to the programme activities at field level.

(vi) Privatization of uneconomic service: Most of the services carried out in Universities are done directly. These cost heavily. The new policy of liberalization can be used for services like construction, maintenance, medical aid, etc.

Human Development Report, 1991, published by UNDP rightly mentions that there is wide potential for restructuring national budgets and international aid in favour of human development. The Report concludes that much current spending is misdirected and inefficiently used. If the priorities are set right more money will be available for accelerated human progress.[13]

In a recent publication of the Department of Education, Published in 1993, "Education For All—The Indian Scene" (pp. 98-99) rightly stressed the need of effective utilisation of resources. To quote:

> "While economic liberalization and the consequent financial restructuring can be expected to facilitate greater resource flow to education, the nation as a whole should assume responsibility for providing the resource support for education, especially as population pressures coupled with budgetary constraints present a constant challenge to the government to maintain the current levels of schooling access and the previous levels of expansion. Achieving a result-oriented balance calls for stress on cost-effectiveness and accountability at every level. In this context, a major challenge consists of reconciling and combining efficient resource utilisation with effective performance and delivery. The tendency to 'rate' programmes and projects by their ability to 'consume' the budget or demand more needs to be replaced by an all pervasive culture in which processes, outcomes and delivery should be the measure of performance rather than mere provision of inputs. As the POA, 1992, points out: "Programmes should cease to be driven by budgets and instead should stress processes and outcomes."

Fred Zindi and Robert Aucoin have rightly stressed the need of support to DE system in the context of African countries but is valid for all the developing countries in the world. To quote them:

"There is a need for governments to adopt a comprehensive policy on distance education as well as effective cooperation with Distance Education Colleges. For as long as distance education is viewed as a poor cousin of the formal education system, it will not be able to fulfil its role of increasing educational opportunities. There must therefore be adequate funding for distance education programmes as well as adequate supply of materials and transport before distance education can realise its potential. For now it will suffice to say that distance education is only being used as a means of sustaining cut-backs in formal education by those governments facing economic hardships or are unable to accommodate their people into formal education institutions as evidenced by the recent (1993) establishments of the Open University in Tanzania and the Centre for Distance Education in Zimbabwe. From recent newspaper reports it is learnt that there is a potential for the development of yet another distance education centre sponsored by the Southern African Development Community (SADC) which consists of 11 countries within Southern Africa. It is envisaged that this will have its Headquarters in Botswana.[14]

The National Knowledge Commission suggest that:

* **Support the Production of Quality Content by a Select set of Indian Institutions**

A set of key institutions should be selected and experts representing diverse knowledge areas like agriculture, engineering, medicine, arts, humanities, science, education, etc. should be asked to develop standards-based content, which can be customized to diverse user needs. This should he made available not only to Indian institutions but also for global use. The efforts made through the project of Ministry of Human Resources Development—National Programme on Technology Enhanced Learning (NPTEL) for creation of OER in the areas of Engineering and technology should be applied in other areas of education also, the content in the repositories should be multimedia interactive and available in different regional languages. These projects should cover a wide range of subjects mentioned above. To speed up the creation, adaptation, and utilization of OER it is necessary to launch a 'National E-content and Curriculum Initiative'.

* **Leverage Global Open Educational Resources**

Sustainable development of quality content relevant to India is a difficult and expensive proposition, given the diverse needs of various sectors in our emerging knowledge economy. Emerging international and national initiatives are offering quality educational content as open resources. It is viral for India to leverage these initiatives as they are readily available for adoption and adaptation and to serve as a model for further indigenous content production. NKC found that there are already 200-300 free knowledge repositories available across the world. The National Knowledge Commission (NKC) is separately disseminating this information through its website.[15]

PART D

FACTS AND SUGGESTIONS

However, we may keep the following facts and suggestions in mind to maintain efficiency within available finances:

(a) We should make use of appropriate technology and not be enamoured under the influence of advertising agencies to go in for higher technology which is not affordable and useful. Thus, we should not make unnecessary investments in costly electronic gadgets.

(b) We should inject improvements in procedures to save on paper and processing. We should have minimum layers and more of decentralization.

(c) We should do small exercises on cost-benefit analysis to the courses being run so that we can cut down on courses which are not being offered by students.

(d) We should develop liaison with Public and private organisations to create demands for their services.

(e) We should make multiple use of our inputs and weed out unnecessary activities.

(f) We should ensure best student support services and there is no need to economise here.

(g) We should encourage students' participation and encourage them to do programmes on contributory basis.

Last but not the least important is the need of accountability, efficiency and transparency to ensure the achievement of the objectives of the distance education system within allocated finance.

Notes and References

1. M.J.K. Thavraj, Financial Management of Government, New Delhi, Sultan Chand, 1978, p. 1.
2. Bakshish Singh, *et al.*, *Indian Journal of Open Learning*, Vol. 3, No. 2, p. 22.
3. M.M. Ansari, Determinants of Costs in Distance Education, in *Studies in Distance Education* by B.N. Kaul, *et. al.* (eds.) New Delhi, AIU and IGNOU, 1998, p. 13.
4. IGNOU, Distance Education Council, Performance Indicators in *Distance Education in National Seminar Report*, 1996, p. 1.
5. F. Jevons, Blurring the Boundaries, Parity and Convergence in R. Garrison and D. Shale (ed.), *Education at a Distance*, From Issues to Practice, Florida, Robert

E. Krieges Publishing Co., 1990, quoted in Eustella a Bhalalusesa The Distance Mode of Learning in Higher Education, The Tanzanian Experience, *Open Learning*, Vol. 14, No. 2, June 1999, p. 22.

6. Rudar Datt: Distance Education *versus* Traditional Higher Education: A cost comparison in B.N. Kaul and *et. al.* (eds.), *Studies in Distance Education*, p. 143.
7. Round Table of Directors of Correspondence Course Institutes, *op. cit.*, pp. 82-83.
8. Bakshish Singh, *op. cit.*, p. 22.
9. *IJPA*, Vol. XXXII, No.3, July-Sept., 1986, pp. 578-79.
10. Ministry of HRD, CABE Committee on Policy, New Delhi, January 1992, p. 74.
11. John M. Pfiffner and R.V. Presthus, Public Administration, New York, the Ronald Press Company, Third Edition, p. 294.
12. Chandigarh Newsline, *Indian Express*, 9th Sept., 1999, p. 8.
13. UNP, Human Development Report, 1991, Oxford University Press, New York, 1991.
14. Fred Zindi and Robert Aucoin, "Distance Education in Tanzania and Zimbabwe" in *Open Learning*, Vol. 10, No.1, February 1995, p. 37.
15. National Knoweldge Commission Report, 2007, p. 51.

Organisation and Management of Distance Education

PART A

(A) INTRODUCTION

The model of an organisation of a DE System can be seen from Chart 11.1. The diagram is based on the model of input and output of an organisation. The diagram reveals the various inputs like structures, resources, and technology used to provide services to the DE Students. The services include Instructional material, students' assignments, audio-visual aids, personal contact programme and other personnel services. There is a need of regular review of services to keep the DE System efficient and effective. Besides, we have to link a distance education institute with students through diffused linkage to gain their support, link it through enabling linkages with DEC, Government, University to get resources and guidance, to link with other distance education institutes through networking, i.e. functional linkages and lastly link it with constant attempt at improvements, i.e. normative linkages.

It has been seen that many DE institutes have become insensitive to students needs over a period of time. What can be done? The answer is analysis and radical reforms at all levels. We have discussed all the inputs and outputs in earlier chapters. Here, we are concerned with the machinery used to conduct distance education programmes.

Organisation and management of Distance Education system involves a great deal of open operations to run the system efficiently and economically. Before we discuss the actual structure and management of Distance Education, let us understand the meaning of an organisation.

According to Dimock and Dimock, "Organisation is the systematic bringing together of inter-dependent parts to form a unified whole through

CHART 11.1

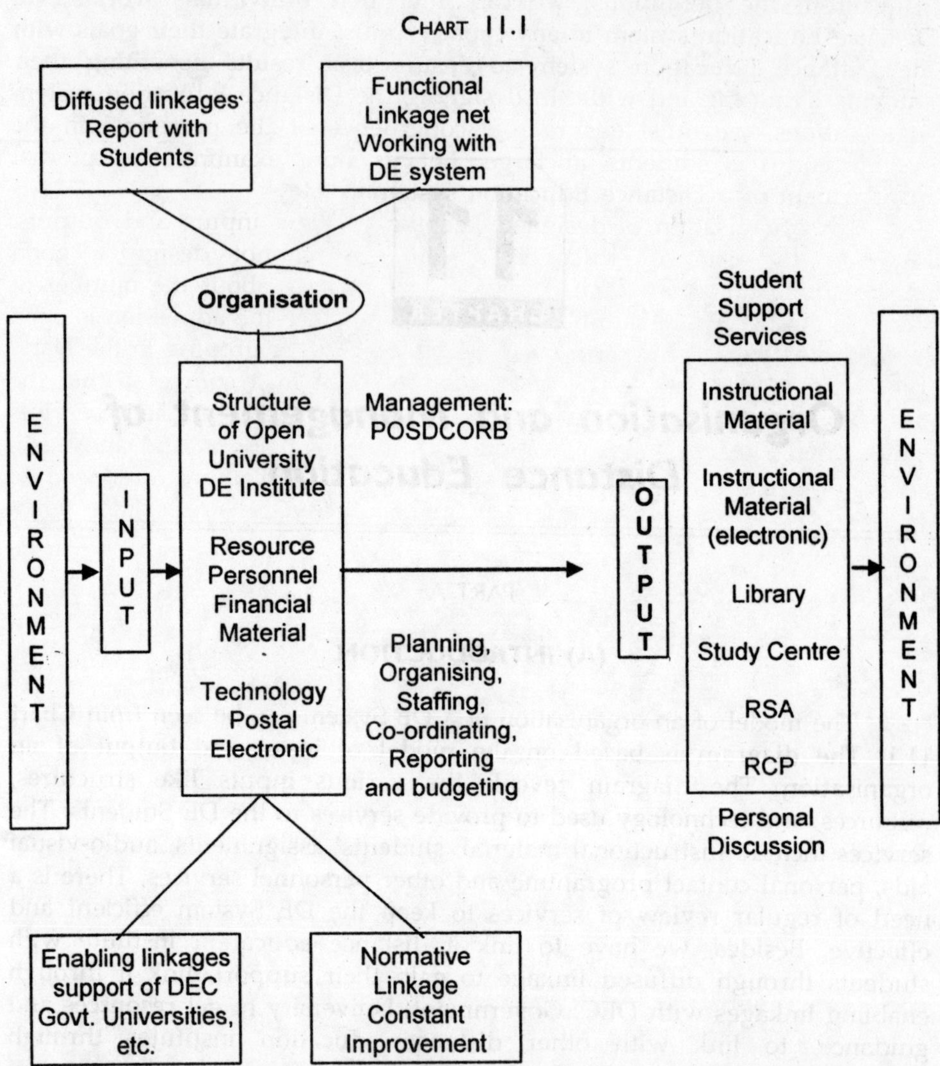

which authority, coordination and control may be exercised to achieve a given purpose. Organisation is both structure and human relations."

Organisations are defined as collectivities that have been established for the pursuit of relatively specific objectives on a more or less continuous basis.[2] A suitable organisation needs to be developed especially for a budding system like DE System wherein, like human body, most of problems are internally and automatically solved. This requires talent, experience and interest in developing an organisation to meet challenging tasks. Organisation building is extremely important to provide decent services. No academic performance is possible without a suitable organisation. Building an organisation is, therefore, the starting point of any academic performance.

From the definitions, we can infer that Individuals working in Distance Education system in any capacity must integrate their goals with the Distance Education system to ensure best results benefiting their students living far and wide. In designing the Distance Education system organisations, we must ensure role congruence of the personnel in the system and the students at large. Let us now examine the internal management of a Distance Education system.

An organisation is designed keeping in view inputs and outputs. However in distance education system, we cannot design a good organisation and administration as we are not sure about the number of students that would be admitted till November, since the admission is open to all. How can one plan and design in advance? It is groping in the Dark. Therefore, there is a need to fix the upper limit in a course so that the distance education institutes can provide effective and efficient services within their capacity. Hence printing can also be planned and above all, faculty arrangements can be done in advance. Thus, there is a need to design clearcut objectives, scope, parameters to avoid crises later when admission goes beyond expectation, students do not get services in time resulting in bad image in the press, public, etc.

(B) TOP MANAGEMENT AND ITS FUNCTIONS

An organisation is like a ladder. At the top is the Vice-Chancellor in the case of an Open University, a Director/Chairman in case of Distance Education Institute. The success or failure of Distance Education system depends, to a great extent, upon the administrative capability and motivation of its top leadership, i.e. Vice-Chancellor in an Open University and a Director in a distance education institute. Administrative capability is an important means of converting or processing programme inputs into outputs such as goods and services meant for the Distance Education students. It has been mentioned by V.L. Gabriel that "What makes the leadership variable so crucial in the implementation process is its dynamic, not passive, quality, i.e., its capability to act and react on these critical inputs. It is this administrative and transferring quality of leadership that could significantly determine the administrative capability of implementing organisastion."[3]

The qualities of a top management would percolate down among the staff working in Distance Education system. In the sacred book, Bhagvad Geeta, Chapter III, Sloka 21, it has been rightly said that whatever a great man (chief executive) does, that very thing other men also do; whatever standard he sets, the generality of men follow the same,

The important functions of the Vice-Chancellor or Director of Distance Education system are given below:

Administrative functions constitute the management of men, money and material. His administrative functions are summed up by Gullick in the word 'POSOCORB'. These elementary functions have become highly complex and developed. The Vice-Chancellor or Director of Distance Education system must understand this complexity with the help of advanced techniques of modern management and use them to discharge administrative functions. Let us mention these briefly as given by Gullick—

(a) Planning that is, working out in outline the things that need to be done and the methods for doing them to accomplish the purpose set for the enterprise.
(b) Organising, that is, the establishment of the formal structure of authority through which work sub-divisions are arranged, defined and coordinated for the defined objective.
(c) Staffing, that is, the whole personnel function of bringing in and training the staff and maintaining favourable conditions of work.
(d) Directing, that is, the continuous task of making decisions and embodying them in specific and general orders and instructions, and serving as the leader of the enterprise.
(e) Coordinating, that is the all-important duty of interrelating the various parts of the work.
(f) Reporting, that is, keeping those to whom the executive is responsible informed as to what is going on, which, thus, includes keeping himself and his subordinates informed through records, research and inspection.
(g) Budgeting with all that goes with budgeting in the form of planning, accounting and control.[4]

No organisation can develop until and unless the personnel working in the organisation are committed to achieve its ideals. An attitude of dedication to the goals of an organisation should be an indispensable trait of the Vice-Chancellor or Director of Distance Education system. This is their primary requisite to operate and function effectively and efficiently to build self-confidence in themselves and, in turn, in the staff.

The most important quality on which their actual role would depend is the integrity. In this context, Peter Drucker rightly observes that a person who does not have the integrity or character is unfit to be a manager and a good educationist.

PART B

(A) INTRODUCTION

Vice-Chancellor or Director functions through faculty in various departments and administrative staff. In Open University, as discussed in Chapter 2, they have their own system—Independent Academic Council, Board of Studies, etc., i.e. they are free to design and carry on their programmes they like. However, in Distance Education system the Director has to function within the constraints of the university framework. The minor details of working differ from one Distance Education institute to another. Let us discuss here the important functions both academic and administrative carried out by the Vice-Chancellor of an Open University/ Director in association with the staff working with him.

(B) ACADEMIC FUNCTIONS OF FACULTY

Below the Director there are coordinators of various programmes. Under him, there are faculty members comprising of Professors, Readers and Lecturers. Coordinator is generally by rotation. This is like other departments in the University system. The functions of departments/ coordinators are as follows:

(a) Preparing, vetting, editing the lecture scripts.
(b) Preparing the material through multi-media medium.
(c) Evaluating the students' assignments.
(d) Conducting personal contact programme.
(e) Preparing broadcasts for students.
(f) Arranging for extracurricular activities.
(g) Institution building.
(h) Arranging seminars.
(i) Removing individual difficulties.
(j) Meeting students for any academic or administrative help.

All these activities would be possible if they, i.e. Coordinators devote substantial time to develop academic excellence in the organisation and strive hard to maintain the tempo once built.

(C) ADMINISTRATIVE FUNCTIONS

Vice-Chancellor or Director is assisted by Registrar, Deputy Registrars, etc. to carry on administrative activities like:

(a) Advertisement for admission;
(b) Preparation of prospectus;
(c) Printing and proof reading of lecture scripts;
(d) Mailing of these units at regular interval of time;
(e) Receipt and sorting out of response sheets;
(f) Despatch of evaluated response sheets;
(g) Arranging for personal contact programme and stay of students in hostel during this period;
(h) Getting examination forms processed;
(i) Sending of examination roll numbers and later results cards;
(j) Keeping accounts;
(k) Helping control over establishment matters; and
(l) Arranging for extracurricular activities.

On critical examination, we find many problems resulting in delays in day-to-day administrative matters causing hardships to students. The administrative staff in the DE system is attuned to the bureaucratic style of functioning resulting in impersonal administration which is highly dangerous in the field of DE system. They are not sensitive to the fact that DE system is time-bound and need-promptness, urgency, sympathy and moral support. We would suggest the need for administrative reforms to keep the system of Distance Education alive and perfect.

No Distance Education system can ever be absolutely perfect, and in order to achieve some sort of perfection, it has to engage itself with the help of innovation cells in devising ways and means for improvement which have to be adopted in the light of open education policies and programmes. The ultimate success of the measures suggested by such cells depends, to a great extent, upon the effective implementation of the measures suggested.

Let us discuss briefly the organisational set-up of two open Universities and a correspondence course department to understand their functioning.

(D) DR. B.R. AMBEDKAR OPEN UNIVERSITY, HYDERABAD

This was the first Open University in the country established in 1982. There is a Vice-Chancellor assisted by four directors managing academic, student services, material production and evaluation. Vice-Chancellor gets policy guidance from Board of Management, Academic Senate, Finance Committee and Planning and Monitoring Board. On the administrative side Vice-Chancellor is assisted by Registrar, Finance officer and in-charge Audio-Visuals. There are 117 study centres at various places.

(E) INDIRA GANDHI NATIONAL OPEN UNIVERSITY (See Chart 11.2)

The India Gandhi National Open University (IGNOU) was established by an Act of Parliament in 1985 with the dual responsibilities of: (i) enhancing access and enquiry to higher education through distance mode, and (ii) promote, coordinate and determine standards in such systems. To fulfil the first objective IGNOU provides opportunities to the students, including those from the disadvantaged groups, physically challenged, home-makers, minority groups and based in remote areas for innovative and need-based general as well as continuing education for their overall development. IGNOU practices a flexible and open system of education in regard to methods and place of learning, combination of courses and eligibility for enrolment, age for entry and methods of evaluation, etc. The University has adopted an integrated multiple strategy for instructions consisting of print materials, audio-visual, radio, educational TV, teleconferencing, video conferencing as also at face to face counselling at its study centres throughout the country. The evaluation system followed by the University consists of continuous assessment and term end examination.

CHART 11.2

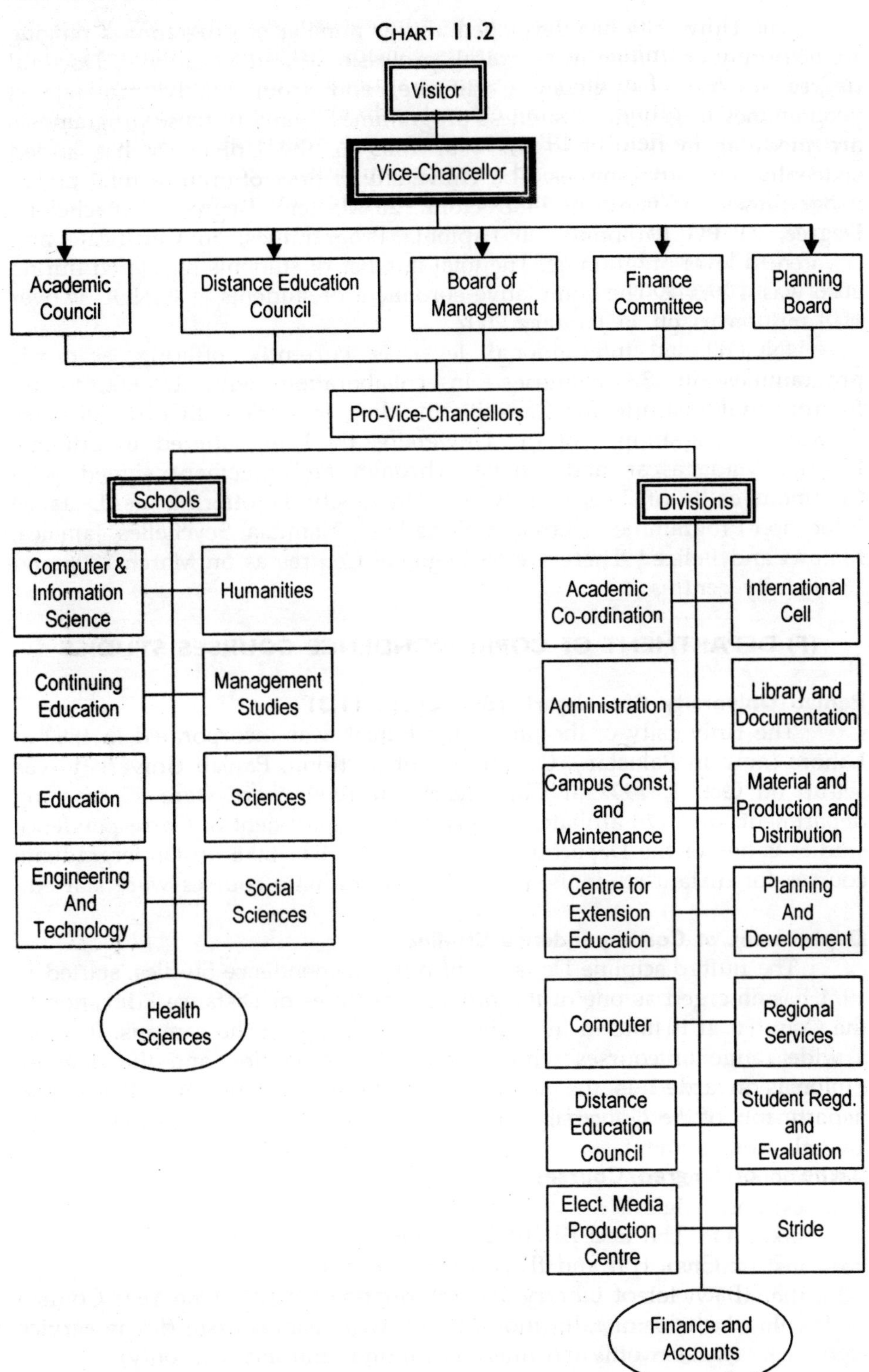

Visitor
Vice-Chancellor
Academic Council
Distance Education Council
Board of Management
Finance Committee
Planning Board
Pro-Vice-Chancellors
Schools
Divisions
Computer & Information Science
Humanities
Continuing Education
Management Studies
Education
Sciences
Engineering And Technology
Social Sciences
Health Sciences
Academic Co-ordination
International Cell
Administration
Library and Documentation
Campus Const. and Maintenance
Material and Production and Distribution
Centre for Extension Education
Planning And Development
Computer
Regional Services
Distance Education Council
Student Regd. and Evaluation
Elect. Media Production Centre
Stride
Finance and Accounts

The University has developed a large number of programmes ranging from: purely academic to technical, professional and vocational; Doctoral degree to the competency Certificate; and from highly professional programmes to general awareness programmes. Many of these programmes are modular in nature. In the year 2005-06, the University has added sixteenth new programmes. The University is now offering a total of 126 programmes consisting of 14 Doctoral, 20 Master's Degree, 15 Bachelor's Degree, 21 PG Diplomas, 20 Diploma Programmes, 36 Certificate and Awareness level programme. The total number of students registered during 2006 was 4,29,542. The cumulative enrolment of students at IGNOU is over 1.48 million as on in January 2007.

INGOU, at International level is currently offering academic programmes in 37 countries. In collaboration with UNESCO and International Institute for Capacity Building in Africa (IICBA), Distance Education Programmes of the University are being offered in Ethopia. Liberia, Madagascar and Ghana. Through an agreement signed with Commonwealth of Learning (COL) University is offering its Distance Education Programme in Lesotho, Swaziland, Namibia, Seychelles, Jamaica, Malawi and Belize.[1] There are 58 Regional Centres as on March 2006 and 1346 study centres.

(F) DEPARTMENT OF CORRESPONDENCE COURSES STUDIES

Panjab University Chandigarh (See Chart 11.3)

The University of the undivided Punjab was incorporated in 1882 at Lahore (now in Pakistan). On the eve of partition, Panjab University was set-up on Oct. 1, 1947 at Chandigarh. In 1999, there were 65 teaching departments and 178 affiliated colleges. The Department of Correspondence studies is one of the Departments set-up in 1971 to take up Undergraduate courses for distant students. In 1977, post-graduate courses were started.

Department of Correspondence Studies

The nulti-discipline Department of Correspondence Studies, started in 1971 has emerged as one of the premier institutes of Distance Education in the Country. It is housed in a sprawling building on the campus. It offers a wide range of courses whose mode of examination and the degree/ diplomas awarded is the same as for those studying in colleges and departments of the University. The Department offers the following courses:

Bachelor of Degree Courses

1. B.A. I, II and III (10+2+3 scheme)
2. B.Com. I, II and III (10+2+3 scheme)
3. Bachelor of Library and Information Science (One Year Course)
4. Bachelor of Education (B.Ed.) (two years course) (for in service teachers only) (Admission through entrance test only)

CHART 11.3

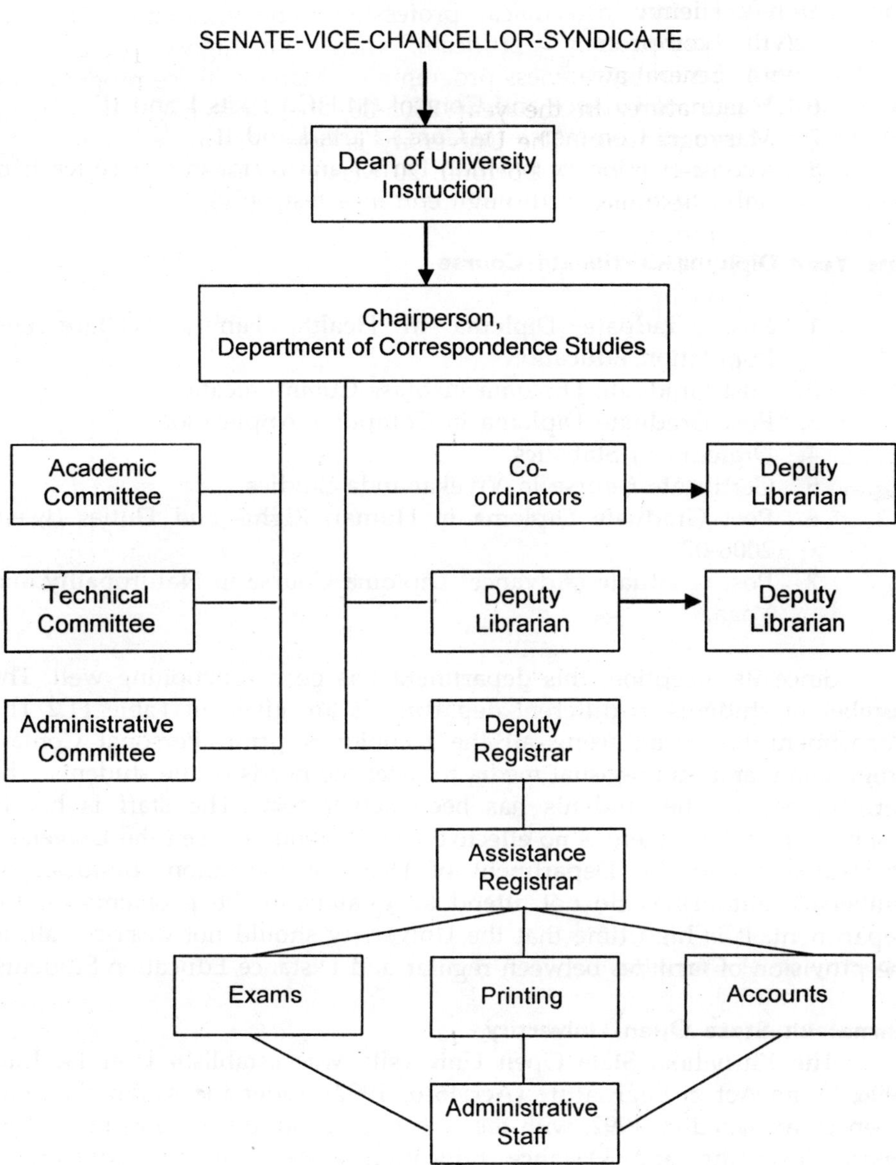

Masters Degree Courses (Annual Examination System)

5. MA. Parts I and II
   - (i) English
   - (ii) Hindi
   - (iii) Punjabi
   - (iv) Public Administration

(v) Political Science
(vi) History
(vii) Economics
(viii) Sociology

6. Master of Finance and Control (M.F.C.) Parts I and II
7. Master of Commerce (M.Com.) Parts I and II
8. Master of Education (MEd.) Parts I and II (for in service teachers only) (Admission through entrance test only)

One Year Diploma/Certificate Course

1. Post Graduate Diploma in Health, Family Welfare and Population Education.
2. Post Graduate Diploma in Mass Communication
3. Post Graduate Diploma in Computer Applications
4. Diploma in Statistics
5. Certificate Course in Vivekananda Studies
6. Post Graduate Diploma in Human Rights and Duties (w.e.f. 2006-07)
7. Post Graduate (Advance) Diploma Course in Naturopathy and Yoga.

Since its inception, this department has been functioning well. The number of students in different departments are given in Table 11.2 The Department has been using all the techniques print, Personal Contact Programme, and audio-visual media to meet the needs of the students. The performance of the students has been satisfactory. The staff is highly qualified. However, there is no effective coordination between the University Departments and the Department of Distance Education. Besides, the University authorities do not attend adequately to the problems of this department. It is high time that the University should not discriminate in the provision of facilities between regular and Distance Education Students.

Karnataka State Open University

The Karnataka State Open University was established on 1st June 1996, by an Act of Legislature (Act 46 of 1992) under the Karantaka State Open University Act, 1992, with the objective of introducing and promoting Open University and Distance Education systems in the educational scenario of Karantaka and also coordinating and determining the standards of such systems. It is the eighth Open University to be started in the country. With over 35,000 students enrolled to a wide range of courses, handled by 48 core faculty and ably supported by over 60 study centres spread across the State of Karantaka and in neighbouring states. Today the University enjoys a prestigious presence in the community of Open Universities in India.

The Karnatkaka State Open University is situated at Mysore in an

Students Enrolled in the Years 2006-07 and 2007-05

Sl. No.	*Class*	*Students enrolled in 2006-07*	*Students enrolled in 2007-08*
1.	BA I	2705	2638
2.	BA II	1619	1478
3.	BA III	1472	1232
4.	B.Com. I	854	961
5.	.B.Com. II	615	553
6.	B.Com. III	500	382
7.	Dip. In HFW and PED	49	24
8.	Dip. In Stat	66	58
9.	B.Lib.	69	45
10.	M.F.C. I	143	135
11.	M.F.C. II	78	87
12.	M.A. I English	321	298
13.	M.A. II English	153	145
14.	M.A. I Punjabi	·119	124
15.	M.A. II Purijabi	86	86
16.	M.A. I Pol. Sc.	94	55
17.	M.A. II Pol. Sc.	94	55
18.	M.A. I History	198	120
19.	M.A. II History	88	87
20.	M.A. I Sociology	232	196
21.	M.A. II Sociology	168	131
22.	M.A. I Hindi	107	71
23.	M.A. II Hindi	82	44
24.	M.A. I Pub. Admn.	115	42
25.	M.A. II Pub. Admn.	78	58
26.	M.A. I Economics	158	150
27.	M.A. II Economics	92	86
28.	B.Ed. Part I	800	611
29.	B.Ed. Part II	518	674
30.	M.Ed. Par Ii	150	120
31.	M.Ed. Part II	131	130
32.	M.Com. Part I	229	208
33.	M. Com. Part II	205	133
34.	Cert. Course in Vivekanand	9	3
35.	MASS Communication	188	142
36.	PGDCA	115	55
37.	PGD in Human Rights	24	16
	Total	12768	11494

area of about fifteen acres along the Mysore-Mangalore highway, in the Manasagangotri campus. The University headquarter houses the Administrative Offices, Academic Block, Lecture halls, a well-equipped library, a few cottages catering to students coming for writing examinations and to attend contact programmes, and all the necessary amenities such as post-office, bank, canteen, etc.

Objectives of KSOU

- To provide an alternative non-formal, non-institutional and cost-effective channel for tertiary education.
- To supplement the conventional university system by releasing undue pressure on the same.
- To provide a second chance to those who have had to discontinue their formal education or could not join regular colleges or universities owing to social, economic and other Constraints.
- To democratize higher education by providing necessary access to the masses particularly to the disadvantageous groups like those living in rural areas, the employed, women and such others wishing to acquire and upgrade knowledge and skills at their doorsteps.
- To promote courses leading to gainful employment, tailored to specific vocational/professional needs, as also being relevant to local needs.
- To provide an innovative system of university level education that is flexible and open in the methods of learning, pace, place, eligibility criterion and they vary in operation of the programme, offering a wide variety of combination of courses and the scheme of conduct of examinations with a view to encourage learning at convenience.
- To help reduce cultural disparities and social imbalance.
- To promote time-honoured values and commitment to quality.

The Karnataka State Open University offers BA with 11 optional to choose from and MA in nine disciplines, M.Phil. and Ph.D. in 11 subjects apart from B.Com., M.Com./MBA, B.Ed., M.Ed. and various other Diploma/ Certificate programmes as detailed below. The University is introducing nationwide. Information Technology (IT) related online programmes through a network of over 150 accredited study centres. In collaborations with IGNOU, KSOU, is launching specialized programmes in areas of contemporary value and interest. Also a unique programme in "Value Education" is being launched globally in collaboration with Prajapita Brahmakumari Eshwariya Vishwa Vidyanilya of Mount Abu from November 2001.

PART C

(A) ACADEMIC PROBLEMS IN DISTANCE EDUCATION SYSTEM

(1) Criteria for Fixing, Quantity and Quality of Teaching, Post

The first important problem is to fix the number of faculty positions. In some institutes the positions are hardly available while in others, there are plenty positions. However, no norms have been fixed. It is high time that the Distance Education council may fix the norms of faculty. It has been suggested that there should be core faculty and part-time faculty. All these difficulties emanate from the fact that the number of admissions is not fixed. Besides, Distance Education system is considered a revenue earning department. In some of the Distance education institutes, distance education is nothing beyond sending third-rate lessons as these institutes are without any faculty position.

> "Expansion without any reference to quality or standards will be counter-productive and will eventually bring disrepute to the system. Good planning. sound policies of recruitment, appropriate staff training, the right kind of curriculum and strict monitoring and evaluation would bring success."[5]

(2) Lack of Discipline among Distance Education Faculty

In the system of Higher Education, as already referred in Chapter 1 indiscipline among faculty is on the increase. This is more serious in distance education. Faculty members do not come punctually and even remain absent without leave. They are not available to distant learners who come from far-off places and go disappointed. We must devise ways and means to create discipline among the faculty. Chin Ning Chu in his book "Thick Face Black Heart" rightly says that whatever your occupation, you will succeed if you properly identify your Dharma to your job. Just the manner in which a chair to be useful must understand its Dharma and allow people to sit on it, so also you must ensure that you do not become useless defunct and redundant. This can happen only if you are in touch with your Dharma. Dharma here means to act in accordance with one's duty decisively and positively.

(3) Lack of Programmes of Staff Development

The process of recruitment in Distance Education is done for core-faculty and the temporary faculty. It is done within the framework of UGC and DEC guidelines. The need is to attract talented personnel who have aptitude for writing, vetting, editing, developing multi-media script besides class room teaching. Since the system in India is already more than three decades old, there is awareness among potential candidates. There is also need to identify personnel available for short duration who can help the Distance Education System both at the headquarters and the study centres. They can provide real lubrication to the system if properly selected.

Besides the minimum academic qualifications prescribed by the UGC, we may suggest their desirable qualifications which can be given extra weightage during selection at the initials stages.

(i) flavour for writing;
(ii) ready to travel to teach away from headquarters;
(iii) good counsellor;
(iv) interest in education of disadvantaged group; and
(v) ready to work on holidays.

The selection through promotion at higher levels may be based on: (i) Contribution to distance education, (ii) Quality of lessons written, (iii) Multimedia talks developed, (iv) Personal Contact Programmes conducted, and (v) Contribution to the subject being taught.

We must be cautious that while promoting a person, we may not select persons from formal system, if we can get persons from within the Distance Education system. If this is not done, frustration would spread.

At present UGC is imparting training to faculty members and educational administrators through 70 Academic Staff Colleges located in various universities and through more than 130 departments of Universities. In the Orientation programmes, there is a component of Distance learning which is taught to all those attending Orientation Training Programme. Distance Education teacher must get two types of training—Refresher and Orientation like other teachers in the higher education system. Madhu Prahar examines the existing situation about the teachers of Distance Education System. To Quote Him: "The Staff Training and Research in Distance Education (STRIDE) was set-up in IGNOU for staff development in the national and state open universities. Although there are stray cases of staff development initiatives for the distance education staff in the dual mode universities, there is no organised mechanism for the same. The only alternative is the Distance Education mode. The distance education mode can be designed in a manner that the strengths of the face to face mode are incorporated.[6] However, orientation programmes in selected staff colleges should be exclusively designed for Distance Education teachers. Such orientation programmes should include:

(i) Scenario of Distance Education in the global context, potentialities and problems of the system.
(ii) Designing of instructional material-lesson writing including editing, vetting, proof reading, etc. Developing New Education Technology-writing of radio programmes, developing of video cassettes, making use of Internet, etc.
(iii) Designing and Evaluation of Response sheets, student services.
(iv) Personal Contact Programmes—teaching methodologies, Art and Science of teaching.
(v) Personality Development.

(vi) Student-teacher relationship through post, telephone, personal contact, etc. Besides, there are some suggestions given below based upon various conferences arranged by UGC.

(vii) Now that we have regular courses like the IGNOU Diploma and MA in Distance Education, the staff members should be required to do one of these courses. As an incentive, the universities concerned should reimburse the course fee, etc. Now that IGNOU has set-up a Distance Education Training Institute (STRIDE) we can expect extensive staff training facilities in due course of time.

(viii) As short-term measures to meet immediate needs of staff development, the following steps need to be taken:

(a) Organising intensive orientation programmes to familiarise teachers with the various aspects of distance education system.

(b) Another way of familiarising teachers with the techniques of various aspects of distance education could be to supply them photocopies of relevant portions of IGNOU course materials for Diploma and MA in Distance Education and some manuals developed by IGNOU for the guidance of Coordinators, Counsellors, etc. In-house seminars should be organised by the CCIs/DDEs to discuss various aspects of distance education. The CCIs may ask UGC/IGNOU for consultants for such seminars.

(ix) As a long-term measure, there is urgent need for organising Workshops, Conferences, etc.

Organising intensive workshops in different regions for providing: (a) Round Table for VCs, Directors of DDEs, Education Secretaries and Directors of Higher Education Councils to highlight the potential of distance education and its role. Developing comprehensive orientation and skills to the CCI teachers concerning various aspects of distance education system with special emphasis on the transformation of printed course material into self-instructional distance education format and improvement of the content of the lessons. At each of these workshops a few lessons of the participating institutes could be improved upon so that these might serve as model lessons. The DDEs, could then improve their other lessons according to their colleagues.

The Round Tables and the workshops suggested above could be combined by devoting the first day to the Round Table, second day to orientation of participants, third day of practical work for converting a few lessons of each CCI into model lessons and giving them the final shape. (6 days in all.) We can cover all the DDEs by organising three or four such workshops. Staff development is of utmost importance for distance education institutes, both for the faculty and the administrative staff. . . . without proper training, a majority of the staff are apt to resist flexibility, openness and innovations with regard to development of curriculum, course material, etc. The teacher from conventional universities are so much used to the closed class-room teaching that they find it difficult to adapt themselves to the multi-media distance teaching methodology.[7]

(4) Promotional Criteria of Distance Education Faculty should give Weightage to Work done in the Distance Education

The recruitment and retention of well-educated, ambitious, capable and talented persons in DE organisation depends to a great extent on the conditions of service, e.g., pay scales and promotion. Adequate in-built promotional opportunities help to a great extent in achieving this objective. Promotion programmes are, in fact, one of the most important aspects of personnel management meant to keep the employees contented, disciplined, efficient and to help retain men of potential ability in service. It serves as a source of inspiration for hard work among employees. The prospects of candidates for a job depends to a great extent upon the promotional opportunities available in an organisation as no qualified and experienced person will join any service and stick to it if the chances of promotion in the service are bleak. The psychological aspects of the promotion system are more important than financial incentives. The Fulton Committee observed: "The right promotion at the right time is an essential: part of the process of developing to the full talents of men and women in the service."[8]

The Capacity Study appointed by the UN commented: "It must be realised that if senior posts are invariably or frequently filled from outside the service, it will prove impossible to retain first class people in the lower ranks, since they will inevitably seek to fulfil their ambitions in other careers which offer better prospects of advancement. Thus, the constraints on efficiency and capacity would be compounded."[9]

We suggest here the following to encourage Distance Education teachers for promotion:

(i) Lessons and New Educational Technology developed by them should be given sufficient weightage in their promotion as they cannot find time for pure research.
(ii) Teaching at the PCP may also be an additional factor which may be given importance.
(iii) Evaluation of Response Sheets also may be added to their credit while appraising them.

His performance, in short, must be judged by his contribution to Distance Education system besides other academic and research qualifications.

(5) Parity of Conditions of Service of DE with the Formal System of Higher Education

Thus, an adequate and sound salary structure together with other working conditions is the *sine qua non* for organisational efficiency and effectiveness. Otherwise, as the Administrative Reforms Commission aptly observes, it has been "one of the major factors for strikes, inter-service tensions and rivalries, indifferent attitude to work, poor performance, frustration and low morale of the employees."[10]

In other words, the aim of the organisation should be to create and maintain such conditions whereby an employee feels like giving his best, gets satisfaction out of his job and is suitably rewarded.

The Faculty and Administrative staff of Distance Education system should be at par with other personnel in the higher education systems. However, no salary structure can satisfy all. It is thus clear that no compensation plan can satisfy all the constituents. The true efficiency of the administrative system can be promoted only through the dedication and loyalty of the DE staff.

In the last resort, the quality of the personnel depends more on the loyalty, faith and sense of mission which they bring into the organisation than on the amount of money expended on them. Nehru rightly said, "The new India must be served by earnest, efficient workers who have an ardent faith in the cause they serve and are bent on achievement, and who work for the joy and glory of it, and not for the attraction of high salaries. The money motives should be reduced to the minimum."[11]

(6) Performance Appraisal

Performance appraisal for faculty in higher education has been stressed by various committees and commissions. Recently Rastogi Committee suggested appraisal by students. This seems to be impractical as students in developing countries are involved in political activities and this may vitiate the atmosphere of the campus. We suggest self-appraisal which is popularly known in management as MBO approach. We can thus say that MBO is a diagnostic tool for self-criticism in the first place, then an action programme for change and improvement and finally a tool for implementation. Although there is a considerable amount of knowledge and understanding required to plan, organize, implement, and operate a performance appraisal system, the application of the process need not be complicated. It has been said that there is an inverse relationship between the amount of paper work involved in the appraisal process and its effectiveness. Consequently, the emphasis of the appraisal process should not be on an elaborate system of forms, procedures and reports. The focus of this approach is the self-development and self-realization among personnel.

HRD is an effort to develop capabilities and competence among faculty and staff of higher education as well as to create an organisational environment conducive to their development. A.D. Moddie has observed that "Good organisation building has to create around it a bracing atmosphere, a prideful tradition of integrity, excellence and fellowship. Human beings breathe this ethos around them almost unconsciously and these traditions make for that ethos."

We may make use of HRD for the development of faculty through training, performance appraisals, potential development exercises, communication policies, job enrichment programmes, etc., and building of an organisational climate which may encourage openness, risk taking, role clarity, awareness of employee's responsibility, increased communication, improvement of personnel policies, management styles, etc., so that they may be effective in translating their potential energy into kinetic energy to make the Higher Education through DE system efficient and effective.

Whether the Distance education system builds up towards positive growth or decays, depends upon the standard practices developed by the faculty. However, sound planning, implementation and monitoring could improve the efficiency of DE system. The faculty of the DE system will have to play a major role.

UNESCO's Report popularly known as Delor's Report summarises the essential ingredients for quality in teacher education. To quote:

> "Improving the quality of education depends on first improving the recruitment, training, social status and conditions of work of teachers; they need the appropriate knowledge and skills, personal characteristics, professional prospects and motivation if they are to meet the expectations placed upon them."[12]

(B) PROBLEMS OF ADMINISTRATIVE STAFF

(1) Dichotomy between Academic and Administrative wing—At present, we have dichotomy between the two, resulting into isolation. Nothing in DE system could be achieved without mutual support of the two. The Vice-Chancellor/Director must ensure fruitful coordination between the two wings.

(2) There is a lack of coordination among different sections of the administration itself resulting in duplication and overlapping.

(3) Effective use of audio-visual aids has not been made.

(4) Administrative staff in DE institute under the control of Registrar causes instability in DE system. Staff in DE institutes (Open Universities do not face this problem) are on deputation to DE institutes. This creates the difficulty of control, continuity and efficiency. It is suggested that the staff need be loaned for a period and need not be withdrawn in between without the concurrence of the Director.

(5) Quantity and quality of administrative staff should be commensurate with the work. It has been seen that the staff remains the same whether the number of students are 10,000 or 20,000. This is quite serious as the quality of the service would go down. Hence, criteria must be fixed for appointment of administrative staff.

(6) Staff deputed to distance education need be given refresher training so that they can work with a sense of understanding and dedication.

Yoginder Verma in his article, "Management of Higher Education Institutions" has rightly said:

> The universities and colleges managed through the application of modern management techniques have excelled in realizing their goals. Unfortunately, in most of the universities and colleges of India educational management has been considered anyone's task. It hardly utilizes the well tried management concepts in educational organisations. It is observed that the decision-making personnel are hardly endowed with the requisite professional knowledge, managerial skills and appropriate temperament. Educational managers tend to believe that knowledge of rules and regulations is sufficient to manage effectively.[13]

PART D

FACTS AND SUGGESTIONS

Conclusion

Organisation set-up of open universities/distance education institutes may not follow traditional university style and structure. The functioning of open universities and distance education institutes are not similar to traditional system of education. We have to deal in these institutes through post and not directly. It requires prompt action on the part of the administration. There is a need of devising methods and procedures to act upon students querries on priority. It should be flexible and student-oriented. Personnel—both academic and administrative—must be responsive, courteous to encourage students in their pursuit of education. Distance education organisations affect the faculty and administrative staff who work for it in five different ways which need improvement:

(i) Distance education organisation should divide work among its members logically giving each employee a particular task, it limits and concentrates his attention on that task.

(ii) The DE organisation should establish standard practices; by working out detailed procedures, it relieves employees of the need to determine such procedure, each time they use crossways;

(iii) The DE organisation should transmit authoritative decisions by despatching such decisions downward, upward and crossways;

(iv) The DE organisation should provide a communication system; and

(v) the DE organisation trains and indoctrinates its members by providing for the internalization of influence relating to knowledge, skills and loyalty; training enables employees to make decisions as the organisation would like them to be made.

It would, therefore, be of utmost significance to stress that DE organisation is not merely a structure; in fact, it embraces a structure as well as the human beings who man and run it in order to realise the pre-conceived objective. We must always strive through administrative improvements and reforms to remove the irritants which creep into the organisations to ensure effective DE organisational climate. We may ensure the following:

(a) Clear definition of objectives of DE.
(b) Systematic grouping of related activities.
(c) Maximum delegation of authority to academic and administrative personnel.
(d) Minimum layering to avoid delays.
(e) Clear demarcation of line and staff functions.
(f) Correct span of control.
(g) Unity of command.
(h) Proper conditions of work.
(i) Provision for easier communication.[14]

The open universities all over the world have become increasingly popular on account of their flexible admission requirements, curriculum and pacing of learning taking education to the very doorsteps of the learner.

As an agency developing human resources and imparting skills it has no parallel. By making proper tie up arrangements and establishing appropriate linkages with industry it has proved that quality education can be imparted through distance education methods.

The strides made by the open university system in China clearly indicate that the economic development and industrial advancement is possible if human resources can be carefully trained in various areas ensuring that the quality of instruction imparted is kept up.

Distance Education today is slowly acquiring the characteristics of industry. Industry is not only cost conscious but also quality conscious. Any dilution in quality will eventually lead to the easing out of the scenario. All out efforts should be made to ensure customer satisfaction. The education offered by open universities has to be designed for the masses, and need be cost effective, customer-oriented, and on top of it all, responsive to the changing needs of the times.

As of now, the hope for the future in the realm of education in terms of access, cost effectiveness and social needs lies in the growth and effective functioning of open universities. They may well serve as a panacea for many of the ills affecting education. Never before has such an opportunity been thrown open. It has to be seized and fully utilised for the good of all.[15]

Vice-Chancellors' meeting of 18 Universities held on 26th May, 1993 have recommended number of Institutional reforms which need to be effected to give a respectable status to the CCls, Directors and the faculty members, e.g.,

1. The UGC should make specific recommendations to the Secretaries of Education in the State Governments and the State Councils of Higher Education wherever they exist, highlighting the need and urgency of revamping correspondence courses institutes so that they may be upgraded to the Distance Education mode and be able to cope with the future educational needs of the people. A data base of Distance Education institutes and the programme/courses offered by them needs to be built up by DEC.
2. In view of the rapid proliferation of distance education since 1962 and the large-scale expansion that is expected by the end of the present century, the organisational side of the DDEs calls for serious attention on the part of the universities concerned to ensure efficiency and time-bound functioning. The CCIs should be re-designated as Directorates of Distance Education. These institutes must have strong and efficient academic and administrative wings which should work as a close knit team.
   (a) A well-planned video cassette should be developed to explain in simple terms what distance education implies, its essential aspects, brief international scenario and the Indian scenario. The purpose of this video cassette should be to create awareness of the innovative distance education system among the public and the potential learners as also to provide information about the programmes/courses offered by CCIs/Distance Education institutes.
   (b) Every DDE should also develop such a cassette highlighting its brief history, achievements, programmes/courses offered, admission criteria, fees, etc.
3. The DDEs must set-up an information and publicity cell for the dissemination of information about their programmes/courses, etc. and for providing guidance to the learners, regarding courses relevant to their need. The cell should also be responsible for supply of information by brouchers, prospectuses and admission forms. Special efforts should be made in collaboration with the State Public Relations Department to reach people in the remote rural and tribal areas and to attract larger number of women and backward sections of society.
4. Every DDE should have an Advisory Committee, for overseeing its performance and looking into problems, programmes innovations, etc. The Advisory Committee should comprise the

Vice-Chancellor as Chairman, two Deans/Professors, two Distance Education experts, a UGC nominee, three faculty members of the DOE and the Director as Convener. The recommendations of the Advisory Committee should go directly to the Academic Council for approval.

5. DDE must be given adequate functional autonomy—academic, administrative as well as financial within the university system. Academic autonomy is very essential to enable the institutes to innovate and launch new job-oriented professional and technical courses.
6. The CCIs be designated as Directorates/Centres of Distance Education. The Directorate must have a full time Director and Core Staff of its own as per UGC norms. The Director should be designated Professor-*cum*-Director and the faculty members as Professors, Readers and Lecturers. The Director and Faculty members of the CCIs should have parity with their counter-parts in the university teaching departments in respect of pay scales, representation on university bodies, etc. Some of the universities have already introduced this reform. Those universities which have not, must do so immediately in order to remove the long-standing irritation and feeling of insecurity among the faculty members of their CCIs.
7. The selection procedure for the post of Director, Professors, Readers and Lecturers in the CCIs should be the same as for the university professors, readers, and lecturers. Some qualifications/exposure to Distance Education should be preferable.
8. Universities offering correspondence courses would allow mobility of students within the existing CCIs and permit migration to the teaching departments and vice-versa. Gradually inter-institutional migration should also be allowed.
9. DDEs must gear up their delivery system for proper assessment of students' assignments and their turn-around time. Complaints, regarding non-receipt of lessons or corrected Response Sheets should be properly attended to. Academic calendar and despatch schedule should be prepared and sent to the students.
10. The universities offering correspondence courses and the State Government should ensure adequate investment/ploughing back of surplus for the development and upgradation of DDEs to the Distance Education mode. A part of the surplus may be kept as a reserve/endowment fund of the institute for meeting unforeseen expenditure.
11. A proper system of feedback from the students should be developed in order to bring about improvements in the teaching-learning operations and methodology. Suitable questionnaires,

students' reactions and suggestions at the PCPs and their response sheets could be good sources for the feedback.

12. It is absolutely necessary that the DDEs must have adequate physical facilities for which a separate and well-planned building is a must for the academic and administrative wings, library, conference room, students' hall, etc.
13. Private appearance at university examinations for which distance education courses are available must be stopped as has already been suggested by the U.G.C.
14. CCIs, with low enrolment (less than 10000) should diversity their courses so as to make them relevant to the needs of people in their areas.

Notes and References

1. Dimock and Dimock, Public Administration, p. 104.
2. Richard W. Scott, Theory of Organisation in Rober E.L. Fairs (Ed.) Handbook of Modern Sociology, Paul McNally & Co., Chicago, 1964, p. 488.
3. Legisias V. Gabriel, College of Public Administration, University of Philippines, Administrative Capability as a Neglected Dimension in the Implementation of Development Programmes and Projects, Seventh General Assembly and Conference of EROPA of the Problems of Achieving Results, Oct. 24-31, 1973, Vol. III, pp. 3-14.
4. Ludhur L. Gullick, Notes on the Theory of Organisation, in Luthur L. Gullick and L. Urwick, papers in the Science of Administration, New York's Institute of Public Administration, 1937, p. 13.
5. P. Ranga Ramanujam, Distance Learning materials of the developing countries: How about their quality, *Indian Journal of Open Learning*, Vol. 2, No. 2, Aug. 1993, p. 12.
6. Madhu Parhar, Human Resource Development in Open and Distance Education, in *University News*, 36 (32), Dec. 28, 1998, pp. 6-7
7. Bakshish Singh *et. al.*, Correspondence/Distance Education in India: Excerpts from a Research Report, *Indian Journal of Open Learning*, Vol. 3, No. 2, July 1994, p. 19.
8. U.K. Fulton Committee, "The Civil Service", Omnd, 3688, London, HMSO, 1968.
9. U.N., A Study of the Capacity of UN System, Vol. I, Geneva, 1969, p. 350.
10. GOI: ARC: Report of the study team on Promotion Policies, conduct, rules, discipline and morale, Vols. I & II, Delhi, 1967, p. 722.
11. J.L. Nehru, An Autobiography, London, The Bodley Head, 1955, p.445.
12. Quoted in K. Walia and J.S. Rajput, Teachers Worldover, *University News*, 36(34), Aug. 24, 1998, p. 4.
13. Yoginder Verma, Management of Higher Education Institutions, in *University News*, 35(28), July 14, 1997, p. 5.
14. S.L. Goel, Modern Management Techniques, New Delhi, Deep and Deep Publications, p. 217.
15. K. Aludipillai, Open Universities in *University News*, July 3, 1995, p. 8. Annual Report, 2006-07, Deptt. of School Education and Literacy, GOI, p. 192.

Qualities of Teachers in Distance Education

Teachers are the pivot round which both the formal and distance education revolve. They are the life and blood of education system. However, teachers in distance education system require more stringent and additional qualifications than the formal system.

The quality of education depends on the quality of teaching. competent, committed and dedicated teachers are the greatest asset for any educational institution. That is why, the role and functions of teachers have been discussed and debated by educationists and educational planners on various occasions and in several committees and commissions. As per consensus the experiences brought by teacher with him as subject expert is not enough for professional development. It was in this context that teacher education programme was introduced for providing directions on how to plan and teach and develop self-confidence.[1]

Thus, it is evident that the logical structure of the written material and provision of opportunities for 'search' in it, contribute to the improvement of learning. Adroitly presented 'orienting instructions' also play an important role in disposing the reader to respond to certain aspects of text. General instructions to learn, advance organizers, various queuing strategies, questions and tutorial letters are some of the important categories of orienting directions. In order to make distance learning more lively and effective these strategies and 'aids to study' should be integrated into the learning material and study guides.

> "The true teacher is he who can immediately come down to the level of the student and transfer his soul to the student's soul and see through and understand through his mind. Such a teacher can really teach and none else."
>
> —*Swami Vivekakanda*

Development of Education is not a mechanical process. It is a human enterprise and its success will depend ultimately on the skill, the quality and the motivations of persons associated with it. Human rather than capital is the key to development. Educational Development prospers where skill is supported by commitment and the human resources exist to translate dreams into reality.

Swami Purnananda in his Article, "Making Life Valuable" by Imbibing Values rightly observes:[2] The relationship between the teacher and the taught is exactly like the relationship of the gardener and the flowers on the bush. The gardener does not create the flowers from the soil and the manure; the flowers must themselves come from the bush. The gardener can only tend its roots, water it, protect it, see that it has the correct amount of sunlight and shade—all these externals he can provide. But no gardener can guarantee the blossom; it can come only from the bush itself.

Similarly, the teacher's job is to nurture the student with right thoughts. The student must be given a conducive and protective environment where he or she need not overstrain to live. But the blossoming—the real fragrance and beauty of the personality must come from within.

The first most important ingredient on which the quality of higher education depends is the faculty of all categories. It is not possible to terminate the services of the faculty, once they are confirmed. Vice-Chancellor and University bodies can ensure future selection on the basis of merit— UGC has laid down some guidelines to ensure quality in faculty recruitment but still favouritism and nepotism play a great role. Vice-Chancellors in the Universities and Public Service Commissions at Union and state level can help in recruitment of teachers of high quality.

We must be clear that faculty is the life and blood of the Education system. It has been rightly said that human rather than capital is the key to development. 80 percent of expenditure in education go in the form of salary to personnel engaged in education.

T.K. Titus in his Article, "The vital role of teachers" feels that[3] the first thing that we teachers require is mentally alert, emotionally vibrant and fully alive to students. For this, the teacher need to be fully alive and must vibrate with real enthusiasm and interest. Our genuine love for teaching and for our respective subjects would never go unnoticed. Obviously the most important task for the teacher is to make his or her teaching truly effective. Here lies the crux of the most vital educational problem. What is the true measure of effective teaching? Who is really an effective teacher? In this context the following passage from a Canadian Education Report (1991) is very illuminating.

It must be clearly understood that teaching consists of more than lecturing. The ability to hold the interest of an audience during a lecture is very valuable but it is neither necessary nor sufficient as an indicator of good teaching. What counts is learning; good teaching is whatever the teacher does that enhances learning on the part of the student . . . the ability to motivate students is the largest part of good teaching.

Teachers are considered nation builders. Kothari Commission rightly mentioned that destiny of a nation is shaped in her classroom. Our ancient literature is full of praise for teachers. Even a day called Guru Purnima is celebrated to pay respects to Guru. Manu has said that a teacher is the image of Brahma.

The Vedas have rightly observed, "Matru devo bhavo, Pitru devo Bhavo, Acharya devo bhavo" i.e., the Mother, the Father and the Teachers have been given the highest regard by the society. Education has always been regarded as a joint venture and as a cooperative process. That is why, the Upanishad enunciates that the teachers and students should live together (Sahna Vabantu), eat together (Sahna Vunuktu), acquire knowledge together (Sahna Veerym Karabavahei), make the education dynamic (Tejaswani Vadhawitamastu).

In the famous birth story of Sutosmu, son of Sudas says, about teacher, "you are my master, my teacher, yea, my deity. I honour your words accepting them with bowed head. Kabir has very nicely said, "If Teacher and God both are standing before me; whom should I pay obeisance? I bow of you my teacher who guides me to God." In the 18th Canto of Bhagwat Gita, Arjun as a true disciple told to Srikrishna, "All my doubts are cleared. I have got Wisdom, my mind is now steady. Your advice will be carried out."

Dr. Radhakrishnan (1949) in the Report of the University Education Commission has aptly observed, "the Teacher's place in society is of vital importance. He acts as the pivot for the transmission of intellectual traditions and technical skills from generation to generation and helps to keep the lamp of civilization burning. He not only guides the individual, but also, so to say, the destiny of the nation. Teachers have, therefore, to realise increasingly their special responsibility to the society. On the other hand, it is incumbent on the society to pay due regards to the teaching profession and to ensure regard to the teaching profession and to ensure that the teacher is kept above want and given the status which will command respect from his students. In the recent past, measures have been taken to improve the economic, social and professional status of teachers and I have no doubt that in the years ahead such difficulties as remain will be removed."

The Secondary Education Commission (1953) succinctly has mentioned, "Every teacher and educationists of experience know that even the best curriculum and the most perfect syllabus remain dead unless quickened, into life by the right methods of teaching and the right kind of teachers."

Plato in his Republic said about the teacher for "improvement of mind and body" and "Promotion of virtue." Teachers lead their students from darkness to light, from untruth to truth.

INTEREST IN INCULCATING CREATIVITY IN STUDENTS

According to Jerome Karle— a Noble laureate in Physics—the main task of a teacher is:

> "to teach students how to think deeply and independently and to enhance their ethical and moral behaviour. The extent to which a society is successful in these matters can have a profound effect on the human and cultural aspects of the society."

C.V. Raman—the only truly indigenous Nobel laureate in Science of our country said:

> "Principal function of a teacher is to discover talent and genius in the younger generation and to provide ample opportunity for its free expansion and expression." "A teacher should not so much supply answers as encourage a student to ask questions to himself."

In order to be successful as a teacher every teacher should have a fund of ready information on which to draw. He should keep the fund supplied regularly by new experiences, new thoughts and discoveries by reading and moving around with people from whom he can acquire such things. He must have a readiness to comment and a willingness to tolerate an opinion diametrically opposed to his own. One should not only be conversant with what is written in standard texts but also about the latest research in the area. He must remain a student all his life. It is only then that we can aspire to what was said of one of the most outstanding teachers of the early part of this century—Lord Rutherford of Nelson.

> "Benevolent guidance, leadership and intellectual authority flowed from him and admiration, respect, trust and loyalty were returned. One would no more question his influence on those around him than one would that of the sun on the planets."[4]

Teaching has been regarded as a noble profession since the advent of civilization. Though every individual is born with a collection of abilities and talents, it is the teacher who helps individuals in identifying their potential, liberalizing their minds achieving heights and making life meaningful. Quality education is a prerequisite for social, economic and material growth of a society along with its cultural refinement. Teaching is basically competence-building, change-fostering and knowledge-enhancing job which has the capability to convert any human being into a wizard. The teacher is bestowed with task of not only training the students in the fundamental field of knowledge, but also, providing them with critical quality of mind and character that will serve them in the hour of crisis (Menon and Dutt, 1996). The teacher is supposed to be endowed with multiplicity of skills and versatility in adapting suitable techniques and methods of teaching according to mental make up, temperament and learning style of the student, should be able to counsel the students as a friend, philosopher and guide, should be able to participate with the students in co-curricular and extra curricular activities and be able to participate in extension programmes, engage in basic and applied research and consultancy and encourage the students in nation-building tasks (Natrajan, 1996).[5]

The qualities required in a teacher are:

(i) who follows a calling or vocation;

(ii) who, according to the demand of one's calling, has specialized knowledge and has had academic preparation;

(iii) who acts not as an isolated individual but as a part of the professional community;

(iv) who conforms to the technical as well as the ethical norms of the profession;

(v) who earns her/his livelihood by adopting a "calling"; and

(vi) who follows a line of exemplary conduct with an unfaltering sense of commitment.[6]

Our students see teachers not only as a vehicle for the transfer of knowledge but also as a role model. Our performance in the classrooms and the laboratories are only effective to a certain extent. Our life styles and behavioural patterns are also important. When our students see and hear us in our strenuous efforts to down size the achievements of our colleagues, when we speak ill of others or when we indulge in petty selfish politicking we lose respect in their eyes. They come to regard us as being as venal and corrupt as the members of the other sectors of the society which we are not tired of criticising.[7]

Let us now discuss the special qualities required to be a distance education teacher:

Harper, the first proponent of correspondence education in USA said that correspondence teacher must be painstaking, patient, sympathetic and alive (STRIDE (1), 2000, 68). Rogers identified four particular personal qualities that appeared to be essential to working as an effective counsellor. They are Warmth, Acceptance, Genuiness, and Empathy. According to Bruner (1966), the task of the distance teacher is to translate information to be learned into a format appropriate to the learners' current state of understanding. Good teaching involves encouraging enthusiasm in students for the subject matter and perceiving why students fail to grasp the relevant concept. (Heerema, Douglas, L. & Richard, L. Rogers, 2002, 35).[8]

Let us now discuss the qualities for Distance Education teachers (See Chart 12.1).

CHART 12.1

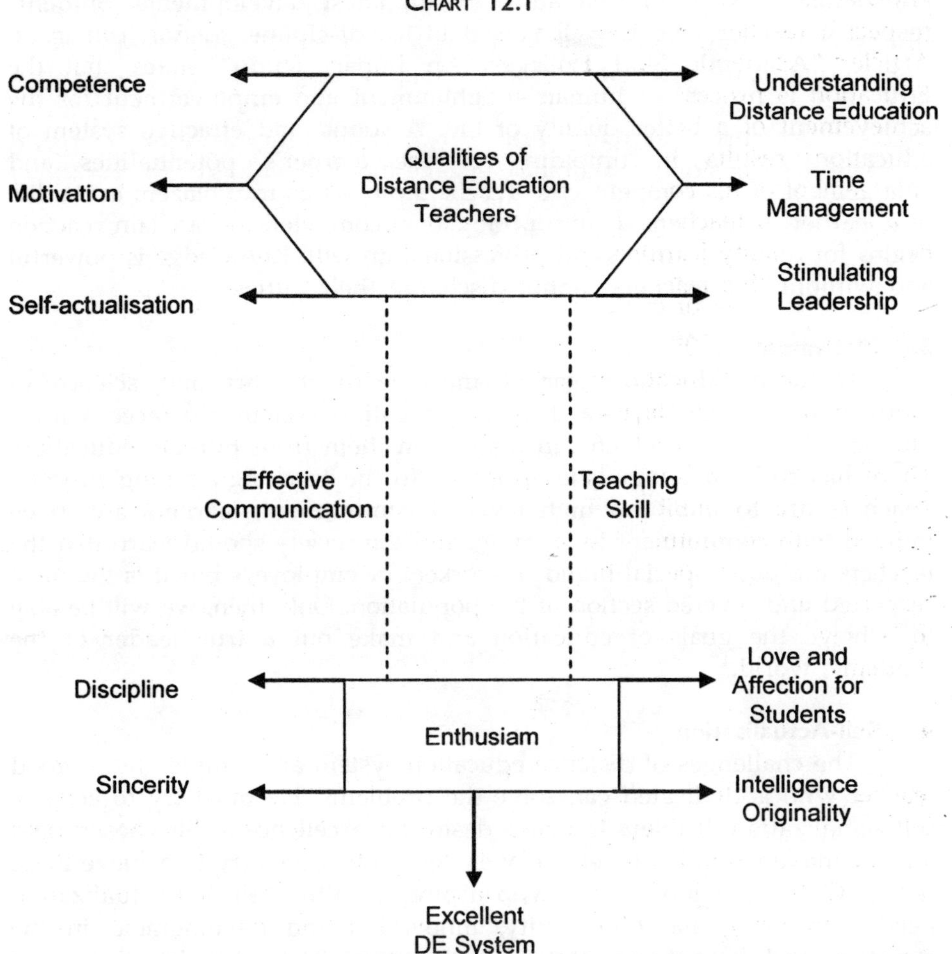

1. Understanding the meaning and scope of Distance Education

The teacher in Distance Education system must understand clearly as to what constitutes a Distance Education System. What are the peculiarities of this system. The students are not with the teacher but are scattered through length and breadth of the country. So, the first quality of the Distance Education teacher is as to how to narrow the gap between him and the student. What are the occasions when he can meet him? How can he develop rapport with his student? The first quality of a distance education teacher is to find ways and means to narrow the gap between students and himself.

2. Competence

The Distance Education teacher must know his subject thoroughly like a formal education teacher and must keep on developing his knowledge to keep himself abreast with latest developments. Students respect a teacher who is well versed in his discipline. *Jeewan Jyoti* in an Article, "Academic Staff Colleges: An Impact study" states that the Education is process of human enlightenment and empowerment for the achievement of a better quality of life. A sound and effective system of education results in unfolding of the learner's potentialities and enlargement of his competencies. Teachers can act as trail blazers in the life of a learner. If teachers acquire professional competencies; a chain reaction begins for quality learning and professional growth. Knowledge is powerful and without this teachers cannot discharge their duties.

3. Motivation

Distance Education teacher must learn the art and science of motivation as students in a distance education system are faced with a number of problems which can dishearten them from pursing education. There has to be a humanistic approach to the teaching-learning process. Teachers are to imbibe a high level of commitment, learners are to be imbued with commitment to learning, and the society should learn that the teachers are not a special brand of workers or employees but it is the most respected and revered section of the population. Only then, we will be able to achieve the goals of education and make out a true leader of the academic world.[9]

4. Self-Actualisation

The challenges of distance education system are complex but a good teacher who is dedicated can solve the problems. He must try to achieve self-actualization. It refers to man's desire for excellence in his chosen field and by maximizing his potential. Very few individuals try to achieve these needs. Only such individuals who aspire to fulfil their self-actualization needs can bring about creativity, innovation and development in the structure and functioning of the organization. The administration must provide congenial and creative environment for them as they are the builders of the organizations. Such individuals may appear to be hostile but they can really contribute to generate social change and modernization.

Such teachers can inject quality in the system and among students joining the system. Excellence, consequently, is not a figment of imagination, incapable of being achieved at any stage; it is a reality capable of being obtained through spiritual growth. And the prescription given by Sanskrit Literatures on attainment of Excellence in all spheres is unique and is itself excellent. Swami Vivekananda was a great exponent of this view.[10]

Human excellence depends upon the will power of human beings which is basic to excellent personality development. Will is the motive power, driving force and takes human beings at a higher plane. Will power strengthens spirituality and character. Human excellence, to become mature needs time and thus patience is required for maturing. Impatience only wastes our vital energy and impairs our will power.

5. Time Management

A distance education teachers has to carry out multifarious activities like preparation of lessons, checking response sheets, conduct PCP, prepare video cassettes, etc. All these require time management. Time is not thought of as a resource. However, it is the most important and crucial factor as time is inelastic and non-renewable. An event cannot take place unless there is a time for it. Time and tide wait for none. We may keep in mind that time is neutral, i.e. it is neither good nor bad by itself. Therefore, to blame the time for any inaptitude or failure will be quite unfair. The Nation must be committed to utilize even a fraction of second for accelerating the tempo of development to usher in socio-economic democracy as enshrined in the preamble to the Indian constitution and further stressed in Fundamental Right and Directive Principles of State Policy. How to go about it? How to ensure optimization of time? How to make the best use of time? The answer to these questions are very simple, i.e., time management at all levels.

6. Stimulating Leadership

The success or failure of distance education system depends to a great extent upon the stimulating leadership, administrative capability and motivation. Administrative capability is an important means of converting or processing programmes inputs into outputs such as good and services. It has been mentioned by V.L. Gabriel that, "what makes the leadership variable so crucial in the implementation process is its dynamic, not passive quality, i.e., its capability to act and react on these critical inputs. It is this administrative and transferring quality of leadership that could significantly determine the administrative capability of implementing organizations."[11] Administrative capability is "the capacity to obtain intended results through organization."[12] Katz says, "Administrative capability for development involves the ability to mobilize, allocate and combine the actions that are technically needed to achieve development objectives."[13] Teachers must be the persons with vision, initiative and desire to achieve the operational goals with dedication and perseverance.

7. Effective Communication

In distance education, students are far away from the teacher. Teachers must communicate in such a way as the students can understand clearly. During the marking of response sheets, remarks should be written in such a way as can be understood by learner. At the PCP also communication should be as per the needs of the students.

8. Teaching Skill

According to Bruner (1966), the task of the distance teacher is to translate information to be learned in to a format appropriate to the learners' current state of understanding. Good teaching involves encouraging enthusiasm in students for the subject matter and perceiving why students fail to grasp the relevant concept (Heerema, Douglas L. and Richard L. Rogers, 2002, 35).[14] The teacher has to teach only for 8-10 days. He must teach in such a way so that the students can be activated and their difficulties are solved. It is called a capsule teaching. The teacher of DE system must learn the art and science of preparing lessons and imparting instructions in a simple and motivating style.

9. Enthusiasm

Students in DE system are disheartened as they lack time and expertise. The teacher must encourage the students to get enthusiasm to work. What is sadly missing today is an enthusiasm to get somewhere, to achieve something? Many people have the potential, they have youth, health, energy, education, training—everything with which to win the race—but they lack drive and determination. They cannot even start because they do not know where they are going. They need a goal, a spark, to set them afire so that they surge forward.

10. Friendliness and Affection

The teacher must develop friendliness and affection with distance students. In this way, the students can feel encouraged and work hard to excel. The quality of teachers in higher education is not satisfactory. We need high quality of teachers. Tagore stressed on role of the teacher as a lifelong learner.

> "A teacher can never truly teach unless he is still learning himself. A lamp can never light another lamp unless it continues to burn its own flame. The teacher who has come to the end of his subject, who has no living traffic with his knowledge, but merely repeats his lessons to his students, can only load their minds; he cannot quicken them. Truth not only must inform but also inspire. If the inspiration dies out, and the information only accumulate, then truth loses its infinity. Tagore stressed that high quality of teachers may be posted in higher education institutions.
>
> "While for the routine work of the university classes men may be appointed as Assistant Professors in consideration of their academic titles and diploma, it would be most serious blunder to select Professors for higher work on the same principle. For the latter they have to be the leader and directors of thoughts. And none but such as have given unquestionable proof of originality and genius be placed in such positions. It is because of this defect in our universities that most of them have not seen the success that they should otherwise have seen. The right methods of appointing professors is to invite the leading writers and thinkers available on any subject irrespective of race, colour, creed and caste to deliver courses of lectures and to select the best from among such lecturers.

Teachers in distance education must possess these qualifications.

The attributes that are required in teachers of DE system may be briefly summarized as: technical competence, missionary zeal, the capacity to motivate others, the ability to get along with students, cultural adaptability, the capacity to organize and manage, the capacity to inspire confidence in others, patience and dignity. Besides, a teacher must believe in the ideals of the organization, be willing to accept hardships and be prepared to work in a spirit of service. His ambition and enthusiasm should not be dampened by local conditions which may not provide him with the necessary facilities. In brief, Distance Education teacher should have:

1. Capacity (Intelligence, alertness, verbal facility, originality, judgement).
2. Achievement (scholarship, knowledge, athletic accomplishments).
3. Responsibility (dependability, initiative, persistence, aggressiveness, self-confidence, desire to excel). Participation (activity, sociability, cooperation, adaptability, humour).
4. Status (socio-economic position, popularity).
5. Situation (mental level, status, skill needs and interests of followers, objectives to be achieved, etc.).

We may conclude with the words that the teachers in DE system are the architect of the DE institutions. On their interest, dedication, perception, attitude and work culture depend the success of DE systems.

Teachers have a big role to play in shaping the future of the nation through their approach to, and performance in teaching. Education is not simply showing your expertise in subject matter knowledge and pedagogy. The essence of teaching lies in creating an insatiable love for knowledge in the learners, a love that will not die when they leave the educational institution, but will continue to influence them till the end of their lives. The real success of a teacher lies in helping children to grow into worthy human beings with courage to face the problems in life, with an inner strength that is the result of good character and community living.

The main aim of education is to shape the character of youth and make them persons of high morality and worthy citizens of the nation. Values have to be inculcated by providing activities and experiences inside and outside the educational institution that promote values. Values are related to both cognitive and affective domains and hence in addition to giving a knowledge of values, integration of value system into the personality of the youth leading to character formation is essential. This can be done by creating an institutional climate wherein the student-teacher relationship is friendly and based on faith. To achieve this the teachers should strive to have a clean image among the students by being honest, sincere and punctual. By following professional ethics and by devoting more time for discussion with students, teachers should present themselves as ideals.[15]

In broader sense, it can be defined as the process by which an organization ensures that it has the right number of people and the right kind of people, at the right places, at the right time, doing things for which they are economically most useful.

There should be only one yardstick to judge the effectiveness of Manpower Planning, namely, continuous improvement of the status and quality of education with the least friction to those who supply the services and most satisfying to the receivers of education. We have to achieve all this with the minimum cost and maximum efficiency. Manpower Planning includes all aspects, i.e. Recruitment, Training, Promotion, Performance Appraisal, Motivation, etc. Let us discuss briefly about them.

Training of Teachers of Formal Education engaged in Distance Education

Formal Education teachers are essential for running distance education system as the number of teachers at the main DE institute level is small as compared to the number of students. At the study centre level, we have to depend on Formal education teachers. The formal education teachers are not well versed with DE system. Therefore, there is a great need of Orientation and training from time to time in the art and science of managing DE system.

Shyani Duggal has developed a model programme scheduled for Orienting Distance Education. The Major Thrust Areas are:

- Philosophical and Psychological Bases of Distance Education;
- Importance of Personal Contact Programs/Counselling;
- Written Communication and Assignment Evaluation;
- Use of Electronic Media;
- Adult Learning Theories; and
- Managerial Skills, etc.

In a nutshell, a well-organized orientation program should always precede a PCP. For meticulously planned and successfully organized PCPs, it is imperative for distance educators to be oriented to the philosophical and psychological bases of distance education, so that they could develop an insight into the system of distance learning. Besides, some specialized skills and strategies, they should also be made aware of SIM (Self-Instructional Material) of both the types—print and electronic media-based SIM, which is a backbone of the entire system of distance education. Though, they have requisite knowledge and skills of theoretical and practical aspects of their respective subjects, still they should be made acquainted with andragogy-based teaching strategies and specialized interpersonal skills for the perpetual growth and amelioration of the system of distance education.[16]

Program Schedule	*Areas of Orientation*	
	Morning Session	*Afternoon Session*
Day I	Need Assessment and Pedagogical Analysis of Needs of Distance Educators	Orientation about Philosophical and Psychological Bases of Distance Education
Day II	Orientation about developmental and Problem Solving Counselling, Role and Tasks of a Counsellor	Understanding the Structure of SIM (Access Devices, Role of Self-Assessment Questions, etc.)
Day III	Understanding the importance of Written Communication (Writing Tutor's Comments and Allotting Grades) in Distance Education	Practical Training in the Skills of Written Communication and Assignment Evaluation (Writing Tutor Comments and Allotting Grades)
Day IV	Understanding the Role of Electronic Media in DE (Role of Electronic Media in Self-paced learning and Interactive Learning, e.g. Teleconferencing, TV and Radio Broadcasts, Computer-based Learning, etc.)	Practical Experience of Using various Electronic Media for Self-paced learning and Interactive Learning, e.g. use of Audio and Video Cassettes, Radio-conferencing, Tele-conferencing, TV and Radio Broadcast Computer-based Learning, etc.)
Day V	Development of Skills in Teaching-learning Strategies more Suitable for Adult Learners based on Andragogical Principles, e.g. Discussion, Brainstroming, Simulation, etc.	Providing need-based training in Core Subjects of the programs for updating their knowledge and skill, Evaluation of Orientation Program: Self, Peer, and Overall Evaluation (Towards end)

"Next millennium is the time for optimizing the interest potentialities of fast growing information technology, scientific development, general education, professional growth and administrative competence through distance education system and usher an era of socio-economic development to make India fit to face the new millennium with courage and determination."—Ministry of HRD

Teachers from formal education need orientation and training so that they can understand the potentialities, capabilities, techniques, quality of students and the way of teaching in a capsuled form. They can also take benefit of this training and use them in improving the formal systems of higher education.

CONCLUSION

To conclude with the remarks by the National Knowledge Commission that faculty development and teacher training is the primary area that needs to be addressed in order to realize the benefits of extended access and improved quality through OER. The training programme must develop domain competencies and teaching skills using new education technologies. The training will also help developers of new OER and in contextualizing existing educational resources. Centres at specific institutions should be identified so that the faculty of these institutions will eventually own, modify, and expand OER repositories. These must be integrated into university curricula and organizational structures. The availability of learning management systems and other quizzing, authoring and collaborating tools should be increased. The evaluation system should be based on the use of the content and the pedagogy in OER.

To implement and monitor the above recommendations urgently and efficiently, the Government of India may designate a suitable organization or establish a new institution with necessary mandate to achieve the above objectives. This institute may serve the following functions:

- Provide leadership and coordination of network-based open education resources.
- Select institutional collaborations for developing content.
- Develop adoption support strategies.
- Recommend and monitor standards for content development and adoption.
- Advise on policy implications *vis-à-vis* licensing, intellectual property rights, etc.
- Identify and set benchmarks based on global best practices.
- Establish relationships with global OA and OER initiatives.[17]

Notes and References

1. G.C. Pal, "Developing Teachers' Professionalism—A Cognitive Science Perspective", *University News*, Oct. 9, 2000, p. 8.
2. Swami Purnananda, "Making Life Valuable by Imbibing Values" in *Journal of Value Education*, Vol. 2, No. 1, January 2002, New Delhi, NCERT.
3. T.K. Titus, The Vital Role of Teachers, in *University News*, Sept. 2. 1996, p. 7.
4. D.K. Raj, Role and Responsibility of a Teacher, in *University News*, Nov. 15, 1999, p. 6.
5. Ajay Rajan and Mukesh Bhurnco, "Job Involvement: A pre-requisite for teacher Accountability" in *University News*, Sept. 25, 2000, p. 12.
6. M. Balasubramanian, Can the Teacher Be A Professional? in *Journal of Higher Education*, Vol. 18, Nov. 1995, UGC, New Delhi, p. 570.
7. D.K. Raj, *op. cit.*, p. 6.
8. B. Prabhuram, Qualities of a Good Distance Teacher in Universities News, Feb. 12-18, 2007, p. 12
9. Meenakshi Sharma, Commitment among Teachers", in *University News*, Jan. 1, 2001, p. 12.
10. Prof. Ramarajan Mukherji, Sanskrit and Human Excellence, in *Souvenir*, ed. (Prof. Vachaspati Upadhyaya, World Sanskrit Conference, 5-9 April 2001, New Delhi, Shri Lal Bahadur Shastri Rashtriya Sanskrit Vidyapeeth), pp. 14-16.

11. Gabriel V. Legisais, College of Public Admn., University of Phillippines, "Administrative Capability as a Neglected Dimension in the implementation of Development Programmes and Project," Seventieth General Assembly and Conference of EROPA on "Implementation of the Problem of Achieving Results", October 24-31, 1973, Vol. III, pp. 3-14.
12. Saul, M. Katz., "A Methodological Note on Appraising Administrative Capability for Development", in *Appraising Administrative Capability for Development*, (U.N. Publication Sales No. E60, II, H2), p. 8.
13. *Ibid.*, pp. 99-100.
14. B. Prabhuram, "Quality of a Good Distance Teacher", *University News*, Feb. 12-18, 2007, p. 12
15. Rajamal P. Devadas, The Essence of Teaching, *University News*, April 17, 2000, pp. 21-23.
16. Shyani Duggal, "Transformation of Regular Teachers of Higher Education into Distance Educators", *University News*, April 16-22, 2007, p. 21.
17. National Knowledge Commission, Report of the Nation, GOI, 2007, p. 52

13
CHAPTER

Organisation and Working of Distance Education Council (DEC)—An Appraisal

PART A

(A) CREATION

Distance Education Council (DEC) is a statutory body created for coordination, promotion and maintenance of standards of Distance Education System in India.

Indira Gandhi National Open University (IGNOU) which was founded on September 20, 1985 by an Act of Parliament is responsible for the promotion, maintenance of standards and coordination of open and distance education in India in addition to functioning as university for open learning and distance education programmes. To carry out its responsibility as an apex body of distance education in India. IGNOU established Distance Education Council (DEC) under Statute 28 of IGNOU, framed under Section 25 of IGNOU Act, 1985. The DEC became operational in 1992.[1]

It was too early to create such a council because as a part of UGC, there were many inherent advantages to DE system. Overhead cost was very little and an isolation from a big parent body would cause great damage to distance education. We must keep in mind that Distance Education is not mere technology but the subject matter also. UGC is dealing with all the subjects taught in the universities. Being independent, we have lost control over substantive aspects of Distance Education system. Technology could be taken care of by UGC also. Since it has been created now, the DE must forge deep bonds with, UGC, AIC, TE, etc. to promote quality of instructional material. Teachers of DE systems generally become outdated and there is need for them to keep in continuous contact with the formal system for quality teaching.

(B) RATIONALE AND STATUS

Consistent with the duty of the University to take all such steps, it may deem fit for the promotion of the Open University and distance education systems in the educational pattern of the country and for the coordination and determination of standards of teaching, evaluation and research in such systems; and in pursuance of the objects of the University to encourage greater flexibility, diversity, accessibility, mobility and innovation in education at the University level by making full use of the latest scientific knowledge and new educational technology, and to further coordination between the existing Universities; it is considered necessary and expedient to establish a Distance Education Council as an authority of the University under Section 16 of the Act.[2]

(C) COMPOSITION

The DEC is a statutory authority consisting of 14 members. The Vice-Chancellor of IGNOU is its *ex-officio* Chairman. The members of the Council include the Union Education Secretary, Secretary UGC, a member of UGC, two members of the Board of Management, two Vice-Chancellors of State Open Universities, two Directors of Correspondence Institutes, three nominees of the visitor and a teacher from the Distance education system. The Director, Distance Education Council is the Secretary of the Council. The Secretariat of the DEC consists of Director, Deputy Director, two Assistant Directors and a complement of supporting staff.[3]

Since the quality of the functioning depends to a Substantial extent upon the interest, attitudes and exposure to Distance Education of DEC members, therefore, the appointing authorities should ensure careful nominations. What has been seen that the authorities take a casual attitude and nominate such persons who cannot contribute in improving the functioning of the Distance Education system, which is the prime objective of Distance Education Council. Besides, the agenda and minutes of the meetings should be promptly despatched to ensure interest of the members. Till now, Distance Education Council has people of eminence as its members.

PART B

(A) FUNCTIONS OF DISTANCE EDUCATION COUNCIL

As stated in DEC Act, the following are the functions of DEC:

(a) It shall be the general duty of the Distance Education Council to take all such steps as are consistent with the provisos of this Act, the Statutes and the Ordinances for the promotion of the open universities/distance education systems, its coordinated development and the determination of its standards, and in particular;

(i) to develop a network of open universities/distance education institutions in the country in consultation with the State Governments, universities, and other concerned agencies;

(ii) to identify priority areas in which distance education programmes should be organised and to provide such support as may be considered necessary for organising such programmes;

(iii) to identify the specific groups and the types of programmes to be organised for them, and to promote and encourage the organisation of such programmes through the network of open universities/distance education institutions;

(iv) to promote an innovative system of University level education, flexible and open, in regard to methods and space of learning, combination of courses, eligibility for enrolment, age of entry, conduct of examination and organize various courses and programmes;

(v) to promote the organisation of programmes of human resource development for the open university/distance education system;

(vi) to initiate and organise measures for joint development of courses and programmes and research in distance education technology and practices;

(vii) to recommend to the Board of Management the pattern and nature of financial assistance that may be sanctioned to open universities distance education institutions and the conditions that may have to be fulfilled by them to receive such assistance;

(viii) to take such steps as are necessary to ensure the coordinated development of the open university/distance education system in the country;

(ix) to evolve procedure for sharing of courses and programmes and for the payment of royalty of other charges to the members of the network whose courses and programmes are used by other members;

(x) to establish and develop arrangements for coordinating and sharing the instructional materials prepared by different open universities/distance education institutions, and the student support systems with a view of avoiding duplication of efforts;

(xi) to prescribe broad norms for charging fees from students who join various programmes offered by the network of open universities/distance education institutions;

(xii) to collect, compile and disseminate information relating to the courses and programmes offered by various open universities/distance education institutions;

(xiii) to advise State Government, universities and other concerned agencies on their proposals to set-up open universities, or to introduce programmes of distance education;

(xiv) to appoint Review Committees from time to time to study and assess the performance of the open universities/ distance education institutions participating in the net work on any aspect relevant to the functioning of the net work;

(xv) to prescribe a broad framework for courses and programmes including their pattern and structure;

(xvi) to evolve norms, procedures and practices in respect of admission, evaluation, completion of course requirements, transfer of credits, etc. of students admitted to the programmes of the open university/distance education network and for the award of certificates, diplomas and degrees to them;

(xvii) to evolve guidelines for the organisation of student support services for the open university/distance programmes;

(xviii) to take such measures as are necessary, consistent with the objects of the University to provide an innovative, flexible and open system of University education, for the promotion, including introduction and continuation, of courses and programmes which conform to the standards prescribed by the DEC, to maintain such standards in the institutions offering distance education programmes and to prevent, through such measures as are considered appropriate, institutions from offering courses and programmes which do not conform to the standards laid down by the Council; and

(xix) to appoint Committees for advising and assisting the DEC in the performance of any of its functions or exercise of any of its powers.

(b) The Distance Education Council shall:

(i) appoint Committees which shall assess, in consultation with the concerned open university/distance education institutions, the development grants required by them for a five-year period and make recommendations to the Board of Management for sanctioning such grants; and

(ii) sanction grants to open universities/distance education institutions for specific projects on the basis of reports by duly appointed committees and in accordance with guidelines prescribed for the purpose and report such approvals to the Board of management.

(c) Financial Assistance under Clause (4)(b) may be sanctioned only to following Categories of Institutions:

(i) An Open University established by or under an Act of a State Legislature, and declared fit to receive assistance from central sources under section 12-B of the UGC Act;
(ii) Any other university as defined in Section 2(f) of the UGC Act provided that such a university is also declared fit, wherever applicable, under Section 12B of that Act; and
(iii) An institution deemed to be a university under Section 3 of the UGC Act.

We can put these functions as:

(i) Coordination of:
(a) common pool courses and their sharing by participating universities and institutions;
(b) development of linkages and networking amongst national/ state open universities and distance education institutions;
(c) sharing of academic services and expertise in delivery system; and
(d) common and transferable credit system for offering wider range of courses to students.

(ii) Promotion:
(a) development of open and distance education institutions;
(b) development of research and expertise in open and distance education system;
(c) development of appropriate facilities required for open and distance education in open universities; and
(d) development of linkages amongst IGNOU and SOUs through open educational networking (OPENET).

(iii) Maintenance of Standards:
(a) development of norms and procedures for quality assurance and quality control;
(b) development of norms and procedures for assessment and accreditation of programmes and their implementation for universities and distance education institutions; and
(c) development of norms in maintaining quality of programmes for export of Indian Distance Education Programmes abroad.

(iv) Central Databases and Information Services:
(a) to establish and maintain the central database of all the relevant information concerning open and distance education institutions in India at tertiary level and offer information services to all; and
(b) this should be achieved by development computer networking amongst all the open universities and distance education institutions.

In the Ninth Plan, the following additional functions were discharged by Distance Education Council:

(i) support in the project formulation of all new state open universities;
(ii) consolidation of the development plans of all open universities, to prepare a national plan for Open University Network (OPENET);
(iii) support and development to distance education institutions of dual mode universities;
(iv) design and development of the operation of the network;
(v) development and management of delivery networks;
(vi) development and management of the common pool of programmes; and
(vii) development and maintenance of database and information dissemination.

All these additional functions are very crucial. The success of the OPENET will depend essentially upon the efficiency and effectiveness of the DEC especially in managing the network and its operations. As the guidelines indicate, DEC will no longer be a dispenser of grants alone, it will, on the other hand, create facilities and systems which the open university can access and use in delivering their programmes.

PART C

(A) WORKING OF DEC

Since its establishment, DEC has been promoting the growth, diversification and guidance to Distance Education System. There had been a difficulty with DEC that Distance Education Institute which command a substantial aspect of Distance Education system are under the control of the University system, i.e. controlled through UGC. Recently, i.e. from IXth Plan onwards, the UGC has transferred the responsibility of funding these institutes to DEC. However, in practice, there would be problems before DEC as to the modality to deal with these institutes through the university. Since its inception DEC has done some pioneering work within all limitations. Let us discuss some of the important achievements:

(I) Maintenance of Standards

Distance Education Council has developed guidelines for design, development and delivery of programmes/courses through distance mode and published these in 1997. Its important contents are—Planning of Academic Programme, Programme Development Strategy, Student support services, Student evaluation, Networking and sharing of resources, Monitoring and performance review, Quality assurance, HRD, Bench-mark for self-assessment and the explanation of standardisation of terms attached as an appendix. In this context, Distance Education Council, as mentioned in the document "DEC" published by IGNOU, provides the following types of assistance to maintain standards:

- Provision of financial support to SOUs and CCIs for infrastructure development (mainly for equipment).
- Provision of support of CCIs for transformation of course material to distance mode (self-learning material).
- Provision of grants for human resource development to SOUs.
- Provision of research grants to SOUs and CCIs.
- Support to SOUs and CCIs for application of new technologies.
- Support for audio-visual facilities.
- Formulation of norms and guidelines for offering programmes of study through distance mode viz., M.B.A., B.Ed., B.C.A., M.C.A., B.Lib., B.Sc. (Nursing).

(2) Establishment of Networking

The DEC has developed a common pool of programmes and courses prepared by different open universities. Guidelines have been prepared to make use of these programmes through adoption, adaptation and translation.

(3) Directory of Distance Education System

A data-base has been developed to provide information about open universities and other distance education institutions in the country, the course contents, student enrolment and faculty positions.

(4) Directory of Experts in Distance Education

DEC has published a directory of eminent persons in the field of distance education in most of the areas. This would provide a ready reference and would promote transparency in putting experts in different committees.

Experts are classified in the following areas:

(a) Planning and Management of Distance Education.
(b) Course Material Development/Instructional Materials.
(c) Materials and Media Production.
(d) Educational Technology.
(e) Tutorial Instructional Support.
(f) Student Support Service.
(g) Research and Evaluation.
(h) Delivery and Assessment of Learners' Responses.
(i) Subject specialists.

(5) Collaborations

The different collaborations of the DEC on national and international level are as follows:

- DECCOL collaboration is continuing since its inception on a number of fronts like exchange of information, data on distance education and quality concepts.
- AICTEDEC collaboration for recognition of MBA programmes offered through distance mode.
- NCTEDEC collaboration for devising norms for recognition of B.Ed. programmes offered through distance mode.
- NAAC DEC are in the process of evolving strategies for self-assessment of the open university system.

(6) Development of Detailed Standards for Running Professional Programmes through Distance Education System

Distance Education Council has brought out some publications wherein detailed standards are mentioned for running professional programmes through distance education mode to ensure quality. Some of these are as follows:

(a) Norms and standards for computer education (MCA, BCA).
(b) Norms and standards for management education.
(c) Norms and standards for library and information science programmes (BLIS and MLIS).
(These were approved by 12th meeting of DEC held on 22nd December, 1996).

Distance Education Council discussed in July 1997 the additional activities to be undertaken by DEC during IXth Plan to promote excellence in distance education.

Future Plans

The scope of activities of the DEC is being broadened to enable it to perform the functions of an apex body for tertiary level open and distance education more effectively. There are proposals to extend the jurisdiction of DEC to Correspondence Course Institutes of Conventional Universities. The private initiatives in tertiary level of open and distance education will also be a concern of the DEC as far as maintenance of standards is concerned. Some of the thrust areas of the projected activities are:

- Development of open education network.
- Technical assistance for establishment of State Open Universities.
- Development of promotional material (Print, Audio-Video) on distance education.

- Encouragement to Research in distance education by instituting Research Fellowships and other awards.
- Development of norms and guidelines for maintenance of standards of programmes offered through distance mode and other quality assurance measures.
- Strengthening of database on open and distance education system.
- Conversion of correspondence programmes into distance education programmes.

The emerging role of the DEC demands that its organisational structure is so designed that it can respond to all these demands. Broadly, the DEC will require additional competence in the following fields:

(i) Education Technology;
(ii) Information Technology; and
(iii) Education Management.

PART D

FACTS AND SUGGESTIONS

1. Distance Education Council an Appendage of IGNOU: Need of ensuring independent and impartial status

The Vice-Chancellor of IGNOU is *ex-officio* Chairman of the DEC which is highly irrational, illogical and improper as it undermines impartiality and independence of DEC. Besides the Vice-Chancellor is too busy as he has to discharge a number of functions of a very complex university. Therefore, he cannot do justice at both the places. Therefore, there is a need to appoint full time Chairman who can devote time to promote distance education in the country and pay equal attention to all institutions.

2. Internal Management of DEC is Restricted to only Processing of Documents and Conduct of Meetings

As already mentioned DEC, in order to meet the growing functions of distance education system, has to diversify its activities independently and not merely endorsing the IGNOU's vision and thinking. Internal management structure need be diversified like the UGC and AICTE to make it fit to discharge its functions. This would add to overhead costs as already discussed. The present structure is only a skeleton with few functionaries engaged in routine activities. We have to create functional bureaus with highly qualified staff which can provide guidance to distance education institutes in the area of information technology, management, financing, research and development.

3. Lack of Monitoring of DE System by Distance Education Council

Majority of the institutes engaged in distance education system are providing sub-standard, services. There is a need to collect data from such institutes—instructional materials, student support services, etc. to find out the reasons of low standards. DEC should earmark funds for this activity as it would help in portraying correct picture of Distance Education rather than projecting it as an highly efficient alternative system of higher education.

4. Meetings are held Haphazardly without much Preparation in Advance

Since the Vice-Chancellor of IGNOU is the Chairman, meetings have to be arranged to his convenience. He being too busy, cannot devote time and attention to this work except harping only on the ideology of IGNOU. Meetings must be held properly and members of DEC must be well received. The venue of the meeting must be spacious and well-equipped and suitable for good discussions and policy formulation.

5. Lack of Coordination and Linkages with UGC, AICTE etc.

There is a need to coordinate with UGC, AICTE as DEC can never be in a position to deliberate on quality of various subjects taught in higher education. For these, DEC has to depend upon the expertise of UGC and AICTE, etc.

6. Documentation not Circulated among DE Institutes

It has been seen that most of the documents developed by DEC are not sent to Distance Education institutes. This deprives the DE system of mature thinking by DEC. It is suggested that all documents must be circulated to all the libraries of DE system rather the libraries of DE system may create a depository section of DEC documents.

7. Future Thrust must be on Improvement Substandard Institutes

The future thinking should be to improve the sub-standard Institutes before launching higher sophisticated programmes. It would be of no use to provide distance education in foreign countries before ensuring good quality distance education in our own country.

8. Lack of Financial and Administrative Autonomy

There is a need to set-up independent secretariat with separate budget. DEC should disburse funds directly. This would require strengthening of the secretariat.

We can thus say that DEC need be made more active, vibrant and independent to take care of the quantity and quality of DE system in the country with impartiality and not restrict itself to the ideology of few open universities.

(B) RECOMMENDATIONS

1. The DEC should be entrusted with an independent status and not an appendage of IGNOU. At present, there is only domination of IGNOU functionaries and most of the advantages coming out of DEC are usurped by IGNOU. This would help it to discharge its functions impartially and meaningfully. This would also involve all open universities and DE institutes on equal basis. Eleventh Five Year Plan has recommended to make Distance Education Council autonomous and not an appendage of IGNOU. There is also a proposal to allocate 700.00 crore during XIth plan to Distance Education Council to promote Quality Distance Education.
2. The present structure of DEC is pathetic. There are only 3 to 4 functionaries on deputation from IGNOU to do administrative work. DEC needs a full-fledged infrastructure to cope with the increasing responsibilities. Internal management structures need be diversified like the UGC and AICTE to make it fit to discharge the functions. There should be experts in planning, financing, development of standards, etc.
3. DEC may be provided with substantial funds to take care of the neglected DE system like monitoring and evaluation of DE system.
4. DEC should ensure equity and quality in higher education through subsidies.
5. DEC should take special interest in development and management of delivery networks, development and management of the common part of programmes, and development and maintenance of database and information dissemination.
6. The Chairman of Distance Education Council should not be the Vice-Chancellor of IGNOU. He should be an independent, whole time, expert in Distance Education.
7. Its meetings are held haphazardly and not well planned. There is no proper secretarial assistance which need be upgraded.
8. There is mushroom growth of Distance Education Institutes with no control on admissions, staffing, student support services leading to dilution of quality of standards. Most of them have become coaching academies. DEC should monitor these institutes and ask them to maintain standards. DEC is only concentrating its activities on selected universities which are well managed. The DEC should concentrate on those institutions which are sub-standards.
9. DEC should establish coordination with UGC, AICTE, etc. to ensure maintenance of standards of correspondence courses under university management.

10. The research reports of DEC and other material useful to DE system should be sent to all to enlighten them on latest thinking and development.
11. The future action of DEC should be on schemes benefiting the sub-standard institutions or devising methods to wind them up to avoid sub-standard teaching.

Even the members of the DEC felt the need of strengthening to play a lead role in the development of the Open University Network (OPENET). For this purpose they recommend that:

(a) The DEC should be restructured to provide it with an independent status. We are conscious of the fact that DEC has been set-up under the provisions of the IGNOU Act. While the DEC owes its existence to the IGNOU Act, it is not necessary that it should be perceived as a sub-structure of the National Open University. Organizationally therefore, it is necessary that DEC is structured as a separate identity through appropriate statutes within the framework of the IGNOU Act.
(b) The crucial functions of the DEC will continue to be promotion and coordination of the distance education system. The directions of development in the Ninth Plan indicate the establishment and development of a substantial infrastructure for the system as a whole consisting mainly of telecasting and computer networks. The management and operationalization of this network will devolve on the DEC and therefore, it is necessary that DEC is strengthened to undertake this task.
(c) Initiatives like mediation of the common pool of programmes, accreditation of programmes to the common pool and facilitating the sharing of delivery networks will require talent and competence of a kind which is new to our education system. It is necessary that the DEC should develop competence in these fields and establish a pool of resource persons to assist the Open Learning System and the DEC in this task.
(d) Simultaneously, the administrative structures within the DEC to perform all these functions will also need to be upgraded and strengthened.

At present, the Distance Education Council (DEC) under IGNOU arbitrates standards and disburses funds for ODE institutions across the country. NKC believes that this arrangement cannot provide adequate and appropriate regulation. A new regulatory mechanism must be established by appointing a Standing Committee on Open and Distance Education under the Independent Regulatory Authority for Higher Education (IRAHE) proposed by NKC. This statutory body would be responsible for developing broad criteria for quality of accreditation as well as laying down standards for quality assurance. It would be accountable to stakeholders at all levels and to IRAHE and have representation from public, private and social institutions involved in the education and development sectors. These include the central open university, state open universities, private open universities, conventional education institutes as well as chairpersons of the specialized bodies to be set-up to look into infrastructural requirement of ODE. In addition, two specialized bodies should be established under the aegis of the Standing Committee:

(i) A technical Advisory Group with representatives from the IT sector, Telecom, space and industry should be constituted to provide guidelines.
Ensure flexibility and track the latest developments in application. The most important function would to be devise common standards for labeling learning content developed by different agencies in order to support indexing, storage, discovery and retrieval of this content by multiple tools across multiple repositories.

(ii) An Advisory Group on Pedagogical Content Management should be set-up to provide guidelines on curricular content and development of repositories, exchange of material, access to students and other such issues. The Standing Committee on Open and Distance Education would also serve as the nodal agency for the National Educational foundation on open educational resources, the National Education Testing Service (NETS) and the Credit Bank.

Notes and References

1. IGNOU, Distance Education Council, a Pamphlet.
2. IGNOU, Statute 28 of the Statutes of the IGNOU (Frame of under-section 25 of the IGNOU Act, 1985.
3. *Ibid.*
4. Round Table of Directors of Correspondence Course Institute, *op. cit.*, pp. 16-17.

Future of Distance Education

Distance Education in higher education is expanding at a very fast rate and at this speed, it is hoped that it may rank equal in number to the formal higher education system in a decade. Every Open University and Distance Education institute is engaged in adding numbers to the present courses and opening new courses at a fast rate. Some experts are praising this system as an alternative higher education system. They feel that this distance education system can bring more and more off campus students to higher education system. The same thing happened to our public enterprises in the Union and State Governments. The result was huge losses and a large number of sick units to whom rehabilitation is becoming difficult. The future, in such a way is good but this expansion of distance education is going to be a liability for higher education and bring a bad name to the system. Let me mention the factors responsible for this undue expansion and uncertain future

1. No core faculty in some Distance Education Institutes causing low quality and a feeling of exploitation

There are many institutes which charge high fees but do not supply the required services. They do not employ the faculty, print the lessons for 5 years etc. and go on distributing the same lessons year after year. They are taking the running of Distance Education as a money making machine at the cost of distant students. I do not understand what is the Distance Education Council doing about it? What is the role of University authorities? Why are they intentionally downgrading the system? The cumulative effect of such a phenomena would be very poor impact on higher education. Later on, when the facts would come before the policy-makers of higher education it would be too late.

2. Faculty where appointed lack commitment, sincerity and identity with the higher education programme

The faculty either remain absent or work for short duration. They take no interest in revising the lecture scripts, checking the response sheets carefully and devising new methodology of teaching at PCP. There is a need to discipline the faculty. The success of personnel administration depends upon the quality of its constituents, i.e. the ability, intelligence and competence of personnel appointed in the organizations. It has been found that a large number of personnel working in organizations are unfit for the assignments they perform. Most of them occupy the positions because of political patronate, corruption, illogical, selections, favouritism, etc. Most of the positions at higher levels are occupied by personnel promoted on the basis of seniority irrespective of their suitability for the job. How to ensure the competence of the personnel in an organization for optimum performance? It can be done through strict tests of recruitment, through promotion based on merit and rigorous training, retraining and refresher courses.

Andrew Carnege has laid great stress on the organization based on the competent people. "Take away all our money, our great works, our mines and coke ovens but leave our organizations and in a few years, I shall have re-established myself. All the personal in an organization must attend seriously to the task of organizational development.

Other Objectives

(i) The personnel at the top level must understand that the most difficult thing in government, as Napoleon said, is not the selection of men but to take work from them. Good administrators know it.

(ii) There is need for delegation of work. The basis of Sardar Patel's success was that he delegated work, trusted the chosen men and that he rarely interfered with them. Nehru said that he did not quarrel with his tools, but he had a way of interfering with them.

(iii) Delay is often the deadliest aspect of administration. Napoelon owned his success to the maxim he prescribed for his men, to be speedy, to use dispatch and not to forget that the world was created in six days.

(iv) To discourage politically motivated intrusions into the career civil services.

(v) To protect personnel from unjust adverse treatment.

(vi) To rationalise the process of sacking incompetent employees.

(vii) To create a basic understanding of modern management especially computer and information technology.

3. Attendance at PCP is only about 20 percent of total enrolled wherever it is not compulsory

The interest of the students in distance higher education can be judged by the attendance of students at PCP. A personal discussion revealed that they find slackness on the part of teachers and thus wastage of time. Without attendance at PCP, students are paying only to make them eligible for appearing in examinations and get degrees. Attendance at PCP is a reflection on the Quality of Distance Education. Many of the students feel that attendance at PCP is wastage of time as the teachers mostly engaged from outside on lecture basis lack knowledge as well as interest.

4. Few students either do not send response sheets or write only patchy answers

The students assignment are an integral part of the higher education. Neither the students take interest in it nor the teachers evaluate them thoroughly. This work is a mere formality. In view of the increasing demand and scope of distance education, it is desirable to review and improve these support services. Research studies should be launched to evaluate the effectiveness of these services and suggest improvements. At the individual student's level there are postal problems faced by them. Generally, there is unusual delay in the postal delivery of material from institution to the student and *vice-versa*. This problem calls for an immediate attention on the part of distance education institutions. One solution, whose feasibility may be examined, is to develop a personal-delivery system in which the Open University may have its own courier services spread over the entire jurisdiction of the University. This should not be impossible because, after all, payments are to be made by the students.

Sometimes, another factor which proves to be troublesome is the delay caused by counsellors in checking the assignments of the students. Regarding this, a large number of complaints are received. In certain cases student's results have been delayed because their assignments were not checked in time. In order to overcome this difficulty, some workable strategy should be devised which may involve introduction of attractive financial incentives.

At the institutional level student support services may be improved by activating the study centres. Library and counsellor-contact services may be improved. Possibilities of sharing of physical and academic facilities with the institution in which the study centre is located my be explored. The Library and Laboratory facilities of the conventional institution may be utilized by the students of open learning system on mutual exchange basis. In turn the study centre may allow the students of the institution to consult open learning material at the study centre. This kind of mutual cooperation will go a long way in the improvement of open learning system.

As suggested by National Advisory Committee (1993) headed by Prof. Yashpal, a special channel meant for education has been launched by Doordarshan and a programme called Gyan Darshan started on the lines of "Krishi Darshan." Such a special channel will serve as an important source of information not only for the students of open learning system but also for the general public.[1]

Students assignments are important yardstick to judge the quality of Distance Education System. Students have no faith in the Distance Education System as their assignments are neither evaluated seriously nor sent in time. Response sheets must create bonds of good relationships among students and Distance Education System. Response Sheets are the real means of communication between teachers and students. They feel a sense of security and good feeling when they get their assignment thoroughly evaluated and get back in time.

5. New Technology is not used and is only an ornamental piece in some of the Distance Education Institutes

New technology like video-conferencing, computer technology, teleconferencing, telemedicine etc. are mere show pieces. These are not being used by most of the distance education institutes and rarely by top level institutions like IGNOU. We have wasted huge money on this technology without much use. In addition, there is a lot of corruption in installing these technologies.

The AVPRC studios were not fully equipped to take up this challenging job of producing Video lessons. There was a shortage of technical staff and in view of the ban on the recruitments by the Govt. of Andhra Pradesh the hands of the University were tied up. Certain facilities like lights, generator, Green Room, Wardrobe, etc. were absent. All these constraints had a telling effect on the quality of production. Further, there was interactive teleconference on every Sunday and the same crew had to run to the Doordarshan Kendra studios to make arrangements for the programs. Resource persons were compelled to work late in the night or to commence the work early in the morning. Also, the bureaucratic rigmaroles were adding fuel to the fire.

Feedback

The costly exercise can be made a qualitative exercise provided, there is a feedback from the learners. A random collection of opinions of learners and teachers revealed that:

- The frequent change in telecast timings is irritating and early morning telecast timing, that is, from 5:30 to 6:00 is not convenient.
- Appearance of the same resource persons time and again is causing monotony.
- In most of the cases communicating skills are absent in the resource persons.
- Repetition of the same lessons is not attracting the attention of listeners.

- Since advance announcement is not made to the students and study centers, many of the learners and academic counsellors are not aware of the program.
- This program is broadcasted through Doordarshan Kendra, channel and which is a satellite channel. All the TV sets can not receive the program unless they have S or H band and cable connection.
- Most of the learners do not own a TV.
- Telecast is not linked to the commencement of academic counselling sessions. In other words, telecast of Video lessons will go on in the air when there are no academic sessions in progress.[2]

Distance Education system takes pride in providing education through New Technology to remove the distance between teacher and students. However, the real picture is quite dismal. Hardly students depend upon this technology. Following are the problems which make the future of distance education uncertain:

(i) Most of the distance education institutes do not possess the personnel and equipment to prepare lessons through this technology;
(ii) There is neither planning for implementation of this technology nor interest to make it effective;
(iii) Students think it as farce and wastage of resources; and
(iv) Most of the institutes of Distance Education institutes realize its Ornamental value.

To improve in future, there is a need of thorough analysis and improvements.

6. Networking has so far taken no roots

It was thought that Open Universities and DE institutes would pool the resources through networking which has not taken place. In addition there are administrative problems like admission for a long time extending even upto December while the examination is in April or so, sending the lecture scripts irregularly, casual arrangements of PCP, etc.

From the above, it is clear that we must analyse the problems of DE system thoroughly, i.e. setting some norms and see those norms are complied. What is need is the organizational analysis of DE system to make future bright for distance education system.

NEED OF ANALYSIS OF EXISTING DISTANCE EDUCATION SYSTEM

Even the best machine gets rusty without timely maintenance. Many aspects of the working of an Organisation have to be examined, to evolve a modified design for an on-going organization, in order to ensure their efficiency. Development in information technology requires further dramatic organizational restructuring through organizational analysis. National competitiveness will increasingly depend on flexibility requiring fast responses from a government that is enabling rather than providing the directions for change.

This includes details about the levels of supervision, the chain of command, the accountability and transparency in the functioning of an organisation and finally the criteria for evaluation. Organisation Building is extremely important in the field of Public Administration. No administrative performance is possible without a suitable organisation.

According to Dimock and Dimock, "Organisation is the systematic bringing together of interdependent parts to form a unified whole through which authority, co-ordination and control may be exercised to achieve a given purpose."[3]

According to Mooney, "Organization is the forum of every human association for the attainment of a common purpose."[4]

The systems approach looks at the organization as a total system, comprising a number of interacting variables. Under this approach, organization is viewed not merely as a formal arrangement of superiors and subordinates or a social system, comprising informal organization and people's influences on each other, but as a total system of formal organization, individuals, social system, the physical setting (man-machine systems) and the environment, all constantly interacting with each other. The systems approach studies the organization as an integrated whole, encompassing many sub-systems, and considers each system as a part of a still larger system.

Organizational analysis is a technique to ensure the achievement of maximum results with minimum costs in terms of human and material resources of the distance education system. The objective of distance education system analysis is to improve pattern of relationships between persons in an organization and to create harmonious arrangement of work with reference to its main objectives. The need for the design of sound DE structures for an enterprise and their continual evaluation in terms of suitability through organizational analysis has been recognized as an effective means to promote improvement in corporate performance. Peter F. Drucker has rightly observed: "Good organization structure does not by itself produce good performance—just as good constitution does not guarantee great Presidents, or good laws a moral society. But a poor organization structure makes good performance impossible, no matter how good the individuals may be."[5]

Organizational analysis is needed in all the distance education institutes/open university system, whether old, or proposed. It should be a continuous activity and should be used at regular intervals of time to ensure that the structure and functions of the distance education organizations are in tune with their objectives. Its purpose is to weed out those activities, which impede the performance of an organization of distance education system. There are, however, certain situations, which warrant immediate intervention of this technique. Let us mention these critical situations:

(a) Change in the Objectives of the DE system

It is not unusual to find distance education system retaining a traditional organization structure, long after its objectives, plans, and external environment have changed. Such mistakes occur when a distance education system fails to plan properly towards a future, substantially different from the past or present. The organizational analysis would help the management to determine as to what kind of DE structure will best serve future needs and what kind of people will best serve the organization.

(b) Change in the Method of Work

The changes in science and technology produce substantial changes in the methods of work, e.g., introduction of new techniques for the promotion of quality would change the working patterns of DE personnel. This automatically requires a different type of organization.

(c) Over-Organization

The existing DE organizations become complicated over a period of time. Over-organizing results from complicating levels of structure and procedures. In such an organization, people are busy in the meticulous application of rules and regulations, rather than focusing on performance. Such a situation immediately calls for organizational analysis, to avoid frustrating results later. IGNOU has expanded so much that it is becoming difficult to supervise them properly.

Besides, the need of organizational analysis is felt under many conditions. Let us mention some of these briefly:

1. Failure to clarify relationships, resulting in friction, politics and inefficiencies.
2. Failure to delegate authority.
3. Confusion of lines of authority and of information.
4. Excessive rigidity in the organization, resulting in operational difficulties.
5. Lack of proper co-ordination.
6. Absence of systematic grouping of related activities.
7. Maximum layering.
8. Authority without responsibility and *vice versa.*
9. Lack of clear-cut demarcation between line and staff functions.
10. Lack of Judicious span of control and unity of command.

Thus, these and many other deteriorating signs can warrant the need of organizational analysis. Madhukar Shukla in his Article "Harnessing Personal Creativity", echoes this viewpoint:

"Managerial functions are no longer confined merely to routine control and co-ordination of activities. Rather, the manager often has to deal with unforeseen situations, where the earlier practices are no longer appropriate, while most managers are potentially capable of coping and responding to situations creatively and of generating new alternatives, very few actually do so. One major reason for this is their own conception of how an Organization functions their own role in it. Most executives think of the Organization as being a systematically designed and highly efficient giant machine. They see themselves as the implementers of Organizational plans and policies by evolving logical procedures and applying rational techniques. It is this kind of 'hardware' view of the managers from being creative. Such a self-image reduces the individual's capacity of play around with ideas, toy with apparently absurd solutions (all innovative ideas look absurd in the beginning), and to take the intellectual risk of imaging far-fetched, though desirable, alternatives."[6]

TECHNIQUES OF ORGANIZATIONAL ANALYSIS

The tools and techniques differ in respect of formal and informal organization. Analysis of formal organization can be done through:

1. Organization Charting
2. Work Distribution Charts
3. Organizational Manuals
4. Checklists of the Principles of an Organization
5. Role Analysis
6. Job Analysis
7. Action Research

Let us discuss these techniques in details:

I. Organization Charting

The organizational chart is a simple form of depicting the various functional groups or departments, which have been set-up to achieve the objectives of an organization. Terry defines chart as: "a diagrammatical form which shows important aspects of an organization including the major functions and their respective relationship, the channels of supervision, and the relative authority of each employee who is in-charge of each respective function."[7]

Chart Contents

Charts may show individually or in various combinations, such information as:[8]

1. Basic organization structure and flow of authority

2. Responsibilities assigned to units and individuals
3. Line and staff relationship
4. Name of components
5. Positions and incumbents
6. Number of personnel
7. Present and/or proposed structure
8. Avenues of promotion
9. Management development requirements
10. Salary data

Too many details should be avoided in the chart. It would be easy to understand and simple to follow.

Advantages

Hicks feels that "Without a chart, many people might view the organization as just a group of people, parts, or activities." The organization charge provides us with a picture of the structure. The chart is a means through which we can better understand the organization as a whole, the components of the organization, and the inter-relationship among these different components. He compared organization chart to a road map and points that just as the road way is not the system of roads itself, an organization chart is not the organization itself.[9]

2. Work Distribution Charts

One of the newest and most promising tools in organizational analysis is the work distribution chart designed for the study of work assignments and job content within any single unit or work group. It shows who does what and for how long. The chart provides useful information pertaining to the ways in which employees spend their time.

In a work distribution chart, the vertical column on the left lists the major activities for which the entire unit is responsible. The other vertical columns are assigned to the employees of the unit in descending order of job rank, from left to right. For each employee, the separate tasks performed and the number of hours devoted to each task during a standard time period are entered. The tasks are classified by the major activities in the left-hand column and totalled by major activity.

The work distribution chart lays down the work assigned in a form that facilitates critical questioning of the existing distribution. It does not provide solution, but it makes finding them a great deal easier.

3. Organization Manual

An organizational chart provides a graphic illustration of the organization. Where a detailed description of organizational relationships is desired to promote understanding of basic organisational structure by means of descriptions of the various jobs that may not be depicted only by title on the charts, manuals are used. These ordinarily are made up of organizational charts, accompanied by descriptions of the different positions charted. A common break down of headings in organization manuals is by general function, responsibilities, authority and relationships with others. Such manuals are generally kept in loose leaf form to facilitate revision. They have come into wide use, particularly in large organizations.

4. Checklists of the Principles of an Organization

Another technique of organization analysis is that of systematic checking of present and proposed arrangements against accepted principles of organization. This will provide a fairly comprehensive audit of the DE organizational arrangements. Such a checklist may be valuable when used in conjunction with charts and manuals of organization.

Several writers have tried to offer principles of organization aimed at smooth functioning of its business operations with a minimum effort.

S. Avery Raube in his paper, "Principles of Good Organization," offers the following principles:

(i) There must be clear lines of authority running from the top to the bottom of the organization.
(ii) No one in the organization should report to more than one line supervisor. Everyone in the organization should know to whom he reports, and who reports to him.
(iii) The responsibility and authority of each supervisor should be clearly defined in writing.
(iv) Responsibility should always be coupled with corresponding authority.
(v) The responsibility of higher authority for the acts of its subordinates is absolute.
(vi) Authority should be delegated as far down the line as possible.
(vii) The number of levels of authority should be kept at a minimum.
(viii) The work of every person in the organization should be confined as far as possible to the performance of single leading function.
(ix) Whenever possible, line functions should be separated from staff function, and adequate emphasis should be placed on important staff activities.
(x) There is a limit to the number of positions that can be co-ordinated by a single executive.
(xi) The organization should be flexible, so that it can be adjusted to changing conditions.
(xii) The organization should be kept as simple as possible.

5 Role Analysis (See Chart 14.1)

Role is the point where the organisation and the individual meet. Role means the pattern of actions expected of a person in activities involving others. Role analysis aims to decode the organisations expectation from the individual and the individual's expectations from his association with the organisation; and brings into focus where these can meet so as to ensure better performance and effectiveness. When expectations of role are materially different or opposite, a person tends to be in role-conflict. This generates psychological reaction slow self-actualisation, low self-esteem, job tensions, job disenchantment/alienation, job dissatisfaction. Role analysis may be used to define a role more clearly to pave the way for effectiveness. The purpose of role analysis exercise is to help the role occupant to clarify his role to reduce role ambiguity, so that he may become more effective.

6. Job Analysis

A job is a collection of tasks, duties, responsibilities, which as a whole, is regarded as the established assignment to an individual employee. Job analysis is the procedure by which the facts with respect to each job are systematically discovered and noted. It is sometimes called Job Study, suggesting the care with which tasks, processes, responsibilities and personnel requirements are investigated.

Job information provided by Job Analysis is used in:[10]

1. Organization and integration of the whole workforce in organizational planning.
2. Recruitment, selection and placement.
3. Transfer and promotions.
4. Training programs.
5. Wage and salary administration.
6. Settlement of grievances.
7. Improvement of working conditions.
8. Setting production standards.
9. Improvement of employee productivity through work simplification and methods improvement.

"Managerial functions are no longer confined merely to routine control and co-ordination of activities. Rather, the manager often has to deal with unforeseen situations, where the earlier practices are no longer appropriate. While most managers are potentially capable of coping and responding to situations creatively and of generating new alternatives, very few actually do so. One major reason for this is their own conception of how an Organization functions their own role in it. Most executives think of the Organization as being a systematically designed and highly efficient giant machine. They see themselves as the implementers of Organizational plans and policies by involving logical procedures and applying rational techniques. It is this kind of 'hardware' view of the managers from being creative. Such a self-image reduces the individual's capacity of play around with ideas, toy with apparently absurd solutions (all innovative ideas look absurd in the beginning), and to take the intellectual risk of imaging far-fetched, though desirable, alternatives."[11]

7. Action Research

Action Research can also play an important role in improving the work system and improve organizational culture. Action research is a process of collecting data about the working relationship of people in an organization. The problems are diagnosed and efforts are made to plan new action and change in behaviour. If needed outside experts can be associated to facilitate to identify the issues and their solutions. It is the process for changing behaviour which emphasizes planning, execution and evaluation.

K. Diesh in his article, "Action Research for Changing Work System" has suggested a model having the following five components:

Diagnostic phase

Feedback phase

Implementation phase

Follow-up phase

Evaluation phase

The organizational analysis by various methods and observations and data analysis would reveal the problems of DE system responsible for diluting the standards of Higher Education. This work can be carried out by Distance Education Council or a specially designed commission by MHRD. On the basis of research, analysis, and inference, we should ask the distance education institute not working well to stop functioning. Where there are minor problems, those distance education institutes may be asked to improve. Since the personnel writing articles and personnel associated with planning and policy-making are from very good institutions like IGNOU where there is no dearth of resource. IGNOU should not be equated with DE system. Before further expansion it is high time to evaluate to maintain standards of higher education.

Efficiency programmes comprise both cost reduction (without lower standards) and performance improvement (at no higher, and preferably lower cost). They question whether a task should be done at all, whether it should be done by government directly or by contractors paid by government, or done by the private sector.

Since government resources are always under pressure (demand exceeds supply and expectations exceed what can be afforded), there is an on-going requirement to review activities to ensure that resources are used to best effect and that government can demonstrate sound stewardship. Consequently, the point of entry for programmes to improve efficiency is commonly a requirement to reduce operating costs as part of budgetary restraint.[12] (See Charts 14.1 and 14.2)

CHART 14.1

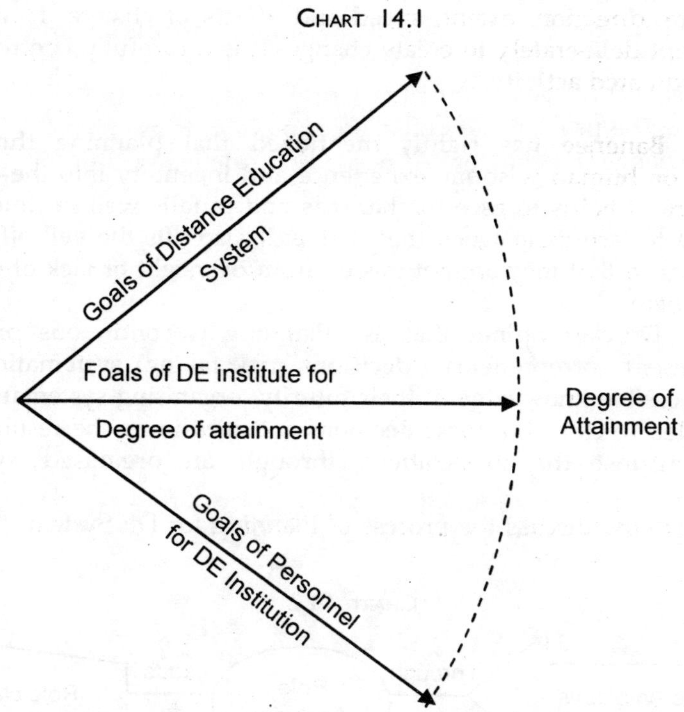

The second approach for the future is planning:

Planning is a Trap

Laid to Capture the Future

According to Henri Fayol: "The plan of action is, at one and the same time, the result envisaged, line of action to be followed, the stage to go through, and methods to use. It is a kind of future picture wherein proximate events are outlined with some distinctness whilst remote events appear progressively less distinct."

According to Terry, "Planning is the selecting and relating of facts and the making and using assumptions regarding the future in the visualization and formulation of proposed activities believed necessary to achieve the desired results." Allen states: "Management planning involves the development of forecasts, objects, policies, programmes, procedures, schedules and budgets. A plan is a trap laid to capture the future."

Cyril, L. Hudson has given a comprehensive definition of planning in the following terms:

> To plan is to produce a scheme for future action, to bring about specified results, at specified cost, in a specified period of time. It is a deliberate attempt to influence, exploit, bring about, and control the

nature, direction, extent, speed and effects of change. It may even attempt deliberately to create change. It is a carefully controlled and co-ordinated activity."

Prof. Banerjee has rightly mentioned that planning throws the searchlight on human wisdom, experience and ingenuity into the darkness of the future; it helps foresee the hazards and pitfalls well in time, so one is equipped to face them when they arrive. It also lifts the veil off possible opportunities so that they are not missed from oversight or lack of readiness to receive them.

Peter Drucker opines that as "Planning is continuous process of making present entrepreneurial decisions (risk taking) systematically and with best possible knowledge of their futurity, organising systematically the efforts needed to carry out these decisions and measuring the result of these decisions against the expectations through an organised systematic feedback."

Let us now discuss the process of Planning for DE System. (See chart 14.2)

CHART 14.2

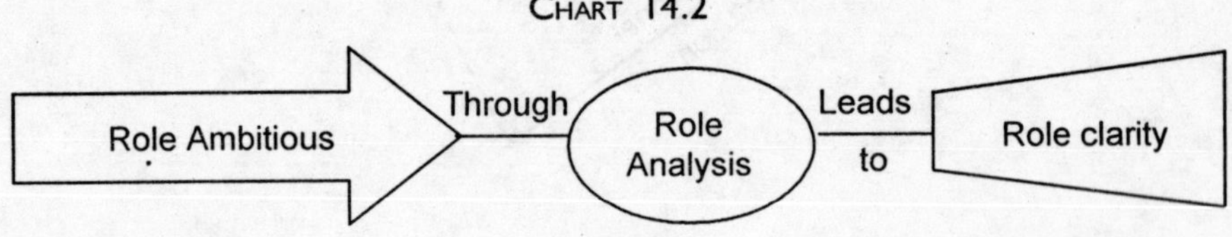

1. Pre-Planning

The effective planning would depend upon the interest of the DE System as manifested by clear policies given by the political authorities and the legislation enacted by the legislature. Administrative capability and skill in planning is the most important attribute of the planning. In order to develop consistent and co-ordinated planning, it is necessary that planning is based upon carefully considered assumptions and predictions devised scientifically. Such assumptions and predictions about the future are known as planning premises.

2. Analysis of Situation in DE System

(a) Assessment of the Present Situation

This relates to a time from which the planning is to be done. It is nothing but setting up of a base line to help the planners to make projections for the planning period and to help in the evaluation of plans. Generally speaking, the data would be required to analyse the present situation. The data collected would serve as the base for planning. Statistics provide the way to a competent, sound and efficient planning. It has been stated officially that planning and effective operation are only possible on the basis of reliable statistics.

(b) Projection of the Situation over the Plan Period

This can be done on the number of assumptions which can predict as to what is likely to happen during and at the end of plan period.

3. Identifying Problems of DE Systems

On the basis of the projected data, we can enumerate the problems which need to be tackled by the plans.

4. Selection of Priorities

Resources in the developing countries are limited. Myrdal has forthrightly said, "The now widely used term 'Developing Countries' is one of these diplomatic euphemisms, the really important aspect of their situation and the meaning that seeks expression is not that they are developing, but that they are underdeveloped, that they need to develop and that they ought to develop, and in some cases are planning to develop."[13]

Thus, available resources are not sufficient to meet the needs of the students. Therefore, there is a need to select the pressing and urgent problems. There are a number of factors (economical, technical, financial, social, political, administrative, ethical, etc.) which must be taken into consideration while laying down the priorities. This can be decided with the help of techniques like cost benefit analysis, cost effectiveness. Priorities have to be determined at different levels.

In developing countries, there are no universal principles to determine priorities. There is a need of research in this area to devise effective methodology or selecting priorities acceptable to political leadership in the country.

5. Definition of Goal and Objectives of DE System

Goal is the direction in which the plan is to proceed. And the term is used more in the case of long-term planning. Goals formulated are generally broad. A goal is usually described in terms of: (1) what is to be attained; (2) the extent to which it is to be attained; (3) the population involved; (4) the geographic areas in which the proposed programme will operate; and (5) the length of time required for achieving those goals. The objective is a precise statement of the ends intended to be achieved. We must build the hierarchy of objectives, ultimate, intermediate and immediate. Immediate objectives are further divided into effort objectives and performance objectives (targets).

6. Write up of Formulated Plan

After deciding the Priorities, Goals, Objectives, the next major step is to prepare a write up of the plan. This may contain a schedule (time sequence for the plan to be implemented) and procedures (a set of rules of implementing the plan) and other details, so that evaluation becomes easy and meaningful.

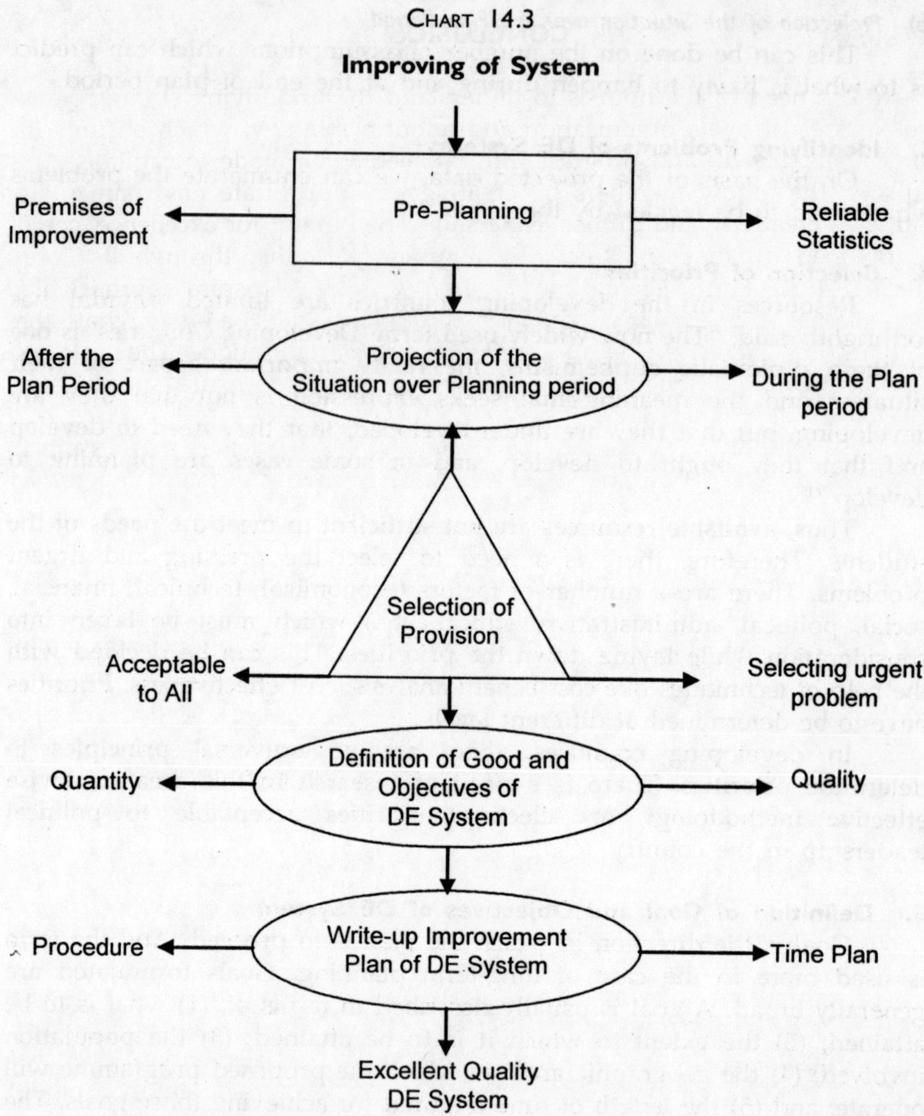

It is clear that poor Planning may upset the programme results. However, we may keep in mind that excessive Planning can divert valuable managerial resources from the present utilization. Rigid enforcement of the detailed plans can kill the programme by stifling initiative. Deviation from detailed task specifications should be allowed, if high level targets are achieved. Therefore, there is a need that planning itself must be clearly anticipated in advance, so as to ensure that it will make a positive contribution to the DE programme.

CONCLUSION

The need of the hour is to understand the underlying strengths and weaknesses of one's organisation and adopt a strategy, which ensures its continuous growth and progress. Efforts need to be made to capitalise the skills of the fellow members by creating an appropriate environment to stimulate creativity and diffuse leadership. The pursuit for excellence, could be imbibed by the rank and file of an organisation, through its core-ideological structure. The structure therefore needs to inspire appropriable; innovations and facilitate their execution in such a way that the organisation is able to sustain its enviable reputation. The role of management, thus, is that of a catalyst, in order to ensure success and survival of an organisation.

The National Knowledge Commission (NKC) believes that a radical reform of the system of Open and Distance Education (ODE) is imperative to achieve the objectives of expansion, inclusion and excellence in higher education. The significance is obvious. For one, more than one-fifth of the students enrolled in higher education are in the ODE stream. For another, ODE has an enormous potential to spread higher education opportunities beyond the brick and mortar world. But there are reasons for concern. First, the quality of higher education provided in large segments of ODE, particularly in correspondence courses in universities, leaves much to be desired. Second, it is not sufficiently recognized that ODE provides educational opportunities not only to those who discontinue formal education on account of economic or social compulsions, but also to young school levers who are simply unable to secure admission in the formal stream at universities. It is time to address these problems. There is a clear need to improve the quality of ODE and to make it more appropriate to the needs of society. It is just as important to expand opportunities in higher education through the use of technology in ODE. It would not be possible to attain a gross enrolment ratio of 15% by 2015 without a massive expansion in ODE. In this endeavour, we must not forget that ODE is seen as inferior to conventional classroom learning. This perception, and the reality, both need change. We must realize that ODE is not simply a mode of educational delivery, but an integrated discipline engaged in the creation of knowledge.[14]

NOTES AND REFERENCES

1. Poonam Chauhan, "Towards Improved Student Support Services in Open Learning", *University News*, January 8, 2001.
2. Shakeela Khanam, "Learning in Future", *University News*, Nov. 20, 2000.
3. Dimock and Dimock: Public Administration, p. 104.
4. J.D. Moony: Principles of Organization, p. 1.
5. Peter F. Drucker: The Practice of Management, Heinemann, London, 1955l, p. 225.
6. Madhukar Shukla, Harnessing Personal Creativity, *Business India*, Feb. 9-22, 1987.

7. Terry George: Principles of Management, Richard D. Irwin Inc. Home-wood, 1972, p. 378.
8. Harry L. Wyllie, Office Managemnet Handbook, ed. 1958, p. 225.
9. Herbert, C. Hick: The Management of Organizations: Systems and Human Resources Appraoch (2nd ed.), New York, McGraw Hill, 1972, p. 259.
10. Dale Yoder: Personnel Management and Industrial Relation (5th ed.), New Delhi, Prentice Hall, p. 281.
11. Madhukar Shukla, Harnessing Personal Creativity, *Business India*, Feb. 9-22, p. 1987.
12. Mohan Kaul, Civil Service Reforms, Learning From Commonwealth Experience, in *IJPA*, July-Sept., 1998, p. 698.
13. G. Myrdal, (1968), Asian Drama, an Inquiry into the Poverty of Nations, New York, Pantheion, Vol. 3, p. 1841.
14. National Knowledge Commission, Report of the Nation, 2007, GOI, p. 48.

Infrastructural Facilities in Distance Education System

So far, there has been no consideration about the infrastructural facilities of DE system. The students are considered as crowd around the DE institutes/Open University, at study centres and at other places where PCP is arranged. No decent arrangement is made for students to stay during the PCP and casual visits. How can students learn in such an environment? Physical amenities are basic necessities. In addition, there are other problems like availability of books in the library and sitting capacities in the library, availability of teachers for discussion and clarification of doubts. Besides, basic amenities like potable drinking water, a clean and cheap canteen, sitting places when periods are vacant. Let us mention these infrastructure requirements before analysis:

1. Building with class-rooms, relaxation rooms.
2. Library—Availability of books and place for reading.
3. Availability of teachers during PCP
4. Good lavatories especially for women students.
5. Basic facilities like potable drinking water.

I. Unsuitable building especially class-rooms and relaxation rooms in DE Institutes

The outlay of DE institutes is dull, shabby and disorderly. The worst positions is of class-rooms which appear to be most repulsive. Various types of furniture do not match in the class rooms which and are so positioned that it appears to be lying scattered and uncared for. Chairs are such that there always remains a danger of falling. In addition, there is no room where students can sit in a vacant period. They just move here and

CHART 15.1

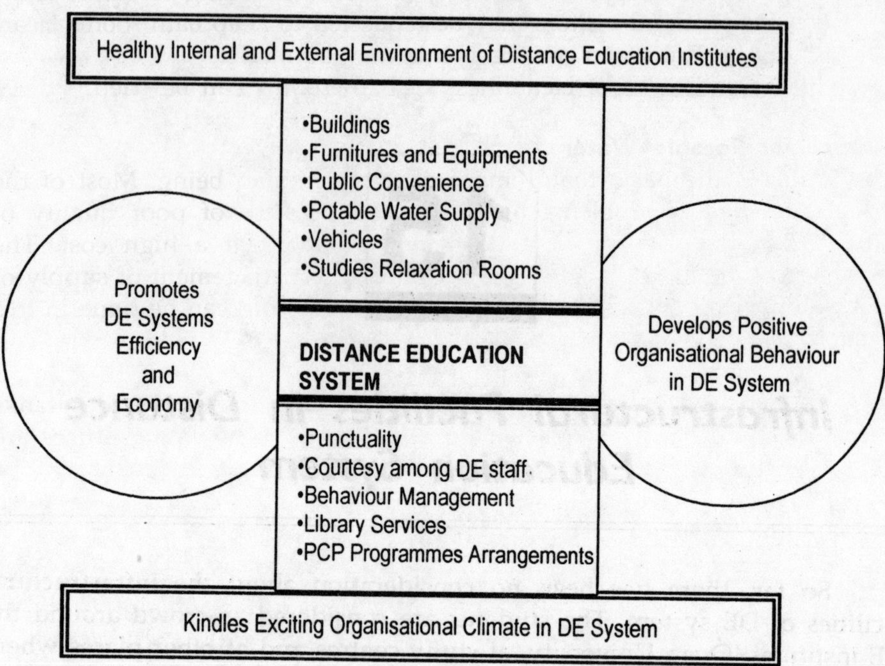

there and thus get tired. Some of them do not attend full PCP and leave in between.

Disorderly parking outside the DE institutes and at the PCP places outside the location of DE institute causes inconvenience to students and the whole place looks like an unorganized market area or worse than that. Besides, buildings are not properly maintained.

2. Poor Maintenance of Public Conveniences

Bath rooms and toilets in DE institute premises are the most essential infrastructural component for students as well as visitors. They should be kept clean, as cleanliness is next to godliness. Many of the diseases are the product of unsanitary conditions prevailing in many DE institutes besides causing physical discomfort and inconvenience to the users. We suggest here the following actions to keep them clean:

(i) Sweepers engaged for cleaning bath rooms may be given training by pinpointing the importance of cleanliness in the upkeep of bath rooms.
(ii) Necessary materials like phenyl, cleansing agents, etc. may be supplied regularly.
(iii) Some persons may be appointed to supervise the rooms regularly and maintaining a record of the action taken.

(iv) Bath rooms may be constructed away from sitting places so that the stink does not adversely affect the working of employees.
(v) Student and visitors may be requested to keep bath rooms clean.
(vi) Sufficient water arrangements may be made.
(vii] Privatisation of cleanliness of bath rooms can be tried.

3. Supply of Potable Water

Water is the basic requirement of every human being. Most of the students get health problems and infections because of poor quality of water. They cannot afford bottled water available at a high cost. The distance education organization should attend to management of supply of good water for all students and visitors. The following can be done in this direction:

(i) Water storage should be done in clean tanks. Besides tanks should be washed on Saturdays/Sundays when DE offices are closed. Besides insecticides like potassium per magnate may be used once a month to keep the water infection free. Tanks which have become too dirty should be discarded.
(ii) Student and visitors should be requested not to waste the precious resource, i.e. water. Taps may not be kept open.
(iii) Plastic jugs and glasses used for taking water in the rooms are mostly dirty. They need be regularly cleaned and well maintained.
(iv) Contract for mineral water at cheap rates may be tried if feasible.
(v) Water testing may be got done through laboratories once in six months to assess its quality.

4. Poor Management Parking of Vehicles

This is an age of vehicles as most of the students and visitors use cars/scooters to come to DE Institutes. Parking of these vehicles has become a big challenge and even nuisance. We suggest the following to manage vehicles:

(i) Parking zones may be earmarked separately for cycles, scooters and cars so that there may be clear cut demarcation.
(ii) Vehicles of the staff who are to park for the whole day should be done separately from students as their movement would be limited.
(iii) Parking rules may be framed and in case of violation, huge fines may be imposed as a deterrent.
(iv) Persons may be engaged to guide the vehicle owners. His salary can be paid from the collections made from vehicle owners.

5. Lack of Punctuality among Teachers/Outside Experts

The PCP time is valuable as the teachers have to finish the course within a short span of PCP. So, the teachers and outside experts must be punctual. The Administration Reforms Commission (ARC) has rightly stated that, "the healthy functioning of the administration depends not only on the competence of its personnel, but also on the maintenance of a high standard of personal conduct and the observance of discipline. It is, therefore, essential that there should be a clearly enumerated code to correct official behaviour and a provision for the punishment of those who deviate thereform. There would, of course, also be provision for punishing slackness and inefficiency."

Punctuality enforcement is not a difficult task provided the culture of non-punctuality is discouraged. Employees are being paid for devoting time and time is money. How can we pay them if they are not producing? DE System is suffering a lot on this count. DE System must give top priority to this issue as we find that because of no punctuality of teachers, administrative staff, students suffer a great agony in waiting for them. The De System must be harsh and no leniency should be exhibited to persons who are not punctual. This is the first and foremost requirement of any administrative success and responsive administration of DE System.

We suggest some of techniques to ensure punctually:

(i) Head of Deptt. should show seriousness about this issue by calling for all employees to observe discipline.
(ii) Induction training may be given to all employees to be punctual as preventive and educational measure.
(iii) Late arrivals should lead to deduction of half day casual leave and 3 consecutive defaults invite censure and adverse entry in SRs and CRs.
(iv) Punching of cards to mark attendance can be introduced.
(v) Habitually non-punctual employees may be served warning/censures/stoppage of increment and even suspension including termination.
(vi) Extra-benefits in the form of deputation for training, other assignments, etc. may be refused to those who are not punctual.
(vii) Strict monitoring may be done to prohibit late coming.

6. Improper Management of Furniture and Equipment

Furniture is essential to provide comforts and working atmosphere to employees and students. Furniture costs money and hence must be used carefully and maintained properly. We can take the following steps to make the furniture serve our purpose:

(i) Proper assessment of the needs of all rooms/employees and students may be done before ordering new equipment. It has been seen that because of lack of coordination furniture at one place is lying surplus while at another place it is in demand causing artificial scarcity. Sometimes the stores are full of old furniture which can be made of good quality with minor repairs and polishing while the orders are placed for buying fresh furniture.

(ii) Peons employed for the upkeep of furniture need be trained in the upkeep of furniture through regular dusting, spraying to avoid rusting, and keeping them in good conditions.

(iii) Furniture should be neatly arranged to provide aesthetic outlook and look presentable.

(iv) Every year/every single article of furniture should be physically counted and examined for repairs, polish or condemnation etc.

(v) Furniture, which is unserviceable and beyond repairs, needs to be condemned rather than piling them up in stores and wasting precious spaces.

(vi) The staff should be convinced about the importance of cleaning, inspecting and keeping equipment in good order; of reporting defects immediately; and of returning equipment to its correct place after use.

(vii) There is no easy way to convince the staff of the need to clean equipment and to keep it in good condition. The best way is for the supervisor to set a good example by ensuring that equipments are cared for and kept in a good condition (dirty or damp equipment deteriorates more rapidly than when it is kept clean and dry).

(viii) An inspection check-list and inspection schedule should be drawn up and duties decentralized among responsible employees irrespective of their administrative charges. These officials should help in detecting discrepancies and taking remedial action.

7. Behaviour Management

DE students must be treated well. Teachers as well as Administrative staff must listen the students properly and solve their problems.

Most of the problems today are the result of rude behaviour of majority of employees towards students. Their behaviour has alienated the students from meeting the personnel of DE System. How to go about it? We may suggest the following remedies:

(i) Training may be imparted in the art and science of communication.

(ii] Employees using filthy language should be dealt strictly by imposition of fines or recording the demeanour in the confidential reports.

(iii) A column about behaviour should be incorporated in ACR.

(iv) Employees should be encouraged to be polite, nice and courteous. Superiors should set a personal example by observing same standards while dealing with their bosses as well as subordinates or students.

(v) Supervision should be done strictly and if required dialogues of students and employees depicting different situations—very negative, negative positive, very positive, be recorded for training purposes. To quote Aristotle, "Anyone can become angry—that is easy. But to be angry with the right person, to the right degree, at the right time, for the right purpose and the right way is not easy."

(vi) A new concept called "Equilibrium Thinking" has been tried out with police trainees both with veterans having thirty years' experience and freshly recruited officer trainees. Several of the trainees reported remarkable breakthroughs in managing anger and other emotions. Equilibrium is produced when positive values or vices are balanced. The positive values need to be affirmed or reinforced and the negative values need to be denied, weakened and uprooted.

Current success literature talks only of the power of positive thinking but mere positive thinking does not generate sufficient power to overcome the challenge of ingrained negative attitudes, habits forces and values. Mere positive thinking does not produce an equilibrium that comes from a habit of self-realisation. The method is quite simple. Continuously hold the words Beat it in one's mind. In order to overcome anger, continually issue the following commands to self:

1. Be calm Beat anger
2. Be gentle Beat stress
3. Be peaceful Beat tension
4. Be patient Beat impatience
5. Be poised Beat imbalance
6. Be tactful Beat tactlessness
7. Be cheerful Beat depression

It takes only about 10 seconds to run the series of commands through one's mind. So even if one repeats the exercise, ten times a day it will take only 100 seconds.

The repetitive reinforcement on a daily and continuous basis will help in internalizing values and overcoming flows and weaknesses. Equilibrium thinking lends itself to the all round development of the human personality and character.[1] Prabhat Kumar, the then Cabinet Secretary of India in his Article,[2] "A Responsive and Effective Government" rightly stresses the need for making the administration sensitive to the citizens needs. To quote him:

> We are now on the threshold of the twenty-first century. In the new millennium, above all, the government would need to re-invent itself to become citizen-centric and citizen-friendly. It would need to limit

its role to core functions such as security, law and order, social services, creation of infrastructure and macro-economic management. Greater delegation and decentralisation of authority and responsibilities would need to be introduced at all levels. A combination of Citizens' Charters and the Right to Information would ensure greater accountability in the administrative systems. The process of consultation with the participation of citizens in decision-making would gradually become more pronounced in order to ensure accountability. At the same time, good citizenry would also need to be emphasised for all round development of the society. Besides enjoying their rights, the citizens would need to behave responsibly and perform their duties to the state. Clearly defined ethical standards would also need to be adopted by the civil servants as well as politicians. In order to achieve all this, innovative use of information technology would be critical. In DE system, we can adopt the same feelings towards students.

Ministry of Personnel, Public Grievances and Pensions (Department of Administrative Reforms and Public Grievances) has given some tips which need be followed to keep offices in order.[3] These steps can also be useful for DE System to deal with the students like celebrations of festivals, discussion etc.

8. Unsatisfactory Library services

With the development of Open Universities (OU) and Distance Education Institutes (DEIs), the number of distance learners has also increased over the years. The distance learners are basically independent self learners, may be employed and with other societal and family responsibilities. They basically depend on the self learning materials supplied by their university/institute. It has been pointed out in the field of education (as opposed to skill training/distance) methods used in a pedagogically authoritarian manner can deprive students of the opportunity to develop a true personal understanding of the ideas and concepts contained in the learning materials. The student runs the risk of being turned into a passive consumer of educational commodities such as packets of knowledge and educational certificates (Kaye and Rumble, 1981, p. 284). In view of this library services to the distance learners has now become one of the most important support services and students are encouraged to undertake projects and use local public libraries for developing their assignments. However, research has shown that normally distance learners do not use library or library services. In a telephone survey of 300 students in Athabasca University (AU) Appavoo and Hansen (1989) found that seventy students never used libraries and another fifty-nine never used AU library. Miller *et al.* (1984) found that about half of the off-campus students attempted to use public libraries but without much success. In fact, library surveys show that most adult students lack

	Do's	Dont's
1.	Make haste, slowly	Don'ts merely make haste
2.	List areas of interface	Don't be unrealistic
3.	Phase out areas for introduction of small steps.	Don't take on more than you can commit.
4.	Involve customer and staff in formulating and implementing it.	Dont's involve only senior officers in the formulation and implementation.
5.	Prepare a Master Plan for formulation and implementation over five years and budget for it.	Don't rush into an overall package for the whole Ministry/Department/ Organization.
6.	Win consumer confidence with small, highly visible measures.	Don't promise more than you can deliver.
7.	Remember, citizen's charter is a process, constantly evolving.	Don't look upon it as a one-time exercise, with a final outcome.
8.	Inform the customer of the proposed commitments.	Don't inform the customer unless you are sure of delivering the service.
9.	Use simple language.	Don't use difficult language or jargon.
10.	Train your staff.	Don't leave yourself out.
11.	Delegate power.	Don't centralize.
12.	Setup system for feedback and independent scrutiny.	Don't continue blindly without regular, periodic reassessment of performance.

independent learning skills which include the ability to select and critically evaluate information and therefore fail to take advantage of the resources available in public libraries (BURGE *et al.*, 1989; Latham, 1985). The process of learning these skills is a key factor in 'learning how to learn' and towards empowering students to become independent lifelong learners (Shklanka, 1990, p. 8). In this context, this paper presents a proposal to teach 'Information Literacy' to all the distance learners.[4]

Libraries are the most important for students of higher education. Library must be the best place in DE Institutes and study centres. However, in practice, libraries are the most neglected. The relevant books are not available as well as seats for studying are limited. The number of DE students are large and more than 10 times of Formal System students but the library facilities are 10 percent of them. Students in DE system must be encouraged to do extensive reading in library. More funds and facilities are required for library.

Open University education has been described more as a process of learning than as a process of teaching, signifying self-efforts to be put in by the students. Thus students in open university education are to be provided with the facilities necessary for mastering the subject matter, technical skills, habits of thought and methods of work in their thrust area. Printed study material alone will not provide all the opportunities needed for attaining the complex objectives.

The library has a prominent role to play in attaining objectives of the open universities. In formal education library is described as heart of educational system; in open university it is more so. The library system caters on-campus teaching community as well as learners residing in remote areas learners having different economic, social and educational background. Now only that, it has to acquire, organize and disseminate information in the form of print materials as well as non-print material. Describing role of library in open university education, Penland asserts as "there has already occurred an increasing acceptance of non-academic programmes, such as the "university without walls as approved avenues to personal improvement, degrees, diplomas. Such activities have placed new responsibilities upon libraries and lead to their further involvement in providing both print and non-print resources and services to meet them."

Highlighting the impact of multimedia, Taylor observed that "A second major impact on libraries will result from the broadening of the communication spectrum from print to sound to image. . . . The capability to transmit non-print forms by video and audio channels opens up, for libraries, a whole new spectrum of services, systems and functions." Thus in open university education the role of the library extends in preparing study packages by the authors, editors, translators, etc.; to supporting intermediaries in completion of learning packages successfully for the self-learning of the students.

A study on Open University library system highlights the following problems:

- The meager budget allotment poses a threat to the very existence of the study centre libraries.
- The holdings of libraries are insufficient to meet users' requirements.
- Periodicals subscribed to are very few and need to be increased;
- Physical facilities are not available;
- Users' need better access to the resources of the library and improvement of services offered;
- Audio-visual materials in the study centres are not sufficient;
- Book lending services are not available; and
- Staff of the study centre libraries are less cooperative.[5]

9. Availability of Teachers

Teachers in DE institutes act like sales-men. They come to teach their class and leave after that. Students cannot meet them. There should be standing instruction to all the teachers of the subject to be present when PCP is being held. There is a need to inject work culture among the DE teachers. Proper work culture in my view should have the following characteristics:

(i) It must be devoid of all the restrictive practices which have crept in our work ethos over a period of time.

(ii) A proper work culture can be built up by reorienting our attitude to work. If we regard work as a curse, we cannot have proper attitude towards work. If we value leisure more than work we will shirk leisurely and easy-going in our habits and will shirk work. Therefore, the basic necessity for building up a proper work ethos is to have a healthy attitude to work itself.

(iii) The proper work ethos can be cultivated if the motivation springs from the work itself or the factors associated with the work such as responsibility, achievement, recognition, accomplishment, etc. and not from the factors external to work such as pay and perks.

As such the work has to be considered as a source of intrinsic satisfaction, a source of status and prestige in the society. In order to achieve this end work has to be made more challenging by proper work design i.e., adopting the method of job rotation, job enlargement, job enrichment and also forming the autonomous work groups. The concept is based on the theory of Fredrick Herzberg.[6]

CONCLUSION

Thus if we want to expand DE system to accommodate increasing number of students as well as maintain quality, then we have to introduce far and reaching changes. We have not simply set-up DE institutes but before being operational we must see that DE institutes possess excellent infrastructure and facilities.

Notes and References

1. Partap Philip, Managing Anger, Aggression and Stress, in *Management in Government*, Jan.-March, 2000, pp. 45-48.
2. Prabhat Kumar, A Responsive and Effective Government, *Management in Government*, Jan.-March, 2000, p. 8.
3. Ministry of Personnel, Public Grievances and Pensions (Deptt. of Administrative Reforms and Public Grievances) Initiatives and Best Practices of GOI for Effective and Responsive Admn. Nov., 1997, p. 4.
4. Sanjay Mishra, "Teaching Information Literacy to Distance Learners", *University News*, May 19, 1997.
5. Dinesh Kumar Gupta, "Open University and Library", *University News*, July 22, 1996, p. 8.
6. B.D. Singh in P.P. Arya, "Human Resource Management and Accounting", *op. cit.*, p. 277.

Dichoyomy between Distance Education System and Formal Education Systems: A Farce

There is a need of developing linkages to bring both at par. There are two parallel systems running to impart higher education, i.e. formal system and distance education system. Distance education system has their own universities as well as these work as a part of formal education system. Both teach the same syllabi and get the same degree. There are many advantages of DE system which can be availed by Formal System while there are many advantages of formal system which can be used for by the DE systems. At present, both the systems are working independently causing great damage to higher education. In order to ensure excellence of higher education, there is a need of forging bonds between the two to ensure academic excellence. The policy-makers and planners must realize this and encourage their collaboration. Let us discuss the advantages of such a system.

I. Both the Formal and Distance Education System stand to Gain to Ensure Quality Higher Education

The formal education system imparts instruction mostly through lecture method which is dull and make teaching dull and uninteresting. In addition, indiscipline among students do not allow the teaching function for minimum number of days essential for academic input.

L.B. Tripathi observes, "I have no hesitation in asseverating that the current state of affairs in most of the Indian universities are frightening as well as depressing. Most of the assumptions of the basis of which universities have been restructured, are not necessarily unjustifiable, but the way they have been implemented, have proven to be deleterious, and have led to corrosion of the basic nature and values of higher education. No

CHART 16.1

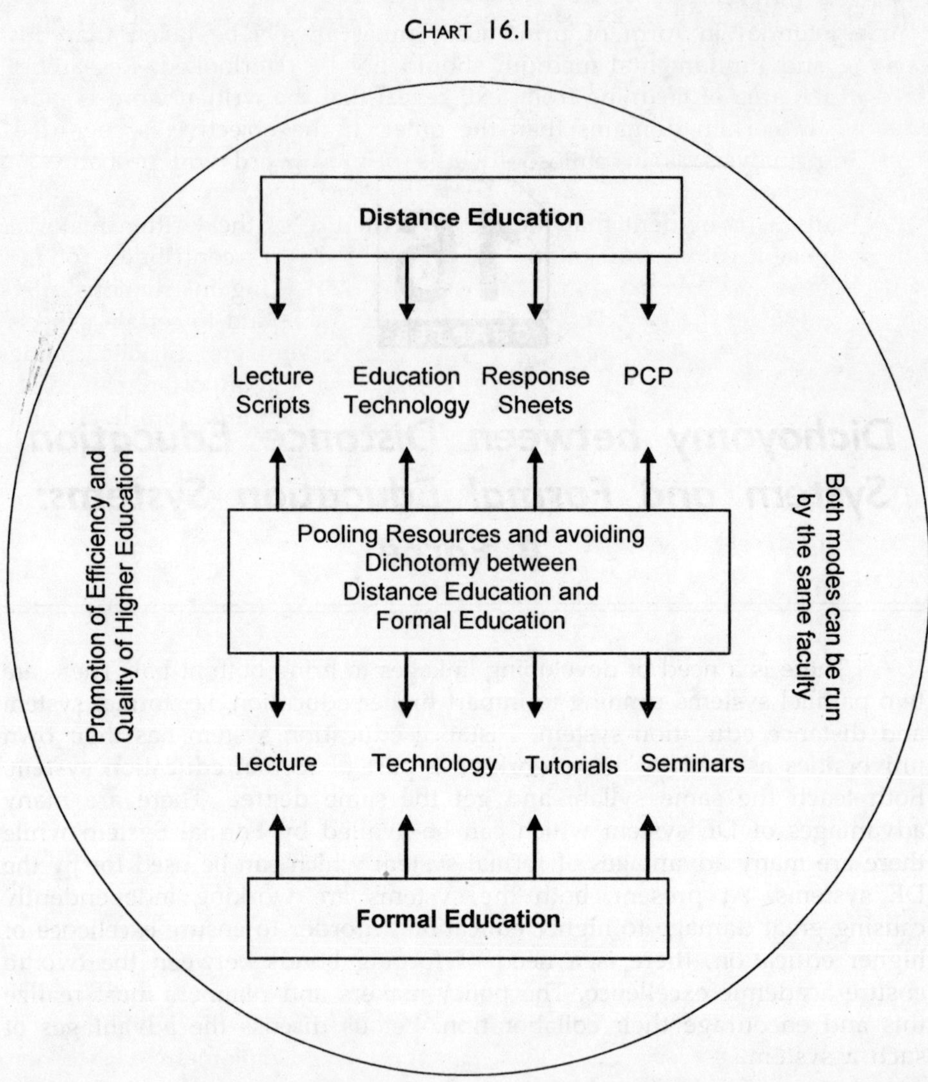

sensible person can deny the importance and value of social justice and equal opportunity to meritorious students, but how to create a socially just system in this country needs serious thinking with a view to developing it with our compromising on the basic values of university education.[1]

On the other hand distance education system provides lecture scripts written by experts and educational technology to make teaching interesting.

By far the most important medium in distance education is the printed word. This applies to conventional correspondence study as well as to highly sophisticated multi-media presentations like courses of an open university. Although the choice of media depends on the nature of subject-matter, print media has been found largely effective in each of the cognitive, affective and connative domains. In fact, medium is just a support for course material in form of print. Care must always be taken that this existing and fundamental medium should not be overlooked. Researches done in the area of 'learning from text' reveal that the written word is more effective in certain domains than the other. If the objective. is cognitive, involving analysis as in philosophy, the printed word will probably be more effective.[2]

Thus, it is evident that the logical structure of the written material and provision of opportunities for 'search' in it, contribute to the improvement of learning. Adroitly presented 'orienting instructions' also play an important role in disposing the reader to respond to certain aspects of text. General instructions to learn, advance organizers, various cueing strategies, questions and tutorial letters are some of the important categories of orienting directions. In order to make distance learning more lively and effective these strategies and 'aids to study' should be integrated into the learning material and study guides.

Thus both formal and Distance Education system can support each other rather than living in independent Ivory towers:

(a) Experts in formal education can help distant education system in preparing printed material which can help both categories of students.
(b) Educational technology developed by DE system can help the formal education system in teaching the students who can be benefited a lot.
(c) *Exchange of Teachers between Formal and DE System can Enrich both*—At present faculty appointed by DE system cannot be transferred to formal system and *vice-versa*. In my view there must be compulsory for teachers of formal education system to learn the art and science of distance education system and for distance education teachers to teach in the class room and becomes active teacher.

2. Distance Education and Formal Education can Supplement each other

However, while talking about distance learning and conventional learning system, it is to be kept in mind that these two systems are not rival to each other. The two systems can move together in order to take benefit of each other in serving the noble cause of providing education to all. However, distance education can achieve much more so far as widening access to education is concerned. This system has the advantage of flexibility in designing and developing course materials relevant to the aspirations of learners and it makes different media available to carry the torch of education to even remote rural and tribal areas which have all along remained neglected. Thus, this innovative system of education will fulfil the aim towards achieving social justice. However, this system needs concerted efforts, good team work, dedication, open mind and broad thinking. Much more requires to be done for achieving the goal of distance education which is not only correspondence education but utilizes higher technologies.[3]

It is of higher consideration that the success of distance education system demands our dedication and commitment to the system which aims at democratisation of educational opportunities for all sections of society without any discrimination. What I personally feel is to educate our people regarding the concept and utilisation of distance learning system which is the latest attraction and innovation in the field of education, specially in developing countries like India. Let us take full advantage of this mode of learning and teaching and fulfil our expectations for achieving the target of higher education of conventional as well as of modern character. Let us plan our career sitting at home and make our future bright. Let us have full faith in distance mode of learning as it has its own significance and attraction.

The system is all poised for a big leap, and it is at this stage decision-makers need to discuss about the strategies to develop the Distance Education system in a more sustainable way. Recognizing that qualified human resource is key to sustainable development of any system would result in a system that provides better qualitative outputs and outcomes at a time when the resilience of the system is subjected to test. Not giving thoughts to the needs of the system in terms of the human resources will bring the system more criticisms in implementation than laurels that the theoretical principles of Distance Education will boast of. As such there is every danger in "Great Plans with little Planning.[4]

3. Each Department of the University can run both the Formal and DE System Profitably as the Knowledge will be Pooled

This is rather better to run both the systems by the same faculty as the teachers become experts in both DE system and formal system and thus they can impart better instruction to formal and DE students. Department of Gandhian Studies, P.U., Chandigarh is running a Diploma in Gandhian Studies through formal and DE mode successfully for the last 20 years. In this way facility can be pooled and more specialization can be created in the department. This device can save the precious resources as well as increase efficiency. For example, in Panjab University, Chandigarh, there are 8 posts of faculty in Public Administration in Distance Education as well as 7 posts in regular department of the university. If they are pooled together, public administration can be run efficiently and its standards can be improved. This model is far better.

4. Resources of Formal Education and DE system can be Pooled to Achieve more which is Vital for a Poor Country like India

India is a poor country and can maintain excellence. States are creating open universities with less resources—less faculty, less financial resources, and less funds for library, PCP, etc. What is the use of creating such institutes which are not viable and are unable to provide excellent higher education? This is the mistake being made by policy-makers and planners. Later on, there is criticism of such institutes in Parliament, Assemblies and other expert bodies appointed to evaluate these institutions. It is high time that we should not compromise on second rate institutions, rather set institutions of excellence provided state governments can afford it.

5. **DE Institutes in a formal university make no difference among the faculty of DE institutes and formal education system**

All the faculty members are treated alike in the formation of Research Degree Committee, Academic Council and representation on other bodies of the university. This is a good system of distance education rather than opening Open Universities which can create isolation for the faculty, students, etc. All the Open Universities created so far except IGNOU are not well equipped to maintain the standards of Higher Education. Distance education institutes get excellent exposure of traditional university and distance education. Thus, they can enjoy the benefits of both.

6. **UGC should be entrusted the task of DEC to improve higher education through DE system by creating a separate body of UGC as all subject panels and experts are in UGC**

The independent creation of a statutory body, i.e. Distance Education Council is serving no useful purpose as their jurisdiction is very limited and is not an independent body because of domination by IGNOU. Both are engaged in higher education. How can we separate higher education simply on the basis of technology. We are in this way loosing contact with the body (UGC) established in 1956 and is the repository of more than 50 years of experience. All those who want the excellence of higher education must advocate for one agency where there is pooled experience and not an isolated body. The UGC can improve the standards of Distance Education alongwith distance education run in traditional universities. Distance education council so far has not contributed for any university except IGNOU. It is high that the Ministry of HRD must examine this afresh and ensure higher standards of education both the Distance Education Organizations as well as General Education.

At present, the Distance Education Council (DEC) under IGNOU arbitrates standards and disburses funds for ODE institutions across the country. NKC believes that this arrangement cannot provide adequate and appropriate regulation. A new regulatory mechanism must be established by appointing a Standing Committee on Open and Distance Education under the Independent Regulatory Authority for Higher Education (IRAHE) proposed by NKC. This statutory body would be responsible for developing broad criteria for accreditation as well as laying down standards for quality assurance. It would be accountable to stakeholders at all levels and to IRAHE, and have representation from public, private and social institutions involved in the education and development sectors. These include the central open university, state open universities, private open universities, conventional education institutes, as well as chairpersons of the specialized bodies to be set-up to look into infrastructural requirements of ODE.

In addition, two specialized bodies should be established under the aegis of the Standing Committee:

(i) A Technical Advisory Group with representatives from the IT sector, telecom, space and industry should be constituted to provide guidelines, ensure flexibility and track the latest developments in application. The most important function would be to devise common standards for labelling learning content developed by different agencies in order to support indexing, storage, discovery and retrieval of this content by multiple tools across multiple repositories.

(ii) An Advisory Group on Pedagogical Content Management should be set-up to provide guidelines on curricular content and development of repositories, exchange of material, access to students and other such issues.

The Standing Committee on Open and Distance Education would also serve as the nodal agency for the National Educational Foundation on open educational resources, the National Education Testing Service (NETS) and the Credit Bank.[5]

7. Vice-Chancellor and Faculty from the formal system can be appointed directly in Distance Education System why they cannot work together

In this quest for knowledge, sharing of information and working together as a team are important pre-requisites. In a recent study on the value of openness in scientific problem, it is said that broadcasting or systematically opening up a problem across the disciplines could successfully solve nearly one-third of the previously unsolved problems. It is said that innovations often happen at the intersection of disciplines. You should share problems and work together for obtaining cost-effective and unique solutions for the good of the society. Only when we learn to solve the problems together, learn to share the knowledge, learn to respect the cultural heritages and ethnic differences, it will be possible to realize the establishment of a genuine global village that enables sustainable livelihood for all. But at the same time, we should remember that our future could continue to be constrained by the self-interests of nations that control technology. We should recognize that in a highly technology-based economic competitive scenario of the future, the advancement of science and technology only could take us to a leadership position.

It can, thus, be seen that there are many opportunities and challenges in the coming years. I am sure, with adequate preparation, passion, commitment, and determination, the challenges can be squarely met. Innovation is the only way to achieve these challenging targets, and the task before all of you is to apply your knowledge and skills to bring out innovative solutions to day-to-day problems the country is facing. As Eric Hofer said, 'In a time of drastic change, it is the learners who inherit the future.' In the globalised competitive world, it only means that a continuous life-long learning, skill updation and teamwork across the multi-disciplinary fields is a must.

My dear friends! Modesty and humility, even as you achieve success, will bring you more laurels and recognition. Living with contentment is the first sign of prosperity and being useful to the people and the society around you will bring you the greatest satisfaction and fulfilment.[6]

Dichotomy of Distance Education and formal education system is bad in principle, wrong in practice and unsound scientifically. The subjects and their contents are the same in both the system. Even New Educational technology is being used in both the systems. The avoidance of Dichotomy would—

(i) Save resources—financial, physical and material.

(ii) Expertise—Better expertise would be available as the faculty of both can be pooled and more variety can be developed.

(iii) Innovations in higher education system can be injected through both the systems.

(iv) Pooling of both the systems can simplify the higher education system.

(v) The spirit of inferiority of DE system can vanish.

(vi) Both the systems can supplement each other and improve quality.

There is a need of appointment of Commission which can go into the working of DE systems in the country as what we read and hear about DE system is not correct. It would be better to allow the students appear in private capacity and one would be wonderstruck that admission of DE system would go down by 75 percent proving thereby that DE system is a path of getting degrees. If one sees how the Regional and Sub-Centres of IGNOU are being run, one would be shocked at the colossal wastage of money without any improvement of academic excellence. This is only the door opening for degrees for those who cannot study themselves.

IGNOU should be engaged more on policy-making rather than running so many Regional and Sub-Centres. These centres may be handed over to State Universities. It is very difficult to supervise the working of so many centres. These in course of time would become liability than an asset: IGNOU can only lay down policies, prepare course designs and not engage itself in running so many courses.

CONCLUSION

To conclude in the word of National Knowledge Commission report "The lack of convergence between programmes run by open universities and correspondence courses offered by the distance education wings of conventional educational institutions is a cause of great concern.

Rather than function as parallel systems at odds with each other, open universities must forge organizational alignment with conventional universities geared towards common goals and strategies. They must engage each other in the collaborative creation of pedagogical resources via OER and its delivery along shared modes. Programmes and courses offered by each should be subject to the same stringent norms of quality assurance. This implies that the distance education departments operating within conventional universities must be encouraged to put correspondence courses through the NETS for purposes of assessment. At the same time, universities must also ensure that their distance education programmes do not stand-alone, but should benefit from regular interaction with university departments in concerned disciplines. The aim of such convergence is to eventually enable learners to move freely from one system to the other.[7]

Eminent scholars A. Gnaman and Antony Stella in their article, "Myths and Realities of Distance Education" in the *University News*, May 24, 2004 rightly observes that it looks as though now the distinction between distance education and campus education itself is a myth, if one considers the convergence between the two already happening in the major universities. When technology is integrated into formal educational processes and used for the 'distributed education' for both on- and off-campus students, the distinction between them gets blurred. This appears to be the general intention of the Indian UGC in diverting enormous funds for ICT ultimately to promote the distributed education in the traditional dual mode universities. That makes one wonder how the stand-alone distance education centers like the national and state Open Universities are going to uphold their relevance and distinct purposes they wish to pursue and how the Distance Education Council is going to steer them.

NOTES AND REFERENCES

1. L.B. Tripathi, "Indian Universities—Underlying Assumptions and Consequences", *University News*, Oct. 9, 2000, p. 7.
2. Umrao Singh Chaudhari, "Distance Education and Print Media—Some Instructional Strategies"—*University News*, Oct. 23, 2000. p. 8.
3. Shamshad Hussain, "Distance Learning—The Latest Attraction', *University News*, Oct. 28, 1996, pp. 15-16
4. Sanjaya Mishra, "Human Resource Planning and Development for Distance Education in India", *University News*, Nov. 17, 2003.
5. National Knowledge Commission, Report of the Nation, 2007, GOI, pp. 48-49.
6. Convocation Address by G.Madhawan Nair, Chairman, Indian Space Research Organisation delivered at the XXXIX Convocation of the IIT, Kanpur on June 1, 2007, *University News*, Aug. 6-12, 2007.
7. National Knowledge Commission, Report of the Nation, 2007, GOI, p. 49.

17

CHAPTER

Conclusion and Recommendations

Education is of cardinal importance for socio-economic development of the country. Inspite of this realisation, traditional system of education failed to equip the personnel with the new developments in all fields as traditional system is only one time education. It is now well-established that education is a life long process. For use and development of human potential engaged in diverse areas of socio-economic development, there is no way out except to depend on Distance Education System to meet the ever changing needs of the people in 21st Century/New Millennium. The Planners, Policy-makers and decision-makers in the sector of Educational development, must give priority to the Distance Education System so that this can have deep roots and is on sound footing having capacity and capability to deliver efficient, effective and latest developments.

Besides, the development of the country depends upon growth of industry, infrastructure, agriculture, horticulture, medical science, etc. Distance Education System can be of great help in all these and other related areas through equipping the personnel engaged in these activities with latest technology, techniques and training in designing new administrative apparatus to suit the requirements of technological changes. We have tried in this book "Distance Education in the 21st Century" to focus the attention of policy-makers, scholars, experts in the field of education to strengthen the system in all its facets as suggested in all the chapters and achieve the results as anticipated.

Since the establishment of the first Open University in UK in 1969, there has been phenomenal growth of Distance Education System in the World—both developed and developing countries. There are at present 1026 institutions in 106 countries offering 31,752 courses, the highest being in Europe 26 with 387 institutions. There has been a parallel growth in India as well. We have at present 8 Open Universities and 50 Distance Education Institutes within traditional universities offering general, professional, science and engineering courses. Many organisations like National Institute of Health and Family Welfare, Industries Department of Karnataka have started Distance Education courses for their employees. Even this mode is being used at school level. National Open School has been set-up by Govt. of India as well as such institutions have been established by State Governments.

Parallel to the rise in number of institutions, courses and students, there have been advances in technology, infrastructure, and knowledge. The distance education, previously restricted to merely depending upon lecture scripts, has been opened to electronic media with tremendous potentialities. There has also been awakening among educationists and change of attitude favouring the role of distance education in higher educational development.

Alongwith these developments, there has been set-up an apex body, i.e. Distance Education Council in 1992 to perform functions relating to distance education which were earlier performed by UGC, i.e. promotion, coordination and maintenance of standards of higher education through distance mode. Though it has functioned for a short duration, it has been able to generate ideas like Networking of courses, study centres, standards of higher education through DE system, student support services, etc. It has also financed the old and new universities for their development programmes. Besides, it has devised guidelines to finance distance education institutes in the country.

There has also been some researches conducted by Indian scholars relating to different aspects of distance education system which are available for guidance and support. Besides, some books on distance education are available. A number of research articles are being published in all the issues pertaining to higher education. All these developments make us feel that distance education system has carved out its place in the system of higher education.

However, when we see around the functioning of DE system in the country, leaving aside 2-3 open universities, we find, hear and see very sad commentaries on their functioning. Why these DE institutes are not adopting standard practices to maintain the standards of higher education? Why are we diluting the quality of higher education? Why are we creating a bad image of the system? The answer to all these questions is that we have designed these institutes well and worked hard in the initial stages but over a period of time, our inaction resulted in a pathetic scenario. We have become very slow in action. We always talk about the big strides about the DE system but we do not see its hollowness from inside. Words, written or spoken are of no use unless put to action. Robert Chambers has rightly observed, "It is action that matters—But knowing does not guarantee a change of feeling and a change of feeling does not guarantee a change of behaviour." So we come to the final paradoxical reversal to start by acting. Not everything can or should be foreseen. It is often best to start, to do something, and to learn from doing.

Let us now mention some facts and suggestions which can help in making the distance education system promote academic excellence and supplement the efforts of traditional universities in their efforts of promoting excellent higher education.

1. Harping the success stories of selected distance education universities, through vocal, print, media publicity while ignoring the wrong practices and poor performance of large number of distance education institutions

The distance education system is not functioning well except in the case of selected universities which have been given huge resources by the Union and State Governments over the years. Most of the distance education institutions have been started without planning, without personnel and financial resources resulting into poor quality of services to distance learners. Many of the distance education institutes, on the other hand, were used as a mechanism to fleece distance learners and collect huge finances to be diverted to meet the deficits of the university. We may appoint a commission exclusively to examine the working of distance education system which can go into all aspects of the system. We should devise ways and means to make all existing distance education institutes excellent and not merely concentrate on selected or pampered few. It is high time to examine whether IGNOU should expand beyond its capacity and capability? Is it possible to keep a control over 400 study centres to maintain quality? To our mind IGNOU should add more to research, philosophy, guidance and new technology to other open universities and distance education institutions rather than engaging itself in these activities which can be implemented by other DE institutes.

2. Lack of motivation and training on the part of the persons associated with distance education system

The quality of teacher surpasses all other factors in making distance education a success. The faculty engaged in distance education has no job satisfaction since this work becomes a drudgery after 2-3 years. I.M. Soni in his article "teaming to tap the power within" in the *Tribune*, Nov. 7, 1999 rightly cautions that lack of action leads to premature fossilisation. Regression sets in and we sink more and more into the quagmire of hoplessness. Distance education system is an art and a science which must be learnt through staff-development programmes. Second, it requires hard work and motivation to work in a challenging task of educating distance learners. Even the best trained persons are of no use if they do not possess high morale, a socio-psychological situation in which men and women voluntarily work on a chosen field because of their intellectual satisfaction. The existing situation is pathetic. Faculty is not punctual and serious in the work. They submit the lessons as it is, for years together without any changes leading to decay and degeneration. There is a need of strict supervision and control to ensure discipline and quality.

The greatest efficiency and productivity will flow from the efforts of those who find satisfaction in their work and conditions of service, who see an awareness of usefulness of their functions, who feel encouraged to move ahead and to meet new challenges, who perceive their working environment as one in which high standards of performance are maintained and rewarded and not one in which indolence and incompetence can be ignored or even protected and rewarded. It is suggested that distance education facility must be kept active and alert through training and motivation.

3. Lack of clarity and even knowledge among the personnel responsible for the delivery of distance education system

The personnel working in the distance education system are not well versed with the latest developments in the area of distance education in India and abroad. They are working like a frog in a well. They neither go through the latest readings in their subject nor in the area of distance education. They have become a part of a bureaucratic set-up like other administrative functionaries on deputation from the university. There is a need to pull them out of this wretched condition to make them fit to deliver education to distance learners.

Administrative staff function in the same way as they were carrying on their work in the university office. They are not sensitive to the needs and aspirations of the distance students approaching them. They should also be given orientation training to make them attuned to the needs of distance education system.

4. Monopoly of vested interests to occupy positions in all the committees/ higher bodies of Union and State Governments making the other eligible persons disheartened and frustrated

Few persons are selected again and again and they usurp all the benefits of Distance Education system, i.e. attending international conferences, National seminars, members of committees, etc. Most of them are nominated from the capital, i.e. Delhi, who in turn oblige persons from their own institution for other nominations. This is a vicious circle which needs be broken. All persons of eminence, wherever they are located and working, should be provided opportunities so that such rewards keep them active and alert.

5. No criteria for enrolment of students, staffing, resources, services resulting in poor performance

At present, there is no criteria about the maximum enrolment, quantity and quality of staff, budget, quantity and quality of student support services. How can we plan without knowing the essential inputs in the system? Rather, we are coping with the given conditions and plan only after admissions, etc. There is no relationship between the core faculty and the number of students. There is a need to design institutes indicating their capacity and capability so that decent student support services can be designed and quality of distance education can be assured.

6. Expansion and diversification without monitoring the existing system causing dilution of services and slackness of supervision

There has been phenomenal expansion of the distance education system in the country and today the distance education system is catering to the needs of large number of students in the higher education system. The system is getting a fillip also because the governments are not in a position to open new colleges on account of financial constraints. However, the quality of the system is going down and Distance Education system is becoming more of a business than education. All the institutes of DE system are exploring the possibility of setting up courses which can sell in the market without the availability of adequate services. This is nothing but cheating the citizens of India. DE institutes are starting the courses without faculty, without library—all on borrowed basis. This is the time for consolidation, introspection and improvements to make the system fit for the delivery of quality higher education.

7. Distance Education Council like UGC has no controlling powers except stopping development grants

Distance Education Council set-up in 1992 to promote coordination and setting standards of DE system in the country is an appendage of IGNOU concentrating mostly on the activities and programmes being conducted by IGNOU. Distance Education Council should be an independent body to cater to the needs of the entire system. It has done a good work by approving what the various organs of IGNOU have already finalised.

More members of the council should be from institutes of DE system and open universities. IGNOU should have no special representation on it otherwise DEC can become a monopoly of IGNOU. DEC should ensure equity and provide its resources in a way that quality of DE system is improved.

8. Networking though highly useful for optimization of resources but very difficult to operate in the Indian context

For a long time, we have been harping on pooling of resources or networking of open universities and DE institutions. It is not easy in practice. If networking is taken to its logical conclusion, it would mean that we may start similar courses at all levels, prepare reading material at one place and then run the courses independently. It would create the problems of control, supervision, responsibility which are very difficult to sort out. Networking can be extended in a limited way, i.e. between 34 open universities or DE institutes which are located geographically nearby or one institute can exchange with another institute. Networking needs well thought out planning, collaboration and sharing of resources and facilities.

9. A fad of new technology dominating the minds of policy-makers of DE system and not the interest of the students

At present, the key exponents are concentrating on providing costly technology in their universities and institutes without examining its utility to distance learners. In one distance education institute in Northern India, the Video-cassette equipment was purchased at a huge cost, Engineer was appointed but there were no programmers. Today, the equipment is lying idle and the engineer is drawing his salary without any output. Only, we should adopt that technology which is feasible, practical, cost effective, and meets the needs of the students. Purchase of costly technology affects the delivery of student support services. A decision on new technology should be taken very carefully.

10. Lack of professional competence and dedication among personnel running DE system

The faculty in distance education is not enthusiastic and has become listless. However, a distance education teacher is expected to be well versed with the new technologies and media besides, being competent in their own fields/specialisations. Regular orientation programmes and workshops can take them out of slumber and inertia. The distance education system requires dedication on the part of the faculty so that they can help the distance students with love and affection. Positive attitudes on the part of the teachers can generate bonds of permanent relationships.

Swami Vivekanand has beautifully summed up the qualities of a good teacher. To quote him, "The true teacher is he who can immediately come down to the level of the student and transfer his soul to the students soul and see through and understand through his mind. Such a teacher can really teach and none else."

11. Enamoured by ideas and researches developed in foreign countries without seeing its feasibility and applicability in the Indian conditions

It has been observed that we are enamored by experiments being conducted in the area of distance education in different countries of the world. It is good that we must keep ourselves aware of the latest developments in the area of distance education. However, we have to examine such experiments and see their applicability in our country keeping in view the environment and availability of resources. What happens is that we initiate new developments but cannot sustain them for long, resulting into failure and loss of huge resources? We are importing a lot of technology from advanced countries without having regard and need for our country. We should be cautious and slow in such actions.

12. Tutors/Part-time teachers/appointed in distance education system already under full employment creates unemployment for new comers and also working half heartedly under stress

IGNOU and other open universities are employing tutors,

coordinators, etc. to manage their study centres. Those who manage these activities are already serving in some educational institutions. Their work in these institutions suffer and in some cases it has been seen that they devote major part of their time in managing this extra work to the utter neglect of their own work. We should ensure to involve fresh persons without any job and train them. This would on the one hand generate employment, while on the other hand this would not disturb the schedule of other educational institutions. We should seriously ponder over this, as such persons who are already employed cannot provide decent services either to their parent institute or to the students at study centres.

It is hoped that some facts and suggestions mentioned above would help the policy-makers, planners, decision-makers of higher education system especially distance education system in ensuring excellence, responsiveness and rationalization of student support services and facilities. Besides the inherent potentialities in the Distant education system can be optimised and potential energy of the personnel involved in the system can be changed into kinetic energy through well designed distance education system. We may briefly conclude with the following pointed suggestions:

(i) A closer focus on results in terms of efficiency and effectiveness and service quality to distance learners.
(ii) The replacement of highly centralised organizational structure with decentralised management environments where decisions on service delivery and resource allocation are taken closer to the point of delivery and which provide feedback from distance learners and personnel engaged in the delivery of distance education system.
(iii) Flexibility to explore alternative methods and technology to provide better services to distance learners economically and efficiently.
(iv) Devising new personnel management policies to provide greater flexibility and motivation to ensure higher productivity and excellence in DE system.
(v) Creating incentives to improve performance through enabling organisations to retain a portion of savings for better student support services.
(vi) Creating greater accountability and transparency through requirements to report on results.
(vii) Equipping policy-making bodies with really eminent educationists visible from their Bio-data.
(viii) The distant learners' interest and satisfaction must be at the centre of all policy-making, planning and decision-making in the area of DE system.
(ix) Constant monitoring and evaluation of the DE system against the norms and standards fixed by DEC should be a regular feature.

Distance Education system has the potentiality, capability and expertise to promote higher education in diverse fields. However, we have to be careful in ensuring quality and effectiveness from the institutions engaged in distance education systems.

13. Instructional Material very poor in quality: Need of Preparing quality Material

As already discussed, the Instructional material supplied is not of good quality. R.D. Pathak, D. Kaul in their article, "Material Production and Distribution of Study Material in an Open University," *University News*, March 29, 1999 has rightly mentioned that preparation and distribution of course material is a crucial aspect of the operations of an open university. An efficient and effective production and material distribution of course material, has to be based on good knowledge of printing and distribution. The preparation of study material has been revolutionised due to the advent of computers and networking in printing, hence it is essential that the Material Production and Distribution Division (MPDD) system should incorporate the latest trends in this field.

Keeping in view the role of open universities in the field of distance education, the MPDD in such a university is expected to fulfil the following objectives:

(a) To provide relevant reading material to the students, regional centres, study centres, open university, other institutions, agents and general public.

(b) To ensure the readability, correctness and understandability of the reading material.

(c) To ensure good presentation of the reading material, using latest quality control techniques.

(d) To adhere to the time schedule, procure paper, identify private presses and distribution of printing material to the above agencies.

14. Fear of loss of contact between students and teachers—Need of devising ways and means

However, we should not forget that we should not alienate the student from the teacher. S.L. Mahajan in his article, "Alienation of Students in Higher Education" in *University News*, June 14, 1999 rightly cautions that distance education is a product of students-teachers alienation and gives solution to alienation of both. It is high time for the system to lift the students from depths of despair to heights of ecstasy to seek better outcome. Same feeling is expressed by R. Natrajan in his article, "Emerging Trends in Technology, Education and Economy" in *University News*, Oct. 14, 1999 that non-traditional education has evolved from correspondence courses to video-based classes taught in a remote location, to online Internet classes which do not meet at a specific time. Different models of Distance Learning share the common feature of a remote place, but are distinguished by pace (scheduling), time (synchronicity), and interactivity. Although faculty can easily create a web-page for their course, incorporating new technology, and converting a class to the distance-learning environment, it requires rethinking the way the course is delivered.

We should endeavour to promote better and good relationship between teachers and students through PCP, personal visits and response sheets assignments.

APPENDIX I

OPEN AND DISTANCE EDUCATION

The National Knowledge Commission (NKC) believes that a radical reform of the system of Open and Distance Education (ODE) is imperative to believe the objectives of expansion inclusion and excellence in higher education. The significance is obvious. For one more than one-fifth of the students enrolled in higher education are in the ODE stream. For another, ODE has an enormous potential to spread higher education opportunities beyond the brick and mortar world. But there are reasons for concern. First the quality of higher education provided in large segments of ODE, particularly in correspondence courses in universities, leaves much to be desired. Second, it is not sufficiently recognized that ODE provides educational opportunities not only to those who discontinue formal education on account of economic or social compulsions, but also to young school Ieavers who are simply unable to secure admission in the formal stream at universities. It is time to address these problems. There is a clear need to improve the quality of ODE and to make it more appropriate to the needs of society. It is just as important to expand opportunities in higher education through the use of technology in ODE. It would not be possible to attain a gross enrolment ratio of 15% by 2015 without a massive expansion in ODE. In this endeavour, we must not forget that ODE is seen as inferior to conventional classroom Iearning. This perception and the reality, both need change. We must realize that ODE is not simply a mode of educational delivery, but an integrated discipline engaged in the creation of knowledge.

In light of the above, NKC constituted a Working Group composed of distinguished experts in this Field, chaired by Prof. Ram Takwale, former Vice-Chancellor, IGNOU. Based on inputs provided by the working group and consultations with stakeholders. NKC recommended the following reforms:

1. Create a National ICT Infrastructure for Networking ODE Institutions

A national Information and Communication Technology (ICT) infrastructure must be set-up through government support for networking all ODE institutions. In this regard, we recommend that the digital broadband Knowledge Network proposed by NKC should have provision for interconnecting (he major ODE institutions and their study centres in the first phase itself. Eventually, minimum connectivity of 2 Mbps must be extended to the study centres of all ODE institutions. A national ICT backbone would enhance access and e-governance in ODE, and enable the dissemination of knowledge across all modes, that is, print, audio-visual and Internet-based multimedia.

2. Set-up a National Education Foundation to Develop Web-based Common Open Resources

A National Educational Foundation with a one-time infusion of adequate funds must be established to develop a web-based repository of high quality educational resources. Open Educational Resources (OER) must be created online through a collaborative process, pooling in the efforts and expertise of all major institutions of higher education. The OER repository would supply pedagogical software for various programmes run through ODE and be available for utilization by all ODE institutions. An enabling legal framework that would allow unrestricted access without compromising intellectual authorship must be devised for this purpose.

3. Establish a Credit Bank to Effect Transition to a Course Credit System

Transition to a course credit system must be carried out to enable the learner to undertake programmes across all ODE institutions and disciplines. As part of this process, an autonomous credit bank must be established for storing and filing credits acquired by every learner. In addition, Admission criteria and the system of credits should be as flexible and adaptable as possible. Provisions must be made for multiple entry points and exit points, a flexible time-table and assessment mechanisms for supporting life-long learning.

4. Establish a National Education Testing Service for Assessing ODE Students

An autonomous National-education Testing Service (NETS) must be established through legislation and Invested with functional powers and responsibility for assessing all potential graduates in ODE. This unified examination system would test the learners' ability to perform intellectual and practical tasks. All courses, degrees and activities offered through ODE should be certified through this system.

5. Facilitate Convergence with Conventional Universities

The lack of convergence between programmes run by open universities and correspondence courses offered by the distance education wings of conventional educational institutions is a cause of great concern.

Rather than function as parallel systems at adds with each other, open universities must forge organizational alignment with conventional universities geared towards common goals and strategies. They must engage each other in the collaborative creation of pedagogical resources via OER and its delivery along shared modes. Programmes and courses offered by each should be subject to the same stringent norms of quality assurance. This implies that the distance education departments operating within conventional universities must be encouraged to put correspondence courses through the NETS for purposes of assessment. At the same time, universities must also ensure that their distance education programmes are not stand-alone, hut should benefit from regular interaction with university departments in concerned disciplines. The aim of such convergence is to eventually enable learners to move freely from one system to the other

6. Set-up a Research Foundation to Support Research Activity in ODE

An autonomous and well-endowed Research Foundation must he established to commission and facilitate multi-dimensional and multi-disciplinary research in ODE. In addition, a favourable environment for research must be created by setting up infrastructure like libraries, digital databases and online journals, holding regular workshops and seminars. granting sabbatical leave for undertaking research, establishing a peer reviewed journal to provide a platform for publication for scholars. And other such measures. A robust research environment is essential to accord ODE value as a discipline, as opposed to it being consigned to a 'mode'.

7. Overhaul Training Programmes for Educators

Training and orientation programmes must be conceptualized to enable educators and administrators to effectively utilize technology to cater to diverse learners' interests. The content of the training modules must promote familiarity with the theories and practices of self-learning. Their delivery should take place through several modes, including web-supported, audio-visual and face-to-face interaction on a regular basis with experts, practitioners and peers. Most importantly, these packages must be updated regularly and administered directly. The B.Ed. curriculum must also be revised, updated and made to emphasize theories and practices of self-learning.

8. Increase Access for Learners with Special Needs

Special Education Committees must be set-up in all ODE institutions to address the needs of learners with disabilities as well as senior citizens. These committees must devise mechanisms to ensure their participation and provide effective mechanisms for monitoring, evaluation of policies, and collection of feedback. Admission criteria and time tables must be flexible enough to provide diverse options for meeting programme requirements to differently able learners and senior citizens. Pedagogical tools and components from the open educational resources must be adaptable to alternative formats for special learning needs. This could include, for example, Braille, colour-contrast texts and voice recordings for the visually disabled.

9. Create a New Standing Committee for the Regulation of ODE

At present, the Distance Education Council (DEC) under IGNOU arbitrates standards and disburses funds for ODE institutions across the country. NKC believes that this arrangement cannot provide adequate and appropriate regulation. A new regulatory mechanism must be established by appointing a Standing Committee on Open and Distance Education under the Independent Regulatory Authority for Higher Education (IRAHE) proposed by NKC, this statutory body would be responsible for developing broad criteria for quality of accreditation as well as laying down standards for quality assurance. It would be accountable to stakeholders at all levels and to IRAHE and have representation from public, private and social institutions involved in the education and development sectors. These include the central open university, state open universities, private open universities, conventional education institutes as well as chairpersons of the specialized bodies to be set-up to look into infrastructural requirement of ODE. In addition, two specialized bodies should be established under the aegis of the Standing Committee:

(i) A technical Advisory Group with representatives from the IT sector, Telecom, space and industry should be constituted to provide guidelines. ensure
Flexibility and track the latest developments in application. The most important function would to be devise common standards for labeling learning content developed by different agencies in order to support indexing, storage, discovery and retrieval of this content by multiple tools across multiple repositories.

(ii) An Advisory Group on Pedagogical Content Management should be set-up to provide guidelines on curricular content and development of repositories, exchange of material, access to Students and other such issues, The Standing Committee on open and Distance Education would also serve as the nodal agency for the National Educational foundation on open educational resources, the National Education Testing Service (NETS) and the Credit Bank.

10. Develop a System for Quality Assessment

Reliable external assessment is valued by employers, students and other stakeholders in the given context of a market driven economy. In view of this, a rating system to assess the standard of all institutions imparting ODE must be evolved and made publicly available. The Standing Committee would stipulate grading norms and independent rating agencies would be licensed by IRAHE to carry out this function. In addition, it is recommended that every ODE institution has an internal quality assurance cell to ensure that statutory quality compliances are regularly met.

Establishment of the new organizations proposed above, namely, the National Education Testing Service, the Credit Bank, the National Educational Foundation for developing common open resources, the Technical Advisory Group and the Advisory Group on Pedagogical Content Management would initially require financial support from the government. Additional finances for networking ODE institutions and creating access centres, developing training programmes for educators and administrators and providing scholarships and services for needy students would also be required.

Source: National Knowledge Commission.

APPENDIX II

OPEN EDUCATIONAL RESOURCES

Our success in the knowledge economy hinges to a large extent on upgrading the quality of, and enhancing the access to, education, One of the most effective ways of achieving this would be to stimulate the development and dissemination of quality Open Access (OA) materials and Open Educational Resources (OER) through broadband Internet Connectivity. This would facilitate easy and widespread access to high quality educational resources and drastically improve the teaching paradigm for all our students. As a part of its consultative process, NKC constituted a Working Group of experts, including distinguished members from the academia, government, private sector and users to suggest necessary measures to improve the quality of Open Access in India, NKC consultations with stakeholders helped identify a few key reform proposals which are elaborated as follows:

1. Support the Production of Quality Content by a Select set of Indian Institutions

A set of key institutions should be selected and experts representing diverse knowledge areas like agriculture, engineering, medicine, arts, humanities, science, education, etc. should be asked to develop standards-based content, which can be customized to diverse user needs. This should be made available not only to Indian institutions but also for global use. The efforts made through the project of Ministry of Human Resources Development—National Programme on Technology Enhanced Learning (NPTEl) for creation of OER in the areas of Engineering and technology should be applied in other areas of education also, the content in the repositories should be multimedia interactive and available in different regional languages. These projects should cover a wide range of subjects mentioned above. To speed up the creation, adaptation, and utilization of OER it is necessary to launch a 'National E-content and Curriculum Initiative'.

2. Leverage Global Open Educational Resources

Sustainable development of quality content relevant to India is a difficult and expensive proposition, given the diverse needs of various sectors in our emerging knowledge economy. Emerging international and national initiatives are offering quality educational content as open resources. It is viral for India to leverage these initiatives as they are readily available for adoption and adaptation and to serve as a model for further indigenous content production. NKC found that there are already 200-300 free knowledge repositories available across the world. The National Knowledge Commission (NKC) is separately disseminating this information through its website.

3. Encourage Open Access

Open Access material stimulates research and helps students, teachers and researchers across the world, as discussed in the attached report. Therefore, at the policy level, all research articles published by Indian authors receiving substantial government or public funding must be made available under Open Access and should be archived in the standard OA format at least on his/her website. As a next step, a national academic OA portal should be developed. The government should allocate resources to increase the current digitization efforts of books and periodicals which are outside copyright protection. Separate funding should be allocated to develop a new high quality OCR software package so that new and old fonts in many different Indian languages can be converted into ISCI/ASCI code and OA portals and servers could be upgraded regularly. Appropriate financial resources should be earmarked for these endeavours. This will also facilitate machine translation of these valuable resources.

4. Develop Network-enabled Delivery Infrastructure

Along with the national initiative for content development, we must develop a network-enabled delivery infrastructure with a focus on two primary areas: access and delivery. For access to the network, High bandwidth connections across institutions and a National backbone that provides advanced networking capabilities are major requirement. Additionally, connectivity to global network is essential. Delivery of the OER consent would be done through distributed repositories of educational resources.

5. Create a Faculty and Institutional Development Programme

Faculty development and teacher training is the primary area that needs to be addressed in order to realize the benefits of extended access and improved quality through OER. The training programme must develop domain competencies and teaching skills using new educational technologies. The training will also help developers of new OER and in contextualizing existing educational resources. Centres at specific institutions should be identified so that the faculty of these institutions will eventually own, modify, and expand OER repositories. These must be integrated into university curricula and organizational structures. The availability of learning management systems and other quizzing, authoring and collaborating tools should be increased. The evaluation system should be based on the use of the content and the pedagogy in OER.

To implement and monitor the above recommendations urgently and efficiently, the Government of India may designate a suitable organization or establish a new institution with necessary mandate to achieve the above objectives. This institute may serve the following functions:

- Provide leadership and coordination of network-based open education resources.
- Select institutional collaborations for developing content.
- Develop adoption support strategies.
- Recommend and monitor standards for content development and adoption.
- Advise on policy implications *vis-a-vis* licensing, intellectual property rights, etc.
- Identify and set benchmarks based on global best practices.
- Establish relationships with global OA and OER initiatives.

Source: National Knowledge Commission Report to the Nation, 2007, GOI.

Bibliography

AIU, Decentralisation of Higher Education System, New Delhi, 1970.

Ahluwalia, S.P. and Bains, H.S., Education Issues and Challenges, New Delhi, Aahish Publishing House, 1992.

Anand, Satyapal, University Without Walls, New Delhi, Vikas, 1979.

B.R. Ambedkar Open University, Andhra Pradesh Distance Education: An Interface, Research Volume Committee, Hyderabad, 1994.

Bates, A. W., Technology, Open Learning and Distance Education, London, Routledge, 1995.

Burt, Gordon, Face to Face with Distance Education, U.K., Milton Keynes, 1997.

Collis, B. Tele, Learning in a Digital World: The Future of Distance Learning, London, International Computer Press, 1996.

Chib, Sukhdev Singh, Teaching by Correspondence in India, New Delhi, Light and Life, 1977.

Datt, Rudar, Cost of Distance Education in India, New Delhi, South Asian Publisher, 1994.

Goel, Aruna, Distance Education in the 21st Century, New Delhi, Deep & Deep Publications Pvt. Ltd., 2000.

Goel, Aruna and Goel, S.L., "Encyclopedia of Higher Education in 21st Century, Deep & Deep Publications Pvt. Ltd., New Delhi, 2005.

Goel, S.L. and Goel, Aruna, Education Policy and Administration, New Delhi, Deep & Deep Publications Pvt. Ltd., 1994.

Gates, B., The Road Ahead, London, Penguin Books, 1996.

Goel, S.L., Modern Management Techniques, New Delhi, Deep & Deep Publications Pvt. Ltd., 1995.

Holmberg, B., Theory and Practice of Distance Education, London, Routledge, 1989.

Harry, K. (ed.), Higher Education Through Open and Distance Learning, London, Routledge, 1999.

Khan, Distance Education, New Delhi, Amar Prakashan, 1991.

Javris Peter *et. al.*, Theory and Practice of Learning, London, Kogan Page, 1998.

Kaur, Ambika Sharanjit, Managing Distance Education, New Delhi, Deep & Deep Publications Pvt. Ltd., 1996.

Kember David, Open Learning Courses for Adults: A Model of Student Progress, New Jersey, Englewood Cliffs, 1995, USA.

Keegan, D., Foundations of Distance Education (2nd Edition), London, Routledge, 1990.

Manohar, K. Murli, Distance Education, Theory and Practice, Prof. G. Rama Reddy Commemorative Volumes I, II, III, 1999, Ministry of HRD, Selected Educational Statistics (1996-97), New Delhi, Department of Education, GOI, 1998.

Nehru, Jawahar Lal, The Discovery of India, London, Meridian Books, 1960.

Peters, Otto, Learning and Teaching in Distance Education: Analysis and Interpretations from an International Perspective, London, Kogan Page, 1998.

Reddy, M. Gurumurthy, Higher Education in India, New Delhi, APH Publishing Corporation, 1997.

Reddy, G. Ram, Open Education System in India, its place and potential, Hyderabad, Andhra Pradesh Open University, 1984.

Rao, M. Satyanarayana, Synergy: Facets of Research in Open Learning, Hyderabad, Dr. B.R. Ambedkar Open University, 1996.

Rathore, H.C.S., Management of Distance Education in India, New Delhi, Ashish Publish House, 1993.

Reddy, G. Ram (ed.), Open Universities, the Ivory Towers Thrown Apex, New Delhi, Sterling, 1988.

Raghunath, K., Management of Distance Education: A Case Study of APOU, Delhi, Ajanta, 1994.

Rao, R.V.R. Chandrasekhra (ed.), Technical and Vocational Programmes through Distance Education, Hyderabad, Book Links Corporation, 1993.

Sharma, D.P., Themes in Primary Health Care, New Delhi, Institute of Research and Action Planning, 1999.

Sen, Amartya, On Interpreting India's Past, Calcutta, Asiatic Society, 1996.

Unnikrishnan, K., Ed., Research Spectrum, Calicut, University of Calicut, 1995.

S. Rana, Open Learning in India, New Delhi, Commonwealth Publishers, 1994.

Sahoo, P.K., Higher Education at a Distance, New Delhi, Sanchar Publishing House, 1993.

Singh, R.P. (Ed.), Indian Universities Towards Nation Building, New Delhi, UGC, 1998.

Sharma, R.A., Technology of Teaching, Merrut, Loyal Book Depot, 1989. Separate New Programmed Instruction, An Instructional Technology, Meerut, Loyal Book Depot, 1989.

Singh, Bakshish (Ed.), New Horizons in Distance Education, New Delhi, Uppal, 1995.

Text Plan, Key Issues in Open Learning, London, Longman, 1993.

UNICEF, Educating Girls and Women: A Moral Imperative, 1992.

UGC, Guidelines for Introduction of Correspondence Courses, Mimeograph, 1981.

Wolf Howard Continuing Education of a Teacher: The Role of the Self in Higher Education, Delhi, Academic Foundation, 1992.

Public Documents

Asian Centre of Educational Innovation for Development, Educational Innovation in India, by Chitra Naik, Paris, UNESCO, 1974, p. 50.

India, Committee of Members of Parliament on Education Report, 1967: National Policy on Education, New Delhi, Ministry of Education, 1967, p. 56.

India, 1992, Director, Publication Division, Ministry of Information and Broadcasting, Govt. of India, February, 1993, p. 910.

India, Committee of Members of Parliament on Higher Education, 1963, Report, New Delhi: Ministry of Education; 1964, p. 65. (Chairman, P.N. Sapru)

India, Committee on the ways and means of financing educational development in India, Report, Delhi: Manager of Publications, 1950, p. 78. (Chairman, B.G. Kher)

India, Department of Education, Analysis of budgeted expenditure on education, 1979-80 to 1981-82, New Delhi: The Department, 1982, p. 184.

India, Educations Commission, 1964, Report, Delhi: Manager of Publications, 1966, p. 692. (Chairman: D.S. Kothari)

India, Lok Sabha Secretariat, National Education Policy, New Delhi, the Secretariat, 1985, p. 41.

India, Ministry of Education, Challenge of Education-Policy Perspective, New Delhi: Ministry of Education, 1985, p. 119.

India, Ministry of Education and Culture, Educational Development of Women in India by R.K. Bhandari, New Delhi, The Ministry, 1983, p. 109.

India, Planning Commission, Eighth Five Year Plan (1992-97), New Delhi, Vols. I & II.

India, Secondary Education Commission, 1952, Report, New Delhi: Ministry of Education, 1953, p. 311. (Chairman, A. Lakshmanaswami Mudaliar). .

India, Special Committee on Reorganisation and Development of Polytechnic Education in India, 1970-71, Report, New Delhi, Ministry of Education and Social Welfare, 1971, p. 212. (Chairman, G.R. Damodaran).

India, University Grants Commission, Report on Standards of University Education, New Delhi: The Commission, 1965, p. 282 (Chairman, N.K. Sidhanta).

Ministry of Human Resource Development: Department of Education.

National Policy on Education, 1986 with Modifications Undertaken in 1992, New Delhi, p. 50.

Programme of Action, 1992, p. 250.

Towards an Enlightened and Humane Society, NPE, 1986, A Review, New Delhi, Dec., 1990, p. 409.

Annual Reports of the Ministry of HRD, New Delhi.

Cabe Committee on Policy, New Delhi, January, 1992, p. 86.

Selected Educational Statistics, 1991-92, New Delhi, 1993.

Books by the Same Authors

1. International Administration: WHO South East-Asia Regional Office, (New Delhi, 1977), Sterling Publishers.
2. Principles, Problems and Prospects of Co-operative Administration, New Delhi (1979), Sterling Publishers, (Co-Author Dr. B.B. Goel).
3. Administration of Personnel in Co-operative, (New Delhi, 1979), Sterling Publishers (Co-Author Dr. B.B. Goel).
4. Health Care Administration: Ecology, Principles and Modern Trends, (New Delhi, 1980), Sterling Publishers.
5. Health Care Administration: Policy-making and Planning (New Delhi, 1980), Sterling Publishers.
6. Health Care Administration: Levels and Aspects, (New Delhi, 1980), Sterling Publishers.
7. International Civil Service: Principles, Problems and Prospects, (New Delhi, 1984), Sterling Publishers.
8. Public Health Administration, (New Delhi, 1984), Sterling Publishers.
9. Public Personnel Administration, (New Delhi, 1984), Reprint 1987, Sterling Publishers.
10. International Civil Services—Principles, Problems and Prospectives, (New Delhi, 1984), Sterling Publishers.
11. Social Welfare Administration, Vols. I and II: Theory and Practice, (New Delhi, 1988), Deep & Deep Publications Pvt. Ltd.
12. Hospital Administration and Management (ed.) Co-Author Dr. R. Kumar in 3 volumes (New Delhi, 1989), Deep & Deep Publications Pvt. Ltd.
13. Policy and Administration: Family Planning & Beyond (New Delhi, 1990), Deep & Deep Publications Pvt. Ltd.
14. Modern Management Techniques, (New Delhi, 1990) Deep & Deep Publications Pvt. Ltd. (Revised & Reprinted).
15. Development Planning and Administration (ed.) S. Bhatnagar (Co-editor), (New Delhi, 1992), Deep & Deep Publications Pvt. Ltd.
16. Financial Administration and Management, (New Delhi, 1993), Sterling Publishers.
17. Advanced Public Administration, (New Delhi, 1993), Sterling Publishers.
18. Personnel Administration and Management, (New Delhi, 1994), Deep & Deep Publications Pvt. Ltd.

19. Educational Policy and Administration, (New Delhi, 1994), Deep & Deep Publications Pvt. Ltd.
20. Slum Improvement Through Participatory Urban Based Community Structures, (New Delhi, 1999), Deep & Deep Publications Pvt. Ltd.
21. Distance Education in 21st Century, (New Delhi, 2000), Deep & Deep Publications Pvt. Ltd.
22. Health Care System and Management: Organization and Structure, (New Delhi, 2000), Deep & Deep Publications Pvt. Ltd.
23. Health Care System and Management: Policies and Programmes (New Delhi, 2000), Deep & Deep Publications Pvt. Ltd.
24. Health Care System and Management: Management and Administration (New Delhi, 2000), Deep & Deep Publications Pvt. Ltd.
25. Heath Care System and Management: Management and Administration, (New Delhi, 2000), Deep & Deep Publications Pvt. Ltd.
26. Management Techniques: Principles and Practices, (New Delhi, 2001), Deep & Deep Publications Pvt. Ltd.
27. Encyclopadeia of Disaster Management in 3 Volumes, (New Delhi, 2001), Deep & Deep Publications Pvt. Ltd.
28. Management of Hospitals: Hospital Core Services, (New Delhi, 2002), Deep & Deep Publications Pvt. Ltd.
29. Management of Hospitals: Hospital Supportive Services, (New Delhi, 2002), Deep & Deep Publications Pvt. Ltd.
30. Management of Hospitals: Hospital Preventive and Promotive Services (New Delhi, 2002), Deep & Deep Publications Pvt. Ltd.
31. Management of Hospitals: Hospital Managerial Services, (New Delhi, 2002), Deep & Deep Publications Pvt. Ltd.
32. Public Personal Administration, (New Delhi, 2002), Deep & Deep Publications Pvt. Ltd.
33. Public Financial Administration, (New Delhi, 2002), Deep & Deep Publications Pvt. Ltd.
34. Urban Development and Management, (New Delhi, 2002), Deep & Deep Publications Pvt. Ltd.
35. Public Administration: Theory and Practices, (New Delhi, 2003), Deep & Deep Publications Pvt. Ltd.
36. Advanced Public Administration, (New Delhi, 2003), Deep & Deep Publications Pvt. Ltd.
37. Panchayati Raj in India, (New Delhi, 2003), Deep & Deep Publications Pvt. Ltd.
38. Encyclopedia of Higher Education in 21st Century, Organisation and Structure, (New Delhi, 2004) Deep & Deep Publications Pvt. Ltd.
39. Encyclopedia of Higher Education in 21st Century, Quality and Excellence, (New Delhi, 2004), Deep & Deep Publications Pvt. Ltd.
40. Encyclopedia of Higher Education in 21st Century, Extension Education Services (New Delhi, 2004), Deep & Deep Publications Pvt. Ltd.

41. Stress Management and Education : An Indian and Perspective, (New Delhi, 2004), Deep & Deep Publications Pvt. Ltd.
42. Human Values and Education, (New Delhi, 2004), Deep & Deep Publications Pvt. Ltd.
43. Public Health Policy and Administration, (New Delhi, 2004), Deep & Deep Publications Pvt. Ltd.
44. Administration and Management of NGO's Text and Caste Studies, (New Delhi, 2004), Deep & Deep Publications Pvt. Ltd.
45. Nursing Services: Management and Administration (New Delhi, 2005), Deep & Deep Publications Pvt. Ltd.
46. Population Policy and Family Welfare Administration (New Delhi, 2005), Deep & Deep Publications Pvt. Ltd.
47. Human Resource Development in 21st Century (New Delhi, 2005), Deep & Deep Publications Pvt. Ltd.
48. Encyclopaedia of Disaster Management, 3 Volumes, (New Delhi, 2006), Deep & Deep Publications Pvt. Ltd.
49. School Health Education, (New Delhi, 2007), Deep & Deep Publications Pvt. Ltd.
50. Health Education : Theory and Practices, (New Delhi, 2007), Deep & Deep Publications Pvt. Ltd.
51. Good Governance : An Integral View, (New Delhi, 2007), Deep & Deep Publications Pvt. Ltd.
52. Right to Information and Good Governance, (New Delhi, 2007), Deep & Deep Publications Pvt. Ltd.
53. Disaster Management: Text and Case Studies, (New Delhi, 2007), Deep & Deep Publications Pvt. Ltd.
54. Hospital Administration : Theory and Practices (New Delhi, 2007), Deep & Deep Publications Pvt. Ltd.
55. Environmental Health Values and Education, (New Delhi, 2008), Deep & Deep Publications Pvt. Ltd.
56. Administrative and Management Thinkers: Revelvance in New Millennium, (New Delhi, 2008), Deep & Deep Publications Pvt. Ltd.
57. Principle and Practice of Human Values, (New Delhi, 2008), Deep & Deep Publications Pvt. Ltd.
58. Distance Education: Principles, Potentialities and Perspectives, (New Delhi, 2008), Deep & Deep Publications Pvt. Ltd.
59. Educational Administration and Management : An Integral View, (New Delhi, 2008), Deep & Deep Publications Pvt. Ltd.
60. Women Health Education, (New Delhi, 2008), Deep & Deep Publications Pvt. Ltd.
61. Health and Hospital Care Administration and Management, Vol. 1, Organizational Structure, (New Delhi, 2008), Deep & Deep Publications Pvt. Ltd.
62. Health and Hospital Care Administration and Management, Vol. II, (*Resources* : Human, Finance and Material), (New Delhi, 2008), Deep & Deep Publications Pvt. Ltd.

63. Health and Hospital Care Administration and Management, Vol. III, (Policy-Making and Programmes), (New Delhi, 2008), Deep & Deep Publications Pvt. Ltd.
64. Health and Hospital Care Administration and Management, Vol. IV, (Emerging and Thrust Area) (New Delhi, 2008), Deep & Deep Publications Pvt. Ltd.
65. Health and Hospital Care Administration and Management, Vol. V, (Primary and Rural Health Care) (New Delhi, 2008), Deep & Deep Publications Pvt. Ltd.
66. Health and Hospital Administration and Management, Vol. VI, (Second ry and Teritary Hospital) (New Delhi, 2008), Deep & Deep Publications Pvt. Ltd.
67. Health and Hospital Administration and Management, Vol. VII, (Management Techniques and Good Governance) (New Delhi, 2008), Deep & Deep Publications Pvt. Ltd.
68. Education of Life Style and Life Time Disease—In Press.
69. Health Education Administration—Process International Level to Village Level—In Press.
70. Health Education for Healthy Cities—In Press.
71. Rural Health Education—In Press.

Index